SUCCESSFUL DIRECT MARKETING METHODS

Bob Stone, Chairman of the Board

Rapp, Collins, Stone & Adler Inc.

Crain Books
A division of Crain Communications Inc.
740 Rush Street
Chicago Illinois 60611

Library of Congress Catalogue Card Number: 74-83058
ISBN 0-87251-016-6

Third printing

Printed in the United States of America

7104

CONTENTS

FOREWORD   ix

PREFACE   EDWARD N. MAYER, JR.   xi

SECTION I THE WORLD OF DIRECT MARKETING

Chapter 1 The Scope of Direct Marketing   Page 1

The Basic Appeals of Direct Marketing
The Credit Card Explosion
The Computer Explosion—Selectivity at
   Last
Six Big Keys to Direct Marketing
   Success
   1. Right Product or Services
   2. Right Media
   3. Right Proposition
   4. Right Formats
   5. Right Tests
   6. Right Analyses
Checklist for Applying the Six Big Keys
   to Direct Marketing Success
The Place of the Consumer Goods
   Manufacturer
The Place of the Retailer
The Place of the Industrial Goods
   Manufacturer

The Place of the Syndicator
The Place of Intangibles
The Place of European Direct Marketing
Eight Major Responsibilities of Direct
   Marketing Executives
   1. Product Selection and Development
   2. Markets and Media Selection
   3. Creative Development and
      Scheduling
   4. Testing Procedures
   5. Fulfillment
   6. Budgeting and Accounting
   7. Customer Service
   8. Personnel and Supplier Relations
Standards of Practice

Self-Quiz
Pilot Project

III

SECTION II MEDIA OF DIRECT MARKETING

Chapter 2 Mailing Lists Page 42

Every List Has a Profile
Working with List Brokers and
  Compilers
Lists as a Profit Center
  32 Questions To Ask a Prospective
  List Manager
Duplication Elimination
Lists Age Rapidly
Analyzing Response by Timing and
  Locale
Determining Proper Test Quantities

Market Segmentation
  Environmental Influences
  Zip Code Areas as Market Segments
  Mailing Lists as Market Segments
Measurement-Identification-Retrieval
  Potential of the Market
  Penetration of the Market
  Market Segmentation
  Retrieval of Market Segments

Self-Quiz
Pilot Project

Chapter 3 Magazines Page 66

Where Do You Go First?
Regional Editions: When Is the Part
  Bigger than the Whole?
Pilot Publications: The Beacons of
  Direct Response Media Scheduling
Bind-in Cards: The Big Guns of Print
  Media Advertising
Magazine Advertising Response Pattern:
  What Do These Early Results Mean?
Timing and Frequency: When Should
  You Run? How Often Should You Go
  Back?

Determining Proper Ad Size: How Much
  Is Too Much?
Four-Color, Two-Color, Black and
  White: How Colorful Should Your
  Advertising Be?
The Position Factor: Where You Are
  Can Mean as Much as What You Say

Self-Quiz
Pilot Project

Chapter 4 Newspapers Page 82

Newspaper Preprints
Syndicated Newspaper Supplements
Comics as a Direct Marketing Medium
Effect of Local News on Results
Developing a Newspaper Test Program
Advertising Seasons
Timing of Newspaper Insertions

Newspaper Response Patterns
Determining Proper Ad Size
The Position Factor
Color vs. Black and White

Self-Quiz
Pilot Project

Chapter 5 Broadcast Page 100

Primary TV Objectives
TV Costs Can Be Low
Determining Length of Commercial
Additional Guidelines
Potentials of CATV
Interactive Cable TV: The Ultimate
Radio: A Powerful Medium

Markets by Formats
Radio Is Audio, Not Visual
Length and Types of Commercials
Five Advantages of Radio

Self-Quiz
Pilot Project

Chapter 6 Co-Ops Page 125

Some Co-Op Myths Dispelled
Special Interest Co-Ops Grow
Growth of Post Card Co-Ops
Package Inserts
Mail Co-Op Costs Enticing

Newspaper Co-Ops
Other Co-Ops
Compiled vs. Direct Response Lists
Some Sobering Thoughts about Co-Ops

Self-Quiz
Pilot Project

Chapter 7 Telephone Marketing Page 137

The Telephone Is a Mass Medium
Varied Uses
Planning and Implementation
Do-It-Yourself or Buy
Telephone Case Histories

Telephone Training
Taped Messages
Summary

Self-Quiz
Pilot Project

SECTION III DEVELOPING THE RIGHT PROPOSITIONS FOR DIRECT MARKETING

Chapter 8 Importance of the Proposition Page 154

Examples of Dramatic Differences
The Key: Overcoming Human Inertia
Danger of Overkill
The "Unique" Proposition
Effect of Terms on Propositions
Importance of the Guarantee
Short- and Long-Term Effects of
    Propositions
Propositions Relate to Objectives

Effect on Bad Debts
Types of Propositions
Checklist of Basic Propositions
    Yes-No
    Free Gift
    Load-Ups
    Get-a-Friend

Self-Quiz
Pilot Project

SECTION IV CREATING AND PRODUCING DIRECT MARKETING

Chapter 9 Techniques of Creating Direct Mail Packages Page

Benefit/Price/Value Equation
Preparation Pays Off
Translate Product Features into Benefits
The Right Copy Strategy
Selecting the Format To Do the Job
The Classic Mailing Package
Self-Mailers—An Inexpensive Favorite
Specialized Formats
Involvement Increases Response
Creating the Classic Mailing Package
Good Typography
Anatomy of a Successful Mailing
Writing a Winning Letter
Pros and Cons of Writing to Formula
Seven-Step Formula
    Classic Sales Letter Fits the Formula

Techniques the Pros Use To Improve
    Letter Copy
Letter Lengths and the P.S.
Developing a Copy Style
Special Types of Letter Copy
The Value of Versioned Copy
Writing Computer-Personalized Letters
How To Improve a Good Mailing
    Package
In Review—How To Create Mailing
    Packages That Sell
    Creative Checklist for Direct Mail

Self-Quiz
Pilot Project

Chapter 10 Techniques of Creating Catalogs Page 211

Catalogs Offer Six Consumer Benefits
Precise Description Is Catalog Forte
Classic Route to Building Successful
    Catalogs
A Look at Specialty Mail Order Firms
The Basics of a Successful Catalog
    Basic Number 1: Right Reason for
                Being
    Basic Number 2: Right Merchandise
                Selection
    Basic Number 3: Right Positioning and
                Grouping of
                Merchandise
    Basic Number 4: Right Graphics

Basic Number 5: Right Use of Color
Basic Number 6: Right Size
Basic Number 7: Right Copy
Basic Number 8: Right Sales
                Stimulators
Basic Number 9: Right Order Forms
Basic Number 10: Right Analysis

Self-Quiz
Pilot Project

Chapter 11 Techniques of Creating Print Advertising Page 233

Visualizing the Prospect
   Selecting Advantages and Benefits
Harnessing the Powers of Semantics
Building in the "Hook"
Writing the Lead
Classic Copy Structure
   Other Ways To Structure Copy
Establishing the Uniqueness of Your
   Product or Service

Effective Use of Testimonials
Justifying the Price
Visual Reinforcement of Words and
   Ideas
The Response Device
"Telescopic" Testing

Self-Quiz
Pilot Project

Chapter 12 Production Techniques Page 263

Personnel and Planning the Answer
Production Knowledge Assures
   Efficiency
Knowledge of Suppliers Is Essential
Art Studios
Typographers
Envelope Manufacturers

List Sources
Printers
Mailing Services
The Importance of Controls

Self-Quiz
Pilot Project

SECTION V THE MATHEMATICS OF DIRECT MARKETING

Chapter 13 Mathematical Criteria Direct Marketers Live By
Page 282

Establishing the Break-Even Point
   Price of Merchandise or Service
   Cost of Filling the Order
   Administrative Overhead
   Estimated Returns and Expense of

   Handling
   Unit Profit and Net Profit
   Establishing Break-Even Point
The Arithmetic of Two-Step Promotions
Improving the Figures

Better Markup as a Key
Projections
Investing in New Customers
The Hard-Core Support Group

How Catalog Firms Rate Customers
Interpretation Is Vital to Success

Self-Quiz
Pilot Project

Chapter 14 Testing Techniques Page 302

Test the Big Things
Questionnaire Mailings
Pretesting for Most Appealing Products
Focus Interviews
Telescopic Testing
Innovative Direct Mail Tests

Testing Components vs. Testing Mailing
    Packages
Determining Sample Sizes

Self-Quiz
Pilot Project

INDEX Page 331

FOREWORD

Many have described direct marketing as a bandwagon, with more and more major marketers getting on.

For most marketers, direct marketing is a bright, new world. A world now inhabited by giants who had heretofore restricted distribution to traditional channels. Giants like Avon, Hewlett-Packard, Polaroid, Bell & Howell, General Mills, and 3M, and would-be giants by the thousands. For the giants in particular, direct marketing provides an additional profit center of major proportions. For uncounted thousands, direct marketing offers a primary source of income and profit.

It has been my rich experience to see the totality of direct marketing grow from a basic concept to an explosion—an explosion spurred by computer oriented market segmentation, availability of consumer credit, mastering of multimedia, and professionalism in direct marketing methods and techniques. Today all the ingredients for accelerated growth exist.

The explosive growth of direct marketing, especially in the past five years, has brought with it an expanding demand for talent with expertise in direct response. Opportunities abound for those who can meet the challenge of the special disciplines of direct marketing.

Direct mail as a single medium never quite captured the imagination of bright marketing students. But direct marketing, with its sophistication, its potential for multimedia application, its *measurable* results, is worthy of the brightest of young minds.

Each year more and more marketing students from the nation's colleges are learning the basics of direct marketing through intensive programs sponsored by the Direct Mail Educational Foundation of the Direct Mail/Marketing Association. Renowned authorities of the caliber of Edward N. Mayer, Jr., former president of DM/MA, John Yeck, famed copy motivator, Bob DeLay, president of DM/MA, and Paul Sampson, formerly of the *Christian Science Monitor,* give freely of their time and experience. It is safe to predict that, before another decade passes, direct marketing will be an accredited course in all major colleges and universities with schools of business.

In structuring *Successful Direct Marketing Methods,* I have divided it into five sections, each related to all the others. It is by design that each major medium of direct marketing is discussed thoroughly following Section I, which is an overview of the scope of direct marketing. Learning the ways to capitalize on each medium is essential to applying the techniques of direct marketing covered in subsequent sections.

Because direct marketing is new, even to many with some years' experience in advertising and marketing, two aids to accelerated learning appear at the end of each chapter. First, there is a self-quiz for each chapter. These quizzes enable the reader to review thoroughly the chapter content. By answering the questions throughout, the reader creates a permanent reference to all of the basic materials in this book.

Every self-quiz is followed by a pilot project. Each pilot project is structured in such a way that the reader can, if he wishes, promptly put into practice the information provided in each chapter.

To take full credit for this book would be a sham. Contributions are all too numerous to record. In a very real way, all who have succeeded in direct marketing have contributed.

If recognition were limited to just one person by name, it would have to be my loyal secretary, Barbara Alberts, who relentlessly kept me on schedule and whose nimble fingers typed every single word of this book.

But I would be remiss indeed if I failed to mention at least some of my wonderful associates. The pages of this book are rich with the wisdom of Aaron Adler, a pioneer in syndication; the planning strategies of Stan Rapp; the lifetime experience of Tom Collins in print advertising. Then there's the in-depth knowledge of all media of two of the brightest gals in the business—Joyce Selcer and Kay Knight. Finally, some of the greatest direct marketing professionals I've known—Jim Kobs, Sol Blumenfeld, Don Kanter, Walter Marshall.

But enough. This book is for you, be you seasoned professional or student looking toward an exciting lifelong endeavor. May this book serve as your blueprint for expanding and continuing success in direct marketing.

BOB STONE

PREFACE

This is a great book for two specific reasons. First, it is the first and only complete, definitive book on the whole technique and study of direct marketing. And second, its author is probably the outstanding professional in the field.

It is also a very timely book. Bob Stone, with a lifetime of experience in the creation and the successful use of direct mail advertising, has, over the past several years, seen the need to move into other media as well. As a result, his agency has been a forerunner in the successful use of the various media available for direct marketing.

This book covers all facets of direct marketing, including the scope of direct marketing; media of direct marketing; propositions or offers pertinent to success in direct marketing; techniques of writing copy, not only for direct mail but for other direct marketing media; techniques of creating catalogs; techniques of creating print advertising; production techniques; and the mathematics of direct marketing. It is replete with facts, figures, techniques, applications of techniques, and case histories. It has been written with both the neophyte and the professional in mind. It is my personal belief that *Successful Direct Marketing Methods* will continue for many years to be the outstanding book on the subject.

I could say a great deal more than these few words about Mr. Stone, his background, and his abilities in the direct marketing field. I suggest, rather, that you read this book and keep it handy for future use.

EDWARD N. MAYER, JR.
Past President, Direct Mail/Marketing Association

SECTION 1 THE WORLD OF DIRECT MARKETING

Chapter 1 The Scope of Direct Marketing

$50 billion plus. That's a lot. But $50 billion is a conservative estimate of the goods and services which were sold via the direct marketing method for the year 1973.

Like so many terms in advertising, "direct marketing" has got into our jargon without being clearly defined in the minds of many. It is important at the outset that we define it. A good definition is in the *Magazine of Direct Marketing:*

The total of activity by which the seller effects the transfer of goods and services to the buyer, directs its efforts to a qualified audience, using one or more media for the purpose of soliciting a response by phone, mail or personal visit from a prospect or customer.

So "direct marketing" is not simply a qualified term for "direct mail" or "mail order." In its total definition, direct marketing consists of the use of one or more media for the purpose of eliciting a direct response.

Direct marketing involves the use of direct mail, to be sure — millions and millions of pieces designed to get a direct response — either inquiry or sale.

Direct marketing is newspapers, too. Hundreds of millions of newspaper inserts appear in Sunday newspapers from coast to coast, Sunday after Sunday. Likewise, direct response ads are part and parcel of every newspaper supplement.

Direct response ads abound in magazines. Small ads. Large ads. Full color. Ads with bind-in cards. Each and every ad with a mission: to get a direct response.

TV is the latest darling of direct marketing. As a matter of fact, of all the media of direct marketing, TV is growing at the most rapid rate. For the year 1973 alone, direct marketers expended $105,576,000 for this exciting medium.

Direct marketing is radio, matchbooks, telephone solicitation, and car cards, too. Direct marketing is indeed controlled messages to defined audiences, each message with a single purpose — to get a response.

What are the expenditures for direct marketing? For the year 1973 it was estimated that the expenditure was $3.4 billion for direct mail alone, with perhaps another $2 billion plus for all other media in the direct marketing mix. So the most accepted estimate is total expenditures of $5.4 billion.

The Basic Appeals of Direct Marketing

Direct marketing, as it is structured, seems to fit the life style of the consumer and the businessman of the '70s. Back in the '50s the shopping center was structured to fit the life style of the consumer. But even the shopping center is proving inconvenient for the consumer of the '70s. The consumer, and the businessman too, can get more specific information through direct mail and other media. Direct marketing offers, above all, *convenience* — getting information, goods, and services without leaving one's armchair. For those who buy via the U.S. mails, the *selection* is tremendous — all the sizes, styles, and colors the consumer wants. And *value* is the watchword of direct marketing.

The Credit Card Explosion

Direct marketing really started to explode in the '60s. The dynamic growth of consumer credit cards was a prime factor in the explosion. It is estimated that there were more than 50 million holders of the two major bank cards—BankAmericard and Master Charge—60.1% of whom were active, as of January 1973, according to the Nilson Report. Nilson shows billing of $5 billion 907 million for Inter Bank (Master Charge), and $4 billion 446 million for BankAmericard, for the year 1972—for a combined total in excess of $10 billion. Inter Bank (Master Charge) cards were honored by 970,903 merchants and BankAmericard by 913,396 merchants as of January 1973. (It is estimated that perhaps 50% to 60% of merchants honoring a bank card accept both cards.)

All the while, the three major commercial cards in the travel and entertainment category—American Express, Diners Club, and Carte Blanche—continue to make additional millions of dollars of credit available. The Nilson report provides these membership counts as of January 1973.

	Share of Total	No. of Card Holders
American Express	76%	4,624,800
Diners Club	13%	827,800
Carte Blanche	11%	647,400
TOTAL		6,100,000

Then we must add to this the great availability of credit offered through the medium of oil company credit cards. It is estimated that some 200 million oil cards are in circulation. (When the fuel shortage became acute, practically all major oil companies stopped soliciting new credit card holders. Hundreds of thousands of $2 and $3 transactions made oil company credit card operations a costly burden. However, it is unlikely that oil companies will ever eliminate their credit card operations in view of the incredible costs they would face in reestablishing them at a later date.) This availability of consumer credit has made it possible to sell big ticket merchandise to the consumer and the businessman without their ever having to leave their premises. Before credit cards, it was difficult indeed to sell any item selling for more than $10 direct in volume. Today, it is commonplace to sell items for $69.95, up to $100 and more, direct to the user on credit.

The Computer Explosion—Selectivity at Last

Concurrent with the credit card explosion has been the development of the mechanical brain of the century—the computer. Today it is possible for any marketer to isolate prime prospects for his products and services, eliminating major segments of our 200 million population who do not have the ability or the propensity to buy what the marketer has to offer. Not only is there selectivity via the mailing list medium, but there is great selectivity in other media as well. Regional editions of magazines abound. *TV Guide,* for example, provides fantastic selectivity by offering 84 regional editions.

Six Big Keys to Direct Marketing Success

What does make direct marketing successful? An oversimplified definition may be:

Offering the right product or services via the right media, with the most enticing propositions, presented with the most effective formats, proved effective as a result of the right tests.

Sounds pretty simple. But, of course, it isn't! The checklist on pages 4–6 explores the six big keys to direct marketing success with 53 basic questions relating to them. Scores more could be added.

Let's explore the basic thinking which has to go into each of these keys to success.

1. Right Product or Services

Success in any endeavor starts with the product. No business can long survive, no matter what the medium of selling may be, unless the product is *right*.

Time was when direct sales of products via mail or space advertising was looked upon as a means of "dumping" merchandise which did not sell well through retail channels. Time was when off-brand merchandise which couldn't get shelf space in retail stores was offered direct to the consumer. That's all changed today. Direct marketers who have really succeeded offer quality merchandise of good value.

2. Right Media

Some authorities give 50% and more of the credit for the success of a given mailing to the lists that are used. You can't prove the figure. But you can bet on this—no key to success is more important than lists!

Likewise, the publications used for print and the stations used for broadcast are vital keys to success. (Chapters 2 through 7 cover each major medium in depth.)

3. Right Proposition

In my book, there is no key to success more important than the proposition. You can have the right product, the right mailing lists, the right print and broadcast media. But you still won't make it big if you don't have the right proposition. You've got to overcome human inertia—whatever the medium.

(Chapter 8 covers 22 different propositions in detail, all of which are designed to overcome human inertia.)

4. Right Formats

The number of formats which may be used for presenting propositions are almost endless. This is particularly true of direct mail, where there are few restrictions on format. The marketer may choose to use anything, from a simple post card to a 9×12 mailing package which could include a giant four-color brochure, letter, giant order card, tokens or stamps, pop-ups, ad infinitum.

Restrictions on print and broadcast advertising are, of course, more stringent, being controlled by the publishers and the stations. But the important point is that there is a *right* format for given mailing packages, given ads, and given commercials. Depending on formats selected, the results can be anywhere from disastrous to sensational.

5. Right Tests

With literally thousands of chances to do the wrong thing, the way to direct marketing success is testing to determine the right thing. Indeed, direct marketing is the most *measurable* type of marketing there is.

Mailing packages can be tested scientifically to determine such vital things as best offer, best format, best lists, best copy, best postage, and so on.

The print medium, with the advent of regional editions, has also made an endless variety of tests possible. Direct marketers now test by regions. They test for size and color. They test for position. They test bind-in cards, bingo cards. They test special interest magazines vs. general. Newspapers can be tested to learn all you have to know.

It is also possible to test, on a control basis, the efficiency of broadcast. Testing is likewise possible when the telephone is used as a selling medium.

(Chapter 14 clearly spells out the techniques developed to enable one to get the right answers.)

6. Right Analyses

There is no key more important to direct marketing success than the sixth — right analyses. Direct marketers live by figures, but figures often lead to erroneous conclusions. Fortunes have been lost by counting *trial orders* instead of counting *paid-ups*. Fortunes have been lost by *averaging* response, by not really knowing break-even points, by never determining the value of a customer, by never preparing cash flow charts.

Section V of this book, "The Mathematics of Direct Marketing," is devoted to applying the mathematics of direct marketing properly.

Checklist for Applying the Six Big Keys to Direct Marketing Success

1. The Product or Service You Offer

- Is it a real value for the price asked?
- How does it stack up against competition?
- Do you have exclusive features?
- Does your packaging create a good first impression?
- Is the market broad enough to support a going organization?
- Is your product cost low enough to warrant a mail order markup?
- Does your product or service lend itself to repeat business?

2. The Media You Use

Customer Lists

- Is your customer list cleaned on a regular basis?
- Do you keep a second copy of your list elsewhere to avoid loss?
- Have you developed a profile of your customer list, giving you all the important demographic characteristics?
- Have you coded your customer list by recency of purchase?
- Have you worked your customer list by the classic mail order formula: recency-frequency-monetary?
- Have you thought of what other products or services may appeal to your customer list?
- Do you mail your customer list often enough to capitalize on the investment?

Prospect Lists

- Do you freely provide facts and figures to one or more competent mailing list brokers, enabling them to unearth productive lists for you?
- Have you worked with competent list compilers in selecting names of prospects who match the profile of those on your customer list?
- Do you test meaningful, measurable, projectable quantities?

- Have you measured the true results of prospect lists, computing for each list inquiries and/or returned goods, net cash receipts per M mailed, and repeat business?
- Have you determined how often you can successfully mail the same prospect list?

Print

- Have you matched your propositions with your markets and used print media with good direct response track records?
- Have you measured the true results of print media, computing, for each newspaper and/or magazine, inquiries and/or returned goods, net cash receipts per insertion, and repeat business?
- Have you determined how often you can successfully use the same print media?

Broadcast

- Have you selected broadcast media which best fit your objective: *(a)* to get inquiries and/or orders; *(b)* to support other advertising media?
- Have you measured the true results of broadcast media, computing, for each station, inquiries and/or returned goods, net cash receipts per broadcast schedule, and repeat business?
- Have you determined the proper times and frequency for broadcast schedules?

3. The Propositions You Make

- Are you making the most enticing offers you can within the realm of good business?
- Does your proposition lend itself to the use of any or all of these incentives for response: free gift, contest, free trial offer, installment terms, price savings, money back guarantee?
- Does your proposition lend itself to the development of an "automatic" repeat business cycle?
- Does your proposition lend itself to a "get-a-friend" program?
- Have you determined the ideal introductory period or quantity for your proposition?
- Have you determined the ideal introductory price for your proposition?
- Have you determined the possibility of multiple sales for your proposition?

4. The Formats You Use

Direct Mail

- Are your mailing packages in character with your products or services and the markets you are reaching?
- Have you developed the ideal format for your mailing packages, with particular emphases on mailing envelope, letter, circular, response form, and reply envelope?
- Do you work with one or more creative envelope manufacturers?
- Are your sales letters in character with your offers?
- Are your circulars graphic, descriptive, and in tune with the complete mailing package?
- Does your response form contain the complete offer? Is it attractive enough to grab attention and impel action?

5

Print

- Are your ads in character with your products and services and the markets you are reaching?
- Have you explored newspaper inserts, magazine inserts, bind-in cards, tip-on cards, dutch door newspaper inserts, plastic records?

Broadcast

- Are your commercials in character with your products and services and the markets you are reaching?
- Have you determined the efficiency of stand-up announcer commercials vs. staged commercials?
- Have you explored the efficiency of noted personality endorsements?

5. The Tests You Make

- Do you consistently test the big things: product, media, propositions, and formats?
- Have you tested to determine the best timing for your propositions, the best frequency?
- Have you determined the most responsive geographical areas?
- Do you consistently test new direct mail packages against control packages, new ads against control ads, new commercials against control commercials?
- Do you use adequate test quantities?
- Do you follow your test figures through to conclusion, using net revenue per M as the key criterion?
- Do you interpret your test figures in the light of the effect on the image and future profits of your company?

6. The Right Analyses

- Do you track results by source, computing front end response, returned goods factor, and bad debt factor for each source?
- Do you analyze results by ZIP Codes, by demographics?
- Do you compute repeat business factor by original source?

The Place of the Consumer Goods Manufacturer

With the tools now available to sell products and services directly to the consumer, direct marketing has attracted major marketers who are household words in both the consumer and the business fields. Marketers like GE, Westinghouse, Polaroid, Bell & Howell, 3M, and Avon—just to mention a few.

But the thought of going the direct marketing route, even as an adjunct, still strikes fear and trepidation in the hearts of most giant corporations that have grown through traditional channels. "Will direct marketing hurt our retail sales?" is the question which brings on chills. This is not a new fear.

A good case in point is the record industry. Traditionally, records were always sold through retail record stores. But, as we all know, record clubs—the direct route between the clubs and the consumer—circumvented the retailer and became a major marketing method back in the '50s. Record dealers registered strong complaints. In 1955, record clubs accounted for $10 million in record sales. By 1968—13 years later—record clubs accounted for $250 million in annual sales. What happened to retail store sales in the interim? From 1955 through 1968, retail record store sales compounded at the rate of 10% a year — right in the face of a tremendous rise in record club sales.

A similar phenomenon occurred in the book industry. Book club sales increased phenomenally, but so did retail bookstore sales. This phenomenon is easily understood when the tremendous amount of advertising done by clubs vs. retail stores is taken into account. A large amount of club advertising rubbed off on retail stores. Millions of people decided to purchase given records and given books in the retail store, all as a result of advertising by book and record clubs. They would never have known about these books and records in any other way.

Two major consumer goods manufacturers who built their business through retail channels, before adding direct marketing as an additional sales avenue, were Bell & Howell and Polaroid. (Both entered direct marketing via the syndicator route.) What most people have not realized is that these firms have, for the most part, offered top-of-the-line cameras by mail. Through deluxe, full color mailing packages, these manufacturers have excited interest among the consumers, thousands of whom could not afford the top-of-the-line models being offered by mail. This has led consumers into the retail stores and accounts for millions of dollars in retail sales of other cameras selling at lower prices. Many consumer goods manufacturers have followed the examples of Bell & Howell and Polaroid.

The Place of the Retailer

While retailers for the most part have shunned or damned direct marketing, some of the most progressive have got on the direct marketing bandwagon.

For years, the great Abercrombie & Fitch played to a select clientele — those who lived in their trading areas and had the wherewithal to cross their threshold. But now Abercrombie & Fitch are taking their image direct to the people across the nation, inviting consumers to trade with them directly by mail. And consumers are buying razors, steak knives, waist trimmers, and a host of other items.

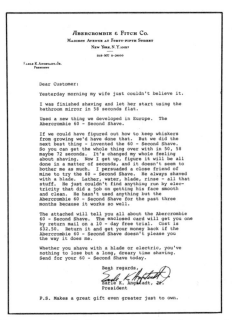

Typical low-key letter by Abercrombie & Fitch Co., soliciting a sale direct by mail.

The giant of giants, Sears, Roebuck, have gone the direct marketing route through individual Sears stores. A typical offer is a $149.95 Argus camera outfit. The charge customer is invited to mail the order card to the individual store or come in to pick up the merchandise.

K Mart (Kresge's) built store traffic among their charge customers with a Realtone radio offer—$24.88 with $5 discount coupon.

Then there's the famed Neiman-Marcus Christmas catalog with "his and her" bath-tubs and a glittering array of merchandise for the affluent of heart.

Retailers like W. T. Grant, Shoppers Fair, and Bond's Kiproe Mail Order Division are selling various camera outfits and a wide selection of other merchandise direct to their charge customers.

What a far cry these examples are from "typical retail direct mail," represented by ill-conceived manufacturer-prepared envelope stuffers. A 1967 survey on direct mail prac-tices, prepared by the National Retail Merchants Association, disclosed that 70% of all direct mail pieces used by retailers were envelope inserts. So, successful direct market-ing efforts by retailers are the exception rather than the rule.

But, as I see it, the time is ripe for retail stores, by the score, to go the direct market-ing route. There are three big pluses for retailers that cannot be matched solely by the mail order method.

1. *The advantage of local identity.* This is a big plus in the local trading area. The reluctance to order by mail from an unknown firm in a distant city is overcome when a mailing comes from a local retailer.
2. *The advantage of additional traffic.* A firm which sells solely through mail order either gets an order direct by mail or it's dead. The retailer, on the other hand, can have his cake and eat it: Orders are generated direct by mail, or by phone. And he can expect additional store traffic as well.
3. *Buying power.* Giant retailers and buying groups have buying power going for them. They have the sources of supply and the possibilities of volume discounts.

With the built-in advantages enjoyed by retailers, plus the buying experience and buying power enjoyed by many, one would think that success is awaiting all who try. But the sad truth is that, beyond the occasional successful Christmas flyer and a few other seasonal promotions, winners have been few and far between. I've seen "big tick-et" offers in the $50 range, that have pulled 15 to 20 orders per thousand from mail or-der lists, pull a dismal three to four orders per thousand from department store lists.

So before examining the ingredients for success, let's pinpoint the prime reasons for failure in retail direct marketing efforts.

Lists: Most retail "customer lists" consist of charge customers—those who have charged purchases at the retail store. They are *not,* for the most part, mail order buyers. Few retail charge lists are arranged by recency, frequency, or amount of purchase. Most retail direct mail promotions are across-the-board: metro areas and suburban alike. And you just don't sell many power mowers to apartment dwellers! Retailers stock dif-ferent merchandise in suburban stores than in downtown stores to cater to different preferences. But they seem to ignore this necessity when it comes to direct mail.

Installment Credit: Without installment credit, the sale of big ticket merchandise by mail is a virtual impossibility. There is a real hang-up for retailers who want to retain their identity with their own charge card—offering 30-day terms—to the exclusion of other charge cards which allow for installment payments. The answer lies in one of two alternatives: a revolving credit plan for the existing store credit card, or working through one of the existing bank credit card systems.

8

Merchandise Selection: Selecting merchandise for mail order sales and selecting merchandise for sale over the counter can be as different as day and night. Few mail order practitioners could earn the right to sit in the chair of the retail store buyer and vice versa! The types of merchandise to be selected, the manner of promotion, the economics involved, vary greatly.

So it may be said the first step for retailers interested in climbing on the direct marketing bandwagon is to recognize why so many have failed.

Since the retailer enjoys the great advantages of store traffic resulting from his direct marketing efforts, there are many objectives which may be explored.

1. *Activating existing charge customers.* The most fertile area in any business is the existing customer. And the charge card list is the prime list. There's no more effective way to activate a charge list than *(a)* to give special recognition to charge customers, and *(b)* to show this recognition with special offers.
2. *Getting new customers.* Close behind the objective of constantly activating existing customers is the constant need for getting new customers. And here's where direct marketing methods can prove a bonanza. Pinpoint marketing makes it possible to seek new customers in the most productive trading areas around existing stores and beyond. Merchandise offers can be tied into efforts to acquire new customers, with the opportunity to make such efforts break even or better.
3. *Increasing store traffic.* Store traffic is still the name of the game. Direct marketing efforts will automatically create store traffic spillover. But beyond this, there can be targeted store traffic mailings — special offers not generally advertised. A well-organized store traffic program can pay off big.
4. *Leveling out sales volume.* The retail sales curve has been a fact of life ever since the early days of Wanamaker, the Penneys, and the Fields. It still is today. Direct marketing efforts can be a big factor in filling in the valleys.
5. *Pretesting merchandise and pricing.* Direct marketing methods offer perhaps the most accurate means of pretesting the appeal of merchandise and the most appealing price level. I have yet to see retailers use direct marketing for this purpose, but it could prove to be imaginative and profitable.
6. *Selling a wider range of merchandise.* This can be the most desirable and most profitable objective of all. Mail order thrives on the sale of merchandise and merchandise combinations not generally available in the retail store. But who is to say that a retailer should not sell merchandise *not generally available in his retail store?* It's being done right now — successfully. Cameras, radios, dinnerware, tool sets, delicacies, paint guns, magazine subscriptions, insurance — an endless variety of merchandise and services — all extra business.

And if the retailer works with a syndicator, there are two distinct advantages. One: properly prepared mailing packages at minimal cost. Two: no inventory or handling by the retail store.

So the time is ripe for retailing to get on the direct marketing bandwagon. The ingredients are all here for those who will grasp the opportunities and run with them. I see three basic ingredients which are vital to success:

1. A separate department headed by a direct marketing manager and/or direct marketing consultant, reporting directly to a store official.
2. An installment credit program in conjunction with the store's own charge card or with one or more charge card systems.
3. A planned continuing program.

The Place of the Industrial Goods Manufacturer

Manufacturers who sell to other business firms, either direct or through dealers, wholesalers, and/or distributors, have likewise discovered that sophisticated direct marketing techniques pay handsomely in sales and profits. Direct marketing techniques apply in four broad categories:

1. Leads for company salesmen.
2. Leads for salesmen of dealers, wholesalers, and/or distributors.
3. Direct sale of supplies and equipment to prospects in territories not covered by company salesmen, dealers, wholesalers, and/or distributors.
4. Direct sale of supplies and equipment which do not lend themselves to sales through salesmen.

It is a difficult task for industrial marketing men today to extract from their universes of potential prospects those who qualify for a full-fledged sales presentation *now*. In most fields of endeavor, the cost of salesmen's ferreting out qualified prospects is so high that the ultimate costs are prohibitive.

The fact is that in most cases sales cost is kept within reason only if salesmen concentrate on qualified leads. Think about the Pitney-Bowes postage meter, for example. There's a size for every office, and theoretically every office should have one. But the cost of calling on every office—even if manpower were available—would be excessive. Experience has shown that qualified leads result in more sales at a lower sales cost.

The importance of lead-producing programs becomes very evident when one takes a look at what it costs for one salesman to make one call. Back in 1955, the average cost of a salesman's call was estimated to be $17.24. Just 14 years later, McGraw-Hill's laboratory of advertising performance pegged the average figure at $49.30 per call. And now it's in the neighborhood of $60 per call—and climbing!

And it is important to note these figures are for cost per call: *not cost per sale*. So the more unqualified prospects a salesman calls on without results, the higher the ultimate sales cost will be. Direct mail and space advertising have the power greatly to reduce the ratio of unqualified prospects to qualified and thereby reduce the cost per order.

Essentials of a Lead-Producing Program

The success of any lead-producing program depends, to a major degree, on the extent of control exercised by management.

Management must hold the cards and play them well. Here are the essentials of a successful lead-producing program:

1. The lead-producing program should be created by the home office.
2. All literature should be pretested to determine maximum sales (at a profit) in ratio to leads.
3. The sales organization should be "sold" the program as one that will increase their selling efficiency and income.
4. All processing of leads should be handled promptly through the home office.
5. Tight controls must be maintained to make certain all leads passed on to salesmen are handled promptly.
6. The objective of management, at all times, should be to put the salesman in a favorable selling position.

There's nothing new about the idea of getting qualified leads for salesmen. The great John H. Patterson, back in the late 1800s, figured he'd sell a lot more of his newfangled cash registers, at a lower sales cost, if he could get qualified leads for his derby-topped salesmen.

Today, almost a century later, the Patterson direct mail principles are still being followed by National Cash Register. The procedures are more sophisticated, to be sure. But the principles remain the same. A study of their procedures shows why they are so successful.

1. Home office direction: All mailing programs are created at direct mail center headquarters at the Dayton, O., home office. And all mail flows through the center. Under no conditions are branch managers or salesmen tied to physically releasing mailings.

2. Branch office and salesmen involvement: The 258 branch offices and 4,000-man sales force decide which campaigns are to be mailed to what categories of business and when. Salesmen can select from some 100 or more campaigns. Salesmen can supply names and specify individual campaigns. Branch managers can order campaigns and specify the lists to be used—either a special compilation or one or more of the lists maintained at the direct mail center. Branch offices are charged for campaigns. Thus they have a vested interest in results.

3. Mail programs tied to marketing objectives: The prime objectives of NCR are to produce qualified leads, to reinforce the salesman after he makes his first call, and to enhance the overall image of NCR. Here's how the objectives are met:
   Mechanized selling campaigns: The prime purpose of these campaigns is to produce qualified leads for salesmen. The salesman calls his shots. He simply fills in a 3×5 card specifying a particular campaign, by number, for a particular line of business. The card goes to the direct mail center.
   Within a week the first mailing in a three-piece campaign is on the way. Other pieces follow on a weekly basis. The 3×5 card is returned to the salesman, so he knows when each specified piece will be mailed.
   Reinforced campaigns: These are known as salesmen's back-up mailings. They follow the salesman's call and help keep the prospect alive. There are usually five pieces to each of these campaigns. The first piece goes out within a week after the salesman's call, the remaining four at weekly intervals.
   Image-building campaigns: Salesmen are urged to request the mailings of these campaigns to anyone they feel may some day become a customer. These campaigns are also used for present customers with the idea of keeping them sold between calls. Campaigns are designed to sell the salesman and the company rather than a product or application.

4. Pretested campaigns: NCR can sell campaigns to branch managers and salesmen with assurance because most inquiry-building campaigns are pretested. Thus, in many cases, NCR can guarantee a given number of inquiries for each 100 pieces mailed.

5. Tight controls to assure follow-through: All inquiries from prospects come directly to Dayton. The branch involved is notified immediately. This puts the branch manager in a position to make sure the local salesman follows through promptly. Nothing is left to guesswork.

Don't let
the rising cost of business
catch you anchored to
outmoded wage policies.

Every retailer is faced with a steadily rising pay scale
for salespeople. Higher wage demands and fringe benefits
are pushing this expense to new heights. And the end is
not in sight.

Because of today's competition, a retailer rarely can
raise prices to offset an increase in payroll. Conse-
quently a retailer should be able to justify the salary
he is paying each salesperson. It's unrealistic for any
modern merchant to assume that he's getting his money's
worth without careful and scientific study of employee
productivity.

To help you establish a realistic wage policy, we have
prepared a special sales productivity chart, "HOW MUCH
SHOULD A SALESPERSON SELL". It contains information that
is vital, revealing and extremely rewarding - in terms of
controlling costs and keeping profits up.

We'll be pleased to send you this chart on the whys, hows,
and wherefores of the modern sales-salary relationship.
Simply give us the signal by mailing the enclosed card
today! And you won't obligate yourself in the least!

Sincerely,

T. E. McCarthy, Vice President
Retail Systems Division

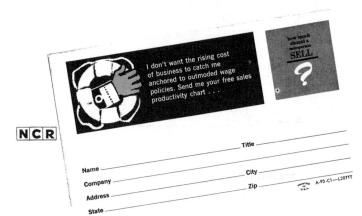

*This mail piece, offering a "sales productivity chart," titled "How Much Should a Sales-
person Sell," goes to National Cash Register customer at salesman's request. It's part of a
three-piece campaign that pulled a 6.5% return.*

Does the NCR direct mail program work? You bet! R. G. Ljungren, director, Corporation Advertising and Sales Promotion, ticks off some interesting figures relating to specific campaigns. He quotes total inquiry responses of from 6.5% all the way up to 14.7%.
Think of what these qualified leads mean to the NCR sales and profit picture!

Finally, Mr. Ljungren points out the wisdom of using up to five pieces in a campaign. He states, "On an average five-piece mailing series (mailed at weekly intervals), if we count all inquiries from the five pieces as 100%, we find that the first mailing accounts for 30.5%, the second for 23.2%, the third for 18.1%, the fourth for 15.2%, and the fifth for 13% of the total."

The Importance of Lists

No one can succeed in direct marketing without a thorough knowledge of mailing lists and their importance to any marketing program. (The mailing list subject is thoroughly covered in Chapter 2.) But a reference to mailing lists as they relate to the importance of lead-producing programs is very much in order at this point.

Ask any manufacturer if he knows who his best prospects are. He'll say "Certainly" without hesitation. Fact is, he knows who his best prospects are in a general sense – not in a specific sense.

Two charts are shown on pages 13 and 14. Both underscore the shortcomings and opportunities related to most direct mail support programs. The charts are based upon actual research. Only the ratios are changed, to screen identity.

Chart 1 was organized under the government's standard industrial classifications which neatly fit all businesses into nine major categories, each divided into hundreds of numerically designated groups.

Headings (1) through (3) show the number of names compiled by the manufacturer for each major SIC classification, number of customers secured from the prospect list, and percent of customer penetration for each major SIC. From all appearances, the manufacturer is doing great: customer penetration from a low of 22.5% to a high of 62.5% penetration, with an average of 39%.

CHART 1.—PENETRATION OF HOUSE LIST VS. TOTAL MARKET POTENTIAL

SIC CLASSIFICATION	1. Names on House Prospect List	2. Customers from Prospect List	3. % of Customer Penetration	4. Un-tapped Names	5. Penetration of Available Names
Agriculture, Forestry, Fisheries	200	45	22.5%	2,810	1.6%
Mining	40	10	25.0%	465	2.1%
Contractors	2,630	870	33.1%	62,580	1.4%
Manufacturers (All types)	8,525	2,655	31.2%	61,385	4.1%
Transportation, Communication, Public Utilities	1,255	785	62.5%	9,270	7.8%
Rated Wholesalers	4,770	1,920	40.3%	32,810	5.5%
Retailers (All types)	8,695	3,130	36.1%	209,705	1.5%
Rated Finance, Insurance, Real Estate	5,410	2,945	54.4%	53,150	5.2%
Rated Service Companies	2,715	1,235	45.5%	83,990	2.6%
TOTALS	34,240	13,595	39.0%	454,780	3.5%

But headings (4) and (5) give dramatic proof that the surface has hardly been scratched. There's 39% customer penetration of the house list. Great! But penetration of total available like names is only 3.5%. House list prospect quantity comes to 34,240 names. The total of available like names comes to 454,780. Untapped names—420,540.

In an interview for *Advertising Age,* Leo Gans, president of National Business Lists, stated, "It's our experience that most direct mail support programs grow like Topsy. Rarely does the manufacturer who offers support programs have a clear picture of customer penetration and total name availability."

Asked how a manufacturer can develop detailed data for distributor-dealer-salesman territories a la Chart 1, Gans said: "This system has evolved over a number of years. With our highly sophisticated computer operation we can profile customer penetration for any manufacturer by territories and project name availability. From the manufacturer's standpoint, it's really quite simple. He provides us with a list of prospects and customers for typical territories. We then compute customer penetration by territory and total available like names. Cost of research is nominal when potential is taken into account."

Don't Get Hung Up on Credit Ratings

CHART 2.—SIC CLASSIFICATION: CONTRACTORS

CREDIT RATING	1. Names on House Prospect List	2. Customers from Prospect List	3. % of Customer Penetration	4. Untapped Names	5. Penetration of Available Names
Listed, but not rated	885	355	40.0%	20,135	1.8%
Not listed	315	65	26.4%	17,465	.4%
Under $5M	40	—	—	4,720	.0%
$5M to $10M	80	15	18.7%	5,885	.3%
$10M to $20M	145	30	20.7%	5,100	.6%
$20M to $35M	110	10	9.1%	2,835	.4%
$35M to $75M	305	135	44.2%	3,405	4.0%
$75M to $200M	240	120	50.0%	1,410	8.5%
$200M to $500M	350	75	21.4%	1,080	6.9%
$500M and over	160	65	40.6%	545	11.9%
TOTALS	2,630	870	33.1%	62,580	1.4%

As revealing as Chart 1 is, Chart 2 is even more so. It dramatically shows what is revealed when SIC classifications are analyzed by ratings or lack of ratings.

In the total research project, all nine major SIC classifications were analyzed by rating or lack of rating. In the chart, we isolate one typical SIC classification—contractors.

Most revealing of all are the first two categories; "listed, but not rated" and "not listed" in credit rating book. Looking at headings (1) through (3), we see 40% of the prospects in the "listed, but not rated" category have become customers. And 26.4% of the prospects in the "not listed" have become customers. When we relate this phenomenon to "untapped names," we find a total of 37,600 available names, which is 60% of all available names for contractors.

14

In this example, which is quite typical, there is a shocker for most manufacturers who have been schooled in the idea that if a firm doesn't carry a rating or isn't listed at all — forget it. False assumption.

I was surprised recently to learn that firms with the stature of Polk Bros., Commonwealth Edison Co. of Indiana, and Ozite Corp. carry no rating in Dun & Bradstreet. Thousands of firms of lesser stature are likewise listed but not rated, or not even listed. The reason I hear most often is that these firms are not about to let their competition know how they are doing. Whatever the reason, nonrated and nonlisted names are obviously a tremendous source for expansion of direct mail support programs.

Probe Your Findings

Market refinement for direct mail support programs can go much deeper than indicated by these two charts. Customer penetration statistics can be developed for the hundreds of subclassifications under the nine major SIC classifications. Data can be developed by number of employees, region, state, standard metropolitan statistical area, county, city, sectional center, or right down to a five-digit ZIP Code area.

Like all research it's great, providing you interpret the figures accurately and apply them intelligently to the advertising sales promotion program. Asked for his expertise in direct mail support programs, Gans comes up with several positive suggestions.

- Find out who your customers really are.
- Use a professional list compiler to determine total availability of names for each list classification.
- Rate prospect value by percent of customer penetration for each list classification.
- Tie your advertising expenditures to prospect value rather than allocating them equally for each list classification. (A prospect list with a 40% rating warrants twice the advertising expenditure as a prospect list with a 20% rating, for example.)
- Learn your "spheres of influence" through studying functional titles, such as systems manager, chief maintenance officer, executive responsible for gift giving, or any title which will help to get a qualified response. Lists having a high percentage of customer penetration often warrant mailings to more than one title within a firm.
- Control your direct mail support program from the home office.
- Settle for nothing less than scrupulous maintenance of your total list, with nonduplication between prospect lists and customer lists.
- See that distributors, dealers, and salesmen all have bound copies of the available names receiving promotions in their respective territories. Provide not only firm names and addresses but telephone numbers as well.

A sound program indeed for manufacturers who are putting important advertising dollars into direct mail support programs.

While it is certainly easier to pinpoint prospects through the medium of mailing lists, the same principles naturally apply to publication advertising available to industrial goods manufacturers.

Mail Order Possibilities for the Industrial Goods Manufacturer

While the consumer goods manufacturer is realizing more and more the potential that mail order has over and beyond the sale of his goods through traditional channels, industrial goods manufacturers have been slow to recognize it. The few who have are, for the most part, enjoying the fruits of an exciting new world.

The cost of person-to-person selling being what it is, many industrial goods manufacturers find themselves in a real quandary. Salesmen will understandably devote the major part of their time to selling basic equipment, where the big commissions are, neglecting the sale of supplies. There is a great after-market for a host of equipment, such as typewriters, duplicating machines, camera equipment, dictating equipment, to mention just a few. This after-market is neglected in industry after industry. Mail order is the ideal way to pick up the lush profits in the sale of supplies.

But mail order possibilities go well beyond the after-market. Many a product or piece of equipment with a great potential has remained on the drawing boards because industrial management has correctly determined the unit of sale would not be sufficient to warrant the time and effort of their own sales force or the sales forces of their dealers, wholesalers, and/or distributors. This is where mail order can do the job.

A classic example is that of Hewlett-Packard, a member of the Fortune 500, who first entered mail order in 1971. Hewlett-Packard are famous the world over for their sophisticated electronic equipment. Most of their equipment, including desk-top calculators, carries a multi-thousand-dollar price tag.

When Hewlett-Packard engineers developed a sophisticated pocket calculator for engineers, the proper selling price was indicated to be in the $400 range — a range far below that typical of Hewlett-Packard equipment. Obviously, it was not for their sales force, particularly if the item were to be sold in volume. Mail order turned out to be the most logical method of selling.

Today, the Hewlett-Packard entry into mail order is a well-known success story. During the very first year, the Hewlett-Packard pocket calculator, known as the HP-35, rolled up approximately $20 million in sales, primarily through the media of direct mail and lead-producing space advertising. The basic mailing package designed to sell this $400 piece of equipment direct, as well as an example of lead-producing advertising, is shown on the following pages.

Mail order opportunities abound for industrial goods manufacturers. It's a new world and a different world, but, for those who will apply sophisticated marketing principles, there's little limit to how far they can go.

The Place of the Syndicator

Direct marketing, as we know it today, would still be in its infancy if it were not for the syndicator. The syndicator enables almost anyone in marketing to enter the field, either by making his product available to other marketers or by enabling the marketer to sell other products to his own customer list. The syndicator is an entrepreneur who has merchandising know-how and market knowledge and is willing to assume risks. Syndicators were a major factor in putting oil companies into direct marketing. They have done the same for many others.

For consumer goods manufacturers in particular, going the syndicated route initially can make eminent sense. There are several advantages for the manufacturer. The manufacturer does not offer his merchandise directly to the consumer; other organizations, with credit checked lists of customers, do so. The syndicator assumes the responsibility of preparing the mailing package. The manufacturer does not assume individual credit risks; the mailers who offer his merchandise to their customers assume those risks.

How profitable syndication can be for a consumer goods manufacturer is illustrated by the case history of Bell & Howell, as told by Aaron Adler, executive vice president of RCS&A (Chicago).

The year was 1959. The sales manager of Bell & Howell called on Al Sloan (a pioneer syndicator) to discuss the possibility of promoting a $150 movie camera outfit by mail. Up to that time, few if any consumer items with prices exceeding $50 had been sold by mail. Al Sloan knew this, but was enough of a gambler to try it.

16

The HP-35 –
A small tribute
to great American
ingenuity. Made in U.S.A.

Don't settle for less.

Hewlett-Packard presents the world's first pocket calculator that challenges a computer

Slide-rule portability and computer-like power for just $395

Hewlett-Packard's HP-35 is a new time-and-work saver that can free you from countless hours of tedious computation. This cordless wonder is just a bit larger than a pack of king-size cigarettes and weighs a mere 9 ounces. Yet it *challenges a computer* in handling complex problems, including log, trig and exponent functions with a single keystroke. Best of all, it solves these problems on the spot—whether in the lab, on a plane, or at a job site. All this highly sophisticated, highly portable calculating power costs a mere $395.00. So why settle for less? Find out now what the HP-35 can do to make your job a little easier . . . and a lot more productive. Write today for your free Capability Report.

HEWLETT *hp* PACKARD

Mail to:
HEWLETT-PACKARD
Advanced Products, Dept.
10900 Wolfe Road, Cupertino, Calif. 95014

Please mail me a free copy
of your in-depth Capability Report
on the HP-35 Pocket Calculator

NAME

TITLE

FIRM NAME

ADDRESS

CITY

STATE   ZIP

Space ad designed to get inquiries for the HP-35 Pocket Calculator.

17

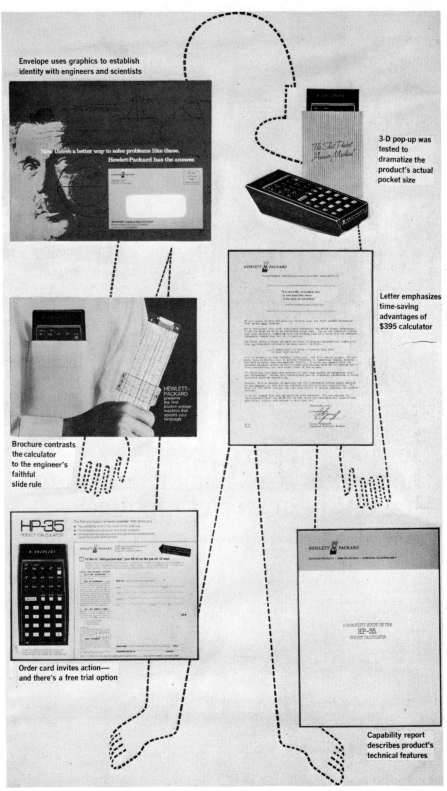

Envelope uses graphics to establish identity with engineers and scientists

3-D pop-up was tested to dramatize the product's actual pocket size

Letter emphasizes time-saving advantages of $395 calculator

Brochure contrasts the calculator to the engineer's faithful slide rule

Order card invites action— and there's a free trial option

Capability report describes product's technical features

Hewlett-Packard's mailing for its pocket calculator was carefully designed to appeal to engineers. Package pulled an incredible $40,000 in sales for every 1,000 inquiries.

Pioneer syndicated mailing package for Bell & Howell created by Aaron Adler.

Under the direction of Aaron Adler, a complete mailing package was prepared, designed to sell the $150 camera directly to the consumer. Al Sloan then presented this package to firms with large lists of credit checked customers. Among the firms to whom the presentation was made were Fingerhut Manufacturing Co., Americana-Interstate, Alden's, and Encyclopaedia Britannica. To everyone's amazement, the mailing pulled in an unprecedented 1% to 2%, or as much as $3,000 revenue per thousand pieces mailed.

With the actual merchandise cost running about $1,900 and the mailing costing about $80 per M (this was in the day of the 2.5¢ bulk third-class postage) the mailer was grossing as much as $1,020 per M profit. Not only did the unprecedented success of this mailing open the direct mail field to the sale of high-priced merchandise, but it brought in many new mailing prospects — firms who had never before thought of using one-shot merchandise promotions.

Now, Some of the Country's Top Journalists (including 3 Pulitzer Prize Winners) will help you

Get More Out of Chicago

We'll sell you the city for 50¢ a month, and give you our charter issue on the house!

Space ad as part of multimedia introductory campaign for "The Chicagoan." *Allowable order cost for this double spread ad in the* Chicago Daily News *was $4; subscriptions were achieved at the remarkable cost of $1.83. The combination of direct mail and space advertising produced in excess of 40,000 charter subscriptions prior to the first issue.*

In the next few weeks, the people who make Chicago what it is will have a new magazine about themselves. Because *you* are one of these people, you are invited to try it—at distinctly favorable, money-saving terms that may never be offered again once the charter issue goes on sale in September.

This new magazine for urban living is called The Chicagoan.

The Chicagoan will be the joint and loving work of some of the best-known names and most polished talents in journalism today.

It will cover all of Chicago and its sprawling environs from the edge of Indiana to the edge of Wisconsin, from where the lake begins to where the outermost suburb leaves off—as they've never been covered before.

It will explore this teeming megolopo-.lis with a zest, curiosity and affectionate realism nobody's ever gotten between the covers of a magazine before.

It will tell you things about the city's pleasures and perils you never knew before—even if you've lived here for years.

And, finally, most important from your standpoint, it will help you make the most of one of the world's most fasci-

nating, habitable cities—or its urbane, informative relevant coverage won't cost you a thing.

To test The Chicagoan's relevance for yourself (and to enjoy some substantial advantages as a charter subscriber) simply mail the coupon below. It entitles you to:

Receive The Chicagoan's charter issue in September without cost—with the compliments of our co-publishers, Jon and Abra Anderson.

Receive a full year of The Chicagoan (11 more monthly issues) at a special charter subscriber's rate that saves you a full $6.00 off the newsstand price and brings you the city at a cost of only 50 cents a month.

Cancel your subscription without cost if you decide The Chicagoan is not for you but keep your "collector's item" charter issue on the house.

This glittering charter issue *already* looks like a sell-out with its newsstand appearance still nearly a month away. To assure yourself of a complimentary copy, clip and mail your reservation coupon today! Then start getting more out of the place where you live—with your satisfaction guaranteed and some of Chicago's most knowledgeable reporters as your guides.

---

5 Good Reasons You'll Want To Try The Chicagoan

1. Pulitzer Prize winner Mike Royko

2. Pulitzer Prize winner Lois Wille.

3. Pulitzer Prize winner Ron Powers.

4. Save 40% off the regular subscription price of $10 per year (and $6.00 a year off the single copy price.)

5. Receive a *complimentary* copy of The Chicagoan's charter issue in September.

A lot of people who make Chicago what it is (from Bill Melton of the White Sox to W. Clement Stone of Combined Insurance, from architect David Haid to rock promoter Frank Fried) have already entered charter subscriptions to The Chicagoan. Join them by mailing the reservation below.

Mail this coupon today
to reserve your complimentary charter issue!

THE CHICAGOAN

Charter Subscriber's Rate:

$6.00

Save $4.00

off the regular subscription price of $10.00 per year. Save $6.00 off the regular newsstand price of $1.00 per issue.

Charter Subscriber's Reservation
The CHICAGOAN
645 North Michigan Avenue, Chicago, Illinois 60611

Yes, please send my complimentary copy of The Chicagoan's charter issue in September. If I like it, bill me for a full year's subscription (11 additional issues) at your charter Subscriber's rate of just $6.00 instead of the regular $10.00 price. If I don't like it, I will write "cancel" across your bill, return it, and that will end the matter. In either case, the charter issue is mine to keep.

☐ I prefer 2 full years, 24 issues, at your Charter rate of $12.00

☐ Bill me later. ☐ Payment enclosed.
(Same trial privilege, of course.)

NAME_____

ADDRESS_____

CITY, STATE, ZIP_____

McGovern
For President
410 First Street, S.E., Washington, D.C. 20003

Mr. Richard Haven
W Pomoroy Lane
Amherst, Mass. 01002

Dear Mr. Haven:

Senator McGovern has asked me to express his deepest thanks to you for the part you played in his great victory in Miami.

"The McGovern phenomenon" was made possible by the support of nearly 110,000 contributors. Without the vision and dedication that all of you displayed, at a time when the odds were strongly against us, it could never have happened.

Now we intend to finance a successful election campaign in exactly the same way -- with thousands of contributions from people in all walks of life.

To compete with the Republican war chest, bulging with ten million dollars in large anonymous contributions from influence-seekers, we aim to gather openly disclosed contributions from one million Democrats, Independents and disenchanted Republicans.

Every contributor will be enrolled in our McGovern Million Member Club.

I know you will want to be a part of this unprecedented and historic event. Obviously we are going to need the help of our most devoted friends more than ever.

One of our friends has come up with an ingenious idea for making it easier to afford a substantial donation. You can send us four checks all at the same time, but date the second check September 1 -- the third check October 1 -- and the fourth check November 1. Then our campaign treasurer will not deposit your second, third, and fourth checks until their effective dates.

If you like the idea, you can use either your own checks or the enclosed blank checks with your name and address already imprinted on them.

This will enable you to make a monthly contribution without having to remember to do so, and will save us the postage and clerical costs involved in contacting you again.

With your help, Senator McGovern has already accomplished the impossible. The half-way point has been passed. Now let's go all the way!

Cordially,

Gary Warren Hart
Campaign Director

P.S. In appreciation of your past help we would like to send you a souvenir of those unforgettable days when the odds against us seemed hopeless and only your steadfast support kept the campaign going. It is a sterling silver lapel pin that says "F.M.B.M." -- standing for For McGovern Before Miami.

Since production will be limited to one pin for each before-Miami supporter, we want to be certain yours does not go astray. So please check your name and address on the enclosed Shipping Label, correct it if necessary, and return it to us for your pin.

A COPY OF OUR REPORT FILED WITH APPROPRIATE SUPERVISORY OFFICE IS (OR WILL BE) AVAILABLE FOR PURCHASE FROM THE SUPERINTENDENT OF DOCUMENTS, UNITED STATES GOVERMENT PRINTING OFFICE, WASHINGTON D.C. 20002

You made George McGovern's nomination possible.

Now we need all "F.M.B.M."s (For McGovern Before Miami) to help make his election possible.

Here's an idea for maximizing your effectiveness.

Here are four blank checks, each dated one month apart.

By filling out all four (or you can use your own checks, of course) you can send us four monthly contributions all at once, and we won't cash the last three until they come due.

If all of our more than 110,000 "F.M.B.M." supporters contribute only $10 a month, this alone would yield more than $4 million.

Or an average contribution of $25 per month per supporter would mean $11 million-or more than all the anonymous donations Nixon got from fat cats before the disclosure law took effect.

So you can see the potential power of your contributions if everyone cooperates.

May we count on you for your share in this great enterprise?

And return this SHIPPING LABEL for your sterling "F.M.B.M." pin →

McGovern for President
410 First Street, S.E.
Washington, D.C. 20003

Mr. Richard Haven
W Pomoroy Lane
Amherst, Mass. 01002

August 1, 1972

PAY TO THE ORDER OF   McGovern for President $
THE SUM OF _____ DOLLARS
YOUR CHECKING ACCOUNT BANK
BANK ADDRESS   SIGNATURE
CITY   STATE   YOUR CHECKING ACCOUNT NUMBER

Mr. Richard Haven
W Pomoroy Lane
Amherst, Mass. 01002

September 1, 1972

PAY TO THE ORDER OF   McGovern for President $
THE SUM OF _____ DOLLARS
YOUR CHECKING ACCOUNT BANK
BANK ADDRESS   SIGNATURE
CITY   STATE   YOUR CHECKING ACCOUNT NUMBER

Mr. Richard Haven
W Pomoroy Lane
Amherst, Mass. 01002

October 1, 1972

PAY TO THE ORDER OF   McGovern for President $
THE SUM OF _____ DOLLARS
YOUR CHECKING ACCOUNT BANK
BANK ADDRESS   SIGNATURE
CITY   STATE   YOUR CHECKING ACCOUNT NUMBER

Mr. Richard Haven
W Pomoroy Lane
Amherst, Mass. 01002

November 1, 1972

PAY TO THE ORDER OF   McGovern for President $
THE SUM OF _____ DOLLARS
YOUR CHECKING ACCOUNT BANK
BANK ADDRESS   SIGNATURE
CITY   STATE   YOUR CHECKING ACCOUNT NUMBER

McGovern
For President 410 First Street, S.E., Washington, D.C. 20003

Mr. Richard Haven
W Pomoroy Lane
Amherst, Mass. 01002

FIRST CLASS MAIL

CONTENTS: JEWELRY

If your name and address are not correct on your shipping label, print them clearly here.

Name _____
_____
City _____ State _____ Zip

010020HVN**W*PR

The famous McGovern fund-raising campaign. *Over $15 million was raised by mail for the McGovern campaign. This computerized letter, mailed to former contributors at a cost of $20,000, raised in excess of $1 million.*

24

DEL MAR, CALIFORNIA 92014

Dear Reader,

Most people, upon leaving school or college, close up their minds exactly as they close up their books. Forever.

The rest of their lives is just running out the string. Intellectual curiosity? Kid stuff. Stimulating ideas? Who needs them. New discoveries about mind and body? Couldn't care less.

If that sounds like you, then you won't have even a passing interest in our offer of a fresh, current <u>complimentary</u> copy of Psychology Today, the liveliest and most widely read magazine of ideas in the world.

Nor will you care so much as a fig for the option that travels with each complimentary copy: an invitation to subscribe for a year at only half the <u>regular</u> rate.

But I don't think you're like most people. If I did, I wouldn't have sent you this letter, which is really an introduction to, and a sampler of, Psychology Today. Just before writing it, I browsed through the last two years of Psychology Today looking for the articles that had, for one reason or another, stuck in my mind.

I'm not on the editorial side here, so I read Psychology Today very much as our regular subscribers do. And during this review, this stroll down Memory Lane, if you will, I realized what our editor, T George Harris, had been up to.

Under the guise of being stimulating and entertaining and thought provoking, he had been secretly educating me!

How much more I know now than I did two years ago about the startling new insights that are coming constantly from psychological and social scientists - about the quirks and quiddities of our amazing species - and about myself!

What Psychology Today has in store for <u>you</u> during the next year or two not even T George Harris could tell you at this point.

(over please)

Unique to direct marketing is the fact that long copy, professionally written, often out-pulls much shorter copy. This 6-page letter, plus order card, is a classic example of the art.

But if it's anything like the last two years, you're going to like it a lot!

There are hundreds of fascination stories buried in the charts and figures and scientific language of learned monographs. The editors of Psychology Today are masters at the art of translating these into readable, narrative form _without_ misrepresenting the serious purpose and conclusions of the original scientist-authors.

Take the article, "How to Quit Smoking" in the January, 1971 issue. It described a research project at the University of Oregon, and it starts with a graphic description of an unusual conditioning technique. Most smokers will instantly see a marvelous logic in this:

> "A metronome ticks back and forth. Every six seconds
> by the metronome's tick the smoker takes a drag on
> the cigarette. Through an opening in the box, puffs
> of heated cigarette smoke blow into his face. Soon
> the combination of rapid smoking and blown smoke causes
> his eyes to water, his nose and throat to burn. He
> begins to cough. He feels nausea developing. Finally
> he cannot force himself to take another drag. He puts
> out the cigarette. The metronome and the smoke machine
> stop. After a brief rest and discussion of his reactions,
> the man lights another cigarette and begins again. The
> man is not a sadomasochist. He is only one of many
> habitual cigarette smokers who want to kick the habit
> but cannot do it on their own."

Sometimes Psychology Today affords insights into mental processes that some of us can put to work in our own lives. "Genius at ZZZ Work ZZZZZZZ" (June, 1970) describes how many famous men solved important problems through dreams. For instance, Elias Howe had been frustrated for years by his failure to perfect the sewing machine. Perhaps one day you'll be able to solve one of your own problems as he did:

> "One night he dreamed he had been captured by savages
> and dragged before their king. The king issued a royal
> ultimatum. If Howe did not produce a machine that would
> sew within 24 hours, he would die by the spear. Howe
> failed to meet the deadline and saw the savages approach-
> ing. The spears slowly rose and then started to descend.
> Howe forgot his fear as he noticed that the spears all
> had eye-shaped holes in their tips. He awakened and

26

realized that the eye of his sewing machine needle
should be near the point, not at the top or in the
middle. Rushing to his laboratory, he filed a needle
to the proper size, drilled a hole near its tip and
inserted it in the machine. It worked well and the
problem was solved."

Sometimes an article is pure fun with, inevitably, a solid
kernel of insightful truth. Have you ever thought of the Wizard of
Oz as a psychiatrist and the Scarecrow, Tin Woodman and Cowardly
Lion as patients with externalized symptoms? Sheldon Kopp did ("The
Wizard of Oz Behind the Couch", March, 1970) and here is his descrip-
tion of the characters' first meeting:

"When they at last arrive at the Palace in the Emerald
City, the Wizard does individual intake interviews with
each of them... The Wizard, good therapist that he is,
quickly comes across as a person who has his own needs.
In therapy country, everyone must pay for what he gets.
That means these poor, helpless patients must give something of themselves if they wish to get something for
themselves. The task that the Wizard assigns is that
they must kill the Wicked Witch of the West. They would
like the Wizard to destroy the bad mother for them, but
no matter how great and powerful a father he seems, he
cannot do for them what they must do for themselves..."

Readers of Psychology Today meet the world's most influential
behavioral scientists: Carl Rogers, J. B. Rhine, Masters and
Johnson, Bruno Bettelheim, Karl Menninger, Norman O. Brown and Erik
Erikson are a few who have either contributed or been featured in
"Conversations" with the editors. Exclusive prepublication excerpts
from important books such as B. F. Skinner's "Beyond Freedom and
Dignity" and Lionel Tiger and Robin Fox's "The Imperial Animal"
appear regularly. You may not always like what these people have
to say, but I guarantee they'll make you think. Take this excerpt
from a January, 1972 conversation with Robert Rimmer, author of "The
Harrad Experiment":

"Many people who hear about the mad proposals of Bob
Rimmer feel that I am trying to undermine the family
structure of this country. Far from it. I believe
that a strong family structure is a sine qua non of
social existence. The trouble with the majority of
homes in the United States today is that they are not
families, they are simply households, most of them

sustained by three or four people, including parents
and children. No man is an island meant to live
alone, and these nuclear households are little better
than islands."

"For most men and women a menage a trois, existing in
the framework of intelligent love, approved by society,
would expand their horizons as individuals, and for
many women in later life, fill out the vacuum of living
lonely, boring days in our suburban wastelands. Man
and woman can love more than each other. A marriage
of three people or of two or three couples could be
lively and exciting. All it takes is men and women
who are willing to use the vast potential of their
brains to reexamine the trivia of their man-made emotions."

I'm surprised at how many times Psychology Today has shown me
that what I thought was fact was really fiction (and vice versa). At
one time the role of erotic literature in generating sex crimes seemed
to me to be beyond question. Then I read "Pornography" in the December,
1970 issue - a report growing out of studies done for the Commission on
Obscenity and Pornography by the Legal and Behavioral Institute. Here's
a short excerpt:

"The rapists, who found it very difficult to talk about
sex, said that there was little nudity in their homes
while they were growing up and that sex was never discussed. Only 18 percent of the rapists said their parents
had caught them with erotic materials; in those instances
the parents had become angry and had punished them. (In
the control group, 37 percent reported that their parents
knew they read erotic materials, but only seven percent
reported being punished. Most reported that their parents
had been indifferent, and some said their parents had
explained the materials to them -- an occurrence not
reported by any other group.) Rapists tended to oppose
premarital sex, and many of them relied on their wives
for a great deal of their sex information... At least
one rapist in the hospital, when he was first admitted,
had had no idea where babies come from."

Sometimes Psychology Today articles help us to better understand
today's headlines. Are you puzzled about the nation's welfare dilemma?
Do you ever wonder whether the "Protestant work ethic" is simply a
legacy from the Puritans or something deeper? Too bad you missed the

report on some ingenious experiments with children and rats in "The Pied Piper vs. the Protestant Ethic," January, 1972. The children were given the choice of getting marbles free or "working" for them by pressing a bar. The rats were given the same options to obtain food. Both showed a positive preference <u>for</u> work. (And it seems unlikely that the rats, at least, were influenced by Protestant conditioning!)

In this same issue was a dark glimpse into a subculture behavior pattern. Entitled "Machismo", it contains this curious definition of a Mexican <u>macho's</u> relationship with women:

> "The <u>machista</u> wants a woman for his personal use in a wholly disrespectful way... The woman, like a toy in a shop, can be selected and relinquished without any participation on her part. But, tragically, as soon as he has possessed her, the wild and petulant <u>macho</u> loses all, or almost all, of the interest he had in her. He regards her mainly as an object of conquest. Nevertheless, he is capable of fighting to the death with another man over her! Both men act as though the woman produces a form of hyperesthesia."

But I can't end on that doleful note. It wouldn't be fair. Because usually Psychology Today cheers me up, sometimes because I come away from it a little wiser, sometimes because I find something <u>I</u> knew confirmed by a famous psychologist. Like this all-too-true observation on bridge players in "Over Troubled Waters", May, 1970:

> "When a game is heated and the competition-cooperation roles are being strained to their limit, a bridge player often reveals a side of his personality that is not evident in his everyday behaviors. He may become irrational and make decisions impulsively, with poor judgment and remarkably limited insight. Defense mechanisms surface -- a player will find elaborate rationalizations for his failures and project the blame for a lost game onto his partner. He becomes suspicious of any inflection or grimace by an opponent and he makes astonished denials when his own play is disputed."

Well, these few examples give <u>my</u> feelings about Psychology Today and why I think <u>you</u> will find it interesting, worthwhile <u>and instructive</u> in its bright, contemporary, unpedagogic way. Perhaps the editors put it better when they wrote: "We want to be less like a classroom than an off-campus eatery where student and teacher gather as people to talk about the consequences of knowledge and ideas..."

I haven't even made an effort to show you the look of Psychology Today. It is quite as striking as the editorial content, but the graphics mesh so intimately with the text that showing them separately does not do them justice. Suffice it to say that in a recent year our magazine received seven awards from the Magazine Design Awards of the Society of Publication Designers.

Now for the moment of truth -

On the card enclosed with this letter you will discern a cut-out token bearing the picture of a hand. If you will detach this token and place it "thumbs up" in the slot marked YES (the work of three or four seconds), the card will bring you a fresh, current copy of Psychology Today with our compliments.

This issue is worth $1.00 on the newsstand, and it is yours entirely without obligation as long as the card is mailed to us before September 30, 1973.

Read the magazine at your leisure. Then if you don't wish to continue with a full year's subscription, just let us know. The complimentary issue is, of course, yours to keep.

If you decide to continue, you will receive the next 11 monthly issues of Psychology Today at a special introductory saving - only $6 for all 12 issues. That's 50% off - a $6 saving! (Send no money now, please. We will bill you later.)

We're quite serious about that cut-off date, though. So why not mail your card right now? How can you lose?

Sincerely,

John Suhler
Publisher

JS/lf

P.S. If, alas, you have decided not to accept our no-obligation offer (a decision I am at a loss to understand) please return the card anyway with the token "thumbs down" in the NO slot. This small courtesy will help us plan distribution of complimentary copies for this special issue. Thank you.

psychology today

Yes

Please send without cost, obligation or commitment my complimentary copy of the current issue. If I like it, bill me for a year's subscription (11 additional issues), for a total of 12, at the special introductory rate of just $6 instead of $12—a 50% saving. If I don't like it, I will write "cancel" across your bill, return it, and that will be the end of the matter. In either case, the issue is mine to keep.

☐ I am enclosing $6, with the understanding that it is fully refundable upon request if I am not delighted with the first issue.

Please

Give us a hand. We will be better able to plan distribution of complimentary copies for this special offer if we have the courtesy of your reply, whether YES or NO, no later than:

Sept. 30, 1973

Just place the token above "thumbs up" in the YES slot or "thumbs down" in the NO slot. Then detach and mail card in the enclosed envelope. Thank you.

DC 1173

J M Kobs
110 Roxbury Lane   9G27
Des Plaines IL 60018

No

Thanks, but I'm not interested.
Remove stub, insert token and return this card in the postage paid envelope enclosed. (Subscriptions outside the U.S. and Canada are $2 extra.)

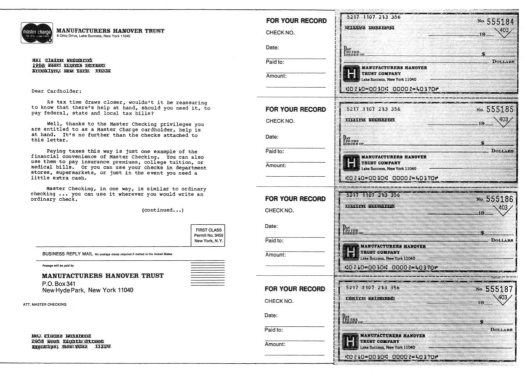

Credit card activation: *Manufacturers Hanover, the Master Charge bank, uses a personalized letter with four "Master Checking Checks" attached at tax time to stimulate account usage and to promote orders for Master checks. The Master Checking Service provides checks which look, and can be used, like regular personal checks but which are charged directly to a Master Charge account rather than a checking account.*

The Place of European Direct Marketing

Direct marketing is becoming global. There's little question about that. Not only are European firms embracing direct marketing. U.S. firms are entering the European direct marketing arena, as well. Here is an overview of direct marketing overseas as gleaned from many contacts I have made with European direct marketing experts.

Q. How would you rate the level of competence in the direct marketing field overseas as compared with its practice in the U.S.A.?

A. The first thing to keep in mind—and it goes for all the myriad aspects of direct marketing—is that in a general way the U.S.A. is still the leader and ultimate source of inspiration for new ideas. But in individual cases highly original designs and unique marketing ideas come out of the U.K., France, and other European countries which compare favorably with the best in the U.S.A. And in some cases, the Europeans are coming up with creative selling ideas and expressing them in original designs which evoke the envy of the best American marketing people and art directors.

Q. What are the most common product lines for European direct mail?

A. In terms of mail quantity, book offers outstrip all others, both in the mails and in media. Then there is a wide range of merchandise, led by records and magazine subscription mail, and, lately, medallions. Then come watches, art prints, and miscellaneous one-shot merchandise offers from power drills to car coats.

Q. Which companies are the leaders in the field?

A. In terms of quantity, in the major European countries we find the first two companies are almost always the local-language *Reader's Digest* operation and the local company of Sam Josefowitz's worldwide network (Concert Hall, in the U.K.; Cercle du Bibliophile, Guilde Internationale du Disque, and others in France; etc.).

Time-Life have often been third, but in France, for example, they may now, by sheer volume, be outdone by the rapidly expanding clubs like those of Tallandier, François Beauval, C.A.L., and others. For an idea of volume, in France the Guilde, and its sister divisions for books and merchandise, mail over 50 million pieces annually— which isn't bad in a country of just that many people (but only 12 million families).

Q. Are there American companies involved in the European direct mail operations?

A. This is partially answered by the previous exchange; the two leaders in the field are American-owned although locally managed, like Time-Life. American investment is only now starting to come in more heavily, both in the book field and in catalogs and merchandise.

Q. Does the extensive American penetration mean that marketing campaigns overseas would simply use the U.S. versions translated into the appropriate language?

A. That used to be the situation 15 or 20 years ago, when direct marketing was relatively new and unsophisticated in Europe. And it still continues in some cases (like subscription promotion for magazines, generally those printed in English but attempting to build a European readership). But creative directors have learned to tailor their messages for the particular market they have targeted. There are even cases where particularly good campaigns worked out for local usage have been picked up by the parent company for use in the United States.

When it comes to merchandise, it is important for U.S. companies to know that different cultures of different European countries dictate different compositions, sizes, patterns, colors. If you were selling tableware, for example, different patterns would be required for France, England, and Germany.

Q. How widespread are consumer credit systems and facilities?

A. Consumer credit is now beginning to grow at a fairly rapid rate from a very small base. Most Europeans still feel it is more honorable to buy for cash than on credit. Daniel Hauguel, president of Fingerhut-France, points out, for example, that the number-one catalog firm in France—La Redoute—does only about 15% of its sales on credit.

Q. Will foreign media permit split-run testing for direct response ads?

A. Yes—depending on the medium. Larger publications, with huge print runs and the power they wield with the printers, will do most of the sophisticated testing that clients want, but even here some are so sought after by advertisers that they simply refuse to do anything to complicate their lives.

Q. What is the list situation overseas: availability, maintenance, cost, etc.?

A. Almost anything you may want is available, and at much lower cost than in the United States—with reservations.

Good lists can be had for as little as $8 to $12 per thousand, but more commonly about $15–20. However, the direct American influence has led to prices like $30–40.

There are great differences from the U.S. situation. Few lists are computerized, so selection of segments is almost always made manually for testing purposes. The breakdowns are excellent geographically, but almost nonexistent when it comes to detailed demographics, and the updating is sometimes very haphazardly done (except where you are buying someone's active files). List brokers, as we know them in the United States, are practically nonexistent.

Q. What does the Common Market mean in terms of mail order in Europe?

A. With the European Economic Community a reality, the market looms as big as the U.S. in terms of population:

Germany	61,000,000
Great Britain	56,000,000
France	51,000,000
Italy	53,000,000
Belgium/Netherlands/Luxembourg	23,000,000
Total	244,000,000

Eight Major Responsibilities of Direct Marketing Executives

The world of direct marketing is a big world, an exciting world, an awesome world for those who have never operated within it. As more and more major corporations enter it — and they are doing so at a rapidly accelerating speed — it is becoming clear that those who are succeeding are doing so by setting up direct marketing separate and apart from other marketing functions. It is safe to predict that in the next decade all major corporations which lend themselves to direct marketing will be staffed by direct marketing experts. The checklist below lists in detail the major responsibilities of the direct marketing executive — a total of 66 individual functions. A review of the eight major responsibility categories with their attendant functions is very much in order.

1. Product Selection and Development

Direct marketing fails right here for many. Selecting or developing the right product or products requires special know-how and special considerations peculiar to direct marketing.

What is the market potential? Is it too small to pursue? Is it too competitive? Can supply sources meet requirements fast? Can they offer good value? Is packaging attractive enough to sell the product or service on its arrival? Is packaging sturdy enough to prevent damage or breakage? Are shipping costs killers to the consumer if he must pay, or killers to the marketer if *he* must pay?

DIRECT MARKETING EVALUATIONS AND FUNCTIONS CHECKLIST

1. Product Selection and Development

Market potential
Competition
Reliability of sources
Value comparison
Packaging
Shipping costs
Unit of sale
Profit margin
Ease of use
Instructions
Refurbishing costs
Repeat potential
Evaluation of syndication

2. Markets and Media Selection

Mailing lists
Magazines
Newspapers and supplements
Radio and TV
Co-ops
Telephone
Car cards, match books, etc.

3. Creative Development and Scheduling

Strategy or concept
Offers
Copy
Layouts
Formats
FTC regulations
Scheduling of ads and mailing
    packages

4. Testing Procedures

Compiled vs. direct response lists
Regional testing
Testing by ZIP Codes
Testing by socioeconomic factors
Seasonal testing
Price testing

34

Offer testing
Establishing control ads and control
  mailing packages
Determining media duplication
Using probability scales
Preevaluation of ads and mailing
  packages
Measuring readership

5. Fulfillment

Shipping facilities
Replacement procedures
Returned goods procedures
Distribution centers
Shipping method (carriers)

6. Budgeting and Accounting

Cash flow charts
Bad debt reserves
Financing costs
Attrition scales
Forms and systems
Commercial credit card affiliations

Credit and collection procedures
Recency, frequency, and monetary
  criteria

7. Customer Service

Sales correspondence
Complaints and adjustments
Activation and reactivation

8. Personnel and Supplier Relations

Advertising department
Fulfillment sources
Accounting department
Customer service
Advertising agency
List brokers
Space reps
Suppliers of merchandise and services
Printers, engravers, and typesetters
Artists and art studios
Envelope houses

What about unit of sale and profit margin? It's hard to chew up selling costs with a small unit of sale, no matter what the profit margin. And if the unit of sale is in the installment credit category, is there an extra margin to carry the costs of an installment credit operation?

Then there's the matter of ease of use. Ironically, while some of the most appealing items are mechanical, give the most astute adult something mechanical and he shows the intelligence of a high school dropout. Getting the consumer to read even the most lucid instructions is a difficult task.

And how about refurbishing costs — the amount the marketer must pay to have returned merchandise checked and refurbished? These can run sky-high, killing off front end profits.

What about repeat potential? Do profits have to come from a one-time sale? Who is to make all these evaluations? If not a company direct marketing executive, a professional direct marketing agency is indicated. Such an organization should be able to match product selection with a company profile and marketing objectives.

2. Markets and Media Selection

When the product or products have been developed or selected, the marketing executive must think in terms of the most profitable route or routes to reach potential buyers. The route can be, and often is, the one to the existing customer list, which is particularly true where syndicated offers are used.

Marketing beyond one's existing customer list may involve a wide variety of media. Direct marketing relies heavily upon lists of mail order buyers and print media with a direct response atmosphere.

3. Creative Development and Scheduling

The creative arm of a direct marketing department is a key factor in the success or failure of a direct marketing operation. It can be said that the creative people who are great in the world of direct marketing are a rare breed of cat. They're creative but they are accustomed to having their creativity measured daily according to traceable results.

Creative development starts with selling strategies and concepts which are translated into propositions. The propositions are presented through copy and illustrations. And the very act of getting copy read and illustrations noted calls for a unique combination of layouts and formats. Copywriters should have at least a working knowledge of FTC regulations—which are becoming increasingly stringent. More and more copy must go through legal channels before release.

The creative people, likewise, have a hand in scheduling and in making certain all their ads and mailing packages appear as conceived and are keyed properly to allow results to be traced.

4. Testing Procedures

Because direct marketing lives by measured results, testing procedures are vital. And it is in this area that many a direct marketing program falls apart at the seams. Erroneous testing procedures lead to faulty conclusions.

There are so many things that must be tested—media, regions, ZIP Code areas, socioeconomic factors. The season of the year can be a key factor. Then there's the whole area of testing for best price and best proposition. Control ads and control mailing packages must be established.

In the case of print media, circulation duplication must be considered. In the case of mailing lists, duplication between direct response lists must be considered. Preevaluation studies and readership measurement may well be considered under testing procedures.

5. Fulfillment

One of the real stumbling blocks to many companies that enter direct marketing is the physical process of fulfillment. I've seen giant corporations flunk out on this. Filling orders promptly, within 48 hours if possible, is critical. Mail order respondents cool off mighty fast.

Of no less importance are prompt replacement and prompt credit for returned merchandise. Lack of efficient systems can lead to nightmares. Distribution centers can alleviate or complicate problems. Having the right carriers is essential for efficient distribution.

6. Budgeting and Accounting

No direct marketing executive can hit the big time without a watchdog treasurer, backed by an efficient force steeped in mail order procedures.

This treasurer will develop cash flow charts which will show management how quickly it will get its money back at various levels of success. He'll be smart enough to set up bad debt reserves that will cover unusually high uncollectables. He'll take the cost of money into account as a direct cost of direct marketing.

And in this very same department, facts and figures will be developed, probably through the computer, which will enable the direct marketing executive to build the business rapidly and profitably. He'll be able to determine acquisition cost and the value of a customer.

7. Customer Service

Probably right down the hall from budgeting and accounting will be "the boys in the white hats," customer service. Direct marketing departments get lots of letters with questions, questions, questions. "How do I put part A into B?" "Where's my free gift?" "How do I stop my membership?" The answers had better be prompt, courteous, and accurate. A good customer service department is a key link in the direct marketing chain.

8. Personnel and Supplier Relations

The ideal direct marketing executive not only must evaluate and know all the functions involved in direct marketing, he must be able to work well with all the internal and external forces involved in his world of direct marketing. And it's quite a world!

His advertising agency should be steeped in direct marketing, as he is. He should have a close relationship with leading list brokers and space reps of direct response publications. A knowledge of suppliers is essential. He should be able to pick the right art studio, engraver, typesetter, envelope house, and printer for each given job.

Direct marketing is indeed a wide, wide world. It requires specialized knowledge and specialized skills, but for those who have them or who will develop them, it's a beautiful world.

Standards of Practice

The world of direct marketing, as this chapter and subsequent chapters will disclose, is a truly exciting world. Its future is very, very bright.

But the future of direct marketing, as with all other phases of marketing, will depend to a great degree on how direct marketers deal with consumers. Consumerism, as all major marketers agree, is here to stay.

The Direct Mail/Marketing Association has, for years, had a watchdog committee who have relentlessly fought for fair standards of practice in the direct mail medium. The standards of practice they have evolved apply to all media of direct marketing. These standards are printed in entirety below.

Operating Guidelines for Ethical Business Practice

1) Advertisers should make their offers clear and honest. They should not misrepresent a product, service or solicitation and should not use misleading, half-true or exaggerated statements. Advertisers should operate in accordance with the Fair Practice Code of the Council of Better Business Bureaus and be cognizant of and adhere to the Postal Laws and Regulations, and all other laws governing advertising and transaction of business by mail.

2) Advertisers should not make offers which purport to require a person to return a notice that he does not wish to receive further merchandise in order to avoid liability for the purchase price, unless all the conditions are first made clear in an initial offer that is accepted by the purchaser by means of a bona fide written order. Attention is suggested to more detailed specifications regarding negative option plans which have been formulated by the Federal Trade Commission.

3) Mailings should not contain vulgar, immoral, profane or offensive matter nor should advertisers use the mails to promote the sale of pornographic material or other matter not acceptable for mailing on accepted moral grounds. Advertisers should not use the mails to promote the sale of products or services by means of lottery.

4) The terms and conditions of guarantee should be clearly and specifically set forth in immediate conjunction with the guarantee offer. Guarantees should be limited to the reasonable performance capabilities and qualities of the product or service advertised.

5) Advertisers should not make exaggerated price comparisons, claims on discounts or savings; nor employ fictitious prices.

6) A product or service which is offered without cost or obligation to the recipient may be unqualifiedly described as "free." "Free" may also

be used conditionally where the offer requires the recipient to purchase some other product or service, provided all terms and conditions are accurately and conspicuously disclosed in immediate conjunction with the use of the term "free" and the product or service required to be purchased is not increased in price or decreased in quality or quantity.

7) Photographs and art work implying representation of a product or service offered should be faithful reproductions of the product or service. Photographs and art work implying situations under which a product or service would be advantageous to the purchaser should be in accord with written claims.

8) If laboratory test data are used in advertising, they should be competent as to source and methodology. Advertisers should not use excerpts of laboratory test material in support of claims which distort or fail to disclose the true test results.

9) Advertisers should not use unsupported or inaccurate testimonials; or testimonials originally given for products or services other than those offered by the advertiser; or testimonials making statements or conclusions the advertiser knows to be incorrect. If testimonials are used, they should contain no misstatement of facts or misleading implications and should reflect the current opinion of the author.

10) Advertisers who sell instruction, catalogs, mailing lists or merchandise-for-resale should not use misleading or deceptive statements with respect to the earning possibilities, lack of risk, or ease of operation.

11) Advertisers should not use promotional solicitations in the forms of bills or invoices (pro forma invoices) deceptively.

12) Advertisers should not mail unordered merchandise for which payment is demanded.

13) Advertisers should not use any list in violation of the lawful rights of the list owner; and should promptly bring to the attention of the lawful owner of any list any information they may have regarding any possible violation of his proprietary rights therein.

14) If products or services are offered on a satisfaction guaranteed or money back basis, refunds should be made promptly on request. In an unqualified offer of refund or replacement, the customer's preference shall prevail.

15) Advertisers should be prepared to make prompt delivery of orders solicited in their copy. Unforeseen contingencies should be reported to the customer promptly when delivery is unavoidably delayed. A reply device should be included, enabling the customer, if he wishes, to cancel the order and obtain a refund of any purchase price already paid.

16) Advertisers should not use misleading or deceptive methods for collecting money owed by delinquent accounts.

17) Advertisers should distribute products only in a manner that will provide reasonable safeguards against possibilities of injury to children and/or adults.

18) All advertisers including those firms who use, create, produce or supply materials and/or lists for direct mail advertising should make conscientious efforts to remove names from their mailing lists when so requested either directly or in accordance with the DMAA Mail Preference Service.

Self-Quiz

1. Define direct marketing.

_____

_____

_____

_____

2. What are the three basic appeals of direct marketing?

1. _____ 2. _____ 3. _____

3. Name the two major bank cards.

1. _____ 2. _____

38

4. Name the three major commercial credit cards.

1. _____ 2. _____ 3. _____

5. What are the six big keys to direct marketing success?

1. _____ 2. _____

3. _____ 4. _____

5. _____ 6. _____

6. Name six major consumer goods manufacturers now engaged in direct marketing.

1. _____ 2. _____

3. _____ 4. _____

5. _____ 6. _____

7. What has been the effect on retail sales in the record and book industry of these industries' selling direct to the consumer by mail?
☐ depressed retail sales ☐ no effect ☐ increased retail sales

8. What are the three major advantages for the retailer in selling the consumer direct by mail?

1. _____

2. _____

3. _____

9. What are the three major reasons why most retail direct marketing efforts fail?

1. _____

2. _____

3. _____

10. Name six major objectives for retail direct marketing.

1. _____

2. _____

3. _____

4. _____

5. _____

6. _____

11. What are the four broad categories for direct marketing techniques to be applied by the industrial goods manufacturer?

    1. _____

    2. _____

    3. _____

    4. _____

12. Name the six essentials of a successful lead-producing program.

    1. _____

    2. _____

    3. _____

    4. _____

    5. _____

    6. _____

13. What is the function of the syndicator?

    _____

    _____

    _____

    _____

14. Why may it be advantageous for the consumer goods manufacturer to explore syndication initially as an entry into direct marketing?

    _____

    _____

    _____

    _____

15. What is unique about an *intangible?*

    _____

    _____

16. What are the most common product lines for European direct mail?

_____

_____

_____

17. What are the eight major responsibilities of direct marketing executives?

1. _____ 5. _____

2. _____ 6. _____

3. _____ 7. _____

4. _____ 8. _____

Pilot Project

Educators agree that the best way to learn is by doing. For the industrious, pilot projects will be suggested for application of the material contained in each chapter.

As the direct marketing manager for Xerox, develop in outline form the basics of a program designed to produce leads for Xerox salesmen. Your outline should include the following information.

1. How you will proceed to determine which prospect lists you will use.
2. How you will test various mailing packages to determine your most effective one.
3. Who will control the lead-producing program — home office, regional offices, individual salesmen.
4. How you will "sell" the program to the sales organization.
5. What controls you will establish to make certain that leads provided to salesmen are followed up.
6. How you will measure the final sales results of the lead-producing program.

SECTION II   MEDIA OF DIRECT MARKETING

Chapter 2   Mailing Lists

Mailing lists—they're the heart of every direct marketing operation. This is true whether the prime medium for getting inquiries and/or orders is mailing lists or print or broadcast. Ultimately every inquiry and/or order ends up on a mailing list.

It's been said that mailing lists may be compared to people. They come in various sizes and shapes. And grooming among them varies tremendously. Some are meticulous. Some are just plain sloppy.

Every List Has a Profile

One isn't in direct marketing very long before one learns that every list of respondents has common characteristics. Thus a profile soon emerges. Once a clearly defined profile emerges, selection of lists for future promotion is simplified.

Consider the profile of 7.2 million active subscribers to *Better Homes & Gardens*, for example. Meredith Direct Marketing of Des Moines provides the following data.

Median family size: 3.5   75% own home
Median household income: $11,700   90% own one or more cars
Median age: 43   42% own two or more cars

The profile of the *Better Homes & Gardens* active subscribers serves two purposes: (1) it provides prospective list renters with statistics necessary for determining whether this list would meet the profile of their customers; and (2) it gives *Better Homes & Gardens* a true picture of the typical subscriber and thus provides direction for selecting lists available from others for prospecting purposes.

A prospective renter of this list with products or services which appeal to home owners (75 percent own their own home) would consider it attractive. Conversely, this list would not be attractive to an organization whose products appeal primarily to consumers in the 18- to 25-year-old bracket (median age is 43).

If *Better Homes & Gardens* were seeking additional active subscribers, they would no doubt consider those like the O.M. Scott & Sons' *Lawn Care* subscription list as testworthy. Note the similarities, as they relate to some of the key demographics.

	Income	Median Age	Two or More Cars	Own Home
BH & G	$11,700 Median	43	42%	75%
Lawn Care	54% over $11,000	50	51%	100%

Direct response lists—names of people who respond by mail—develop profiles as a result of propositions. It is axiomatic, for instance, that an inquiry list of a home study school will predominantly constitute names of people who have not gone to college and in most cases have not completed high school. So the educational level of a home study inquiry list would be on the low side. Another example—the customer list of a classics book club would almost certainly contain in its profile a high educational level, with a major percentage having attended college.

While profiles of a direct response list are dictated by the proposition, compiled lists have various profiles within the universe which can be selected separately.

A good example of selectivity within a compiled list is the "Young Family Index" maintained by Market Development Corporation of Hazelwood, Missouri. The Young Family Index is a birth list. Market Development Corporation assembles approximately 2 million new names each year. Selectivity is possible by region, by state, by city, by size of city, by sales area, by income, and so forth. The data which follow show the variety of selectivity.

TOTALS BY STATE	Yearly Totals	Monthly Average
Alabama	23,238	1,936
Arizona	18,303	1,525
Arkansas	15,789	1,316
California	217,561	18,130
Colorado	16,024	1,335
Connecticut	28,919	2,410
Delaware	5,633	469
District Columbia	5,070	422
Florida	41,910	3,492
Georgia	42,820	3,568
Idaho	9,434	786
Illinois	113,396	9,442
Indiana	65,190	5,432
Iowa	30,620	2,552
Kansas	23,231	1,936
Kentucky	31,288	2,607
Louisiana	23,081	1,923
Maine	8,244	687
Maryland	37,620	3,135
Massachusetts	63,037	5,253
Michigan	118,820	9,902
Minnesota	40,316	3,360
Mississippi	5,131	428
Missouri	49,629	4,136
Montana	7,559	630
Nebraska	16,795	1,400
Nevada	3,050	254
New Hampshire	9,492	791
New Jersey	55,837	4,653
New Mexico	10,218	851
New York	165,598	13,800
North Carolina	48,556	4,046
North Dakota	7,615	635
Ohio	137,702	11,475
Oklahoma	23,729	1,977
Oregon	16,736	1,395
Pennsylvania	114,413	9,534
Rhode Island	8,879	740
South Carolina	10,259	855
South Dakota	5,872	489
Tennessee	34,331	2,861
Texas	150,106	12,509
Utah	18,907	1,576
Vermont	4,857	405
Virginia	25,967	2,164
Washington	35,231	2,936
West Virginia	19,619	1,635
Wisconsin	54,748	4,562
Wyoming	3,421	285
Alaska	1,405	117
Hawaii	9,253	781
TOTALS	2,034,459	169,538

SELECT BY
TEN INCOME GROUPS
(Highest to Lowest Income)

Group #	Monthly	Yearly
1	41,004	492,044
2	10,460	125,522
3	13,728	164,738
4	14,735	176,827
5	19,572	234,863
6	14,322	171,868
7	13,549	162,595
8	12,352	148,219
9	8,561	102,726
10	21,255	255,057
TOTALS	169,538	2,034,459

SELECT BY
% NONWHITE POPULATION

	Monthly	Yearly
0%	49,800	597,601
1-5%	76,829	921,958
6-9%	12,285	147,416
10-13%	6,331	75,969
14-17%	4,328	51,926
18-21%	3,583	42,993
22-25%	2,739	32,871
26-29%	1,772	21,268
30-35%	3,069	36,826
36-39%	1,363	16,361
40% and over	7,439	89,270
TOTALS	169,538	2,034,459

SELECT BY
MULTICHILDREN FAMILIES
(Families with 2 or more children)

Quantity	395,000

SELECT BY
NIELSEN MARKET AREA

	Monthly	Yearly
A	66,039	792,472
B	49,406	592,866
C	33,229	398,750
D	20,864	250,371
TOTALS	169,538	2,034,459

SELECT BY REGION

Region	Monthly	Yearly
New England	10,286	123,428
Mid Atlantic	27,987	335,848
East North Central	40,828	489,856
West North Central	14,506	174,078
South Atlantic	19,787	237,454
East South Central	7,832	93,988
West South Central	17,722	212,705
Mountain	7,241	86,916
Pacific	23,349	280,186
TOTALS	169,538	2,034,459

SELECT BY
PARENTS LIVING IN SMALL TOWNS

Monthly	Yearly
54,093	649,121

SELECT BY FIRST BIRTHS

Monthly	Yearly
9,154	109,851

SELECT BY
PREVIOUS-YEAR NAMES
AVAILABLE

1971	2,051,468

Reviewing the data, we see clearly the wide variety of profiles which exist within a compiled list. If a proposition caters or appeals to high-income groups only, then maybe only Groups 1, 2, and 3 will respond satisfactorily. If nonwhite population is required, then it can be selected. If a proposition appeals only to multichildren families, only their names can be selected. It is this great selectivity available in most compiled lists which make them profitable for many marketers.

One final example of selectivity within a compiled list. One would certainly think that all attorneys are pretty much the same. But they aren't. Approximately 270,000 attorneys have sheepskins, but only about 40% are members of the Bar Association. Of

43

the 270,000, there are 123,936 who go it alone, with one man per office. There are about 26,000 attorneys in government, 27,000 in industry, 3,000 in education, 5,000 patent attorneys, and 13,000 nonpracticing attorneys. It's axiomatic: The closer you can get to matching your customer profile to segments of a list, the better your response is likely to be.

Working with List Brokers and Compilers

No one succeeds in direct marketing without working with one or more competent list brokers and compilers. The more precise the direct marketer can be in providing the list broker and compiler with a profile of his typical customer, the more likely it is he will be provided with good, responsive lists. It's a case of saying, "Here is who my customers are. I want more customers just like them."

Lists as a Profit Center

While the primary purpose of compiling a house list—customers and/or inquiries—is to generate in-house sales, an important secondary factor is the possible income from the rental of such names to noncompeting advertisers. Indeed, profits from mailing list rentals are without exception at a much higher percentage than the percentage of profit realized in the sale of goods or services. A list renting for $30 a thousand will gross the advertiser $24 per thousand after payment of 20% brokerage commission. So rental of one million names will produce $24,000 in gross revenue, with a fulfillment cost of approximately 10%. Profits derived from mailing lists rental can mean the difference between profit and loss on a direct marketing operation. Also, when a marketer knows his potential revenue from new names he can, if he wishes, use a part or all of this profit for investment in new customers.

There are different schools of thought about renting mailing lists. One is that it is harmful to the prime business to make customer names available to other advertisers. Another school holds that it is not harmful, providing those who use the list are not in any way competitive. Then there is yet another which has a policy against renting lists of current or active names. For example, a publisher may not offer current subscriber lists for rental, but he will offer lists of former subscribers.

Most major direct marketers who have assembled large lists of customers and/or inquiries have come to the conclusion it is not harmful to their prime business to rent these lists—but only to noncompetitive, reputable firms.

Many direct marketers also exchange lists with both competitors and noncompetitors. When such exchanges are arranged through a mailing list broker, each member of the exchange customarily pays a brokerage commission. So that, for a list which normally rents for $30 a thousand, each participant in the exchange would pay only the 20 percent brokerage commission of $6 a thousand.

It is not unusual for two direct competitors to exchange lists, particularly of their older names. For example, two firms sell Christmas greeting cards by mail. Each has a list of approximately 100,000 customers who have not bought from it in three years. These are qualified names for each of the competitors in that these customers have previously purchased Christmas greeting cards by mail. But, obviously, they have not chosen to repeat. Therefore, after exchanging lists, each competing firm is mailing to a prime prospect list with a good chance for success, because its proposition may have basic ingredients of appeal which were lacking in that of its competitor.

During the past few years there has been a trend toward list management, whereby a given list broker takes over the complete management of a list for rental purposes. Under this arrangement, the list manager performs all or almost all of the following functions:

44

1. He, rather than the list owner, handles all contacts with all list brokers and processes their orders.
2. He likewise solicits his own list brokerage customers direct.
3. At his own expense, he regularly places advertising on behalf of the list owner in appropriate advertising journals, and consistently promotes the list owner's list, by mail, to prospective users and other list brokers.
4. He and his sales force consistently call on prospects in person and by phone.
5. He maintains the list owner's list, if the list owner wishes, either in his own shop or with an experienced computer service organization.
6. He analyzes the results of each mailing when they are available and often makes suggestions for segmented use of the list with a view to increasing profitability.
7. He usually handles all billing to other brokers or his customers, remitting to the list owner, less commissions.
8. He provides a detailed report of list activity, usually on a quarterly basis, to the list owner.

While the normal commission to a list broker is 20% of gross, the list manager usually earns a commission of 10% of gross when rental is arranged through another broker, and list brokerage commission plus management commission when he rents directly to one of his customers.

List rental business is a part-time activity for most list owners. The extra business realized by putting this function into the hands of a competent list manager usually more than warrants the compensation the manager receives for his specialized services.

It should be noted that this extra profit potential exists only when a list is put into the hands of a *competent* list manager. Bob Kestnbaum, a leading direct marketing consultant, recommends that prospective list managers be carefully screened. These questions should be put to each.

32 Questions To Ask a Prospective List Manager

Services Provided

1. What method and equipment will be used to maintain the list?
2. Does the manager have the capability to add demographic data on the basis of ZIP Codes or census tracts?
3. Could the list be merged into a larger data base for additional rentals or could it be unduplicated against similar lists being managed by the same organization?
4. What clerical and reporting functions would be assumed (see below, Order Processing and Reports)?

List Preparation and Maintenance

5. Is there sufficient flexibility in the system to establish and use all the selection factors appropriate for the particular list?
6. How are test panels selected and controlled? What system is used to avoid providing names delivered on previous orders?
7. What controls exist to avoid excessive mailing to the same name?
8. In what forms can the list be delivered (label, direct impression, heat transfer, magnetic tape)?
9. What time service would be given on normal orders and rush orders, e.g., how rapidly would addressed material be delivered?

Security Procedures

10. Are magnetic tapes or address masters retained in a safe place that is kept locked?
11. How is access to the locked storage area limited and controlled?
12. Are magnetic tapes or address masters logged out and in when they are removed from the locked storage area?
13. What procedures exist for seeding the list with decoys and for being sure that decoys appear on every test panel or list segment delivered?
14. What procedures are used to identify and mark labels or magnetic tapes shipped out?

Order Processing and Reports

15. What procedures are used to be sure that necessary approvals are secured for each rental order?
16. What records of list rental orders are maintained?
17. What summary counts of names delivered are supplied with each rental order?
18. What types of sales reports and analyses are supplied to the list owner?
    By month
    By offer type
    By broker
    By user
    By industry
19. What efforts are extended to collect rental accounts receivable and to provide accounts receivable aging reports?

Sales Effort

20. Does the prospective list manager have special experience, knowledge, and contacts with and of the most likely types of users of the list in question?
21. Are there salesmen who call on potential list users and brokers? How many? Where located?
22. What types of mailings and advertisements will be used to promote the list? How frequently will they be used?

Costs and Revenue

23. Will there be a charge for special computer programming?
24. Will there be a charge for generating, inputting, or converting the list?
25. What is the cost of selecting names, producing test panels, or skipping names?
26. How much does it cost to change names, add names, and kill names?
27. What are the charges for running labels or producing magnetic tape?
28. What fees will be charged for managing or promoting the list?
29. If the list is managed on an exclusive basis, how will broker's commission be divided?

Other Considerations

30. How much experience and knowledge do the employees of the list management firm have?
31. What reputation does the firm have in its field?
32. Are there people in the firm who have the capability to provide sound advice and guidance?

Duplication Elimination

1968 will go down in the history of direct marketing as the year of the breakthrough for overcoming mailing duplication. Prior to 1968, it was either impossible or impractical to remove duplicate names from mass mailing programs. But in 1968 several systems evolved for removing duplicate names by using the computer. The processes employed are commonly known as "merge and purge." Here, very simply, is how merge and purge works.

1. You rent your lists through the brokers involved in the usual way. Almost all lists on magnetic tape or punch cards are suitable.
2. The tapes or punch cards provided for rented lists, as well as those for the mailer's customer and/or prospect list, are sent to the service organization designated.
3. The service organization puts the tapes through a computerized matching process which compares the names on each list with every name on every other list, including the mailer's customer list.
4. The mailer receives one set of labels with no duplication whatever between the rented lists (no matter how many may be involved) and the customer list.
5. In addition, the mailer receives a second nonduplicating set of labels representing names of known mail order buyers which appear two or more times on the multiplicity of rented lists.

The chart which follows details possible savings through the elimination of duplicates. Figures are based on a mailing cost of $100 per thousand for simple computation, although most mailings today cost at least $125 per thousand and more. Looking at the chart, let's take a reduction in duplication of just 15% and note the savings across the chart as they relate to the quantity mailed. A one-million-piece mailing can save $15,000; a five-million-piece mailing, $75,000.

SAVINGS POTENTIAL By Eliminating Duplicate Mailings

Mailing Quantities

Percent of Duplication	1,000,000	2,500,000	5,000,000	10,000,000	25,000,000	50,000,000
10	$10,000	$ 25,000	$ 50,000	$100,000	$ 250,000	$ 500,000
15	$15,000	$ 37,500	$ 75,000	$150,000	$ 375,000	$ 750,000
20	$20,000	$ 50,000	$100,000	$200,000	$ 500,000	$1,000,000
25	$25,000	$ 62,500	$125,000	$250,000	$ 625,000	$1,250,000
30	$30,000	$ 75,000	$150,000	$300,000	$ 750,000	$1,500,000
35	$35,000	$ 87,500	$175,000	$350,000	$ 875,000	$1,750,000
40	$40,000	$100,000	$200,000	$400,000	$1,000,000	$2,000,000
45	$45,000	$112,500	$225,000	$450,000	$1,125,000	$2,250,000
50	$50,000	$125,000	$250,000	$500,000	$1,250,000	$2,500,000

Based on a mailing cost of $100 per thousand.

One case history will show the dramatic savings possible when the merge and purge system is put into effect. *Southern Living* applied merge and purge to 17 lists totaling 1.4 million names. They found the duplication rate between the 17 lists was 13.5%, plus an additional 17.3% on their house list. *Southern Living* saved $44,643 on this one mailing. They cut their customer acquisition cost by 25%.

47

MERGE AND PURGE PROGRAM

List Number	Total Input	Exclusive List	Multi-buyer	Total Output	Percent of Duplication
1.	48,000	47,641	30	47,671	1
2.	27,646	21,232	811	22,043	18
3.	24,837	20,016	833	20,849	17
4.	43,899	33,461	1,288	34,749	19
5.	25,220	18,647	614	19,261	22
6.	12,595	11,410	206	11,616	12
7.	100,220	73,445	2,700	76,145	25
8.	58,006	43,188	1,859	45,047	23
9.	24,527	20,435	598	21,033	13
10.	63,000	53,595	1,228	54,823	15
11.	25,230	18,281	968	19,249	24
12.	23,750	19,611	524	20,135	12
13.	25,272	18,158	1,319	19,477	21
14.	64,460	47,904	1,812	49,716	24
15.	47,480	42,621	600	43,221	10
16.	70,590	63,567	721	64,288	9
17.	16,700	15,432	203	15,635	6
18.	72,000	54,720	2,251	56,971	19
19.	6,000	4,544	197	4,741	49
20.	239,430	202,885	4,537	207,422	13
21.	58,682	50,035	1,077	51,112	10
22.	51,150	31,374	1,886	33,260	40
23.	32,800	24,393	1,149	25,542	22
Grand Totals	1,161,494	936,595	27,411	964,006	16.5%

The total number of rented names processed (total input) was 1,161,494 names. There were 936,595 names, in total, on the exclusive lists (names which appear on the original source list, but not on any other lists). There were a total of 27,411 multibuyer names (names which appeared on two or more lists). The rented lists were also matched against the mailer's customer list of 1,441,000 names with the result that a total of 146,522 house names were suppressed. The net result was that 964,006 nonduplicating names were used.

Note: Percent of duplication for each list reflects duplication against all other rented lists as well as the house list of the mailer.

Source: System Dupli-Match from Alan Drey Co.

A bonus feature of any merge and purge program is the list which emerges of names which appear on two or more lists. Such names constitute choice prospects. They qualify for follow-up mailings on the same proposition. So merge and purge not only improves the image of direct mail but saves untold dollars as well.

A truly exciting application of duplication elimination is a cooperative effort between the May Co. in Los Angeles and the *Los Angeles Times*. A sophisticated program has been worked out. Computer matched tapes have enabled the May Co. to distribute their catalogs to their customers through home delivery subscribers of the *Los Angeles Times*. The May Co. customers who are *Times* subscribers get their catalogs in the paper. May Co. customers who are not *Times* subscribers get their catalogs by mail. It costs the

May Co. $57 a thousand to mail a printed catalog. That same catalog inserted in the newspaper (going to May Co. customers only) costs the company $32 a thousand—saving $25 per thousand. It is a safe prediction that this unique computer matched system will ultimately be offered by scores of newspapers across the country.

Lists Age Rapidly

One of the most basic lessons to be learned about mailing lists is—the more current the names, the better the response is likely to be. Lists age rapidly. This is a mobile country. Consumers move at a fantastic rate. Address changes on some lists are as high as 25% a year. So every list is, in effect, a moving target.

Forgetting the ever existent problem of address changes for a moment, let us note a very important axiom about customer lists and inquiry lists which should be indelibly printed on the mind of every direct marketer. It is this: The longer the period from the time of the last response, the less responsive that customer is likely to be. The best way to demonstrate this is to test any given list of respondents by years of last response. Rating the most current year as 100%, response is likely to break into this type of pattern:

```
1974 names . . . . . . . . . . . . . . . . .  100%
1973 names . . . . . . . . . . . . . . . . .   80%
1972 names . . . . . . . . . . . . . . . . .   60%
```

Since the most current names are likely to bring the best response, it is wise to test lists by them, not testing the older names until most of the current names have met or exceeded quota. One can be quite certain that, if the most current names do not meet quota, it will be a waste of money to test the older names.

Analyzing Response by Timing and Locale

When and where you mail is also a big factor in response. "What are the best mailing months?" is a perennial question at direct mail seminars. The chart which follows was provided by Ray Snyder, a direct mail consultant and former sales manager of the Direct Mail Department of *World Book*. It resulted from a three-year test program for a nonseasonal item. The mailing was made to an equal quantity of like names from a given list every month of the year. The best-pulling month was rated 100%.

Month	Comparative	Month	Comparative
January	100.0%	July	73.3%
February	96.3%	August	87.0%
March	71.0%	September	79.0%
April	71.5%	October	89.9%
May	71.5%	November	81.0%
June	67.0%	December	79.0%

This chart, in my opinion, is truly meaningful, for it closely coincides with the experience of most mass mailers. Seasonal goods—Christmas items, for example—aside, January is traditionally the best responsive month of the year for a wide variety of mail offers.

June is traditionally the worst month. Note the variance of 33% on the chart. The theory most often advanced to explain why mail dropped in June does so poorly is that this is the start of the vacation season.

It must be emphasized that the chart applies to general offers as opposed to seasonal offers. Rare is the power mower offer that will succeed in January, no matter what the discount! And it's pretty difficult to get the consumer whipped up about Christmas cards in July. But there are sales variation swings by months for mailers with seasonal offers, too. And it is vital that all mailers, those with nonseasonal offers as well as those with seasonal offers, have a performance chart by months.

A performance chart is a key factor in projecting test results. Every mailer is faced with the fact that, if he is to mail in volume in his best month or months, his test must be made two to three months previous to his best month or months. He must be able to project accurately how much greater his response will be in his best months over his test months. A performance chart, based on experience, enables him to make projections with confidence. For example, on the basis of the chart, an offer which is tested in July will do 16.6% better in October. This better performance could well be the difference between profit and loss. Many a test dies aborning because the mailer lacks performance figures by months from which he can project.

Just as there is a pattern of best mailing months for each mailer, so there is a pattern of best states. And varying degrees of responsiveness can be considerable. In addition to a seasonal chart, Snyder also developed a chart which showed the ranking of states by response. It resulted from a total of some 33 million mailing pieces covering 20 different offers of various types of books and merchandise mailed by companies for whom Snyder has worked or acted as a consultant. State rankings will vary considerably among marketers, but there is a ranking for every marketer. Later we shall deal with much more sophisticated rankings by ZIP Codes within states.

Position	State	Position	State
1	Alaska	29	Oklahoma
[2	Washington, D.C.]	30	New York
3	Hawaii	31	Rhode Island
4	California	32	Georgia
5	Nevada	33	Ohio
6	Arizona	34	Delaware
7	Wyoming	35	Virginia
8	New Mexico	36	Pennsylvania
9	Idaho	37	Arkansas
10	Montana	38	Missouri
11	Utah	39	South Carolina
12	Florida	40	Connecticut
13	Nebraska	41	North Carolina
14	Louisiana	42	New Hampshire
15	Oregon	43	North Dakota
16	Illinois	44	Minnesota
17	Indiana	45	Kentucky
18	Texas	46	Vermont
19	Colorado	47	Tennessee
20	Washington	48	Iowa
21	Maryland	49	Mississippi
22	Wisconsin	50	Massachusetts
23	West Virginia	51	Alabama
24	South Dakota		
25	Maine		This chart reflects the ranking
26	New Jersey		of states (based upon sales re-
27	Michigan		sponse) for a total of 20 mailings
28	Kansas		offering various types of books and merchandise.

Determining Proper Test Quantities

Perhaps one of the most frequently pondered questions about list tests is deciding how big or how small a quantity of names should be used. Many rules of thumb for establishing test quantities have been used by mailers for years. Some mailers say, "I always test 10% of the list." Others say, "We never test more than 1,000 names on a list." Neither approach is mathematically sound.

Certainly those who follow the rule of 10% of the list are not wise in testing a quantity of 100,000 names when the total list is one million. If the test fails, $15 to $20 thousand dollars could go down the drain. And what confidence can we have about a test of 1,000 names from a universe of one million names? Testing too large a quantity forces us to spend more than is necessary to obtain reliable test results; testing too small a quantity wastes money, since we cannot have much confidence in our results.

Sophisticated mailers today rely on test sizes and results based on the laws of probability. To make the scales work for you, you first need to know three things which determine the size of your test:

1. What is your anticipated response?
2. What level of confidence do you require? (Must you be right 99 out of 100 times, or can you risk being right 95 out of 100 times?)
3. By how much can you miss the anticipated pull and still be within an acceptable lower response limit? (Can you live with 1% plus or minus 0.2%, or can you still profit if your mailing pulls 1% plus or minus 0.5%?)

Because of the time required to compute a probability equation for each individual mailing made or contemplated, it is usually easier to refer to probability tables for which the calculations have already been figured for various percentages of response and limits of error. (The probability equation is included in this chapter for those with an exceptional mathematical IQ.)

Probability tables are made up of four elements: test sample size; level of confidence; response; and limit of error. At the top of each probability table is a notation about the level of confidence on which it is built. Running horizontally across the top of the page are the limits of error, expressed in percentage points. The column headed "R" is the percent of response or results. Figures within the table where the "response" and "limit of error" intersect are the sample sizes required.

To illustrate the use of probability tables, let us take an actual sample of a test mailing and determine the limit of error which we could expect on a larger mailing. For convenience, we'll use the small table which follows. In this case, we mailed 10,000 pieces and received a 1% response. Now we want to find the limits of error for an identical mailing with a 95% confidence level. (Statistically, this means results will be as indicated 95 out of 100 times.)

Using the table on page 52, we would read down the R column until we came to 1% response. Then, we would read horizontally until we came to the closest figure to our 10,000-piece sample size. Then, reading vertically to that column's heading, we find 0.20 as the possible limit of error we could expect on a larger mailing to the same size list under identical circumstances.

In like manner, suppose we want the number of pieces we should mail on a proposed list if we anticipate an .8% response, cannot afford a limit of error greater than plus or minus .25, and want to be sure that 95 out 100 times we will stay within the .25 limit of error. First we read down the R column until we find the .8% response figure. Then we read horizontally until we locate the sample size required under the column headed by the .25% limit of error. We find that we would require a test mailing of 4,877 pieces, or,

PROBABILITY TABLE BASED ON 95% CONFIDENCE LEVEL

R Response	Limits of Error (as percentage points) 0.16	0.18	0.20	0.25	0.30
.1	1,499	1,184	958	614	426
.2	2,994	2,366	1,917	1,226	852
.3	4,467	3,546	2,872	1,838	1,276
.4	5,977	4,723	3,826	2,448	1,700
.5	7,464	5,897	4,777	3,057	2,123
.6	8,948	7,070	5,727	3,665	2,545
.7	10,429	8,240	6,675	4,272	2,966
.8	11,907	9,408	7,621	4,877	3,387
.9	13,382	10,573	8,564	5,481	3,806
1.0	14,854	11,736	9,506	6,084	4,225
1.1	16,322	12,897	10,446	6,686	4,643
1.2	17,788	14,055	11,385	7,286	5,060

Source: Alan Drey Co., Chicago.

for convenience, 5,000 names. This means that if this test mailing pulls an .8% response, an identical larger mailing will produce results falling between .55% and 1.05% —95 out of 100 times.

Included on pages 54 and 55 are two comprehensive probability tables, one at 99% confidence level, and the other at 95% confidence level.

It must be remembered that probability tables are constructed on pure statistical probabilities. They can predict, within certain limits of error, the results that can be expected from a larger mailing *exactly identical* to the test, but only if a good random cross-section has been used in creating the test sample.

It should also be remembered that probabilities work only when your continuation mailing is made under identical circumstances. Any changes in copy, format, or offer to the same list will invalidate the statistical study. Seasonal variations in mailing response must also be considered. When a scale of seasonal variations exists, these can be weighted into the figures.

Probability Equation

Formula for determining sample size is:

$$N = \frac{(R)\,(1-R)\,(C)^2}{E^2}$$

where (R) is the frequency of response, a percentage expressed as a decimal; $(1-R)$ is the frequency of *non*response, also a percentage expressed as a decimal; (C) is the confidence level, expressed as a number of standard deviations; (E) is the error limit, expressed as a decimal; and (N) is the sample size, the number of pieces to be mailed.

To illustrate the use of the above formula, determine the sample size required in terms of mailing pieces when the expected response is 1% and the desired error limit is ±.2% at a confidence level of 95%. Thus:

R = 1% . . . or .01, expressed as a decimal.
1 − R = 99% . . . or .99, expressed as a decimal.
C = 1.96 statistic deviations, assuming a 95% confidence level.
E = .2% . . . or .002 expressed as a decimal.
N = to be determined.

Substituting the above values into our formula, we have:

$$N = \frac{(.01)(.99)(1.96)^2}{(.002)^2}$$

$$= \frac{(.01)(.99)(3.8416)}{.000004}$$

$$= \frac{.03803184}{.000004}$$

$$N = 9,508 \text{ pieces to be mailed}$$

Suppose that, in the above experiment, we had actually mailed 9,508 pieces . . . and the actual response turned out to be 1.5%. Now, still at a 95% probability level, what would be the error limit of continuation mailings projected from this experiment? The formula for determining error limit follows:

$$E = \sqrt{\frac{(R)(1-R)}{N}} \times C$$

Substituting the new values (with the same notation as before) into this formula, and solving for error limit, we have:

$$E = \sqrt{\frac{(.015)(.985)}{9,508}} \times 1.96$$

$$= \sqrt{\frac{.014775}{9,508}} \times 1.96$$

$$= \sqrt{.000001554} \times 1.96$$

$$E = .00124 \times 1.96$$

$$E = .00243 \text{ or } .243\% \text{ error limit}$$

These two examples illustrate the statistical importance of setting up direct response tests, first of all, in such a manner as to assure a sample size adequate for meaningful projection of response within acceptable tolerances. Second, they demonstrate the need for accurate determination of the error limit, the variation which could occur by chance alone and not as a result of a significant difference in particular marketing efforts. When comparing the response from two diverse market segments, for example, we must recognize such "error by chance" difference during the evaluation process. In the example above, where response was 1.5% and the error limit was calculated to be .243%, then any response from continuation mailings, or comparative tests, within the range of 1.257% and 1.743% would be statistically "the same as" 1.5% and such variation could have occurred sheerly by statistical chance, at a 95% level of confidence.

Market Segmentation

Market segmentation has long been recognized as a key to maximizing response in ratio to advertising expenditures. It is through understanding market segments and developing and applying techniques for isolating the segments that maximizing is reached.

An acknowledged authority in the theories and techniques of market segmentation is Martin Baier, vice president of marketing of Old American Insurance Co. of Kansas City, Missouri. His thoughts and applications, which follow on page 56, merit deep study.

SAMPLE SIZES FOR RESPONSES BETWEEN 0.1% and 4.0%
CONFIDENCE LEVEL—99 PERCENT

LIMITS OF ERROR (EXPRESSED AS PERCENTAGE POINTS)

R (Response)	.02	.04	.06	.08	.10	.12	.14	.16	.18	.20	.30	.40	.50	.60	.70
.1	165,709	41,427	18,412	10,357	6,628	4,603	3,381	2,589	2,046	1,657	736	414	265	184	135
.2	331,087	82,772	36,787	20,693	13,243	9,197	6,756	5,173	4,087	3,311	1,471	827	529	368	270
.3	496,132	124,033	55,126	31,008	19,845	13,781	10,125	7,752	6,125	4,961	2,205	1,240	794	551	405
.4	660,846	165,212	73,427	41,303	26,434	18,356	13,486	10,325	8,158	6,608	2,937	1,652	1,057	734	539
.5	825,228	206,307	91,692	51,577	33,009	22,923	16,841	12,894	10,187	8,252	3,667	2,063	1,320	916	673
.6	989,279	247,320	109,919	61,830	39,571	27,480	20,189	15,457	12,213	9,893	4,396	2,473	1,582	1,099	807
.7	1,152,997	288,249	128,111	72,062	46,120	32,027	23,530	18,015	14,234	11,530	5,124	2,882	1,845	1,281	941
.8	1,316,384	329,096	146,265	82,274	52,655	36,565	26,864	20,569	16,251	13,164	5,850	3,291	2,106	1,462	1,074
.9	1,479,439	369,859	164,381	92,465	59,178	41,095	30,192	23,116	18,264	14,794	6,575	3,698	2,367	1,643	1,208
1.0	1,642,163	410,541	182,463	102,635	65,687	45,616	33,513	25,658	20,273	16,422	7,299	4,105	2,627	1,825	1,340
1.1	1,804,554	451,138	200,505	112,784	72,182	50,126	36,827	28,195	22,278	18,045	8,020	4,511	2,887	2,004	1,473
1.2	1,966,614	491,654	218,512	122,913	78,665	54,628	40,134	30,728	24,279	19,666	8,740	4,917	3,146	2,185	1,605
1.3	2,128,342	532,085	236,482	133,021	85,134	59,121	43,435	33,255	26,275	21,283	9,459	5,321	3,405	2,365	1,737
1.4	2,289,739	572,435	254,414	143,108	91,590	63,603	46,729	35,777	28,268	22,897	10,176	5,724	3,663	2,544	1,869
1.5	2,450,803	612,700	272,310	153,175	98,032	68,077	50,016	38,293	30,256	24,508	10,892	6,127	3,921	2,723	2,000
1.6	2,611,536	652,884	290,170	163,221	104,461	72,542	53,296	40,805	32,241	26,115	11,607	6,529	4,178	2,901	2,132
1.7	2,771,937	692,984	307,992	173,246	110,877	76,997	56,569	43,311	34,221	27,719	12,319	6,930	4,435	3,079	2,263
1.8	2,932,007	733,002	325,777	183,250	117,280	81,444	59,836	45,812	36,197	29,320	13,030	7,330	4,691	3,257	2,393
1.9	3,091,744	772,936	343,527	193,234	123,670	85,881	63,096	48,308	38,169	30,917	13,741	7,729	4,946	3,435	2,523
2.0	3,251,150	812,788	361,238	203,197	130,046	90,309	66,350	50,799	40,137	32,512	14,449	8,128	5,202	3,612	2,654
2.1	3,410,224	852,556	378,912	213,139	136,409	94,728	69,596	53,284	42,100	34,102	15,156	8,525	5,456	3,789	2,783
2.2	3,568,967	892,242	396,551	223,060	142,759	99,138	72,836	55,765	44,061	35,690	15,862	8,922	5,710	3,965	2,913
2.3	3,727,377	931,844	414,152	232,961	149,095	103,537	76,068	58,239	46,016	37,273	16,566	9,318	5,964	4,141	3,042
2.4	3,885,456	971,364	431,716	242,841	155,418	107,929	79,294	60,710	47,968	38,855	17,268	9,714	6,216	4,317	3,172
2.5	4,043,203	1,010,800	449,245	252,700	161,728	112,311	82,513	63,174	49,915	40,432	17,970	10,108	6,469	4,492	3,300
2.6	4,200,619	1,050,155	466,734	262,538	168,025	116,682	85,726	65,634	51,859	42,006	18,669	10,501	6,721	4,667	3,429
2.7	4,357,702	1,089,425	484,187	272,356	174,308	121,046	88,932	68,088	53,798	43,577	19,367	10,894	6,972	4,842	3,557
2.8	4,514,454	1,128,614	501,606	282,153	180,578	125,402	92,131	70,538	55,734	45,145	20,064	11,286	7,223	5,016	3,685
2.9	4,670,874	1,167,718	518,984	291,929	186,835	129,745	95,324	72,982	57,664	46,708	20,759	11,677	7,473	5,189	3,812
3.0	4,826,963	1,206,741	536,327	301,685	193,079	134,081	98,508	75,421	59,591	48,270	21,453	12,067	7,723	5,363	3,940
3.1	4,982,719	1,245,679	553,635	311,420	199,309	138,409	101,687	77,854	61,514	49,827	22,145	12,457	7,972	5,536	4,067
3.2	5,138,144	1,284,536	570,903	321,134	205,526	142,725	104,858	80,284	63,433	51,381	22,836	12,845	8,221	5,709	4,194
3.3	5,293,237	1,323,309	588,135	330,827	211,729	147,034	108,024	82,706	65,348	52,932	23,525	13,233	8,469	5,881	4,321
3.4	5,447,999	1,362,000	605,333	340,500	217,920	151,333	111,183	85,124	67,258	54,480	24,213	13,620	8,716	6,053	4,447
3.5	5,602,428	1,400,607	622,490	350,152	224,097	155,621	114,334	87,537	69,165	56,024	24,899	14,006	8,964	6,224	4,573
3.6	5,756,526	1,439,132	639,611	359,783	230,261	159,903	117,479	89,945	71,067	57,565	25,584	14,391	9,210	6,395	4,699
3.7	5,910,292	1,477,573	656,699	369,393	236,412	164,174	120,616	92,347	72,966	59,103	26,268	14,775	9,456	6,567	4,824
3.8	6,063,727	1,515,932	673,746	378,983	242,549	168,435	123,749	94,745	74,860	60,637	26,949	15,159	9,702	6,737	4,949
3.9	6,216,829	1,554,207	690,756	388,552	248,673	172,688	126,872	97,137	76,750	62,168	27,629	15,542	9,947	6,907	5,074
4.0	6,369,600	1,592,400	707,733	398,100	254,784	176,933	129,991	99,525	78,636	63,696	28,309	15,924	10,191	7,077	5,199

SAMPLE SIZES FOR RESPONSES BETWEEN 0.1% and 4.0%
CONFIDENCE LEVEL—95 PERCENT

R (Response)	LIMITS OF ERROR (EXPRESSED AS PERCENTAGE POINTS)														
	.02	.04	.06	.08	.10	.12	.14	.16	.18	.20	.30	.40	.50	.60	.70
.1	95,929	23,982	10,659	5,995	3,837	2,665	1,957	1,499	1,184	959	426	240	153	106	78
.2	191,666	47,916	21,296	11,979	7,667	5,324	3,911	2,994	2,366	1,917	852	479	307	213	156
.3	287,211	71,803	31,912	17,951	11,488	7,978	5,861	4,487	3,546	2,872	1,276	718	459	319	234
.4	382,564	95,641	42,507	23,910	15,303	10,627	7,807	5,977	4,723	3,826	1,700	956	612	425	312
.5	477,724	119,431	53,080	29,858	19,109	13,270	9,749	7,464	5,987	4,777	2,123	1,194	764	530	390
.6	572,693	143,173	63,632	35,793	22,908	15,908	11,687	8,948	7,070	5,727	2,545	1,432	916	636	467
.7	667,470	166,867	74,163	41,717	26,699	18,541	13,622	10,429	8,240	6,675	2,966	1,669	1,068	741	545
.8	762,054	190,514	84,673	47,628	30,482	21,168	15,552	11,907	9,408	7,621	3,387	1,905	1,219	847	622
.9	856,447	214,112	95,160	53,528	34,258	23,790	17,478	13,382	10,573	8,564	3,806	2,141	1,370	951	699
1.0	950,648	237,662	105,628	59,415	38,026	26,407	19,401	14,854	11,736	9,506	4,225	2,376	1,521	1,056	776
1.1	1,044,656	261,164	116,072	65,291	41,786	29,018	21,319	16,322	12,897	10,446	4,643	2,611	1,671	1,160	853
1.2	1,138,472	284,618	126,496	71,155	45,539	31,624	23,234	17,788	14,055	11,385	5,060	2,846	1,821	1,265	929
1.3	1,232,097	308,024	136,899	77,006	49,284	34,225	25,145	19,251	15,211	12,321	5,476	3,080	1,971	1,369	1,006
1.4	1,325,529	331,382	147,280	82,845	53,021	36,820	27,051	20,711	16,364	13,255	5,891	3,314	2,121	1,473	1,082
1.5	1,418,769	354,692	157,640	88,673	56,751	39,410	28,954	22,168	17,515	14,188	6,305	3,547	2,270	1,576	1,158
1.6	1,511,818	377,954	167,980	94,489	60,473	41,995	30,853	23,622	18,664	15,118	6,719	3,780	2,419	1,680	1,234
1.7	1,604,674	401,168	178,297	100,292	64,187	44,574	32,748	25,073	19,811	16,047	7,132	4,012	2,567	1,783	1,310
1.8	1,697,338	424,334	188,592	106,083	67,894	47,148	34,639	26,521	20,955	16,973	7,543	4,243	2,716	1,886	1,385
1.9	1,789,810	447,452	198,868	111,863	71,592	49,717	36,526	27,966	22,096	17,898	7,955	4,474	2,863	1,988	1,461
2.0	1,882,090	470,523	209,121	117,631	75,284	52,280	38,410	29,407	23,235	18,821	8,365	4,705	3,011	2,091	1,536
2.1	1,974,178	493,544	219,352	123,386	78,967	54,838	40,289	30,846	24,372	19,742	8,774	4,935	3,158	2,193	1,611
2.2	2,066,074	516,518	229,564	129,129	82,643	57,391	42,165	32,282	25,507	20,661	9,182	5,165	3,306	2,295	1,686
2.3	2,157,778	539,444	239,753	134,861	86,311	59,938	44,036	33,715	26,638	21,578	9,590	5,394	3,452	2,397	1,761
2.4	2,249,290	562,322	249,920	140,581	89,972	62,480	45,903	35,145	27,769	22,493	9,997	5,623	3,599	2,499	1,836
2.5	2,340,609	585,152	260,068	146,288	93,624	65,017	47,767	36,572	28,896	23,406	10,403	5,851	3,745	2,600	1,911
2.6	2,431,737	607,934	270,192	151,983	97,269	67,547	49,627	37,996	30,021	24,317	10,807	6,079	3,891	2,702	1,985
2.7	2,522,673	630,668	280,296	157,667	100,907	70,074	51,483	39,416	31,144	25,227	11,211	6,307	4,036	2,803	2,059
2.8	2,613,416	653,354	290,380	163,339	104,537	72,595	53,335	40,834	32,264	26,134	11,615	6,534	4,181	2,904	2,133
2.9	2,703,968	675,992	300,440	168,998	108,159	75,110	55,183	42,249	33,382	27,039	12,017	6,760	4,326	3,004	2,207
3.0	2,794,328	698,582	310,480	174,645	111,773	77,620	57,026	43,661	34,497	27,943	12,419	6,986	4,471	3,105	2,281
3.1	2,884,495	721,124	320,499	180,281	115,380	80,125	58,867	45,070	35,611	28,845	12,820	7,211	4,615	3,205	2,355
3.2	2,974,470	743,618	330,496	185,904	118,979	82,623	60,702	46,476	36,721	29,745	13,220	7,436	4,759	3,305	2,428
3.3	3,064,254	766,063	340,471	191,516	122,570	85,118	62,535	47,878	37,830	30,642	13,619	7,660	4,903	3,404	2,501
3.4	3,153,845	788,461	350,427	197,115	126,154	87,607	64,364	49,278	38,936	31,538	14,017	7,884	5,046	3,504	2,574
3.5	3,243,244	810,811	360,360	202,703	129,730	90,089	66,188	50,675	40,040	32,432	14,414	8,108	5,189	3,603	2,647
3.6	3,332,452	833,113	370,271	208,278	133,298	92,568	68,009	52,069	41,141	33,325	14,811	8,331	5,332	3,702	2,720
3.7	3,421,467	855,367	380,163	213,842	136,859	95,041	69,825	53,460	42,240	34,214	15,207	8,554	5,474	3,801	2,793
3.8	3,510,290	877,572	390,031	219,393	140,412	97,507	71,638	54,848	43,336	35,103	15,601	8,776	5,616	3,900	2,865
3.9	3,598,921	899,730	399,878	224,932	143,957	99,969	73,446	56,233	44,430	35,989	15,995	8,997	5,758	3,998	2,938
4.0	3,687,360	921,840	409,706	230,460	147,494	102,426	75,252	57,615	45,522	36,874	16,388	9,218	5,900	4,097	3,010

The increasing complexity of direct response marketing activities has brought about an increasing need for segmentation of the heterogeneous total market into smaller and more homogeneous units, in terms of either specific, qualified mail response lists or clusters within generally larger compiled lists. Frequently such market segmentation has been geographic—by region, state, county, and metropolitan area. Sometimes it has been demographic—by sex, age, marital status, and occupation. Recently it has been psychographic—by habits, attitudes, life styles, and behavior patterns of consumers.

To be truly meaningful, too, the resultant market segments should constitute a unit whose physical definition is not only readily identifiable geographically but is also one whose homogeneity enables us to measure it in economic and cultural as well as demographic and psychographic terms.

Environmental Influences

People with like interests tend to cluster. Their behavior, including their buying habits and attitudes, tends to be influenced by their environment—of which, in effect, they themselves are a part. So the need is to be able (a) to identify areas where such groupings occur; (b) to classify them in terms of economic potential; and (c) to measure their cultural pattern—all the effects of their environments on their buying behavior—or, to sum it up in one term, to measure them *culturologically*. Then, once the marketer has determined the common denominator—or tone—of one or more of these cultural units in relation to his product, he can apply this indicator to all other units, use it to locate those units with similar characteristics, and expect the same kind of reactions to his marketing moves.

Purchase decisions are not so much dependent on income—which is generally assumed in economic theory—as on the buyer's perception of his relative position, or that to which he aspires, in his environment. The behavior of consumers must thus be related to their environment—to select reference groups, social classes, and cultural influences—and their *ability to buy* must be distinguished from their *proneness to buy*. Such measurement enables direct response marketers to define their best prospects, seek them out, establish sales potentials, predict consumer behavior, and consider penetration in relation to potential in a manner which can be statistically evaluated.

The basic concept of human ecology—that man's behavior is a response to environmental influences—tells us that a household with a $6,000 annual income located in an area where the mean household income is $8,000 is prone to emulate the $8,000 level. The reverse also is true—a $10,000 household tends to behave like its $8,000 neighbors. It is this tendency which contributes to the homogeneity of behavior within an area, even though absolute characteristics among individual households vary. Discretionary purchases by households under such circumstances are dependent not just on the *ability* to buy but also on the *proneness* to buy.

Thorstein Veblen's concept of conspicuous consumption, with its emphasis on the social character of consumption decisions and the interdependence of consumer choices, has proved important and durable. As Veblen put it more than half a century ago, "The accepted standard of expenditure in the community or in the class to which a person belongs largely determines what his standard of living will be."

Many types of face-to-face reference groups exert strong influences on consumer decisions. Such groups include families, social clubs, work associates, church members—and, of course, neighbors. "Keeping up with the Joneses" helps to explain the marketing success which a prestigious magazine is reported to have had when it mailed a subscription offer to the next-door neighbors of its present subscribers. The invitation was on the order of: "Your next-door neighbor reads *National Geographic*. Shouldn't you?" Another similar marketing effort was a letter from an automobile manufacturer which started out with "Have you noticed that new Rambler in your neighbor's driveway . . . ?" So-called referral selling – the use of a third party directly or indirectly to recommend a product or service – is a notable example of reference group influence. A consumer is inclined to respect the judgments of those with whom he associates.

A buyer is strongly influenced, too, by his social class or that to which he aspires, rather than by income alone. Culture also exerts a strong influence on buying decisions. Social class has been seen by many as the most meaningful manner of market segmentation. Noting that income level alone does not determine social class, these researchers point to such things as educational level and occupation as more important variables which determine class membership. The beginning plumber and the young lawyer, for instance, possibly have comparable incomes, although they do not command the same prestige or social class membership.

ZIP Code Areas as Market Segments

Because people with like interests *do* tend to cluster and because their purchase decisions are frequently influenced by their desire to emulate their friends, neighbors, and community innovators, ZIP Code areas are now being used by many direct response marketers to provide the means to identify meaningful market segments. The homogeneity of ZIP Code areas also makes it possible to classify and qualify them in such a manner as to measure the effects of economic and cultural environment – along with demography and geography – on buying behavior within these marketing units.

Generally, geographic units which have heretofore been used in segmenting markets have lacked *homogeneity* as well as ready *identity* with a consumer. The need has been for a marketing unit whose physical boundaries could be defined in terms which were *economically meaningful* and *environmentally measurable*. ZIP Code areas fulfill the need on both counts.

An obvious convenience of these geographic units – setting them apart from commonly used units such as counties or metropolitan markets – is that each household and business within the unit is easily identifiable by the five-digit number assigned to it as a part of its address. The first digit of the code identifies one of ten (0 through 9) geographical areas of the nation. The first three digits combined identify a major city or major distribution point (sectional center) within a state. The full five-digit ZIP Code represents either an individual post office for a small town and/or rural area served from the sectional center transportation hub or else a specific delivery unit or area within a city.

The homogeneity of these units, of special interest for effective and efficient direct response marketing, results from the fact that each sectional center radiates from a transportation hub. This tends to reflect the economic facts of life and cultural environment of the area – key factors that, in turn, influence buying behavior. Within metropolitan areas, the units constitute neighborhood clusters.

This is not to say that there is not considerable spread among households within and between three-digit or five-digit ZIP Code areas. There is, just as there is among households within and between cities, towns, and counties. The marketer should be aware of this in weighing his relative need for three-digit versus five-digit units or unit groupings. The opportunities for measurement are desirable in either instance – owing, let us repeat, to the ready *identity* and *homogeneity* of ZIP Code areas, coupled with a *convenience* heretofore lacking for defining geographic areas.

It is well to keep in mind, too, that while we recognize the basic homogeneity of households within a ZIP Code area, not *all* households have the *same* characteristics.

Rather, it is a basic concept of human ecology that clusters of households, even though each household has different demographics, tend to emulate each other. As previously mentioned, both the $6,000 and $10,000 households behave like the $8,000 households where the mean household income of the marketing unit is $8,000. It is the *environment* which is being measured, *not the individual household.*

Mailing Lists as Market Segments

For those engaged in direct response marketing, various structures of mailing lists (or subscriber lists, for newspapers and magazines; or viewers/listeners, for broadcast media) evolve quite naturally, as well as logically, into market segments. Such structures may be categorized as *house lists, mail response lists,* and *compiled lists.* Let's look at each of these categories individually:

House Lists: Within the direct marketer's own firm resides his most valuable asset — his list of customers. They may be active, recently active, long-since active, or have merely made inquiries. They may have made many purchases or just one or maybe none at all, as in the case of inquiries. Individual purchases may have been quite large or small, in monetary terms. Customers may be differentiated by the types of product lines in which they expressed interest. Or, possibly, by the promotional strategy used to obtain them: direct mail, space advertisements, broadcast media, or personal salesmen. Furthermore, they may be considered in terms of a host of other variables: how long they have been customers, their credit vs. cash experience, etc.

In addition to all these factors, which relate to them as *customers,* they have still other characteristics as *individuals:* geographic, demographic, psychographic. They may be located in a certain geographic area of the country where climate influences purchase behavior. They may be a certain age or subject to environmental influences. There is one thing they have in common, however, and that is their relationship with your firm. This intangible, sometimes called goodwill, is your most valuable asset, even though it never appears as such on your balance sheet.

Mail Response Lists: Next in importance to those who have made a direct response to your own promotional efforts are probably those who have responded to another firm's direct response offer, preferably somewhat related in terms of buyer qualification. There are thousands of such so-called mail order lists available from an endless array of firms. Such lists are most commonly rented (they are rarely sold) through mailing list brokers. In effect, they are the house lists of other direct response marketers. That is what makes them of value to you — a history of direct response, especially if the offers are similarly qualified. Such lists can also be further qualified into market segments, just like your own lists, in terms of geography and demography. Frequently, the type and nature of their purchases may even qualify them psychographically, in terms of life styles and values.

Compiled Lists: Next in terms of direct response expectations, but generally first in terms of potential volume, come a great variety of lists which have been compiled for one purpose or another from one or more sources. Examples of such lists would be automobile registrations and telephone directory, city directory, or crisscross directory listings. There are also major compilations, for example, by age or occupation or educational attainment or even manufacturer warranty cards. A variation could be the merger of one or more such compiled lists — auto registrations by age of owner, for example — into a further qualified list. Sometimes, large mail response lists are similarly merged to identify *multiple appearances* on such lists in the manner we have described earlier. The sophistication of computer routines makes such qualifications — or, as we prefer to call them, market segmentations — increasingly possible.

58

Measurement-Identification-Retrieval

If, from what has been presented thus far, the possibility of finding relative homogeneity of consumer behavior in ZIP Code areas has been established, then it remains to develop a methodology for measuring the environment of these areas in such a manner that consumer decisions can be predicted. This calls for not only recognition of the psychographic (as opposed to simply demographic or geographic) nature of such measurement but also a scientific approach to decision making.

Old American Insurance Co. has developed a model for such market measurement. It is called ZIP Code Segmented Marketing Evaluation. Through it, the marketer is able to analyze marketing effectiveness and thus determine those market segments in which his firm may more effectively direct its efforts. Basically, the model is concerned with:

Potential of the market
Penetration of the market
Market segmentation
Retrieval of market segments

The procedural flow of the model is visualized below and on page 60.

Potential of the Market

The accumulation of market data is, of necessity, the first step in calculating the potential for the individual firm. With such a data bank at hand, the firm can define its own market segments or territory assignments in terms of environmental characteristics or psychographic life style. These segments may be collections of either three-digit or five-digit ZIP Code areas or, for that matter, other suitable marketing units for which data are available. In this sense, the system is quite flexible.

ZIP CODE AREA
SEGMENTED MARKETING EVALUATION
PROCEDURAL FLOW CHART
EXHIBIT I

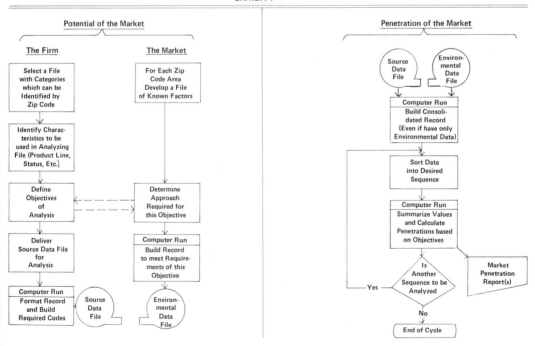

59

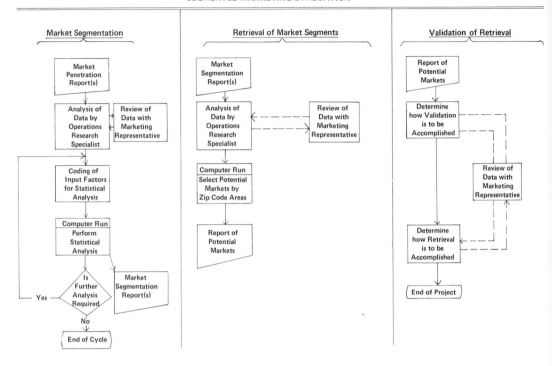

At Old American Insurance Co., a unique data bank stores up to 125 bits of *manifest* (observed) data about each ZIP Code area. This information is extracted from Bureau of Census data as well as Internal Revenue Service income statistics and R. L. Polk automobile registrations. The data bank thus lists potential marketing units (ZIP Code areas) in terms of their environmental characteristics. These characteristics, when *combined into factors,* provide the *latent* (underlying) dimensions of life style and are thus used to explain consumer behavior.

The ultimate objective of segmenting the total potential in this manner is to arrive at an array of market segments manageable in size and suited to the needs of the individual marketer. The key results to be examined will be the number of households (or individual consumers) that qualify as potential buyers. Competitive, economic, and other uncontrollable conditions, of course, should receive due consideration as the total potential, divided into suitable segments, is evaluated.

A broad manner of segmenting the total market for measurement, which many direct response marketers will find usable and pertinent to their needs, is that which separates central city, urban fringe, and rural areas. A suggested definition for such a division of the total market in terms of ZIP Code areas by metropolitan type is this:

Central City: Five-digit ZIP Code areas within multicoded cities (those which have postal carrier routes) which have a population of more than 50,000 and are within the boundaries of a standard metropolitan statistical area.

Urban Fringe: Five-digit ZIP Code areas within multicoded cities which have a population of less than 50,000 as well as those areas which are not within multicoded cities—both categories being within standard metropolitan statistical areas.

*Rural:*Five-digit ZIP Code areas which are beyond standard metropolitan statistical areas.

60

This manner of grouping five-digit ZIP Code areas to evaluate a firm's total potential market results in a fairly even three-way split of all U.S. households. Note, however, that "urban fringe" does not necessarily mean "suburban." A suburban ZIP Code area of more than 50,000 population within a standard metropolitan statistical area is considered as a central city. The broad geographic environs of most standard metropolitan statistical areas put many suburbs as well as more remote small towns into the category of urban fringe.

Three case studies are typical of the value inherent in even such a broad analysis of sales within ZIP Code areas, when segmented as described above. All involve the direct sale of products or services by mail. Both the exposure of the offers to prospects as well as the tabulation of sales response were accurately recorded and analyzed. A comparison summary of the results of the three cases follows:

Direct Response by ZIP Code Areas, Grouped According to Central City, Urban Fringe, and Rural Types
(Central City Sales Response = 100)

Type of ZIP Code area	Sales Response as a Percent of Mailed Offers		
	Case 1	Case 2	Case 3
Central city	100	100	100
Urban fringe	109	104	89
Rural	136	138	142

Such division of the total market into segments is purely geographic. A more definitive method of segmenting markets for measurement is also somewhat more complex. It involves identifying, for each five-digit ZIP Code area, a level of response to an individual marketing effort. The environmental characteristics of each ZIP Code area are then related to response, to determine those characteristics which differentiate the best from lesser levels of response. Having thus defined the relevant factors affecting response, one must then identify other ZIP Code areas with similar factors.

The environmental characteristics—up to 125 of them, in the Old American model—are grouped through a statistical process called factor analysis. Using this technique, we can mathematically correlate the 125 environmental characteristics of the ZIP Code areas of interest (many of which inevitably occur with others) with each other and thus condense them into a dozen or more uncorrelated factors which are much more meaningful and manageable in subsequent analysis. One such factor, for example, may comprise several characteristics which manifest minimal education, below average income, largely unskilled occupations, low amounts of rent paid, low percentage of homeownership, high nonwhite population, absence of telephones and household appliances, etc.

Because each factor so defined appears to some greater or lesser degree within each five-digit ZIP Code area of interest, these can then be considered as independent variables to be correlated with penetration, the dependent variable, which is defined as a measure of marketing success in terms of either customers or response. We especially want to observe the *interactions* of the various factors within each individual ZIP Code area—that is, a high level of one particular life style factor in concert with a relatively low level of another factor.

Penetration of the Market

The direct response marketer, in measuring the penetration of his potential market (the dependent variable) and then searching for correlation with factors defined by environmental characteristics (independent variables), may want to catalog his current customers or measure his direct response within certain broader groupings. Such groupings may be according to product lines or by degree of sales activity (recency/ frequency/monetary). Within each of these subcategories, then, the individual marketer may look at his own penetration (in terms of customers or new buyers) as a percentage of total potential (in terms of households or potential buyers). He can then seek, through statistical analysis, to establish and explain the correlation between the varying degrees of penetration and measurements of the environment within the ZIP Code areas in which he now sells or hopes to sell.

Calculating penetration is a relatively simple arithmetical process. Within each ZIP Code area, responses are related to mailings or customers are related to households, as follows:

ZIP Code	Total Mailed	Total Responses	Percent Responses/Mailed
A	5,793	60	1.04
B	2,735	33	1.21
C	6,731	138	2.05
D	4,341	119	2.74

Our concern to this point has been primarily measuring a firm's *penetration* of its *potential* market — its marketing effectiveness, in terms of ZIP Code areas. When significant differences of penetration are observed, the need for explanation becomes apparent. Explanatory factors have been suggested that can be used either alone or in combination. Let's turn next to the *measurement* of the significance of penetration vs. potential in terms of the chosen factors.

Market Segmentation

Once the direct response marketer's most productive market segments have been identified (in terms of percentage penetration of the market) and classified (even so simply as by central city/urban fringe/rural types of areas, or perhaps by the firm's product lines), then qualification and explanatory measurement in terms of factors defining psychographic life styles are necessary. The validity of such measurement is directly related to the homogeneity of the marketing unit used. One reason measurement is needed is that it makes it possible to transfer marketing results, within units which have been productive, to other units where prior experience is lacking but where similar environmental characteristics are observed.

Our objective is to determine the degree of explanation between our factors (clusters of common environmental characteristics — the independent or explanatory variables) and our penetration percentage (the dependent variable). These coefficients are expressed in decimal form, ranging from 0 to 1 (for positive correlation), and 0 to −1 (for negative correlation). In both instances, 1 (positive *or* negative) indicates perfect correlation and 0 indicates no correlation.

Regression analysis, in general, describes a functional (mathematical) relationship between one dependent and one or more independent variables. In our model, stepwise multivariate regression is used. This consists of fitting a line to the observed points

62

(penetration percentages related to potential) in such a way that the sum of the squares of the differences between the observed points and the values estimated by the regression line is minimized. (This technique is known as the "least-squares" method.)

In using the stepwise analysis, we allow the independent variables (factors defining life style) to enter the regression *in the order in which they most explain* the penetration variations observed; that is, the more predictive (or explanatory) enters first and the least predictive enters last.

If the process isn't clearly understood, one result can be a rank ordering of ZIP Code areas, from the highest to the lowest *estimated* penetrations, along with accumulated availabilities within ZIP Code areas with similar factor definitions. Such a rank ordering of relevant ZIP Code areas on the basis of estimated penetration visualizes, also, the correlation of such ranking with the independent variables. Decide how big a market segment is needed and determine what the overall penetration would be. Or set a minimum marketing requirement and determine how big the market segment could be.

Retrieval of Market Segments

Unless the findings from the measurement and evaluation procedures described can be practically applied in some sort of mechanism for retrieving the most desirable market segments for the individual marketer, the wisdom of the process can and should be questioned. A firm which sells its products largely through direct response has mailing lists of its customers and prospects that are entirely identified by five-digit ZIP Codes. It is thus a relatively simple matter to select only those ZIP Code areas which have the characteristics desired.

This model is not, of course, limited to direct response application. A knowledge of market segments affording the individual firm its greatest potential for penetration is a prerequisite for *any* marketer. Such knowledge enables optimum location of dealer outlets, franchises, and salesmen, as well as pinpoint distribution of direct mail or other promotional efforts.

A *market segment,* in our present sense, is a cluster of ZIP Code areas with factor definitions relevant for the individual marketer. When these relevant characteristics have been identified, that segment must be retrieved in terms of ZIP Code areas.

Of course, the system cuts across any known characteristics of the prospect as an individual, such as age or sex. The process is *additive* — designed to *improve* marketing direction. There's got to be validation, to be sure . . . . test marketing to confirm. Because no warranties are ever expressed or implied in such a system as this. And it should be remembered that such scientific decision making is an *aid* to sound executive judgment, not a substitute for it!

Self-Quiz

1. In addition to median age, name five other factors which are significant in establishing a list profile.

   1. _____ 2. _____

   3. _____ 4. _____

   5. _____
2. When may it make sense to exchange lists with a direct competitor?

   _____

3. Describe the principal functions of a list manager.

_____

_____

_____

_____

4. Define "merge and purge."

_____

_____

_____

5. What is the first rule for testing lists?

_____

6. Historically, which is the best month, and which the poorest month, to mail?

Best month: _____   Poorest month: _____

7. In order to make probability scales practical, what are the three things you must know to determine the size of your test?

1. _____

2. _____

_____

3. _____

8. Market segmentation can now be measured by *psychographics*. Define the term.

_____

_____

9. A household with a $6,000 annual income located in an area where the mean household income is $8,000 is prone to spend at the $_____ level.

10. A household with a $10,000 annual income located in an area where the mean household income is $8,000 is prone to spend at the $_____ level.

11. Why do ZIP Code areas serve as an ideal means for identifying meaningful market segments?

_____

_____

_____

_____

12. Name the three types of lists available to every direct marketer.

1. _____

2. _____

3. _____

13. The model for ZIP Code Area Segmented Marketing is concerned with four basic factors. Name them.

1. _____

2. _____

3. _____

4. _____

14. Total markets in terms of ZIP Code areas should be defined by three metropolitan types. Name them.

1. _____

2. _____

3. _____

15. Define *regression analysis.*

Pilot Project

You are the advertising manager for a publisher of children's books. You have a new set of books for preschool children. You want to test in July to determine if you can mail in large quantities in October.

Your assignment:

With a total test budget sufficient to mail 50,000 pieces, set up a set of tests for the Young Family Index birth list, determining the quantity for each test. Make your decisions from the following criteria.

1. The quantity you will have to mail to each test segment with *(a)* an anticipated response of 1%; *(b)* a 95% confidence level; *(c)* a margin of error of 20%.
2. Decide whether you want to test by first births, by multichildren families, or by both.
3. Decide whether you want to test by selected states or selected regions.
4. Decide whether you want to test by small towns or by large cities.
5. Decide whether you want to test by income groups and, if so, which income groups.
6. Decide whether you want to test by Nielsen market areas.
7. Decide whether you want to test by percentage of nonwhite population.

Note: Your total mailing budget of 50,000 pieces clearly obviates the possibility of making all the tests you may want to make. Therefore the tests you do make should be those you consider most important.

Chapter 3 Magazines*

Where Do You Go First?

The advertising pages of magazines are to the direct response advertiser what the retail outlet is to the manufacturer selling through the more traditional channels. A magazine that performs consistently well for a variety of direct response advertisers is like a store in a low-rent, high-traffic location—far more profitable than a store selling the same merchandise on the wrong side of town.

Such a magazine just seems to have an atmosphere which is more conducive to the mail response customer. The mail order shopping reader traffic is high in relation to the publication's cost per thousand. Magazines in this category (and this is by no means a complete list) at this time are *Psychology Today, Cosmopolitan, Woman's Day, Seventeen,* and the mighty *TV Guide.* Women's publications also doing well for mail order advertisers are *Family Circle, Better Homes & Gardens, Ladies' Home Journal,* and *Glamour.* Men's publications include *Esquire, Popular Science,* and *Penthouse.* (For a comprehensive list of magazines which provide a structured mail order atmosphere, see the list on the following page, "Magazines with Shopping Advertising Pages.")

But just as retail locations come into and go out of favor with each passing decade, so do the trends that determine which publications work well in the mail order marketplace at a particular time. For example, coming into favor right now are *Time, Newsweek, Penthouse, Psychology Today,* and *Ms.* In the '60s there was much greater interest in such publications as *McCall's, Ladies' Home Journal, House & Garden, House Beautiful,* and the *National Observer.*

And I can remember, in the '50s, looking to *Living for Young Homemakers, Harper-Atlantic, Saturday Review*—and a publication called the *Saturday Evening Post* could be counted on for good results.

There are some publications which appear at first glance to be just great for the mail order advertiser—but on close examination of past performance figures for many different advertisers, they rate a great big WARNING sign for the direct marketing advertiser. Here are a few places to go right now at your own risk: *Reader's Digest, National Geographic, New York,* and the *New Yorker.*

Regional Editions: When Is the Part Bigger than the Whole?

For the buyer of space in magazines today, most publications with circulations of over 1.5 million offer the opportunity to buy a regional portion of the national circulation. But it was not always so.

Although it has been said that the *New Yorker* was the first to publish sectional or regional editions, in 1929, it wasn't until the late 1950s that major magazines began selling regional space to all advertisers, not just to those who had distribution limited to a particular section of the circulation area.

The availability of regional editions for everyone opened important opportunities to the mail order-advertiser which had not been available before. Here are a few of the things you can do with regional buys:

*I am grateful to Stan Rapp, president, and Joyce Selcer, vice president and director of media services, of the New York office of RCS & A, for their great contribution to this chapter.

Magazines with Shopping Advertising Pages

A. D. (Mail Order)
After Dark, The Magazine of Entertainment (Mail Order)
Airline Publishing, Inc. (Gourmet Page)
Air Progress (Mail Order)
American Boating (Boat Mart; Boating Supplies)
American Girl (Mail Order)
American Home (Market Place)
American Home Crafts (Mail Order)
American Horseman (Mail Order)
American Legion Magazine, The (Mail Order)
Antique Trader Weekly, The (Antiquers Directory)
Apartment Life (Mail Order)
Architectural Digest (Mail Order)
Argosy (Stop to Shop Section)
Army Times Military Group (Times Shopper)
Audubon (Mail Order)
Auto Racing Digest (Mail Order)
Baby Talk (Mail Order)
Baseball Digest (Mail Order)
Basketball Digest (Mail Order)
Better Homes and Gardens (Mail Order)
Better Homes and Gardens Christmas Ideas (Mail Order)
Better Homes and Gardens Garden Ideas and Outdoor Living (Grower and Mail Order)
Better Homes and Gardens Home Furnishings Ideas (Mail Order)
Big Bike (Mail Order)
Bon Appetit (Mail Order)
Bon Voyage (Mail Order)
Boy's Life (Gifts and Gimmicks)
Brides Magazine (Mail Order)
Camera 35 (Spot Shopping)
Canadian Reader's Digest (Views on Values)
Car Craft (Mail Order)
Car and Driver (Mail Order)
Century Sports Network (Mail Order)
Charlton Comics Group (Shop-By-Mail)
Chicago Today Magazine (Mail Mart)
Chicago Tribune Magazine (Please Send Me)
Children's Christmas Group (Shopping Section)
Children's Day (Shopping Section)
Christian Life (Mission/Non-Profit Organizations)
Columbia (Shopping Section)
Competition Press & Autoweek (Mail Order)
Correspondence Education Magazine, The (Mail Order Market)
Cosmopolitan (The Cosmopolitan Shopper)
Cycle (Mail Order)
Cycle Guide (Mail Order)
Cycle Illustrated (Mail Order)
Cycle World (Mail Order)
Decorating & Craft Ideas Made Easy (Mail Order)
Desert Magazine (Trading Post)
Dirt Bike (Mail Order)
Dirt Cycle (Mail Order)
Down Beat (Mail Order)
Down East (Mail Order)
Eagle Magazine (Eagle Easy Shopper)
Elks Magazine (Elks Family Shopper)
Empire State Mason (Mail Order)
Esquire (Talking Shop with Esquire)
Essence Magazine (Mail Order)
Exploring (Marketplace Section)
Family Circle (Mail Order)
Family Handyman (Mail Order)
Family Motor Coaching (Motor Coach Mart)
Fave (Mail Order)
Fawcett Christmas Group (Shopping Section)
Federal Times (Times Shopper)
Field and Stream (Sportsman's Shopper)
Fishing and Hunting Guide (Mail Order)
Fishing and Hunting News (Outdoor Outlet)
Flip Magazine (Mail Order)
Flower and Garden Magazine (Shopping With Ed & Betty Jackson)
Football Digest (Mail Order)
Glamour (Glamour Aisle)
Go Boating (Brokerage)
Golf (Golf Shopper)
Golf Digest (Golfers Shopping Guide)
Golf Guide Magazine (Mail Order)
Good Housekeeping (Mail Order)
Good Housekeeping Needlecraft (Mail Order)
Gourmet (Garden of Eating)
Handymanual (Mail Order)
Harper's Bazaar (Shopping Bazaar)
Hockey Digest (Mail Order)

Holiday Inn International Magazine (Mail Order)
Horticulture (The Garden Shop)
Hot Rod Magazine (Mail Order)
Hounds and Hunting (Beagler's Shopping Guide)
House Beautiful (Window Shopping)
House Beautiful's Decorating for Brides and Young Marrieds (Mail Order)
House Beautiful's Gardening and Outdoor Living (Mail Order)
House Beautiful's Home Decorating (Mail Order)
House & Garden (Shopping Around)
House & Garden Decorating Guide (Mail Order)
House & Garden Guide (Mail Order)
House & Garden Second House Guide (Mail Order)
Human Behavior (Mail Order)
Invitation to Snowmobiling (Mail Order)
Kitchen and Bath Improvements (Mail Order)
Ladies' Home Journal (Journal Store)
Ladies' Home Journal Needle & Craft (Mail Order)
Ladycom (Mail Order)
Lady's Circle (Shopping Section)
Lady's Circle Needlework (Shopping News Section)
Leisure Home Living (Mail Order)
Letterman (Mail Order)
Los Angeles Times Home Magazine – (Shopper's Mart)
Mademoiselle (Shop Here Department)
Marvel Comic Group (Shop By Mail)
McCall's Magazine (Mail-Away Shop)
McCall's Needlework & Crafts (Gifts and Things)
McCall's Pattern Fashions (Mail Order)
McCall's You-Do-It Home Decorating (Shopping Section)
MD's Wife (Mail Order)
Mechanix Illustrated (Mail Order)
Michigan Out-Of-Doors (Mail Order)
Mobile Living (Mail Order)
Model Railroader (Commercial Classified Marketplace)
Modern Bride (Mail Order)
Modern Needlecraft (Mail Order)
Modern Photography (Mail Order)
Moose Magazine (Moose Home Shopper)
Motor Boating & Sailing (The Sea Bag)
Motorcycle World (Mail Order)
Motorcycle World's Special Choppers (Mail Order)
Motor Trend (Mail Order)
New England Guide, The (Gift Page)
New Ingenue, The (Mail Order)
New Republic, The (Mail Order)
New York Times Magazine (Shopping Mart)
Official Detective Group (Mail Order)
Off Road Vehicles and Adventure (Mail Order)
101 Home Plans (Mail Order)
1,001 Decorating Ideas (Mail Order)
1,001 Fashion & Needlecraft Ideas (Mail Order)
Organic Gardening and Farming (Mail Order Market Place)
OUI (Mail Order)
Our Sunday Visitor (Mail Order)
Outdoor Life (Mail Order Shopping Section)
Parents' Magazine & Better Family Living (Shopping Scout)
Penthouse (Mail Order)
Petersen Action Group (Mail Order)
Petersen Automotive Group (Mail Order)
Petersen's Photographic Magazine (Mail Order)
Philadelphia Inquirer Magazine Today (Mail Order)
Phoenix Magazine (Shopping Section)
Plane & Pilot (Mail Order)
Playboy (Mail Order)
Popular Cycling (Mail Order)
Popular Electronics (Electronics Marketplace)
Popular Hot Rodding Magazine (Mail Order)
Popular Mechanics (Bargain Hunters)
Popular Photography (Photographic Market Place)
Popular Science (Mail Order)
Popular Snowmobiling (Mail Order)

Power Boat Annual and Accessory Directory (Displays)
Presbyterian Survey (Mail Order Shopper)
Prize Winning Homes (Mail Order)
Pro Football Weekly (Mail Order)
PV4 (Mail Order)
Railroad Model Craftsman (Hobby Dealer)
Redbook Magazine (Tops in the Shops)
Right On! (Mail Order)
Road & Track (Mail Order)
Rotarian (Sale by Mail Section)
Rudder (Sea Chest Shopping)
Sail (Brokerage)
Sailboat & Sailboat Equipment Directory (Brokerage, Fixed Format Sailboat Pages)
Sailing (Yacht Brokerage)
Saturday Evening Post (Shoppers Section)
Scholastic Coach (Buyer's Guide)
Science Digest (Mail Order)
Science & Mechanics (Mail Order)
Sea & Pacific Motor Boat (Yacht Broker)
Seventeen (Shop-Wise Section)
Signature (Mail Order)
Ski (Ski Shop Section)
Skier (Where To Shop)
Skin Diver Magazine (Treasure Chest)
Southern Living (Mail Order, Southern Living Shopper)
Southern Outdoors (Shopper Section)
Sphere (Mail Order)
Spinning Wheel (Antiques Buy-Ways)
Sportsfishing (Yacht Brokerage)
Sports Afield (Sportsman's Bargain Counter)
Sports Car (Mail Order)
Sports Illustrated (Mail Order)
Street Chopper (Mail Order)
Street & Smith's College Football Yearbook (Mail Order)
Street & Smith's College & Pro Basketball Yearbook (Mail Order)
Street & Smith's Pro-Football Yearbook (Mail Order)
Sunset Magazine (Shopping Center)
Super Stock & Drag Illustrated (Mail Order)
Teen (Mail Order)
Tiger Beat (Mail Order)
Tiger Beat Group II (Mail Order)
Tiger Beat Spectacular (Mail Order)
Today's Homes (Mail Order)
Trailer Life (Mobile Bazaar)
True (Retail Shopping Center)
Vacation Vehicles (Mail Order)
Venture/Dash (Mail Order)
V.F.W. Magazine (Mail Order)
Vintage Magazine (Wine Retail & Restaurant)
Viva (Mail Order, The Company Store)
Vogue (Shop Hound)
Western Horseman (Shopper's Corral)
Western Outdoors (Shopper Section)
Westways (Mail Order)
Woman's Day (Shopper's Showcase)
Woman's Day Apartment Living (Shopping Section)
Woman's Day Decorating Guide (Shop For Your Home – At Home)
Woman's Day Home Decorating Ideas (Shopping Section)
Woman's Day Knit & Stitch (Shopping Section)
Woman's Day Knitting Book (Shopping Section)
Woman's Day New Craft Ideas for Under $50 (Shopping Section)
Woman's Day 101 Crafts Ideas (Shopping Section)
Woman's Day 101 Gardening and Outdoor Ideas (Shopping Section)
Woman's Day 101 Sweaters You Can Knit & Crochet (Shopping Section)
Woman's Day Needlework Ideas (Shopping Section)
Woodall's Trailering Parks and Campgrounds (Market Place)
Words & Music (Mail Order)
Workbasket (Shopping With Ellen Jordan)
Workbench (Shopping With Bob Edwards)
World (Book Mail Order, Retail)
Writer's Digest (Swap & Shop)
Yachting (Yacht Brokerage)
Yacht Racing (Trader's Horn)
Ziff Davis Magazine Network, The (Mail Order)

Source: Standard Rate & Data

67

1. *You don't have to invest in the full national cost* of a publication to get some indication of its effectiveness for your proposition. In some cases, such as in *Time,* by running in a single edition you can determine relative response with an investment of less than 20% of what it costs to make a national buy.
2. Some regions traditionally pull better than others for the mail order advertiser. For many mail order products or services, nothing does better than the West Coast or worse than the southeast region. *You can select the best response area for your particular proposition.*

   Remember you will be paying a regional premium in most publications for the privilege of buying partial circulation. If you are testing a publication, putting your advertising message in the better-pulling region can offset much of this premium charge.
3. Availability of regional editions makes possible multiple copy testing in a single issue of a publication. Some magazines which offer A/B split-run copy testing offer this possibility in each of the regional editions published. For example, in *Newsweek,* you can test one piece of copy against your control in the eastern edition, another against your control in the east central, another against your control in the southern, and so on. As a result, you can learn as much about different pieces of copy in a single issue of one publication as you could discover in several national A/B copy splits run in the same publication over a time span of two years or more.
4. If you have a product with a purely regional appeal, you may hit the jackpot by placing your ad in that region. For example, the Southern Living Cookbook Club could be advertised in southern editions of national magazines with an acceptable cost per response but would not bring an acceptable cost in national schedules. If you have a regional proposition, try to find a national advertiser who would prefer not to advertise in your "natural" region. Then go partners by splitting the circulation between you—and do it at the national rate without paying any regional premium charge.

Warning: Buying regional space is not all fun and games. You will have to pay for the privilege in a number of ways. As mentioned, regional space costs more. How much more? You can get an idea of what to expect from these representative examples:

> *Woman's Day* ..... from 10% to 59%
> *Time* .... from 7.6% to 40%
> *Popular Science* .... from 17.8% to 36%
> *TV Guide* .... from 3% to 182% (Hawaii edition)
> *Reader's Digest* .... from 64.5% to 180%

The minimum and maximum figures relate to the number of regions you may be buying for any one insertion.

Another factor to keep in mind is the relatively poor position regional ads receive. The regional sections usually appear far back in the magazine. As you will see later in our discussion of position placement, the poor location of an ad in a magazine can depress results as much as 50% below what the same advertisement would pull if it were in the first few pages of the same publication. If you are using regional space for testing, be certain to factor this into your evaluation.

An example of how various factors must be weighed in utilizing regional circulation for test purposes follows:

68

Redbook

Space	Full page 4-color insert
Position	4th card position
Issue	May 1973
Space cost	$7,950 (printing cost not included)
Editions used	Newsstand circulation – one million (21.2% of total circulation)
Regional premium	68%

Family Circle

Space	Full page 4-color insert
Position	Back of main editorial
Issue	June 1973
Space cost	$4,646 (printing cost not included)
Editions used:	

Los Angeles:	666,000
San Francisco:	378,000

Total test circulation	1,044,000 (13.8% of total circulation)
Regional premium	None. This publication offers a special test rate for full page inserts.

Since full page 4-color inserts have been extremely profitable for some of the larger mail order advertisers, this unit was tested for the Washington School of Art to see if such inserts could bring in a lower lead cost than obtained from a black and white page and card.

The most successful media for this advertiser are women's publications, so the school went to two that offered the mechanical capabilities for regional testing of such an insert. Although May and June are not prime mail order months, it was necessary to test then in order to allow turnaround time for the next season's scheduling. Therefore, the following factors would have to be taken into consideration in projecting test results to learn whether this unit would be successful in prime mail order months with full circulation: (1) regional premium; (2) month of insertion; (3) position in book; and (4) relative value of specific media.

Pilot Publications: The Beacons of Direct Response Media Scheduling

When planning your direct marketing media schedule, think about the media universe the way you may think about the view of the universe that you get looking up at the sky in the evening. If you have no familiarity with the stars, the sky appears as a jumble of blinking lights with no apparent relationship. But as you begin to study the heavens, you will soon be able to pick out clusters of stars in constellations which have a relationship to one another.

You will recognize the stars that make up the Big Dipper in Ursa Major, the Hunter Orion, the Swan, the Bull, and other familiar constellations. If you were to go on to become a professional astronomer, you would eventually recognize 88 distinctly different relationships. Once you know the various constellations, a star within a particular grouping inevitably leads your eye to the other related stars.

The magazine universe is no different. There are about 200 consumer magazines published with circulations of 100,000 or more. The first step in approaching this vast list is to sort out the universe of magazines into categories. Although this process is somewhat arbitrary, and different experts may not agree entirely as to which magazines fall into which category, we are going to set down a chart of the major publications which you can use like a chart of the skies to map out particular magazine groupings. Once you begin to think of magazines as forming logical groupings within the total magazine universe, you can begin to determine which groupings offer the most likely marketplace for your product or proposition. What follows is a basic magazine category chart for the direct response advertiser.

Basic Consumer Magazine
Categories

Dual Audience Publications

1. General entertainment
2. News
3. Intellectual
4. General editorial

Men's Publications

1. General
2. Entertainment
3. Special interest
   a. Automotive
   b. Fishing & hunting
   c. Mechanics & service
   d. Sports

Youth Publications

1. Male
2. Female
3. Male and female

Women's Publications

1. General
2. Fashion
3. Service
4. Special interest
   a. Baby care
   b. Brides
   c. Dressmaking & needlework
   d. Shelter (home service)
   e. Romance

Special Interest (Dual Audience)

a. Arts & antiques
b. Boating & yachting
c. Aviation
d. Business & finance
e. Camping & recreation
f. Crafts & hobbies
g. Dressmaking & needlework
h. Dogs & other pets
i. Fraternals & clubs
j. Horses
k. Music
l. Photography
m. Religious
n. Sports
o. Travel

Here is what a closer look at the dual audience categories reveals:

A. *Dual Audience Categories*
   General Entertainment
   1. *Cue*

   2. *Home Life*
   3. *TV Guide*
B. News

1. *Newsweek*
2. *Time*
3. *Sports Illustrated*
4. *U.S. News & World Report*

C. Intellectual
   1. *Human Behavior*
   2. *Psychology Today*

3. *Smithsonian*
4. *Saturday Review/World*

D. General Editorial
   1. *Ebony*
   2. *Harper's*
   3. *Mankind*
   5. *National Lampoon*
   6. *National Observer*
   7. *New York*
   8. *New Yorker*
   9. *Reader's Digest*

Here are two examples of dual audience special interest categories:

A. Business and Finance
   1. *Barron's — National Business and Finance Weekly*
   2. *Business Week*
   3. *Dun's Review*
   4. *Forbes*
   5. *Fortune*
   6. *Wall Street Journal*

B. Music
   1. *Audio*
   2. *Downbeat*
   3. *FM Guide*
   4. *Hi Fidelity*
   5. *Opera News*
   6. *Rolling Stone*
   7. *Stereo Review*

Each of the other headings has its own grouping of similarly oriented publications. And within each category there is usually one publication which performs particularly well for the direct response advertiser while at the same time it may cost less to try than some other publications in the group. We call that magazine the pilot publication for the group. If you use the pilot publication and it produces an acceptable cost per response, you can then proceed to explore the possibility of adding the other magazines in that category to your media schedule.

Here is an indication of how *Field & Stream* was used as a pilot publication in a test schedule for the Time-Life American Wilderness program and the roll-out schedule which followed in that category:

Time-Life Books

American Wilderness

Spring	April 1972	4-color page/2-color w/card	*Field & Stream*
Fall	Oct. 1972	4-color page/2-color w/card	*Field & Stream*
	Sept. 1972	4-color page/2-color w/card	*Outdoor Life*
	Oct. 1972	4-color page/2-color w/card	*Sports Afield*
Spring	April 1973	4-color page/2-color w/card	*Outdoor Life*
	March 1973	4-color page/2-color w/card	*Outdoor World*
Fall	Sept. 1973	2-color/4-color spread w/card	*Field & Stream*
	Sept. 1973	2-color/4-color spread w/card	*Sports Afield*
	Sept. 1973	2-color/4-color spread w/card	*True Hunting Yearbook*
	Sept. 1973	2-color/4-color spread w/card	*Alaskan Magazine*

In selecting the pilot publication in a category, keep it in mind that you are not dealing with a static situation. As indicated earlier, a publication's mail order advertising viability changes from year to year, and what is a bellwether publication this season may not be the one to use for that purpose next year. What is important is that you check out your own experience and the experience of others in determining the best place to advertise first in each category, and the next best, and the next best, and the next best, and the next best.

The following chart indicates a current view of what pilot publication you may want to use in several major categories:

Examples of
Pilot Publications
in Major Categories

Dual Audience

General & entertainment — *TV Guide*
News — *Time*
Intellectual — *World*
Ethnic — *Ebony* (note: choice of pilot
   publications depends upon specific
   ethnic categories desired)

Men's Publications

General — *Esquire*
Entertainment — *Penthouse*

Women's Publications

General — *Redbook*
Fashion — *Mademoiselle*

Examples of Some Special Interest Pilot
   Publications

Dressmaking & needlework — *McCall's*
   Needlework
Fraternal & clubs — *Elks*
Music — *High Fidelity*

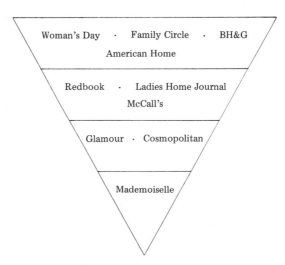

Example of inverted triangle approach to media selection: Start with pilot publication and, using results from pilot test, expand media selection to succeeding levels.

Think of your expanding media buying program as an inverted triangle:

At the apex of the triangle — the narrowest part at the bottom — insert the name of the pilot publication you decide to use first. If this publication pays off, you will want to expand your schedule to the next level of the pyramid when planning the follow-up campaign.

In the same way you can continue to rise to successively wider levels of the media category from campaign to campaign until you have reached the widest possible universe.

Bind-in Cards: The Big Guns of Print Media Advertising

Today's young media buyer cannot remember a time when preprinted insert cards were not part of the world of print media advertising. It must appear to newcomers to print media advertising that insert cards crop up naturally in publications, like weeds in suburban lawns. But it was not always so. Insert cards began to appear as recently as 1958 and magazines at first were slow to accept this radical innovation.

What makes the insert card so commonplace today was the eventual realization that the considerable investment in printing, binding, and space more than paid for itself if your goal was getting a direct response from the insertion.

The reason for the success of the insert card is self-evident. Pick up a publication, thumb through its pages, and see for yourself how effectively the bound-in cards flag down the reader. Each time someone picks up the publication, there is the insert card pointing to your message.

Before the development of the insert card, the third and fourth covers of a magazine were the prime mail order positions and were sold at a premium. The bind-in insert card has created a world in which three, four, five, or more direct response advertisers can all have the same position impact once reserved for the cover advertisers alone.

When you go out to purchase space for a page and an accompanying insert card, you come up against the familiar truism that the best things in life are *not* free. Insert card advertising costs more. You must pay a space charge for the page and the card and sometimes a separate binding charge, and you must then add in the cost of printing the cards. How much you pay, of course, depends on the individual publication, the size of the card, and a number of other factors. There is no rule of thumb to follow in estimating the additional cost for an insert card. Space charges alone can be as little as 40% of the black and white page cost to as much as the full cost of a black and white page *plus* additional binding costs, for a standard business reply card.

When the cost of the insert unit adds up to two to three times the cost of an ordinary black and white page, you will have to receive two to three times the response to justify the added expense.

For most direct response advertisers, the response is likely to be four to six times as great when pulling for an order and as much as six to eight times as great in pulling for inquiries. As a result, you can expect to cut your cost per response by 50% or more with an insert card as opposed to an ordinary on-page coupon ad.

Magazine Advertising Response Pattern: What Do These Early Results Mean?

There is a remarkable similarity from one insertion to another in the response curve from most magazines. Monthly publications generally have a similar pattern for the rate of response from week to week. However, publications in different categories can vary in their pattern of response. For example, a fashion magazine (*Glamour, Mademoiselle,* etc.) will pull a higher percentage of the total response in the first few weeks than a shelter book (such as *House & Garden* or *Better Homes & Gardens*). A shelter book has a slower curve but keeps pulling for a long period of time because it is kept much longer and is not so seasonal as a fashion magazine.

If you are running an ad calling for direct response from a monthly magazine, here is a general guide to the likely response flow:

After the first week	3–7%
After the second week	20–25%
After the third week	40–45%
After one month	50–55%
After two months	75–85%
After three months...................	85–92%
After four months	92–95%

From a weekly publication, such as *Time* or *TV Guide*, the curve is entirely different; 50% of your response comes in the first two weeks.

These expectations, of course, represent the average of many hundreds of response curves for various different propositions. You may see variations up or down from the classic curve for any single insertion.

As a general rule, for monthlies, you can expect to project the final results within 10% of accuracy after the third week of counting responses. If you are new to the business, give yourself the experience of entering daily result counts by hand for dozens of ads. Before long you will develop an instinct for projecting how an ad for your particular proposition is doing within the first ten days of measured response.

Timing and Frequency: When Should You Run? How Often Should You Go Back?

Once you determine where you want to run, timing and frequency are the two crucial factors in putting together an effective print schedule.

Of course, there are some propositions which have a time of the year when they will do best (e.g., novelty items are likely to be purchased in October and November for Christmas gifts). But for the nonseasonal items, you can look forward to two major print advertising seasons for direct response.

The first and by far the most productive for most propositions is the winter season, which begins with the January issue and runs through the February and March issues. The second season begins with the August issue and runs through the November issue.

The best winter months for most people are January and February. The best fall months are October and November. For schools and book continuity propositions, August frequently does as well or better.

If you have a nonseasonal item and you want to do your initial test at the best possible time, use a February issue with a January sale date or a January issue with a late December or early January sale date of whatever publication makes the most sense for your proposition.

How much of a factor is the particular month in which an ad appears? It could be 40% or even more. Here is an example of what the direct response advertiser may expect to experience during the year if the CPR in February were $2: January, $2.05; February, $2; March, $2.20; April, $2.50; May, $2.60; June, $2.80; July, $2.60; August, $2.40; September, $2.60; October, $2.20; November, $2.20; December, $2.40.

These hypothetical relative costs are based on the assumption that the insertion is run one time in any one of the 12 issues of a monthly publication. But, of course, if you are successful you will want to run your copy more than once. So now we are faced with the other crucial factor—what will various rates of frequency do to your response? Should you run once a year? Twice? Three times? Or every other month?

74

The frequency factor is more difficult to formularize than the timing factor. Optimum frequency cannot be generalized for print media advertising. Some propositions can be run month after month in a publication and show very little difference in cost per response from issue to issue. Other products or services require six months' to a year's wait between insertions for any expectation of maintaining the previous cost per response. At one time, Doubleday & Co. had worked out optimum frequency curves for some of its book clubs which required a 24-month hiatus between insertions.

How, then, do you go about determining ideal frequency of insertion? Try this procedure. The first time your copy appears in a publication, run it at the most likely time of the year for your special appeal. If you have a nonseasonal proposition, use January or February issues.

If the cost per response is in an acceptable range or up to 20% better than expected, wait six months and follow with a second insertion in the second half of the year. If that insertion produces within an acceptable range, you probably are a twice-a-year advertiser.

If the first insertion pulls well over 20% better than allowed order margin, turn around and repeat within a three- or four-month period.

If the response to the test insertion in January or February was marginal, it usually makes sense to wait a full year before returning for another try in that publication.

The best gauge of how quickly you can run the next insertion aimed at the same magazine audience is the strength of the response from the last insertion. What you are reading in the results is a measurement of the saturation factor as it relates to that portion of the circulation which is interested in your selling message.

Of course, like all the other factors which affect response, frequency does not operate in a vacuum. The offer of a particularly advantageous position in a particular month or a breakthrough to better results with improved copy can lead you to set aside whatever carefully worked out frequency formula you had adopted earlier.

Determining Proper Ad Size: How Much Is Too Much?

A crucial factor in obtaining an acceptable cost per response is the size of the advertising unit you select. Ordinarily, the bigger the ad the better job the creative people can do in presenting the selling message. But there is one catch. Advertising space costs money. And the more you spend, the greater the response you need to get your money back.

What you want to find is the most efficient size for your particular proposition *and for the copy approach you have chosen.* Just as with frequency, there is no simple rule of thumb here.

Generally speaking, advertising for leads or prospects or to gain inquiries requires less advertising space than copy which is pulling for orders. Many companies seeking inquiries or running a lead item to get names for catalog follow-up use advertising units of less than one column. Only a handful of companies looking for prospects can make effective use of full page space. Going one step further and using a page and insert card to pull for leads runs the risk of being too good. This unit can bring in inquiries at very low cost, but there is always the danger that the quality would be very poor. Find out at your own peril.

For example, a lead cost of $5 from a black and white page with a tear-off coupon which converts at a 10% rate produces an advertising cost per sale of $50.

Take the same insertion and place it as a page and insert card, and the cost per response may be as low as $3. If the conversion rate held up to 10%, the advertising cost per sale would be only $30. But it is more likely that the advertiser would experience a sharp drop in conversion rate to perhaps 5%, with a resultant $60 cost per sale plus the cost of processing the additional leads.

When a direct sale or a future commitment to buy is sought, the dynamics usually are different from those when inquiries are sought.

As a general rule, the higher the unit of sale or dollar volume commitment, the larger the unit of space which can be afforded—right up to the double page spread with insert card. However, there are a number of additional factors to be considered as well:

1. The nature of the product presentation may inherently require a particular space unit. For example, in record club and book club advertising, experience has shown that a maximum number of books and records should be displayed for best results. As a consequence, many of these clubs run a two-page spread as their standard ad unit. And in a small-size publication, such as *TV Guide,* they may take six or even eight pages to display the proper number of books and records.
2. Some propositions, such as Time-Life Books in the continuity bookselling field, require four-color advertising in order to present the beautiful color illustrations which are an important feature of the product being sold.
3. Usually full page ads appear at the front of a publication and small-space ads at the back. So going to a full page unit is often related to the benefits you can expect from a premium front-of-book position.
4. If you are successful with a single page ad with coupon, test going to an insert card before you try to add a second page. If the page and insert card work for you, give the spread and card a try.
5. Most mail order advertising falls into one of three size categories: *(a)* the spectacular unit—anything from the page and standard card insert to the four-page preprinted insert; *(b)* the single full page unit; and *(c)* the small-space unit less than one column in size.

The awkward size in pulling for an order appears to be the one-column and two-column units. These insertions seldom work better than their big-brother pages or little-sister 56-line, 42-line, and 24-line units.

Always remember, space costs money. The objective is to take the minimum amount of space you need to express your proposition effectively—and return a profit.

Start by having the creative director at your advertising agency express the proposition in the amount of space needed to convey a powerful selling message. Once you have established the cost per response for this basic unit, you can experiment with other size units.

If you have two publications on your schedule that perform about equally well for the basic unit, try testing the same ad approach expressed in a smaller or larger space size in one of those two publications, while running the basic control unit in the same month in the other publication.

Four-Color, Two-Color, Black and White: How Colorful Should Your Advertising Be?

All magazines charge extra for adding color to your advertising. And remember there will be additional production expense if you go this route.

Usually the cost of adding a second color to a black and white page does not return the added costs charged by the publication for the space and the expense of producing the ad. If the copy is right, the words will do their job without getting an appreciable lift from having a headline set in red or blue or green.

It is with the use of four-color advertising that the direct response advertiser has an opportunity to get his money back—and maybe a profit on the investment in color, too.

A number of publications (for example, *Esquire*, *Time*, *Woman's Day*, *Ladies' Home Journal*) allow you to run a split of four-color vs. black and white, in an alternating copy A/B perfect split-run. Test results indicate an increase of anywhere from 30% to almost 60% where there is appropriate and dramatic utilization of the four-color process.

Given a striking piece of artwork related to the proposition or an inherently colorful product feature to present, you can expect an increase in response when you use four-color advertising. Since you will need more than 20% increase in most publications to make the use of color profitable, it is wise to pretest the value of this factor before scheduling it across the board.

Now just what can you expect the cost of four-color advertising to be? Here is a scale of four-color charges from a representative group of consumer publications:

Four-Color Rate Examples*

Publication	Black and White Page Rate	4-Color Page Rate	% Increase for 4-Color
Woman's Day	$26,825	$31,825	18.6
Family Circle	26,900	31,750	18.0
Ladies' Home Journal	29,575	38,600	30.5
Seventeen	7,325	10,900	48.8
Redbook	19,640	26,025	32.1
McCall's	30,750	40,500	31.7
Good Housekeeping	22,765	29,680	30.4
Glamour	7,350	10,750	46.3
Newsweek	17,155	26,680	55.5
Time	25,560	39,615	55.0
Sports Illustrated	16,310	25,280	55.0
Popular Mechanics	8,090	11,465	41.7
Mechanix Illustrated	6,645	9,795	47.4
Reader's Digest	51,375	61,765	20.0
Esquire	10,490	15,860	51.2

*Current rates at time manuscript was prepared.

If you plan to use four-color advertising, the increase in publication space cost is only one of the cost factors to be weighed. The cost of the original four-color engravings for a 7×10 page runs from $2,000 to $4,000, depending on the copy and artwork being used. This compares with a black and white engraving cost which could be from $150 to $250. In addition, any dye transfers and other four-color preparatory work will probably increase mechanical preparation costs by 50% or more over a comparable black and white insertion.

The Position Factor: Where You Are Can Mean as Much as What You Say

Position in life may not be everything—but in direct response it often means the difference between paying out or sudden death. By "position" we mean where your advertisement appears in the publication. There are two rules governing the position factor. First, the closer to the front of the book an ad is placed, the better the response will be. Second, the more visible the position, the better the response will be.

The first rule defies rational analysis. Yet it is as certain as the sun's rising in the morning. Many magazine publishers have offered elaborate research studies demonstrating to the general advertiser that an ad in the editorial matter far back in a publication gets better readership than an ad placed within the first few pages of the publication. This may well be true for the general nonresponse advertiser — it is not true for the direct response advertiser.

Whatever the explanation may be, the fact remains that decades of measured direct response advertising tell the same story over and over again. A position in the first seven pages of the magazine produces a dramatically better response (all other factors being the same) than if the same insertion appeared farther back in the same issue.

How much better? There are as many answers to this question as there are old pros in the business. However, here is about what you may expect the relative response to be from various page positions as measured against the first right-hand page arbitrarily rated at a pull of 100.

First right-hand page	100
Second right-hand page	95
Third right-hand page	90
Fourth right-hand page	85
Back of front of book (preceding editorial matter)	70
Back of book (following main body of editorial matter)	50
Back cover	100
Inside third cover	90
Page facing inside third cover	85

The second rule is more easily explained. An ad must be seen before it can be read or acted on. Right-hand pages are more visible than left-hand pages. Therefore, right-hand pages pull better than left-hand pages — by as much as 15%. Insert cards open the magazine to the advertiser's message, and thereby create their own "cover" position. Of course, the insert card introduces the additional factor of providing a postage-free response vehicle as well. But the response from insert cards, too, is subject to the influence of how far back in the magazine the insertion appears. Here is what you can expect in most publications (assigning a 100 rating to the first card):

First insert card position	100
Second insert card position	95
Third insert card position	85
Fourth insert card position	75 (if after main editorial)
Fifth insert card position	70 (if after main editorial)

The pull of position is as inexorable as the pull of gravity. Well, almost, that is. There are a few exceptions. In the fashion and the mechanics magazines, card positioning seems to make little or no difference. Another exception may involve the placement of an ad opposite a related column or feature article in a publication. For example, a *Home Handyman's Encyclopedia* ad opposite the Home Handyman column. Another exception may involve placement of your ad in a high-readership shopping section at the back of a magazine.

Magazine advertising for the direct response advertiser, tested properly, used properly, represents a vast universe of sales and profit potential.

Self-Quiz

1. Name five magazines which provide a conducive atmosphere for direct response advertisers.

   1. _____ 2. _____

   3. _____ 4. _____

   5. _____
2. Name the four major advantages of using regional editions of magazines.

   1. _____

   _____

   2. _____

   _____

   3. _____

   _____

   4. _____

   _____

3. What are the two negative factors involved in buying regional space?

   1. _____

   _____

   2. _____

   _____

4. Name the five basic consumer magazine categories.

   1. _____ 2. _____

   3. _____ 4. _____

   5. _____
5. Give the definition of a pilot publication.

   _____

   _____

   _____

   _____

6. What is the theory of an expanded media buying program based on an inverted triangle?

_____

_____

_____

_____

7. What is the principal advantage of an insert card in a magazine?

_____

_____

_____

8. When direct response advertisers use insert cards, the response is likely to be _____ to _____ times as great when pulling for an order and as much as _____ to _____ times as great in pulling for inquiries.

9. As a general rule, when a direct response advertiser uses a monthly magazine, he can usually expect to have about 50% of his total response after _____ weeks.

10. For weekly publications, 50% of total response can be expected after _____ weeks.

11. From a timing standpoint, which is the most productive season for most direct response propositions? _____

12. Which is the second most productive season? _____

13. When is the best possible time to test a nonseasonal item? _____
_____

14. How much is the cost per response (CPR) likely to vary between the best pulling month and the poorest pulling month? _____%

15. Provide guidelines for frequency factors in magazine advertising.
    a) If the cost per response is in an acceptable range or up to 20% better than expected, wait _____ months and follow up with a second insertion in the second half of the year.
    b) If the first insertion pulls well over 20% better than allowed order margin, turn around and repeat within a _____ or _____ month period.
    c) If response to the test insertion in January or February was marginal, it usually makes sense to wait _____ before returning for another try in that publication.

16. Generally speaking, which requires more space for effective direct response advertising?
    _____ Pulling inquiries   _____ Pulling orders

80

17. What is the prime advantage of a full page ad vs. a small ad in a magazine?

    _____

18. If a single page ad with coupon is successful, what is the next logical test?

    _____

19. What are the three size categories for most mail order advertising?
    a) _____

    _____

    b) _____

    c) _____

    _____

20. When four-color vs. black and white is tested, results indicate an increase of any-where from _____% to almost _____% where there is appropriate and dramatic utilization of the four-color process.

21. What are the two rules governing the "position" factor for the direct response advertiser?
    1. _____

    _____

    2. _____

    _____

22. Right-hand pages pull better than left-hand pages by as much as _____%.

23. If a 100 rating is assigned to a first insert card position in a publication having five insert card positions, what would the fifth insert card rate pull? _____

Pilot Project

You are the advertising manager of a mail order firm that has exclusive rights to the U.S. sales of a unique set of hard steel kitchen knives, being offered under the trade name, "MacKnife." The set consists of paring knife, fillet knife, utility knife, and carving knife. Selling price is $19.95. Outline a plan for advertising this in magazines.

1. What pilot publication or publications could you use?
2. Will you use any regional editions?
3. Prepare a inverted triangle indicating how you will expand your media buying program if your pilot publication indicates expansion possibilities.
4. Prepare a timing schedule, indicating when your pilot ad (or ads) will break and when your expanded media buying program will take place.
5. Consider the product being offered: what ad size will you use and will the ad be black and white, two-color, or four-color?

81

Chapter 4 Newspapers

For sheer circulation in print, there is nothing to compare with the daily and Sunday newspapers. There are 1,761 daily newspapers in the U.S. with an average daily circulation of 62,510,242. Thus the circulation available through newspapers offers an exciting opportunity for direct response advertisers. It is significant that among the top 100 national newspaper advertisers for the year 1972, as reported by *Media Records,* some of these advertisers spent all or a significant portion of their newspaper dollars for direct response advertising:

Columbia Broadcasting Systems	$5,158,100
Union Fidelity Life Insurance Co.	$3,704,700
Doubleday & Co.	$3,457,500
National Liberty	$3,070,300
Time, Inc.	$2,465,000
Greenland Studios	$2,112,000
Franklin Mint	$1,852,200
Reader's Digest Association	$1,756,000

Total newspaper expenditure for mail order in the year 1972 was reported to be $28,725,000.

Newspapers are unique in that they can and do serve as a vehicle for carrying direct response advertising formats foreign to their regular news pages. Remarkable results have been achieved by using these special formats.

Newspaper Preprints

Use of preprints by direct response advertisers is a phenomenon of this decade. The Newspaper Preprint Corporation of New York City estimates that 11.8 billion preprints circulated in 1972. Preprints became a viable method for direct marketers back in 1965. In the first five months of that year there was only one preprint mail order advertiser (Time-Life Books) in million-circulation newspapers.

Columbia Record Club followed Time-Life Books in 1965. Their agency, Wunderman, Ricotta & Kline, first tested preprints in newspapers in six markets (Akron *Beacon,* Dallas *Times Herald,* Des Moines *Register,* Minneapolis *Tribune,* Peoria *Journal Star,* and Seattle *Times*). Since then, hundreds of millions of preprints have been run in newspapers by Columbia Record Club. There are two obvious advantages to preprints such as those used by Columbia. First, they provide abundant space for the detailed listing of items available. Second, a perforated postpaid return card may be imprinted which, because of the weight of the stock used, closely resembles an ordinary post card and can be mailed by the respondent with a minimum of effort.

The dramatic impact of preprints in a newspaper must be measured against the greatly increased cost. Comparing a four-page preprint with a fourth cover in a syndicated Sunday supplement, one finds the preprint costs almost six times as much. The tremendous volume of preprints found in the Sunday newspaper is good evidence that the increased cost is often more than warranted.

Newspaper Preprint Corporation furnishes the following estimated space costs for inserts for the top 100 markets based on a tabloid size of $10\frac{3}{4} \times 12\frac{3}{4}$.

2 pages plus flap	....						$14.03 per M		
4 pages	....						14.43 per M		
4 pages plus flap	....						15.23 per M		
6 pages	....						16.20 per M		
8 pages	....						17.70 per M		
12 pages	....						21.49 per M		
16 pages	....						25.60 per M		
24 pages	....						32.92 per M		

It should be noted that these estimated costs in the 100 top markets are for *space only*. Printing costs of the inserts must be added to space costs.

Starting below on this page, there is a breakdown of costs for space, depending on the sizes of preprint, for 39 representative newspapers.

Careful note should be taken of the fact that the CPM tends to be lower for large metro papers. Thus if a direct marketer has a proposition which appeals to small towns only, the chances for successful use of preprints are greatly diminished. Other facts about preprints, their use and trend, as provided by Newspaper Preprint Corporation, are these:

Acceptable Size: Size depends on the newspaper's policy and equipment, but, generally speaking, minimum sizes are 5½ × 8⅛. Maximum size is 10¾ × 14½. These minimum and maximum sizes are folded sizes — unfolded size could be larger. For example, a standard format size of 21½ × 14½ printed on a heavy stock could fold in half to 10¾ × 14½.

Sunday vs. Weekday Inserts: From 1970 to 1972, while total circulation of preprints at national rate increased about 60%, the increase on weekdays has been over 90%.

Card vs. Multipage Insert: A survey shows that 83% of total preprints used are of multipage formats. Since just about all Sunday newspapers accept preprints and between 60% and 70% of daily newspapers accept inserts, it behooves all direct marketers who have products or services appealing to mass markets to explore this selling vehicle.

NEWSPAPER	SINGLE SHEET	CPM	4-PAGE	CPM	6-PAGE	CPM	8-PAGE	CPM	SUNDAY CIRCULATION
ASHEVILLE CITIZEN TIMES Asheville, North Carolina (Available Daily)	850 lines or less ... $1,225	17.09	850 lines or less ... $1,250	17.44	850 lines or less ... $1,637	22.83	850 lines or less ... $2,025	28.25	71,690
ATLANTIC CITY PRESS Atlantic City, New Jersey (CPM - based on press run of 72,000) (No Daily)	8 x 11" w/flap	9.20	8 x 11"	17.34	6 x 10¼"	17.05	6 x 10¼" 8 x 11"	22.37 33.62	60,962
BANGOR DAILY NEWS Bangor, Maine (CPM - based on circulation day of insertion)		14.50		16.50		20.00		22.00	78,258
CHARLESTON GAZETTE DAILY MAIL Charleston, West Virginia	$1,715.78	18.19	$1,715.78	18.19	$1,715.78 (UP TO 4,100 LINES IN TOTAL)	18.19	$1,715.78	18.19	94,336

CHICAGO ZONE NEWSPAPERS
  AURORA BEACON NEWS
  Aurora, Illinois
	$1,479	34.83	$1,479	34.83	$1,479	34.83	$1,479	34.83	42,465

ELGIN COURIER NEWS JOURNAL & WHEATON JOURNAL	$1,785	41.77	$1,785	41.77	$1,785	41.77	$1,785	41.77	37,437 - Elgin 5,295 - Wheaton

NEWSPAPER	SINGLE SHEET	CPM	4-PAGE	CPM	6-PAGE	CPM	8-PAGE	CPM	SUNDAY CIRCULATION
CHICAGO ZONE NEWSPAPERS JOLIET HERALD NEWS Joliet, Illinois	$1,581	32.64	$1,581	32.64	$1,581	32.64	$1,581	32.64	48,442
THE CINCINNATI ENQUIRER Cincinnati, Ohio (CPM - based on press run day of insertion) (Available Daily)		16.00		16.00		16.00		16.00	303,826
DAYTON NEWS & JOURNAL HERALD Dayton, Ohio (Available Daily — 8-Page min.)	Less 800 lines $3,587 801 to tabloid $4,477	15.82 19.74	Less 800 lines $3,587 801 to tabloid $4,477	15.82 19.74	SAME AS 4-PAGE RATE. MINI-PRINT LESS than 8-pager 5½ x 8½'' $3,080	 13.58	Less 800 lines $4,140 801 to tabloid $5,170	18.25 22.79	226,806
THE DETROIT NEWS Detroit, Michigan (Envelope inserts not accepted)	$8,976	10.78	$8,976	10.78	SAME AS 8-PAGE RATE.		Up to 979 lines $10,752.50	12.91	852,801
DULUTH HERALD & NEWS TRIBUNE Duluth, Minnesota	$1,454.78	17.15	$1,454.78 w/env. takes 6-page rate.	17.15	$1,734.55 w/env. takes 8-page rate.	20.44	$2,014.31	23.74	84,848
GARY/HAMMOND NEWSPAPER UNIT (Available Daily)	$3,100	20.35	$3,100	20.35	$3,100	20.35	$3,100	20.35	79,020 - Gary 73,312 - Hammond

NEWSPAPER	SINGLE SHEET	CPM	4-PAGE	CPM	6-PAGE	CPM	8-PAGE	CPM	SUNDAY CIRCULATION
GRAND FORKS HERALD Grand Forks, North Dakota (Available Daily)	$689.92	18.13	$602.16 (up to 11 x 15'')	15.83	$689.92 (up to 6 x 8¾'')	18.13	$1,075.86 (up to 11 x 15'') $869.39 (6 x 10½'' w/env)	28.27 22.85	38,052
GREEN BAY PRESS GAZETTE Green Bay, Wisconsin (Available Daily)	$1,222	19.64	$1,222	19.64	$1,222	19.64	$1,222	19.64	62,232
THE RECORD Hackensack, New Jersey (CPM - based on circulation day of insertion)		14.00	w/envelope . . .	14.00 16.00	w/envelope . . .	16.00 17.00		18.00	185,282
THE HOUSTON CHRONICLE Houston, Texas (CPM - based on latest Publisher's Statement) (Available Daily Wed/Thurs)		16.85		16.85		16.85		16.85	359,638
HUNTINGTON HERALD-DISPATCH & ADVERTISER Huntington, West Virginia (Available Daily)	8 x 11'' . . . $808.40 11-1/8 x 9¼'' . . . $736	13.71 12.48	8½ x 11'' . . . $1,316.80 5½ x 8½'' . . . $662.40	22.28 11.23	6 x 10½'' . . . $1,357.92 8 x 9'' w/env. . . . $1,475.57	23.03 25.02	6 x 10½'' . . . $2,144.40 850 lines . . . $2,503.00	36.37 42.45	58,964
THE STATE JOURNAL Lansing, Michigan (Available Daily)	$2,293	27.08	$2,293	27.08	$2,293	27.08	$2,565	30.29	84,684

84

NEWSPAPER	SINGLE SHEET	CPM	4-PAGE	CPM	6-PAGE	CPM	8-PAGE	CPM	SUNDAY CIRCULATION
THE ARKANSAS GAZETTE Little Rock, Arkansas (Available Daily)	$2,356.53 Envelope Inserts NOT accepted.	16.70	850 lines or less $2,356.53 (N/C for env.)	16.70	$2,356.53	16.70	850 lines or less $2,356.53 w/env. $2,651.10 1,000 lines w/env $2,771.28 w/env. $3,117.70	16.70 18.79 19.64 22.09	141,125
LONG BEACH INDEPENDENT PRESS TELEGRAM Long Beach, California (CPM - based on print order of 165,000)		15.00		15.00		16.00		17.50	146,268
MANCHESTER UNION LEADER Manchester, New Hampshire (Available Daily)	$1,645	26.82	$1,645	26.82	$1,645	26.82	$1,645	26.82	61,330
NEWPORT NEWS PRESS & TIMES HERALD Newport News, Va. (CPM - based on actual paid circ. of previous Sunday rounded to nearest thousand.)	70/80 lb. stock w/flap +$300 net stuffing	14.00 17.00	w/env. . . .	17.00 18.00	w/env. . . .	18.00 19.00		19.00	87,261
THE SUNDAY OKLAHOMAN Oklahoma City, Oklahoma (Available Daily)	$5,490	18.77	$5,490 Mini-print 4½ x 6" . . . $4,270	18.77 14.60	$6,100 w/env.	20.89	$6,100	20.89	292,488
THE OMAHA WORLD HERALD Omaha, Nebraska	$3,522	12.40	$3,522	12.40	$3,522	12.40	$5,259 (Insurance size 6 x 10½" takes 4-Page rate)	18.51	284,076

NEWSPAPER	SINGLE SHEET	CPM	4-PAGE	CPM	6-PAGE	CPM	8-PAGE	CPM	SUNDAY CIRCULATION
PALM BEACH POST-TIMES W. Palm Beach, Fla. (CPM - rate based on print order of 95,000) (Available Daily)	850 lines w/flap	10.00 12.00	850 lines Mini-Print	14.00 10.00	Up to 6 x 10½" Over . . .	14.00 16.00		16.00	98,926
THE PASADENA STAR NEWS Pasadena, California (Available Daily)	$1,200	20.99	$1,200	20.99	$1,200	20.99	$1,200	20.99	57,164
RICHMOND NEWS LEADER & TIMES DISPATCH Richmond, Virginia (Available Daily)	8½ x 11" $1,756 . . . 10 x 12" $1,946 . . .	8.81 9.76	8½ x 11" $2,808 . . . 10 x 12" $3,418 . . . 5½ x 8½" $1,634 . . .	14.09 17.15 8.20	6¼ x 12" w/e $3,211 . . . 8 x 9" w/e $2,858 . . . 6 x 8 - 3/4 w/e $2,501 . .	16.11 14.34 12.55	8½ x 11" $4,753 . . . w/env $4,878 . . . 6 x 10½" w/e $3,652 . .	23.85 24.48 18.33	199,287
ST. PAUL DISPATCH & PIONEER PRESS St. Paul, Minnesota (No Daily)	$3,720	15.77	$3,720 w/card $4,885	15.77 20.71	$4,162.50 w/card $5,327.50	17.65 22.58	$4,605 w/card $5,770	19.52 24.46	235,890
SAN BERNARDINO SUN-TELEGRAM San Bernardino, California (CPM - based on latest SRDS) (Available Daily)		13.50		13.50		18.00		23.00	85,490
SAN DIEGO UNION TRIBUNE San Diego, California (Available Daily)	$4,227	14.58	$4,227 . . . up to 1,000 lines $5,495 . . . over	14.58 18.95	$4,227 . . . up to 1,000 lines $5,495 . . . over	14.58 18.95	$4,227 . . . up to 1,000 lines $4,499 w/e $5,495 . . . over $5,767 w/e	14.58 15.52 18.95 19.89	289,911

NEWSPAPER	SINGLE SHEET	CPM	4-PAGE	CPM	6-PAGE	CPM	8-PAGE	CPM	SUNDAY CIRCULATION
SAN FRANCISCO CHRONICLE/EXAMINER San Francisco, California (CPM - rate based on latest Publisher's statement rounded to nearest thousand).		16.00		16.00		16.00		16.00	661,016
THE SCRANTON TIMES Scranton, Pennsylvania (Available Daily)	5 x 7 " to 8½ x 11" $1,100 ... 8½ x 11" to 10 x 15" $1,140 ...	20.17 20.90	5 x 7" to 8½ x 11" $1,160 ... 8½ x 11" to 10 x 15" $1,240 ... 10 x 15" to 15 x 21½" $1,400 ...	21.27 22.73 25.67	5 x 7" to 8½ x 11" $1,200 ... 8½ x 11" to 10 x 15" $1,320 ... 10 x 15" to 15 x 21½" $1,560 ...	22.00 24.20 28.60	5 x 7" to 8½ x 11" $1,240 ... 8½ x 11" to 10 x 15" $1,400 ... 10 x 15" to 15 x 21½" $1,720 ...	22.73 26.67 31.53	54,543
SPRINGFIELD SUN NEWS Springfield, Ohio (No Daily)	----		----		----		$1,882	41.57	45,276
THE TACOMA NEWS TRIBUNE Tacoma, Washington (Available Daily)	$1,592	15.95	$1,592	15.95	$1,942	19.46	$2,193	21.98	99,790
TAMPA TRIBUNE AND TIMES Tampa, Florida (CPM - rate based on press run day of insertion). (Available Daily)	TAB SIZE Less Tab Size Mini-Print (7½ x 11" or less)	15.16 14.47 10.60	TAB SIZE Less Tab Size Mini-Print	16.32 15.58 10.60	TAB SIZE Less Tab Size Mini-Print	17.76 16.97 11.93	TAB SIZE Less Tab Size Mini-Print	19.24 18.37 12.83	212,706
THE TRENTON TIMES Trenton, New Jersey (CPM - based on circulation day of insertion). (Available Daily)		12.95		12.95		16.48		18.83	104,402

NEWSPAPER	SINGLE SHEET	CPM	4-PAGE	CPM	6-PAGE	CPM	8-PAGE	CPM	SUNDAY CIRCULATION
THE WASHINGTON POST Washington, D.C. (CPM - rate based on press run day of insertion).		13.78		13.78		13.78		13.78	710,148
WINSTON SALEM JOURNAL SENTINEL Winston Salem, N.C. (Available Daily)	$1,260 (Up to 1,500 lines)	12.51	850 lines $1,839 w/env. $2,013 Mini- 5½ x 8½" $1,260 ...	18.26 19.98 12.51	6 x 8¾" w/env. $2,013	19.98	850 lines $3,318 w/env. $3,492 6 x 10½" w/env. $2,100	32.94 34.67 20.85	100,734
THE NEWS TRIBUNE Woodbridge, New Jersey (NO SUNDAY . . . Saturday & Daily Rates).	$1,920.05	34.14	$1,920.05	34.14	$1,920.05	34.14	$1,920.05	34.14	56,248

Syndicated Newspaper Supplements

Imagine, if you will, placing three space insertion orders and buying newspaper circulation of 50 million plus! This is indeed possible if you place insertion orders in the three major syndicated newspaper supplements. Branham-Moloney, Inc., major newspaper reps, present these figures:

PUBLICATION	CIRCULATION	FOUR-COLOR PAGE	CPM	BLACK AND WHITE PAGE	CPM
Sunday-Metro	23,000,000	$102,135	$4.44	$ 85,454	$3.72
Parade	17,900,000	78,895	4.41	64,185	3,59
Family Weekly	9,500,000	38,950	4.10	33,250	3.50
Total	50,400,000	$219,980	$4.36	$182,889	$3.63

Distribution of the three syndicated supplements breaks down about this way. *Sunday-Metro* is distributed by approximately 51 member newspapers. Those carrying *Sunday-Metro* supplements offer a choice of 50 or 60 top metro areas for advertising. *Family Weekly* has approximately 281 member newspapers. *Family Weekly* is generally carried by the newspapers with smaller circulations, many of which publish within the top metro areas. The majority of the newspapers distributing *Family Weekly* are outside the top 150 metro areas. *Parade* has approximately 105 member newspapers. *Parade* is included in some of the *Sunday-Metro* newspapers, but generally it is more evenly distributed among the top 100 metro areas.

Obvious advantages of syndicated supplements are their relatively low CPM and the possibility of reaching top metro areas as well as smaller cities, depending on the supplement used.

One thing going for the syndicated supplements is their mail order atmosphere. *Parade,* for instance, points out that 60% of the advertising in it carries some kind of coupon which enables the advertiser to get a measurement of results. Jay Norris, a major mail order newspaper advertiser, spent approximately $2 million of a $3-million budget in *Parade* in 1972.

Among the syndicated supplements, *Parade* is unique in having a mail order booklet regularly inserted. This booklet, commonly called a dutch door, runs 12 pages. Its page size is one-half the page size of the supplement. *Parade* does not sell space in this booklet. It is contracted by Fairfax Agencies of New York City. Some issues are taken over entirely by one advertiser (other issues contain a variety of small mail order ads).

It goes without saying that no direct marketer who has not previously placed space in one of the syndicated supplements would go full run without testing. *Parade,* for example, offers remnant space to mail order advertisers at a 38% discount. This is advertising space left over when package goods advertisers buy only those markets where they have distribution. Second to testing in remnant space is testing in regions.

With approximately 550 Sunday and weekend magazines, both syndicated and locally edited, a direct response advertiser has an incredible amount of distribution available at low cost.

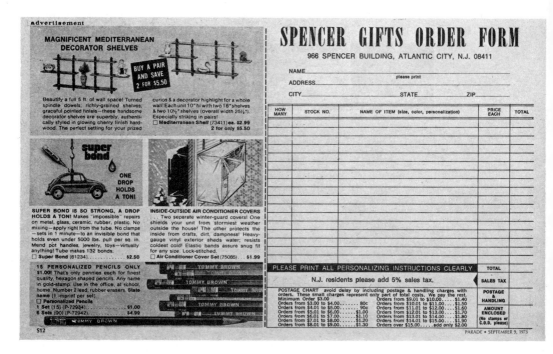

Dutch door insert in Parade *(newspaper supplement). Illustration shows the first page and the last page of a 12-page insert for Spencer Gifts.*

Comics as a Direct Marketing Medium

Perhaps the biggest sleeper as a medium for direct marketers is the comic section of weekend newspapers. Comics are not glamorous, nor are they prestigious. But their total circulation, readership, and demographics, as well as low CPM, constitute an exciting universe for the direct response advertiser. The prestigious media department of N. W. Ayer & Son has produced some fascinating facts and figures about comics as an advertising medium.

Each week, usually on Sunday, 48.8 million of color comics are distributed through 454 different newspapers. These comics literally saturate the major and secondary markets, providing 50% or better coverage in 278 of the 300 strategical metropolitan markets of the country. There are two major comic groups — Puck and Metro.

The Puck Group is available through two networks: the National Network and the American Network. The National Network, made up of newspapers which almost all have circulations of over 100,000, is distributed through 47 papers in 46 cities. The American Network, made up of newspapers with circulations of under 100,000, is distributed in 48 papers in 48 cities. Also available through Puck are two geographically concentrated editions: the West Coast edition, made up of eight West Coast newspapers, and the California/Nevada group, with 12 papers.

Metro Sunday comics are available on the basis of newspaper networks. There are three networks: (1) basic network of 42 newspapers; (2) Pacific network of 14 newspapers; (3) selective network of 12 newspapers. Total circulation for all three networks, comprising 68 newspapers, is 21,030,804.

Standard Rate & Data Service also lists 18 other smaller comic groups, regionally oriented. The size of these groups ranges from the Texas Sunday Comic Section, with a circulation of 919,123, to the Wyoming Color Comic Group, with a circulation of 36,122.

Combined, Metro and Puck have a total circulation of 36,904,635. And perhaps most enticing of all is the CPM of one page printed in four colors. Metro's cost for a four-color page comes to $2.59 CPM; Puck's cost comes to $2.50 CPM.

Demographics of comic readers is quite a surprise to most advertisers, who seem to have ill-conceived ideas about this type of reader. The median age of the adult comic reader is 41.7, slightly younger than the U.S. median age of 43.

Age	Comics	U.S. Average
18–24	18.9%	16.9%
25–34	18.6	18.8
35–49	28.1	27.0
50–64	22.0	22.4
65+	12.4	14.9
	100%	100%

One of the major misconceptions about comic readership is that the higher one's education, the less likely one is to read the comic pages. N. W. Ayer statistics dispel this:

Education	Comics	U.S.
Graduated from college	12.3%	10.6%
Attended college	15.2	12.9
Graduated from high school	37.9	35.3
Attended high school	17.7	19.0
Did not attend high school	16.9	22.2
	100%	100%

Finally, there has been the misconception that the higher one's income, the less likely one is to read comics. Once again, the figures contradict this.

Income	Comics	U.S.
$25,000+	5.6%	5.1%
$15–24,999	20.7	18.2
$10–14,999	27.8	25.0
$8–9,999	14.0	13.4
$5–7,999	14.9	17.1
Under $5,000	16.9	21.2
	100%	100%
Median income	$10,740	$9,775

Among direct response advertisers, the largest users of comic page advertising in the past have been photo finishers. Huge photo finishing businesses have been started from scratch, using comics as a prime advertising medium. Availability of ad-an-envelope in conjunction with comic page advertising serves a genuine need of photo finishers, because they are able to provide an envelope in which the prospect can return completed film rolls. The standard charge for affixing a card or envelope to the ad averages about $2.50 CPM, plus the cost of printing the card or envelope. With ad-a-card and ad-an-envelope, the direct response advertiser provides the same impetus to response as he does when he sends a standard direct mail package with a reply card or reply envelope.

Following the photo finishers with comic page advertising have been insurance companies and land developers. The opportunities are obviously there for a host of other direct response advertisers seeking mass circulation at low cost.

Comic page advertising traditionally limits advertising to one advertiser per page. Thus full page advertising is not essential to gain a dominant position.

Comics, not unlike syndicated supplements, should be tested before going full run. You can test individual papers among the Metro Group, the Puck Group, and the independent groups.

ROP Advertising

We have been exploring formats carried by newspapers – preprints, syndicated supplements, and comics. Not to be overlooked, of course, is run-of-paper advertising. Generally, direct response advertisers have not got the type of results with ROP advertising that they have obtained from newspaper preprints and syndicated newspaper supplements. One obvious reason is that four-color advertising is not generally available for ROP. Another is that ROP ads don't drop out for individual attention.

But there are many success stories for small-space ROP advertising, small-space ads that have run frequently year after year in hundreds of newspapers. When small-space ads are run over a long period of time with high frequency, the number of reader impressions multiplies rapidly in proportion to the cost.

Effect of Local News on Results

If there is a major difference between newspaper advertising and all other print media, it is that the newspaper reader is more likely to be affected by local news events. All newspaper advertising appears within the atmosphere of the local news for a given day.

A major scandal in local politics, a major catastrophe in a local area, such as a tornado, can have a devastating effect on the advertising appearing in a given issue. Magazines, on the other hand, do not tie in closely with local events. Magazines are put aside to be read during hours not taken up by involvement in local events.

It is because local events have a strong effect on response, positively or negatively, that markets with like demographics don't always respond in like manner. All newspaper advertising tends to be *local*, even though a schedule may be national.

Developing a Newspaper Test Program

When a direct response advertiser first considers testing newspapers as a medium, he has a myriad of decisions to make. Should he go ROP, the newspaper preprint route, local Sunday supplements, syndicated supplements, TV program supplements, comics? What papers should he test? Putting ad size and position aside for the moment, we have two initial considerations: (1) the importance of advertising in a mail order climate; and (2) the demographics of markets selected as they relate to the product or service you are offering.

If I had one simple product, a stamp dispenser, for instance, and a tiny budget, I'd place one small ad in one publication. I'd run the ad in the mail order section of the *New York Times* Sunday magazine. Generally, but not always, if you don't make it there, you won't make it anywhere. Running such an ad would give a "feel." If it works, a logical expansion would be indicated in like mail order sections in major cities like Chicago, Detroit, and Los Angeles.

Simple items, which lend themselves to small-space advertising in mail order sections, greatly simplify the testing procedure. But, more often than not, multi-city testing in larger space is required.

Prime direct response test markets in the United States include Atlanta, Buffalo, Cleveland, Dallas–Fort Worth, Denver, Des Moines, Indianapolis, Omaha, and Peoria.

In a test market, the newspaper selected should be analyzed to make certain it has advertising reach and coverage and offers demographics which are suitable to your product. If there are two newspapers in a market, it is worthwhile to evaluate both of them. For instance, a leisure-craft item, appealing to women, is to be tested in Buffalo. Let us say that because of budget, advertising can be placed in only one newspaper in the Buffalo market. Such criteria as circulation, household penetration, women readers, and advertising linage relating to the product to be advertised should be measured for both papers.

In the metro zone, we find the *Evening News* in Buffalo has a circulation of 252,646 and the *Courier Express,* the morning newspaper, has a circulation of only 120,091. The *Evening News* has a metro household penetration of 59% as compared to the *Courier Express* penetration of 28%. (Source: SRDS Circulation Analysis 1972)

As for women readers in the 18–34-year age group, the *Evening News* has 140,000, according to *Simmons Local Index Study 1972.* In the 35–49-year age group, the *News* has 120,000 and the *Courier* 46,000. In the 50-year or older age bracket the *News* has 110,000 and the *Courier Express* 94,000. In 1972, retailers in the classification which can be best related to a leisure-craft item placed as much as ten to 20 times more advertising linage in the *Evening News* than in the *Courier Express.* The Buffalo *Evening News* ranked first in all criteria measured.

These facts indicate that the *Evening News* is the more efficient buy of the two newspapers for the leisure-craft item. The *Evening News* line rate of 60¢ offered a $2.75 cost per thousand (based on a 1,200-line ad), net unduplicated women readers. The *Courier Express,* with a line rate of 43¢, offered a cost of $7.37 per thousand women readers.

So demographics is a major consideration market by market, whether you are going ROP, preprints, local supplements, syndicated supplements, or TV program supplements.

Once an advertiser develops a test program which closely resembles the demographics for his product or service, expansion to like markets makes possible the rapid acceleration of a full-blown program. But selecting newspapers is tedious, because there are hundreds from which to choose as compared with a relative handful of magazines whose demographics can be more closely related to the proposition. If we use the leisure-craft item as our example, a test newspaper schedule could be placed in the following markets.

Markets

Atlanta, Georgia	Dallas – Fort Worth, Texas	Indianapolis, Indiana
Buffalo, New York	Denver, Colorado	Omaha, Nebraska
Cleveland, Ohio	Des Moines, Iowa	Peoria, Illinois

(If there is more than one newspaper in a test market, the paper with the most likely demographics should be selected.)

Formats To Test

Market	Format
Atlanta	Preprint
Buffalo, *Courier Express*	*Parade* remnant
Cleveland	Metro Comics
Dallas – Fort Worth	ROP
Denver	Preprint
Des Moines	ROP
Indianapolis	Preprint
Omaha	Metro Comics
Peoria	*Parade* remnant

A test schedule such as this would be ambitious in terms of total dollars, but it would have the advantage of testing markets and formats simultaneously. Once a reading has been attained from the markets and the formats, the advertiser can then rapidly expand to other markets and will have the advantage of using the most productive formats.

Advertising Seasons

Rather as in direct mail and magazine direct response advertising, there are two major newspaper direct response advertising seasons. The fall mail order season begins for the most part with August and runs through November. The winter season begins with January and runs through March.

The chart on page 93 shows the insertion pattern of 18 advertisers using preprints in million market newspapers. Particular note should be made of the insertions in July. A July insertion is often possible, particularly where you have a pretested piece.

Exceptions to the two major direct response seasons occur in the sale of seasonal merchandise. Christmas items are usually promoted from September right through the first week of December. A nursery, on the other hand, will start promoting in late December and early January, then again in the early fall. Many nurseries follow the practice of promoting by geographical regions, starting earlier in the south and working up to later promotion in the north.

92

Preprint Insert Sections In Million Market Newspapers

18 Advertisers — 57 Preprints — 245,486 Lines

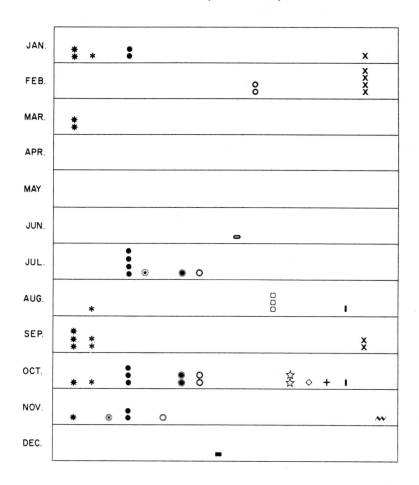

93

Timing of Newspaper Insertions

Beyond the seasonal factor of direct response advertising in newspapers, there is timing as it relates to days of the week. According to the *E & P Yearbook 1968*, Bureau of Advertising Circulation Analysis, the number of copies of a newspaper sold per day are remarkably constant month after month — despite such things as summer vacations and Christmas holidays. And people buy the copy of the newspaper to read not only the editorial matter but also the ads. According to an *Audits & Surveys Study* in 1964, the percentage of people opening an average ad page any day Monday through Friday varies less than 3%, with Tuesday ranking the highest at 84%.

Tuesday, Wednesday, and Thursday are favorite choices of many direct response advertisers for their ROP advertising. Many direct response advertisers judiciously avoid the weekday issue containing grocery advertising. There is no question that the local newspaper is an integral part of practically everyone's daily life. While magazines may be put aside for reading at a convenient time, newspapers are read the day they are delivered or purchased, or not read at all.

As we have seen, more newspapers are accepting preprints for weekday insertions. This can be a major advantage in view of the larger number of preprints appearing in most large Sunday newspapers.

Newspaper Response Patterns

Newspapers have the shortest closing date of any print medium. In most cases, ads appear in the newspaper within 48 hours after placement. Depending on the format used, up to 90% or more of responses will be reached for a typical direct response newspaper ad within these time frames.

ROP	After second week
Preprints	After third week
Syndicated newspaper supplements	After third week
Comics	After second week

The chart which follows tracks responses from an identical direct response ad placed in two Chicago newspapers over a weekend.

Paper	Percent of Total Response by Days and Weeks								
	1st Day	3d Day	5th Day	7th Day	9th Day	10th Day	3d Week	4th Week	5th Week
Chicago *Daily News*	7.1%	50%	65%	72%	83%	85%	93%	97%	98%
Chicago *Tribune*	1.4%	46%	63%	76%	83%	85%	93%	96%	98%

In reviewing this chart, we note that the first day of response, a Monday, showed 7.1 of total response for the *News* against 1.4% for the *Tribune*. This is accounted for by the fact the *News* is a Saturday paper and the *Tribune* a Sunday paper (thus *News* responses had a weekend in the mail compared to one day for the *Tribune*). But the truly significant figures are 50% of total for only three days of response for the *News* and 46% for the *Tribune*, 85% of total for both papers by the tenth day, and 93% in three weeks. Readings from direct response newspaper ads come lightning fast.

Naturally, response patterns vary according to the proposition. It is important that each advertiser develop his own response pattern. But the nature of newspaper adver-

94

tising almost always lends itself to a quick turnaround. *Dow Theory Forecasts,* for instance, have run ads in hundreds of newspapers and they are able to project results, determining whether to repeat or not, within a week after first orders are received.

Determining Proper Ad Size

In direct response newspaper advertising, as in retail or national newspaper ads, few people dispute the feeling that generally the larger advertisement will get more attention than a smaller one. But whether the full page ad gets twice the attention of the half, four times the attention of the quarter, is debatable. In the final analysis, it is cost per response that counts. Just as in magazine advertising, less space is usually indicated for inquiry advertising and more space is dictated for a direct order.

According to a study conducted by the Bureau of Advertising in 1971 relating to mailback newspaper coupons, the size of the space seems to be a factor in the reader response only to the extent that it is a factor in initial reader attention. In this study, 85% of newspaper inserts ran ads of 1,000 lines or more. Only 50% used fewer than 1,000 lines, with a minimum of 500 lines per ad.

A low-budget advertiser often has to choose between a single full page ad and several small ads over a protracted period of time. The proper guide to follow in determining initial size of ads is to base the size on the space required to tell *the complete story.*

It would be ludicrous to try to sell membership in a record and tape club in a small space. Experience shows one must offer a wide selection of records in the ad to get memberships. The same is true of a book club.

On the other hand, if you are selling a single item at a low unit of sale—a cigarette lighter for $4.95, for instance—common sense says the complete story can be told in a small space. Where small-space advertising can tell the complete story, consistency and repetition often prove to be keys to success.

Outside of the obvious requirement of a full page or more for a proposition, constant testing of ad sizes will establish the proper size to produce the most efficient cost per inquiry or per order.

The Position Factor

There are many similarities between the importance of position for direct response advertising in a newspaper and in a magazine. Research showing high readership of newspaper ads regardless of position notwithstanding, direct response advertisers prefer right-hand pages.

Generally, they find ads are more effective in the front of the newspaper than in the back. And coupon ads appearing in the gutter of any newspaper page are to be avoided like the plague.

Since all newspapers are in sections, special consideration should be given to reading habits of men and women as they relate to specific sections of a newspaper. Three major sections of any given newspaper are sports, women's pages, and general news. A study by *Million Market Newspapers* of 32,000 ads showed the following statistics:

Products of Interest to Both Men and Women		
	Median Performance Index	
Type of Page	Men	Women
Sports	114	49
Women's	63	101
General news	100	101

Source: MMN Starch Studies of 32,000 Ads (1961–63)

What this study obviously says is—if you have a product which appeals to sports-minded men, you are going to get high readership on the sports pages. If you have a product which appeals to women, you are going to get high readership in the women's section. If you have a product which appeals to both men and women, running the ad in the general news section makes eminent sense.

Color vs. Black and White

The possibilities of color in newspaper advertising may be considered in the same manner they are for magazine advertising, with one major exception. If you are using one or more colors other than black in a ROP ad, you just can't get the quality that you get in a color magazine ad. This does not mean ROP color should not be tested. A majority of newspapers which offer color will allow A/B splits of color vs. black and white.

According to a December 1970 Bureau of Advertising Study (1969 cost figures), using the top 100 markets as a group, one-color ROP costs 19% more than the same full page in black and white. Use of three-color ROP costs 30% more than the same full page in black and white. In both cases, these comparisons are based on cost per thousand copies of the newspaper. On the same cost per thousand copies basis (in the same market), Preprint Corporation estimates hi-fi costs 129% more than black and white (cost of space and production). In other words, for every $100 spent in the top 100 markets to buy a full page in black and white, it costs $119 to buy the same full page in one-color ROP; $130 to buy it in three-color ROP; and $229 to buy it in hi-fi.

A number of studies have been made, via split-runs and the recognition method, to test the attention-getting power of both one-color and full-color ROP. They have shown increases of 58% for one color and 78% for full color above the level of results for black and white versions of the same ads. Comparable cost differences are 19% and 30%. When Starch "noting score" norms are used to estimate the same attention-getting differential, a different conclusion is reached. The differences are about 10% and about 30% (when size and product category are held constant). Using norms means comparing a black and white ad for one product in one city at one time with an ad in color for another product in another city at another time. These variables inevitably blur the meaning of the comparisons.

For the direct response advertiser, these studies are interesting. However, genuine controlled testing is the only way to get true figures.

Mass circulation at low CPM is the potential offered by newspapers. With the right propositions, the right formats, the right newspapers, the results can be great.

Self-Quiz

1. Name four prominent direct marketers who spent $1 million or more in newspaper advertising in 1972.

   1. _____ 2. _____

   3. _____ 4. _____

2. Name the two obvious advantages of preprints.

   1. _____

   _____

2. _____

_____

3. Which is the most popular format for a preprint?
   ☐ Card   ☐ Multipage
4. Name the three major syndicated newspaper supplements.

   1. _____   2. _____   3. _____
5. Indicate major market penetration for each of the supplements.

Supplement	Top 50–60 Metros	Top 100 Metros	Below Top 100
Sunday Metro	_____	_____	_____
Parade	_____	_____	_____
Family Weekly	_____	_____	_____

6. Define a dutch door.

_____

_____

7. What is remnant space?

_____

_____

8. What are the names of the two major comic groups?

   1. _____   2. _____
9. The higher one's education, the less likely one is to read the comic pages.
   ☐ True   ☐ False
10. The higher one's income, the less likely one is to read the comic pages.
    ☐ True   ☐ False
11. What is the advantage of the ad-a-card and ad-an-envelope for comic page advertisers?

_____

_____

12. How many advertisers will comic groups allow per page? _____
13. What major advantage to direct response advertisers is offered by preprints and supplements over ROP advertising?

_____

_____

97

14. What major difference is there between newspaper advertising and all other print advertising as related to possible results?

_____

_____

15. What are the two initial considerations in developing a newspaper test program?

   1. _____

   2. _____

16. If you had a single item which lent itself to advertising in small space, and a limited budget to test, which one publication would you test first? _____

17. Name nine prime test markets for newspaper direct response advertising.

   1. _____   2. _____   3. _____

   4. _____   5. _____   6. _____

   7. _____   8. _____   9. _____

18. What are the two major newspaper direct response seasons?

   1. _____

   2. _____

19. Name the preferable weekdays for ROP advertising.

   _____   _____   _____

20. Depending on the format used, up to 90% or more of responses will be reached for a typical direct response newspaper ad within these time frames.

   ROP . . . . After _____ week(s)

   Preprints . . . . . After _____ week(s)

   Supplements . . After _____ week(s)

   Comics . . . . After _____ week(s)

21. The size of newspaper space seems to be a factor in reader response only to the extent it is a factor in _____ _____ _____.

22. When running ROP, direct response advertisers should specify
   ☐ Left-hand page   ☐ Right-hand page.

23. What is the major disadvantage of running color ROP?

   _____

   _____

98

Pilot Project

You have a $50,000 newspaper test budget. You are the advertising manager of a unique book club, called New Life Style Book Club. You have enjoyed unusual success in two media: direct mail and consumer magazines. But you have never used newspaper advertising.

Outline a newspaper test plan.

1. In which cities will you test?
2. Will your tests run in the Sunday or the weekday edition, or both?
3. What formats will you test—preprints, supplements, comics, local TV books, ROP?
4. What size preprints or ads will you test?
5. At what time of the year will you run your tests?

Note: In structuring your $50,000 test budget, keep in mind the fact that if you use preprints or ad-a-card, your total space budget should allow for printing costs.

Chapter 5 Broadcast

One of the most glamorous breakthroughs in direct marketing over the past five years has been the emergence of TV as a viable direct response medium. TvB (Television Bureau of Advertising, Inc.) reports direct marketing investments in television for 1973 to be:

Records and tapes	$ 62,800,000
Key outlet items	17,889,000
Schools, colleges	10,712,000
Books and magazines	8,405,000
Resorts, cruises	5,770,000
	$105,576,000

This figure of $105 million plus for 1973 compares with a figure of $22.5 million reported for 1969. And these figures do not include local direct response TV advertising. TvB regards direct marketing as television's number-one growth area.

It is significant that better than 59% of the total reported direct marketing investment in television for 1973 has been expended by direct marketers selling records and tapes to the consumer, who is induced to order by mail or phone. It is likewise significant that key outlet items — items which best lend themselves to heavy TV promotion on behalf of major retail chains like Walgreen Drugs — rank second. In the case of items available through key retail outlets the thrust is the same — strong TV promotion — but the consumer completes the transaction at the outlet rather than by mail or phone.

Responding Advertisers' Annual Direct Marketing Sales

Annual Sales	% Respondents
Under $1,000,000	17
1,000,000–5,000,000	26
5,000,000–10,000,000	17
10,000,000–50,000,000	22
Over 50,000,000	9
No answer	9

Responding Advertisers' Television Ad Budgets

TV ad budget	% Respondents
Under $100,000	39
100,000–250,000	13
250,000–1,000,000	22
Over 1,000,000	17
No answer	9

Television Is a *New* Medium for Direct Marketers
6 out of 10 have used TV 5 years or less

Used TV	%
1 year or less	17
2–5 years	43
Over 5 years	26
No answer	13

The Median Number of TV-Promoted Items per Advertiser Is Three

No. of items	%
1	26
2–5	43
6–10	9
Over 10	17

Half of Respondents Use TV for *Both* Selling & Inquiries

Use TV for	%
Selling and inquiries	52
Selling only	39
Inquiries only	9

"Mail Only" Response Was Voted Most Productive

Viewer response	%
Mail only	39
Phone only	9
Both mail and phone	17
"Depends on item"	30

Note: Four percent did not answer.

30% of Respondents Use Payment After Receipts Exclusively

Payment Techniques	%
Exclusively prepayment	35
Exclusively bill enclosed	30
Exclusively C.O.D.	9
Combination of these	22

Note: Four percent answered "inquiries only."

Half of Respondents Use TV for Producing Inquiries

TV used to produce inquiries for:	%
Leads for interest in merchandise*	30
Leads for salesmen	13
Other	9
Not used for inquiries	48

*Includes catalogs.

39% of Advertisers Use a Combination of 120s and 60s

Commercial length	% of Advertisers Using
120s only	26
120s and over	4
60s only	4
60s and 120s	39
60s and shorter	17
90s and shorter	4
Neither 120s nor 60s	4

Two-Thirds of Respondents Promote *Both* Mail & Phone Response via TV

Viewer response	%
Both mail and phone	65
Mail only	35
Phone only	0

Over Half of Advertisers Require Cash Up Front

Payment techniques	%
Prepayment	57
C.O.D.	26
Payment after receipt	43
Inquiries only	4

Note: Total percent exceeds 100% because of multiple answers.

17% of Advertisers Accept Credit Card Orders

Mention credit card in commercials	%
Yes	17
No	83

The 120-Second TV Commercial Is Most Used

Length of commercial	% of Advertisers
120-second	70
60-second	65
30-second	22
90-second	13
Under 30-second	9
Over 120-second	4

Late Night and Daytime Most Popular Day Parts

TV Day Part	%
Late night	78
Daytime	70
Early evening	61
Prime time	48

101

More Advertisers Concentrate on Daytime Television

50% or More of TV Commercials in:	% of Advertisers
Daytime	30
Late night	22
Early evening	13
Prime time	9
None dominates	17
No answer	13

More Advertisers Schedule Weekdays as Dominant Choice

	% of Advertisers
Weekday dominant	39
Weekend dominant	22
Weekday and weekend equal	35
No answer	4

83% of Advertisers Ranked Cost per Response as Most Important Factor in Buying TV

No. 1 Factor in Importance	% Advertisers
Cost per response	83
Audience characteristics	13
TV ratings	4
Cost per 1000	0

Audience Characteristics Was Second Most Important Factor in Buying TV

	Percent Ranking		
	2d	3d	4th
Audience characteristics	39	17	4
Cost per 1000	22	35	13
TV ratings	4	17	48

35% of Respondents Invest over Half Their Direct Marketing Budgets in Television

% of Ad Budget in TV	% Advertisers
Over 50%	35
31–50%	0
30% or less	48
No answer	17

30% of Respondents Increased Their TV Budget in 1972

1972 vs. 1971	% of Advertisers
TV increased	30
TV same	22
TV decreased	9
No answer	39

Over Half of Respondents Said Television's Cost per Response Is Equal to or Lower than Direct Mail

Cost per Response TV vs. Direct Mail	% Respondents
TV is lower	20
TV equals mail	34
TV is higher	40
Varies by item	6

Primary TV Objectives

To explore the possibilities for TV, we should first of all explore the objectives to which TV may be applied. There are three main areas.

1. *To sell products.* Selling products via TV is not new, of course. Direct response advertisers started using TV back in the days when wrestling matches were more popular than pro football and Milton Berle was a bigger attraction than Archie Bunker.

    One of the new breed of direct marketers of merchandise via TV — Ronco Products Co. — budgeted about $7.5 million for the medium in 1971 alone. They have sold tons of items such as Amazing Spray Gun, Dial X Knife Sharpener, and London Aire hosiery.

    In the recording field — major user of TV — Columbia House has taken the lead. They've been strong in 150 to 200 markets.

    Competition has been quick to follow.

    There are two basic lessons to be learned from these two successful TV marketers. In Ronco's case, their best-selling items lend themselves to dramatic demonstration. Demonstration in full color is a TV plus not available in any other medium.

    In the case of Columbia House, it should be noted their TV success lies in selling record albums rather than record club memberships. The lesson to be learned here is that complicated offers via TV are death. To quote Jacob A. Evans of the Television Bureau of Advertising: "Good direct response commercials are simple, clearly written and spoken direct person-to-person communication."

    If one is to succeed in selling items in the $29.95 and over category via TV, credit terms should be a major consideration. And with credit terms there are credit problems — big credit problems if applicants aren't carefully screened. Credit turndowns of 40% aren't unusual.

    Referring back to the survey of TvB, we should note that over half of the advertisers require cash in advance.

2. *To give support.* As direct marketing has matured, TV has become a part of the multimedia approach. TV fits the mix beautifully as a support medium, to reinforce mass direct mail and/or newspaper distribution in selected markets.

    I have read of one large consumer magazine which has found its mail response is up 20% in cities where it runs TV support during the mail delivery period.

    Direct response insurance firms have embraced TV as a support for their newspaper inserts. Harry Hites, advertising director of Physicians Mutual, is quoted as stating, "Television has become a major part of our media mix." Art Linkletter has appeared in scores of markets urging viewers to look in their Sunday newspapers for an insurance offer.

    TV advertising makes sense when you can use it to support blanket mail and/or newspaper advertising in given markets. I've seen support budgets of 5% to 10% increase response 25% to 50%.

The script which follows was used to support inserts in selected Sunday newspapers.

VIDEO	AUDIO
ANNCR. IN FRONT OF REAR-PROJECTION SCREEN, FOOTAGE OF CROWDED EXPRESSWAY TRAFFIC SCENE	Ever stop to think how dangerous it is to drive today? That's why I hope you'll take a few minutes this weekend, to read this very important letter. It's from Old American Insurance Company, and you'll find it right in your weekend newspaper. Old American tells how you can apply for *twenty-five thousand dollars* worth of protection against the crippling costs of death or dismemberment from a fatal traffic accident. And the premium for the first month is just twenty-five cents!
CHROME-A-KEY OF LETTER INSERT	
CHROME-A-KEY: OLD AMERICAN INSURANCE COMPANY	
CHROME-A-KEY ON RIGHT: $25,000 TRAFFIC AND TRAVEL ACCIDENT PROTECTION	
CHANGE CHROME-A-KEY: JUST 25¢ FOR THE FIRST MONTH	

	(TAG)
SLIDE OF LETTER INSERT AND NEWSPAPER LOGO	It's an offer that's too good to pass up . . . so be *sure* to look for this letter in the [name of paper]!

3. *To get leads.* Acquiring leads through TV is mushrooming along with other uses. Bankers Life has long used Paul Harvey as spokesman to get leads for salesmen. Columbia School of Broadcasting (not an affiliate of CBS) reportedly spent in excess of $1 million in TV during a six-month period to get leads.

   TV is an ideal lead-producing medium for programs and propositions where you have to reach the masses to ferret out the prospects. Correspondence and vocational schools are good examples, as are land operations and investment programs. The thing going for such programs is the large unit of sale involved, which makes a lead cost of $6, $10, or more, acceptable for many.

   On the other side of the scale are propositions with mass appeal. H&R Block, the tax service people, reportedly get leads for new customers in existing markets at an average cost of $3.22, with costs in new markets as low as $1.20.

TV Costs Can Be Low

When the potential offered by TV is mentioned to most direct marketers who have never used the medium, they turn pale at the thought of the cost. Their thinking goes something like this: "I heard that one minute on 'Marcus Welby, M.D.' costs about $85,000. Good God, I can't afford that!" And indeed they can't. But such a program in prime time would probably be a very poor medium for a direct response advertiser.

TV spot costs on any given station vary over an incredible range. Jacob Evans points out that a one-minute spot on the most highly rated show on a given station may cost $1,200, whereas the same one-minute spot on the show with lowest ratings may cost $10. That's a ratio of 120 to one!

Fortunately, the lower-cost spots play into the hands of direct response advertisers. Evans explains this phenomenon: "We have been told that response is not efficient from live sports events or newscasts, particularly the high-rated 10 o'clock news. It seems that sports and news viewers are too absorbed to break away from the program for pencil and paper to write down the address or phone number."

Evans also says that stations tell the TBA that types of programming most in demand among direct response advertisers are movies, game shows, and talk shows, followed by syndicated shows of various types.

TV time periods favored by most direct marketers are late night, weekend, daytime, and especially early morning and prime time on *independent* stations. Prime time on independent UHF stations has proved particularly effective because these stations' rates are much lower than network affiliates'. And frequently UHF programming provides the same environment for good response that late night or daytime does on network stations.

To put costs into perspective for a prospective direct marketer, let's explore TV support for a newspaper insertion in one market.

Let's say our hypothetical direct marketer has an insurance firm. He's running newspaper inserts and soliciting insurance applications in a number of markets, including Abilene, Tex. For Abilene and other selected markets, he decides to develop a 30-second TV commercial in support of the insert which will appear in the Sunday paper. Objective: To reach as many viewers as possible in the Abilene area, urging them to look for the insert in the Sunday paper.

There are two TV stations serving the Abilene area, an NBC affiliate and a CBS/ABC affiliate. Client experience indicates the prime market lies with adults 35 and older. So the agency is asked to prepare a schedule which will saturate the prime market for insurance to a major degree and have a cumulative impact over a wide time span.

The table which follows shows the type of schedule the agency could put together for this 30-second support commercial.

Station A

Time Slot	Days	Show Adjacencies	Rate Card Cost/Spot	No. Spots	Total Rate Card Cost
7:00-9:00 a.m.	Fri.	"Today Show"	$15	2	$ 30
9:00-9:30 a.m.	Fri.	"Dinah's Place"	15	1	15
9:00-9:30 a.m.	Sun.	"Oral Roberts"	15	1	15
9:30-10:00 a.m.	Fri.	"Concentration"	15	1	15
10:00-10:30 a.m.	Fri.	"Sale of the Century"	15	1	15
11:00-11:30 a.m.	Fri.	"Jeopardy"	15	1	15
11:30-12:00 Noon	Fri.	"Who, What, Where"	15	1	15
12:00 Noon-12:30 p.m.	Sun.	"Meet the Press"	15	1	15
12:15-12:30 p.m.	Fri.	"Sunday Chapel"	23	1	23
			Total	10	$158

Station B

Time Slot	Days	Show Adjacencies	Rate Card Cost/Spot	No. Spots	Total Rate Card Cost
7:00-8:00 a.m.	Fri.	"CBS Morning News"	$ 7	1	$ 7
8:00-9:00 a.m.	Sun.	"Roller Derby"	7	2	14
9:00-9:30 a.m.	Fri.	"Lucy Show"	7	1	7
9:00-9:30 a.m.	Sat.	"Bewitched"	7	1	7
10:00-11:30 a.m.	Fri.	"Password"	7	1	7
12 Noon-12:30 p.m.	Sun.	"Film Feature"	14	1	14
12:30-1:00 p.m.	Fri.	"As the World Turns"	14	1	14
			Total	8	$70

Here's a saturation schedule that a direct marketer could use for a support spot.

A recap shows the advertiser would be able to run a total of 18 spots in time slots adjacent to programs with a concentration of viewers in the 35-year-plus age category for a combined total of $228. The cost of the insert in the Sunday paper, including space cost, would run about $2,000. So if the full TV support program were used, TV would run about 10% of the total budget. (In larger markets, TV support may come to an even smaller percentage.) So anything better than a 10% increase in newspaper pull would make TV support very worthwhile.

Determining Length of Commercial

TvB's survey showed that the 120-second TV commercial was most used—by 70% of direct response users. However, as with all phases of direct marketing, averages can be misleading. The commercial's objective should be the determining factor in deciding the proper length of the commercial.

On the average, a 30-second spot should be adequate for support TV; a 60-second, for inquiries; 60s and 120s, for direct sale of merchandise. A limiting factor in using 120s is the fact that such time periods are not readily available from all stations.

The necessity for longer spots can best be illustrated by this commercial prepared to sell a set of knives.

VIDEO	AUDIO
1. OPEN ON MCU PROFESSIONAL DEMONSTRATOR IN KITCHEN, HACKING AT WOODEN BLOCK	DEMONSTRATOR: I'm purposely chopping this hardwood block to smithereens to demonstrate an amazing new product: MIRACLE MAC KNIVES!
2. ZOOM TO ECU DEMON. STILL HACKING AT BLOCK. SUPER CARD # 1 (FLASHING): (WARNING)	DEMON. (VO): Ladies and gentlemen, please don't try this on the knives in your kitchen drawer. MIRACLE MAC KNIVES are the *only* knives in the world that can take this kind of punishment, and keep coming back for more!!
3. CUT TO DEMON. CUTTING PAPER INTO STRIPS	The secret is space-age, chrome molybdenum steel— the hardest steel ever made—that stays sharp, for *life*, without any grinding or sharpening tools!
4. CUT TO ECU DEMON. GESTURES TO BLADE	
5. HANDS DEMO SHARPENING	Imagine! Just a simple pass over the back of a china plate restores the original cutting edge.

6. PULL BACK FOR MCU DEMON.	DEMONSTRATOR:	Grab a pencil and paper folks because I want to send you a set of these amazing MAC KNIVES for 30 days *free!* But first, watch . . .
7. DEMO TOMATO	DEMO. (VO):	You can: cut a tomato paper-thin slice after slice — and never lose a drop of juice . . .
8. DEMO ROAST		carve meat from the bone as clean as a whistle . . .
9. DEMO RADISHES		decorate radishes like an expert . . .
10. DEMO BREAD IN MID-AIR		cut bread a sixteenth of an inch *thin* . . .
11. DEMO TURKEY		carve a turkey clear down to the bone in seconds . . .
12. DEMO POTATO		even take an eye out of a potato so easy you won't believe it!
13. CUT TO ECU HANDS DEMO BLADE		*And just look at this:* Each knife is scientifically designed to keep your fingers away from the cutting board.
14. HANDS DEMO TIPS		with safe rounded tips
15. HANDS DEMO HOLE		and handy hanging hole,
16. HANDS DEMO HANDLES		*plus* teak handles that are *permanently* bonded to the steel for *super* strength.
17. PULL BACK TO DEMON. WHO DISPLAYS KNIVES ONE AT A TIME	DEMONSTRATOR:	And now, during this special TV offer, you can own *one* . . . two . . . three . . . four . . . MIRACLE MAC KNIVES for just $19.95.
18. DISS TO KNIVES + BOX. SUPER CARD #2: (30-DAY FREE TRIAL)	DEMON. (VO):	But first, try them at home for 30 days free! No need to send any money!
19. CUT TO KNIFE RACK DEMO. SUPER CARD #3: (FREE! WHEN YOU SEND $19.95 PLUS $1 SHIPPING & HANDLING)		However, if you use your credit card or include payment with your order, we'll

20. DEMON. ASSEMBLES
    SANDWICH AND CUTS IT

21. CUT TO SLIDE: (PHONE
    NUMBER & ADDRESS). SUPER
    CARD #4: (OFFER FOR CABLE
    TV VIEWERS ONLY)

include this handsome hardwood knife rack at no extra cost! If not fully satisfied, return the knife set . . . keep the knife rack and we'll refund your purchase price of $19.95. Try the knives that are so *hard, so sharp,* they slice through a Dagwood sandwich in one stroke!

Order your set today. Give them a real workout for 30 days Here's how: Call 000-0000 *right now* or write MAC KNIVES, care of station 000, Charleston West Virginia. Send only $19.95 plus $1 shipping and handling. That's: MAC KNIVES, care of STATION 000, CHARLESTON, WEST VIRGINIA or call 000-0000 now.

Additional Guidelines

A number of guidelines have been established for considering TV for direct marketing.

1. For direct sales of merchandise, TV ratings have little, if any, correlation with results. Lowest-cost time spots are often the most effective.
2. TV stations whose audiences are oriented to direct response are usually better if the objective is to get inquiries or orders via TV.
3. If the objective is to support direct mail and/or newspaper advertising, the best buy is time adjacent to shows with broad viewing audiences that closely fit the customer profile.
4. Production costs for TV commercials need not be expensive: $4,000 or less for a 30- or 60-second spot is often adequate.
5. Nationally known personalities can and often do add believability and credibility to TV commercials.
6. Since time is a perishable commodity, TV rates are often subject to negotiation.
7. Generally, the same principles of motivation to action used in direct mail and print advertising prove effective for TV.
8. Programs involving passive viewing, such as movies, game shows, and talk shows, are usually more effective in getting response than programs with active viewing, such as sports events.
9. Simple, direct commercials are usually most effective.

108

Potentials of CATV

While commercial TV, as we have known it, is understood and used effectively by many, cable television is still in its infancy. Yet many believe, and with good reason, the ultimate potential of CATV is vast.

Elliott Guzofsky, founder of Mark/James, Inc., a merchandise syndicator, has pioneered in testing the medium as a direct marketing vehicle. In March 1973, Guzofsky was interviewed by *Direct Marketing* magazine. In this interview, he provides an insight into the methods to be considered in testing cable TV and the potentials which exist.

Q. Let's talk about how you became interested in cable TV, and how you got involved with the Times Mirror.

A. In 1964, I saw a demonstration of phonevision and fell in love with the idea that this was the ultimate method of convenience marketing to show and sell merchandise.

We were in San Francisco one day working with Gousha. They are map people and also a subsidiary of the Times Mirror. We had worked a program for them, run by Herb Drake. He said, "Why don't you see our cable people in LA?"

This was in '69 and Herb Drake took the time and trouble to come up to LA to make the introduction personally to Robert Beckner, at that time president of TM Communications, the Los Angeles Times Mirror subsidiary running cable systems in cable TV. They are operating approximately 50 to 60,000 homes.

They are wiring up south of Los Angeles and also have systems in Florida and Eastern Long Island which are growing rapidly. At the present time approximately 11% of the homes in the U.S., about 7 million, are on cable.

Q. And where is progress taking it to by 1980?

A. Best estimates are between 40 to 60 million homes on cable. That's about 80%.

Q. How many cable systems are serving now and how many will be needed to serve 60 million households?

A. At this point there are approximately 4,500 systems with approximately 4,000 more just starting. The number of systems is unpredictable because each community gives out its own franchise. As new communities enter into it, you are going to have multiple systems operating. The way most of the systems are operating is that the main company may have many systems all over the country in different areas.

Basically they are non-exclusive contracts, but if one fellow is wiring the city nobody else will go into a fight with him over who is going to get the customer. These cable systems are looking to 80 channels in the foreseeable future and approximately 200 channels within 3 to 4 years.

Q. An almost unlimited capacity to communicate, in other words?

A. Just about. You could get any information you want over the channels.

109

Q. Let's go back to '69 and your first meeting with the Los Angeles Times Mirror. I am not sure you really explained why they wanted you to come down. You're a merchandiser, a manufacturer's rep; you know direct mail, direct marketing. They knew this, so that is why you went to Los Angeles.

A. That's correct. We laid out the type of program we wanted to test on their systems. They agreed to the test. In 1970 we laid out the basic program, including cost, and in April of '71, the test was launched.

On the test we used single item mailings, multiple mailings, statement stuffers, bangtail envelopes, package stuffers, bounce back programs, all backed up by commercials on the particular items that we were promoting.

Q. You are talking about a mailing list of cable TV subscribers?

A. Yes. Each system's mailing list is their subscriber list, and we set up the Cable Family Shopping Center which would be the catch-all to do all the promotional work to the individual subscriber. Our role is to test merchandise, locate the merchandise, develop the direct mail—or really the marketing program.

Q. What did you test?

A. A broad range of products from $19.95 to $300 in single item mailings. We ran a multiple once which ranged from $19.95 to $39.95. This was a standard direct mail package. We also ran single item mailings which ranged up to $300.

Q. And in this test how many subscribers were you dealing with?

A. Approximately 25,000.

Q. What kind of results did you get?

A. The average results on the single item mailings ran about 1.4%. On the multiple mailer they ran 1.6 to 1.7% in orders. On the statement stuffers results ranged from .9 to 1.2%.

Q. What did you say in the mail? Did you say, "Dear cable customer?" Did you say something to involve and convince them that you were really doing something for them?

A. On the current test we are. On the original test, we just wanted to see what the cold results would be and tie them in together with the commercial shown on video as to what we could expect from them.

On each item for which we ran a mailing piece there was a back-up color commercial. This ran all month long. Whatever month the item ran, the commercial also ran at least once a day.

We also ran some tests on doing the mailing before the commercial, showing the commercial first and then making the mailing, and also sending out the mailing at the same time as the commercial.

110

Q. What did you find out?

A. It seems that if they could read the direct mail piece, and then see it on the tube, that it would activate them. They would look for the card and mail it in.

Q. What about phone orders?

A. Lots of them, especially on the commercials. Higher than two-to-one.

Q. Did you organize it to the station?

A. It was organized at that point because we had a central location, so that they could call the station.

Q. This must have opened your eyes, because you're going to a metro mail list, a cold list. You didn't know which were mail order buyers.

A. That's correct and the amazing thing about it is that taking a city like Long Beach, which is a metropolitan area highly discount store oriented, depressed economic level, we got the same responses you would from an ordinary mail order list.

Q. What about credit terms? Was it credit or cash-with-order?

A. It was on credit and the credit experience was comparable to the regular mail order list, a little less than 5%.

Q. What about return of merchandise?

A. Returns averaged a little higher than the average oil company or finance type mail order list.

Q. What was the most exciting product that you promoted in that test—the price, the return, the percentage and that kind of thing?

A. The best product from a standpoint of total dollars was the $200 Keystone movie outfit. We did about 1.1% on that, returns were very low, and credit turn-downs nil.

Q. What was the arrangement with the station, a percentage of sales?

A. That's correct. The stations get a percentage of the retail price and are entitled to bonuses as they draw a better percentage, so they feel they have an interest in seeing more and better promotions so they can earn a higher income.

Q. The test turned out that the station did as well as if they had charged a regular commercial rate?

A. No, much greater. The time on cable right now is so cheap, $6 a minute, $3.50 a minute, whatever, that all they had to do was sell one item to be ahead of the game.

Q. What are the cable systems billing subscribers, $5, $6 a month for service? This gives you really an access as a merchandiser to supply the BRE in color and offer additional merchandise. Allows the cable company to send BRE's and BRC's on an omnibus basis, so that any advertiser can use the omnibus cable card or envelope. What is your view on that?

A. The cable companies today are looking for any kind of income to facilitate laying more cable and getting more subscribers. They do not have marketing people as such, and they are looking for ways and means to get additional income from their subscribers. This marketing route here is a fund raising deal to raise money to lay cable.

Q. Well, then, you ran your test and that was . . . April of '71, and the reason we got together today really is that you made your first cable family mailing right after the first of October, 1972. Your first day of return was 8 days later. Let's describe the mailing first and where the test market is.

A. The test market is in 18 states across the country. Cablemart, which is a new subsidiary of the Times Mirror and a joint venture between them and ourselves, has signed up multiple system operators on an exclusive basis across the country.

Any merchandise or services to the subscribers will go through Cablemart. They in turn are giving the system operators their percentage off the top of the retail sale, acting as the syndicator.

And the first mailing includes a letter describing the concept of the Cable Family Shopping Center.

Q. This is a two page letter here in blue and black and the letterhead is Cable Family Shopping Center, P.O. Box 8537, Fountain Valley, Calif. 92708. Telephone number is 714-557-6407. That's where the shopper would phone if she had any questions. What's the letter all about?

A. It explains the concept of a Cable Family Center and some of the additional services that will be offered to them in the future, such as the travel club of the air. Being a member of the center qualifies them for affinity charter groups, meaning the cheapest charter rate available.

Also we have started health/accident insurance and local promotional deals. Auto and even life insurance will be part of the club program.

We're tying in local promotions with the local merchants to promote cable both ways. The local merchant is able to promote on the cable and also give the cable family member a special bonus for dealing with him. As a member of the local family cable center they present their membership card and get their coupons, which is sort of a stamp plan.

Q. Is the cable family system then an umbrella marketing organization for not only national mail order but also local business?

112

A. That is correct. We feel that the local merchant will become as important as the national, and the national will bring in merchandise ideas, services that aren't available locally. Also it brings home to the consumers the method of convenience marketing that we feel is the ultimate.

Q. On this test mailing, I see a 4-color brochure. It looks like an 8-page, 8½″ × 11″ fanfold, and it's a multiple product offering, isn't it?

A. Yes. We have a vacuum cleaner, floor polisher, clock radio, socket set, flatware, toaster-oven, meat grinder and multi-year calendar watch.

It went out to almost 300,000 subscribers as a basic example of the type of offerings and values that we would be offering in the foreseeable future.

Q. What are the prices?

A. The price range is from $29.95 to $49.95. We have also given them the option of having credit or charging it to their BankAmericard or Master Charge account. Also, there were credit applications for both Master Charge and BankAmericard in the offering. Mark/James handled all packaging and marketing.

Q. So you had to get everybody into this package. I notice that in the 6″ × 9″ package is a card with a bunch of numbers on it. Would you explain those?

A. This is the Cable Family Shopping Center membership card with a cable account number. The first two numbers are a code for the multiple system operator or the main company that is handling a number system.

The next three digits designate the exact system in the multiple system. In other words, the local system perhaps might be Peoria or Fergus Falls or Cleveland or some place like that.

98% of the cable systems, the individual systems, are in a single ZIP Code area, which gives you the benefit of having some demographics as to what type of merchandise to beam toward that particular audience.

Q. Can you split ZIP? We have heard some conversation about being able to quarter towns or divide them up in eights or something like that.

A. We are not looking for that. If there are two different ZIP Codes we can split promotions from one ZIP Code to the other, in the same system, but we cannot split within the ZIP Code.

Q. Your broadcast, then, is all city, but your mailings can be split by ZIP Code, so you can try the same commercial, and with different mailings to different sections.

A. That's correct. The results of testing on that have given us quite an insight into what can be done in the future.

Q. One question that might occur to a retailer in these markets is, "What's happening?"

113

A. Probably the same thing that has happened over the years when the discount houses started, when the mass merchandisers started, when the rack merchants started: the regular retailer will hide his head in the sand and say it will go away.

Q. Won't it be too late to get into this game?

A. No. He is really right at the beginning of it if he wants to be aggressive. He can lease a channel. We would be happy to help him and to run a store promotion on the lease channel.

Q. What do you see when this is in full flight? Can A Hutzler's in Baltimore lease a channel for 8 hours a day, 5 or 7 days a week, and run a catalog on a cable TV thing?

A. They could lease it for 24 hours a day and do whatever they want. It is their channel and they could run various promotions. You will be able to eventually dial a code to bring up whatever specific item you want to see.

Q. Now you are talking about a subscriber retrieving information, right?

A. That's correct. The subscriber will be able to dial a code if he wants to see a refrigerator, as an example, and they will show him 10 refrigerators of the type that he wants to see.

Q. You're changing the whole darn ballgame of retailing.

A. Well, it's been changed before, but you will have eventually 200 channels, and I'm sure that eight or ten channels will be leased to various merchants.

They could have a fashion show every afternoon at 2 o'clock. They could have a homemaking binge every day at 4 o'clock. They could have an interior decorating course and sell the viewers on whatever they are demonstrating.

There is nothing that can't be done in this medium. It goes as far as your imagination will take you.

Q. How many other people are testing the medium in the way you are?

A. Nobody. Nobody seems to really appreciate the vast way in which cable is going to change our lives in the near future.

Q. One of the things I hear is that not many people are watching cable, but take Sterling in New York.

A. Sterling in New York is getting beautiful listenership because they have tied up Madison Square Garden on home games.

Q. But how do you know when to run your commercial and how do you know you are going to have at least one person watching your commercial?

A. How do you know when Ford Motor Company runs on NBC how many people are watching? They are paying for that. Here you are not paying for a thing.

Q. I see, so you hope whoever is watching will respond.

A. It is all gravy.

Q. But then your mail could almost help you build an audience for certain segments.

A. Right. The mail has to be an integral part of this to start with.

Q. So that your package on merchandise could go out and key into a certain program either directly or indirectly, and they would see the commercial as part of the program you suggested they watch. Then it would be synergistic with the mailing.

A. That's correct. The second part of the test is the inclusion of a statement stuffer, like the Keystone camera offered at $39.95, with the monthly billing. On the original test, this camera pulled 1.1%. The cost of the circular is about $6/M.

Q. Describe it, Elliott.

A. It's a $2\frac{1}{2}'' \times 5''$ 4-color 4-fold with a perforated return order card as the bottom fold. Figure the cost of stuffing somewhere about $12-13/M.

Q. So that's another dimension of using a family of TV subscribers. What do you see down the road?

A. Down the road we see that the visual end of it will become more important as the technology becomes perfected.

Q. Are you saying also that the mail end of it will be any less important? You don't see cable TV doing-in direct mail or the printing industry as we know it today?

A. No, the mail end of it, especially the monthly stuffer type program or the bangtail envelope, will continue to be important, because as people see it in the mail and then see the commercial, it reinforces and accentuates the promotion.

The cable industry will hurt the network TV more than they will hurt the printing industry because this kind of communication system is going to take up more time. Cable TV has the capability to get tremendous listenership on local issues, town meetings, high school and college athletic events, and thereby fracture the audience from the network audiences.

Any system with over 3,500 subscribers is required by law to do local origination, and as programming becomes more sophisticated it will get a larger listenership and this together with the mail and commercials on the cable will help divert some of the listenership and make it profitable for the cable system to do more programming and keep diverting people from the network channels.

Q. Is it technologically feasible today to retrieve, if you have a cable sub, a certain program at will?

A. Yes. They are testing this in Orlando, Florida, and El Segundo, Calif., using two-way communications with which the viewer can vote, purchase, let his wishes be known.

Q. Who's doing this?

A. The System in Orlando, Florida is run by American Television & Communications. The system in California is run by Theta-Com.

Q. What's next? You have made this test of 300,000 of multiple merchandise. What are you playing with next?

A. We are visualizing somewhere between 3 and 4 million homes by the end of 1973. We are opening a subsidiary in Canada and will start with approximately a half million to 750,000 homes for April.

Q. Do you see any limit, Elliott, in the range of merchandise that you can offer?

A. No limit whatsoever: anything can be sold — mink coats, cars, refrigerators, watches. You can sell anything that anyone will buy if you make it appealing to them.

Q. What do you think is going to happen to shopping centers and the retailers? Will they change?

A. We hope they do, because they sure have a place in this world. One of the things that we have found out is that the average person can't find out what he is buying in a shopping center. The average sales clerk does not have the technical knowledge.

One of the things we also found in our test, which I think is important from the mailer's standpoint, is buying habits. Over 50% of the people on the first 6-month test bought at least 3 times.

Q. So we are living in a new age indeed. Cable is growing. Direct marketing on the cable is assured and you're in the catbird seat on this one.

A. So far it is a lonely seat. We would like some company.

As Elliott Guzofsky points out, the combination of CATV commercials plus direct mail opens the opportunity for direct marketing success.

The letter which follows explains the Cable Family Shopping Center concept to the subscriber.

Interactive Cable TV: The Ultimate

For a number of years now, direct marketers have dreamed of the day when viewers will be able to see their merchandise on the screen, push a few buttons on a home console, and place an order instantly. The El Segundo, California, pilot project may well prove to be the final link in making the dream come true.

Present plans are for a pilot test among 1,000 subscribers in El Segundo, to be launched by January 1975. Each home will be equipped with a console, making interactive cable TV a reality. Through use of the console, among other things, subscribers will be able to:

116

Cable Family Shopping Center

P.O. BOX 8537
FOUNTAIN VALLEY, CALIFORNIA 92708   (714) 557-6407

Welcome to the new world of convenience shopping

..............the CABLE FAMILY Shopping Center!

Dear Friend:

What is the "Cable Family" Shopping Center? Why is it the fastest-growing shopping idea sweeping the Country today?

Cable Family Shopping, as its many satisfied member-families will tell you, is not only the most <u>convenient</u> but a most economical and time-saving way to shop.

Cable Family Shopping means you have merchandise to use in your home for 15 days with no obligation to keep it---compare that to a fast look at an item on a store shelf before you buy.

Cable Family Shopping is the world of tomorrow---in your home today!

Cable Family Shopping offers you:

> <u>Convenience shopping from your own living room---</u>
> <u>convenience never before available anywhere. Complete</u>
> <u>description of the construction of the merchandise---</u>
> <u>what it can do and what it can't do---in print and on</u>
> <u>your TV screen.</u>

Cable Family Shopping eliminates:

> <u>Merchandise that does not live up to its advertised</u>
> <u>claims. When you order "Cable Family" products, you</u>
> <u>know they are quality...guaranteed or your money back.</u>
> <u>No questions...no "stalling". And you actually use the</u>
> <u>merchandise in your home for 15 days before you decide</u>
> <u>to keep it!</u>

Cable Family Shopping offers you:

> <u>Convenient credit terms through either Master Charge or</u>
> <u>Bank Americard in addition to a 15 day free trial.</u>

And that's only a few of the many reasons more and more families, many of them, no doubt, friends and neighbors of yours, are participating in the Cable Family club!

Among the enclosures was a multimailer with eight individual merchandise offers, as well as an explanatory letter from the cooperating CATV outlet, a membership card, and an order card, as illustrated.

Here are just a few other services this new, tuned-to-the-times buying organization plans to make available to members:

- An exclusive Cable Family TRAVEL CLUB that offers you special excursion rates...for trips all over the world and travel service for all of North America.

- Low cost Life, Hospitalization and Accident Insurance.

- Complete product description shown on your T.V. set. No more wondering about specifications or product use.

As a member of the Cable Family Shopping Club, you are part of an exclusive family! Your personal membership card is enclosed with a special, multi-page brochure which will show you just a few of the many values membership in Cable Family can bring you.

How do you order? Just fill in the enclosed order card and your order will be processed immediately. You can order through your Bank Americard or Master Charge card. Both are accepted from Cable Family members. If you don't presently have a Bank Americard or Master Charge card, just fill in the enclosed application and we will have it processed for you immediately. The normal processing time is approximately four (4) weeks.

Remember, ALL Cable Family Shopping Center merchandise is quality merchandise with exclusive features you won't find elsewhere. All products fully guaranteed, returnable. All products on a NO RISK - FREE TRIAL basis.

We strongly urge you to take advantage of these opportunities for the Cable Family members! Check the enclosed brochure for outstanding buys. Just fill in the enclosed order card and you'll find out why Cable Family shopping is becoming a delightful habit with so many people.

Very truly yours,

R. A. Johnson
Vice-President

Cable Family Shopping Center
P.O. BOX 8537 · FOUNTAIN VALLEY, CALIFORNIA 92708 · (714) 557-6407

Cable Account No.

12-012　　№　3875

Signature

Dear Cable Subscriber:

We have made special arrangements for you
and your family to receive information
concerning the Cable Family Shopping Center.
We have studied this plan and believe that
it will offer you a convenient opportunity
to select high quality, fully-guaranteed
merchandise in the comfort of your home.

This exclusive service will be available to
cable subscribers only.

After you have had an opportunity to study
the enclosed material and if you have any
questions, don't hesitate to call your local
cable system office.

LVO CABLE, INC.

Cable Family 15-DAY FREE HOME TRIAL Certificate
Sale ends November 30, 1972

Gentlemen: Yes, send me the following item(s) for a 15-day free trial period. I understand that if I am not delighted with it, at the end of that time, I will return it, at no cost or obligation to me.

VACUUM CLEANER
☐ The purchase price of $39.95* plus any applicable State and local sales tax and $4.95 for shipping and handling charges for each ordered.

50-Pc. Monogrammed Tableware
☐ *Antoinette* ☐ *Marbella* with the initial of_____
☐ The purchase price of $29.95* plus any applicable State and local sales tax and $2.95 for shipping and handling charges for each ordered.

FLOOR POLISHER
☐ The purchase price of $29.95* plus any applicable State and local sales tax and $4.50 for shipping and handling charges for each ordered.

TOASTER OVEN
☐ The purchase price of $29.95* plus any applicable State and local sales tax and $2.95 for shipping and handling charges for each ordered.

AM-FM CLOCK RADIO
☐ The purchase price of $39.95* plus any applicable State and local sales tax and $2.95 for shipping and handling charges for each ordered.

Meat Grinder & Salad Maker
☐ The purchase price of $29.95* plus any applicable State and local sales tax and $2.95 for shipping and handling charges for each ordered.

136-Pc. Socket Wrench & Tool Set
☐ The purchase price of $49.95* plus any applicable State and local sales tax and $4.00 for shipping and handling charges for each ordered.

Multi-Year Calendar Watch
☐ Yellow Gold Finish ☐ Chrome
☐ The purchase price of $29.95* plus any applicable State and local sales tax and $2.50 for shipping and handling charges for each ordered.

☐ Enclosed is a check or money order for $_____ which includes charges for shipping, handling and State and local sales tax.

PLEASE CHARGE MY
☐ BankAmericard　　☐ Master Charge

_____
Credit Card No. (give all numbers)

Interbank No. _____
(Master Charge only)

Card Expiration Date _____

Cable Account No. _12-012_ __ __ __ _____

_____
Signature

PLEASE ALLOW TWO WEEKS FOR DELIVERY

119

1. Place orders for merchandise direct through their consoles.
2. Request further information about given propositions.
3. Ask for a salesman to call.
4. Ask questions and get immediate answers.
5. Select seats and order tickets for the theater and sporting events.
6. Order airline tickets, reserve hotel rooms, learn about vacation facilities.
7. Place orders from other than television stimuli, such as catalogs and print advertising.
8. Get speedy credit verification for in-store purchases.

A tremendous benefit which interactive cable TV makes available to the marketer is the system's capacity to take program viewing polls every three seconds, to select randomly households for A/B commercial testing. Thus the advertiser will be able to quickly determine his most effective commercials, his most effective appeals. Indeed, the potential for direct marketers is tremendously exciting.

Radio: A Powerful Medium

TV is the glamour medium of broadcasting. Hence the potential of radio is often overlooked by direct marketers. This is a mistake. Radio can prove to be a very powerful medium.

The Radio Advertising Bureau provides these interesting statistics.

1. America now has 368,577,000 working radios—more than $1\frac{1}{2}$ sets for every man, woman, and child in this country.
2. As of January 1, 1972, 67,382,000 homes had at least one radio in working order, with an average of 5.3 radio sets per home!
3. 99% of all autos are now equipped with radios.

Radio is everywhere. The audience is vast.

Markets by Formats

While radio reaches every ear in America every day, program formats and types of stations make it relatively simple to target markets for products. Complete audience demographics are readily available for radio stations, both AM and FM, as well as the best time periods for each defined audience.

Consider just three of the formats available and note the types of products and/or services which logically fit these formats.

Format:	Product Related to Format:
All news	Stock market services News magazines Merchandise for the home
Classical and semiclassical music (older audience)	Classical record albums News magazines General magazines appealing to older audiences Insurance offers for older people Merchandise for the home Retirement home offers
Contemporary music (younger audience)	Contemporary record albums Home study schools Apparel for youth

120

Radio Is Audio, Not Visual

The audio nature of radio dictates the types of products or services which best lend themselves to this medium.

If yours is a product which must be demonstrated to be sold, radio is obviously not your best medium. You can't demonstrate the 15 or more things you can do with a blender on radio, nor can you show how to use a paint gun, hedge trimmer, a new power mower, or a host of other demonstrable products.

But if you can do the job with audio, sans video, radio is a most attractive medium. You can talk to school dropouts about completing their high school education at home. You can talk to older folks about retirement homes. And you can sell record albums and tapes because you can "demonstrate" with audio. You can even sell well-known publications by radio, if your proposition is one which offers a savings from established price. (Kiplinger has successfully used radio as a prime medium for its *Changing Times* magazine for years.)

Length and Types of Commercials

As in TV, the length of commercials is dictated by the objective. For support, a multiplicity of 30-second spots can often do the job. For inquiries, phone or write-in, 60-second spots make sense. But if you are trying to effect a sale through radio, you will probably find you need one minute and 20 seconds, or longer. (Not all stations will accept commercials exceeding 60 seconds.)

Both commercially produced spots and live copy have their advantages. While commercially produced spots have the advantage of being *the same quality* each time used, the value of live spots lies in the fact that a station personality can deliver a message which provides two things — a seemingly uninterrupted flow from music to talk to commercial, and a believability not usually so inherent in a taped message.

Many talk shows are taped for syndication to radio stations across the country. The leading talk show, the one syndicated to more radio stations than any other, is the Earl Nightingale program. Here is an example of how Nightingale tailors commercials to local sponsors, furnishing the spot announcements to the local station to follow the syndicated message.

Copy for:	Decatur Federal
J.O. No.:	DF-552
Draft No:	3
Date:	June 28, 1972
Job:	60-Sec. Recorded Radio Earl Nightingale Luggage Promo

EARL NIGHTINGALE: I'd like to take a minute of your time to tell you about something you'll enjoy for years. It's a free gift from Decatur Federal: a beautiful, "carry on" Travel Bag . . . when you open or add to a Decatur Federal Savings account in the amount of $1,000 or more. These free travel bags — in two smart styles for men and women — are durable yet light-weight, easy to keep clean . . . and they're made of luxurious, glove-soft vinyl. The men's flight bag has three outside zipper pockets, the inside is lined, contains a hanger . . . and comes in a variety of colors. The ladies' tote bag is also available in a variety of colors . . . it zips and locks . . . and has two outside and one inside pocket — plus double-riveted straps. Believe me, they're *really* good looking and wonderfully practical. Federal regulations limit free gifts to one per customer per year. So stop by any Decatur Federal office now — deposit $1,000 or more in a new or existing savings account — and pick out your Travel Bag — free.

Five Advantages of Radio

Radio will never be the glamour medium of broadcast. But the Radio Advertising Bureau presents these points to be remembered by direct marketers.

1. Radio is a selective, personal medium.
2. You can target your potential market.
3. Radio has great reach and frequency.
4. Radio can be low in cost. (BBD&O figures show that to reach men 18 and older, the cost is $1.70 CPM. To reach women only, $1.60 CPM.)
5. Radio offers opportunity for great creative ability.

Broadcast today — both TV and radio — is a definite part of the direct marketing media mix. For the right products, for the right propositions, the media are structured for expanding markets.

Self-Quiz

1. During the year 1973, more than $100 million was invested in TV by direct marketers. More than 59% of the total was invested in the sale of _____

   _____

2. Which of these methods of requested response is considered most productive by users of TV? _____ Mail only? _____ Phone only? _____ Both mail and phone?
3. According to a TvB survey, what percentage of advertisers require cash in advance when soliciting orders via TV? _____%
4. What are the three primary objectives to which TV may be applied?

   1. _____   2. _____

   3. _____
5. Name the four types of TV programming most in demand among direct response advertisers.

   1. _____   2. _____

   3. _____   4. _____
6. Why is it that the most expensive TV time spots often prove less effective for direct marketers than low-cost time spots?

   _____

   _____

   _____

7. Time periods favored by direct marketers using network TV stations usually rank in this order:

   1. _____   2. _____

   3. _____

8. Time periods preferred on independent stations are:

   1. _____ 2. _____

9. On the average, a 30-second spot should be adequate for _____;

   a 60-second spot for _____; 60s and 120s for

   _____

10. Production costs for TV spots need not be expensive. An expenditure of $_____
    for a 30- or 60-second spot is often adequate.

11. It is estimated that by 1980 there will be _____ to

    _____ million homes on cable TV.

12. How can a direct marketer reach cable TV homes other than through the medium
    of TV commercials?

    _____

    _____

13. What advantages are promised direct response advertisers through the medium of
    interactive cable TV?

    _____

    _____

    _____

    _____

14. Name the three major radio formats available to all direct response advertisers.

    1. _____ 2. _____

    3. _____
15. What types of merchandise do not readily lend themselves to direct sales via radio?

    _____

    _____

    _____

16. What types of merchandise and/or propositions do readily lend themselves to direct

    sales via radio? _____

    _____

    _____

17. What is the determining factor in establishing the length of a radio commercial?

_____

_____

18. What is the principal advantage of a commercially produced radio spot?

_____

19. What is the principal advantage of a live radio spot?

_____

_____

Pilot Project

Interactive cable TV is now an ongoing test program in El Segundo, California. You have an opportunity to reach 1,000 homes, each equipped with a console, enabling subscribers to "converse" directly with the station about your proposition.

Your product, called Rapid-Read, is a self-study rapid reading program selling for $69.95 (either one payment of $69.95, or 12 equal monthly payments of $6.50, including interest. Monthly payments may be added to the subscriber's monthly bill).

The program consists of 12 booklets, plus a timing device to measure reading speed. Rapid-Read is to be offered on a 30-day free trial basis.

Your assignment:

1. Prepare one 120-second commercial designed to get trial orders.
2. Prepare two 30-second commercials, to be tested against each other in obtaining inquiries.

When writing the commercials, be sure to take full advantage of the opportunities of interactive cable TV that let the subscriber "talk" directly with the station.

124

Chapter 6 Co-Ops

The use of co-ops by direct marketers has been expanding at an increasing rate over the past several years, especially as postage rates have risen. Best "guesstimate" is there are more than 300 co-ops available at present. Most marketing men have thought of co-ops primarily as cents-off coupons mailed to Mrs. Homemaker by the millions via a Donnelley or Metromail co-op. And this is still the major route for the package goods marketer. But direct marketers do not use co-ops for the purpose of creating store sales. Direct marketers use co-ops to get inquiries or sales direct.

Some Co-Op Myths Dispelled

Over the years some myths have developed about co-ops, particularly consumer co-ops. Two major misconceptions, according to the market research firm R. H. Bruskin Associates, are:

1. Response decreases as number of inserts increases; and
2. Inclusion of mail order offers, such as film and magazine offers (which solicit mail response), with cents-off offers (which solicit in-store redemption) has a negative effect on cents-off offers.

Research on Metromail co-op mailings resulted in some surprising findings. For the average coupon, the total recognition level was actually slightly higher, with 12 inserts over six inserts. Total recognition was only 7% less for 15 to 18 inserts when compared to six inserts. And mail order offers seemed to have no adverse effect on store coupon offers. Coupon redemption rates for store coupon offers are surprising to many. For example, typical redemption rates are 15% to 17% on a Birds Eye coupon in a Donnelley co-op, and a similar figure for the Rise N Dine General Foods co-op in conjunction with Metromail.

Special Interest Co-Ops Grow

A spate of special interest co-ops has become available in the past decade. Through special interest co-ops, direct marketers can reach clearly identifiable audiences with common interests at low cost. A classic example of a special interest co-op mailing is the one offered by Joe Kayser of Teen Mail. Kayser claims the all-time response record from a co-op mailing.

He reports that a mailing to one million college girls — 500,000 known to be mail order respondents — produced over 750,000 total replies. There were 21 individual inserts, offering 21 different products, all carried in one envelope. Kayser points out that college girls are ultraresponsive to mail, far more than they are to magazine offers of like ads. He quotes Starch *read most* figures of 8%, 9%, or 10% for magazines against Teen Mail average readership of about 50%.

But as dramatic as the front end response figures are for the youth market co-op, the advertiser's prime interest is the back end — conversion to regular customers at the retail store level. According to Kayser, respondents choosing from an average of 21 inserts will redeem about 4$\frac{1}{2}$% of them, with a 69–70% conversion to regular customers.

There are special interest co-ops for practically every age and life style. Folks in the older age market can be reached through a co-op beamed at 2,800,000 buyers of a health product by mail. There is a baby product co-op—about three million names yearly; a newlywed co-op—about 1,200,000 names yearly.

One page of post cards from The Physicians' Market Place—*a post card publication beamed at the special interests of physicians.*

126

Growth of Post Card Co-Ops

Co-ops that use a post card as the format instead of loose sheets have grown by leaps and bounds to special interest lists. North American Publishing Co. of Philadelphia is a leader in post card co-ops for special interest markets. Post cards appear in bound booklets. Advertisers may purchase a full page, two-thirds of a page, or one-third of a page. All post cards are perforated. The advertising message appears on the front of the card, the return address on its back.

Among North American's co-ops is one for the educational market circulated to 67,000 grade schools, one for the data-processing field circulated to 68,000 data-processing executives, and one for the industrial field circulated to 40,000 purchasing agents or office managers. A post card co-op distributed by Thomas Publishing Co. goes to 210,000 buying influences from 104,000 manufacturing plants, none with fewer than 20 employees. And geographical splits are available, since the list is divided into four U.S. regions.

Many trade publications have seen the wisdom of providing a post card mailing program to their subscriber list. *Training in Business and Industry* is an example. They provide a booklet with direct response post cards, three-up, which they send to their subscription list. Thus all participating advertisers are assured that their message on a post card is going to readers with a special interest in training in business.

BUILDING OPERATING MANAGEMENT

407 E. Michigan St.
Milwaukee, Wis. 53201
414/271-4105

BUILDING OPERATING MANAGEMENT (est. 1954; published by Trade Press Publishing Co.)

EDITORIAL PURPOSE: Edited for administrative and middle management to help them improve the efficiency, economy and appearance of their buildings, including: commercial, industrial, educational and institutional.

TYPES OF ADVERTISERS: Mfrs. of building remodeling and replacement products; building interior and exterior housekeeping and maintenance products.

CIRCULATION: Audited by BPA. Pub. statement for 6 mos. ending Dec. 31, 1972: Average—62,650. Nov. issue analysis: Total—62,650. Commercial—19,775; Industrial—13,582; Hospitals/Nursing Homes—9,424; Hotels/Motels/Clubs/Restaurants—6,745; Religious Institutions—1,526; Schools—9,647; Architects—1,951.

DATA: Pub. monthly. Issued 1st of mo. Ad closing—5th of preceding mo. 1-time B/W nonbleed pg.—$1,200. Nonbleed ad size—7" x 10". Editions—National only. AIA.

Here's My INDUSTRIAL MARKETING Action Request! Please Send Your Media/Market Kit:

Name _____ Title _____

Company _____ Phone _____
(area)

Street _____

City _____ State _____ Zip _____

——————————————Detach And Mail Today——————————————

THE OFFICE

1200 Summer St.
Stamford, Conn. 06904
203/327-9670

· LATERAL FILES ·
WRITING INSTRUMENTS

THE OFFICE (est. 1935; published by Office Publications, Inc.)

EDITORIAL PURPOSE: To provide executives and administrators authoritative articles and the necessary product information required to improve their business systems and reduce office, data handling and paperwork costs.

TYPES OF ADVERTISERS: Mfrs. of Office Equipment and Machines, Furniture, Data Processing Equipment and Supplies, Business Forms and Papers, Management Services.

CIRCULATION: Audited by BPA. Pub. statement for 6 mos. ending June 30, 1972: Average—107,323. May issue analysis: Total—108,248. Corporate Management—32,367; Financial Management—18,409; Purchasing Management—6,750; Administrative Executives and other Personnel—50,722.

DATA: Pub. monthly. Issued 1st of publ. mo. Ad closing—1st of preceding mo. 1-time B/W nonbleed pg.—$1,385. Nonbleed ad size—7" x 10". Editions—National; Demographic/Regional Editions—contact publisher for rates. AIA.

Here's My INDUSTRIAL MARKETING Action Request! Please Send Your Media/Market Kit:

Name _____ Title _____

Company _____ Phone _____
(area)

Street _____

City _____ State _____ Zip _____

Industrial Marketing's *Media Market Action Cards offer data on scores of business papers. Even though only two are shown, the co-op booklet is bound with four post cards to the page.*

Post cards illustrated are typical of 34 single post cards bound into one edition of "The Marketing Man's IDEA FILE," published by Potentials in Marketing.

Industrial Marketing provides a unique direct response card program which it mails to its subscription list in February and August. The action post cards enable the publication's readers to get media/market data and full information about marketing products and services.

Almost all post card co-ops are available through mailing list brokers. Standard Rate & Data also publishes a list.

Package Inserts

Still another medium for co-ops comprises package insert programs offered by many firms who sell through the direct response method. These co-ops have a special interest nature, in that the type of products a firm sells identifies the interests of the market.

Virgil D. Angerman, sales promotion manager of Boise Cascade Envelope Division, has compiled a comprehensive list of firms who offer the availability of package inserts. These data appear on the following page.

Acceptable inserts for package insert programs are usually folders, brochures, or wallet-type envelopes. Some firms limit the number of inserts they will enclose in a shipment. Others accept inserts only if they do not increase the postage on shipments.

As Angerman points out, "The planning of a package insert program is much like planning a direct mail campaign. The advertiser should evaluate the type of persons who will receive the package insert. The advertiser should ask if he or she is the logical prospect for a particular merchandise or service. The question should be raised, will the insert do a thorough selling job? Is the offer attractive? Have you made it easy to send an inquiry or order?"

128

FIRMS ACCEPTING PACKAGE INSERTS

Armstrong Nurseries, Inc.
Ontario, CA 91761
Tel. 714/984-1211, Ext. 30 or 48

John B. Tucker, Adv. Mgr.
Roses, dwarf fruit trees
Can insert: 200,000 yearly
Inserting charge: Inquire
Minimum test: 50,000

Berkey Prof. Processing, Inc.
130 Front St.
Hemstead, NY 11550
Tel. 516/486-3800
Harry Egelman, Mgr.
Prof. photographic processing
Customer profile: 90% male
Can insert: Inquire
Inserting charge: Inquire
Minimum test: Inquire

Best Photo of California
4782 Alvarado Canyon Road
San Diego, CA 92120
Tel. 714/286-0500
James C. Adamson, Mkt. Dir.
Mail order photo service
Customer profile: mostly female
Can insert: 25,000 monthly
Inserting charge: $25.00 M
Minimum test: 10,000

Best Photo Service, Inc.
100 Summer St.
Coolville, OH 45723
Tel. 614/667-3141
A.K. Summers, Pres.
Photofinishing
Customer profile: 75% female
Can insert: 2,000,000 yearly
Inserting charge: $25.00 M
Minimum test: 5,000

Broadway Photo Service
217 Darling Ave.
Nutley, NJ 07110
Tel. 201/777-3400, Ext. 9
Milton D. Goldsmith, Dir.
Photo service to teenagers
Customer profile: 95% female
Can insert: 250,000 yearly
Inserting charge: $25.00 M
Minimum test: 5,000

Calev Photo Labs, Inc.
21-20 45th Rd.
Long Island City, NY 11101
Tel. 212/361-1513
Benjamin B. Calev, Pres.
Film processing
Customer profile: 80% female
Can insert: 500,000 yearly
Inserting charge: $25.00 M
Minimum test: 10,000

J. Carlton's, Inc.
176 Madison Ave.
New York, NY 10001
Tel. 212/683-8180
Paul A. Goldner, Pres.
General Mdse. & gifts
Customer profile: 60% female
Can insert: 300,000 yearly
Inserting charge: $35.00 M
Minimum test: 5,000

Colorcraft Corporation
3000 Croasdaile Rd.
Durham, NC 27705
Tel. 919/383-5596
Donald D. France, V.P. Marketing
Photofinishing
Customer profile: 60% female
Can insert: 600,000 yearly
Inserting charge: $25.00 M
Minimum test: 25,000

Colorcraft Corp. - New Haven Div.
290 Grand Ave.
New Haven, CT 06513
Tel. 203/562-3161
Nate Maresca, Div. Mgr.
Photofinishing
Customer profile: 70% female
Can insert: 60,000 yearly
Inserting charge: $25.00 M
Minimum test: 5,000

Colorcraft Corp., Rockford Div.
214 N. Church St., Box 102
Rockford, IL 61105
Tel. 815/962-5507
Thomas G. Krause, Vice-Pres.
Photofinishing
Customer profile: 70% female
Can insert: 10,000 monthly
Inserting charge: Inquire
Minimum test: 10,000

Combine Camera
225 Hempstead Turnpike
West Hempstead, NY 11552
Tel. 516/481-4500
Henry Becker
Photographic supplies
Customer profile: 70% female
Can insert: 50,000 yearly
Inserting charge: $25.00 M or exchange
Minimum test: 3,000

David C. Cook Publishing Co.
850 N. Grove Ave.
Elgin, IL 50120
Tel. 312/741-2400
Bob Westenberg, Adv. Mgr.
Religious Lesson Material & Mdse.
Customer profile: 85% female
Can insert: 6,000-20,000 monthly
Inserting charge: $25.00 M
Minimum test: 5,000

Joan Cook Co.
1241 N.E. 8th Ave.
Fort Lauderdale, FL 33304
Tel. 305/764-0171
James T. Cook
Gifts & housewares
Customer profile: 90% female
Can insert: 2,000 monthly
Inserting charge: $25.00 M
Minimum test: 5,000

Data Color
1236 S. Central Ave.
Glendale, CA 91204
Tel. 213/245-7711
G.E. Keeney, Pres.
Prof. M.O. photofinishing
Customer profile: 90% male
Can insert: 5,000 monthly
Inserting charge: $25.00 M
Minimum test: 1,000

Walter Drake & Sons , Inc.
Drake Building
Colorado Springs, CO 80940
Tel. 303/596-3140
Carl H. Mott, Gen. Mgr.
Mail Order Mdse.
Customer profile: 85% female
Can insert: Inquire
Inserting charge: Inquire
Minimum test: 10,000

Elan Cosmetic Corp. Intl.
200 East Ontario St.
Chicago, IL 60611
Tel. 312/943-4177, Ext. 22
S.M. French, List Mgr.
Cosmetic items of our mfgr.
Customer profile: 99% female
Can insert: 120,000 yearly
Inserting charge: $30.00 M
Minimum test: 2,000

Farmer Seed & Nursery Co.
Faribault, MN 55021
Tel. 507/334-6421, Ext. 23

George L. Wiberg, Exec. V.P.
Seed & Nursery Supplies
Customer profile: 50% male
Can insert: 75,000 yearly
Inserting charge: $20-30 M
Minimum test: 5,000

James G. Fast Company
1820 W. Roscoe Ave.
Chicago, IL 60657
Tel. 312/248-3660, Ext. 34
Martin Michalek, Circ. Mgr.
Professional Apparel
Customer profile: 95% female
Can insert: 25,000 monthly
Inserting charge: $30.00 M
Minimum test: 5,000

Earl Ferris Nursery
811 Fourth St., N.E.
Hampton, IO 50441
Tel. 515/456-2563
Earl Ferris, Vice-Pres.
Nursery stock
Can insert: 20,000 Spring only
Inserting charge: $25.00M
Minimum test: 3,000

Fiesta Photo
2304 Santa Maria
Laredo, TX 78040
Tel. 512/722-5161
Dennis Meurer
Photofinishing
Customer profile: 60% female
Can insert: 10,000 monthly
Inserting charge: Inquire
Minimum test: 1,000

Fingerhut Products Company
3104 W. Lake St.
Minneapolis, MN 55416
Tel. 612/927-8471
Al Kauder, Mktg. Acq. Mgr.
Household Pdts. & Apparel
Customer profile: 50% male
Can insert: 5,000,000 yearly
Inserting charge: $25.00 M
Minimum test: 10,000

Foster & Gallagher, Inc.
6523 North Galena Rd.
Peoria, IL 61601
Tel. 309/691-4610, Ext. 242
    William Spray, Circ. Mgr.
    Mail order gifts & housewares
    Customer profile: 90% female
    Can insert: 2,500,000 yearly
    Inserting charge: $30.00 M
    Minimum test: 10,000

Foster-Trent, Inc
2345 Boston Post Rd.
Larchmont, NY 10538
Tel. 914/834-7370
    William M. Kenny, Media Dir.
    Sporting goods, housewares,
        novelties & gift items
    Customer profile: 50% male
    Can insert: 79,000 monthly
    Inserting charge: $25.00 M
    Minimum test: 5,000

Fotomat Corporation
920 Kline St.
La Jolla, CA 92037
Tel. 714/459-2360, Ext. 367
    Gerald M. Hatfield, Dir. of Merch.
    Photo Processing
    Customer profile: 55% female
    Can insert: 15,000,000 yearly
    Inserting charge: $25.00 M
    Minimum test: 10,000

Frederick's of Hollywood
6608 Hollywood Blvd.
Hollywood, CA 90028
Tel. 213/466-5151
    Joseph Nussbaum, Vice Pres.
    Ladies apparel & accessories
    Customer profile: 90% female
    Can insert: 40,000 monthly
    Inserting charge: $25.00 M
    Minimum test: 10,000

Fulltone Photo Co., Inc.
1404 S. Shelby St.
Louisville, KY 40217
Tel. 502/634-9471
    R. Paul Baker, Gen. Mgr.
    M.O. Photofinishing
    Customer profile: 75% female
    Can insert: 50,000 yearly
    Inserting charge: $20.00 M up
    Minimum test: 1,000

Gift-Pax, Inc.
Hand-Mail, Inc. Division
29 Hempstead Gardens Drive
West Hempstead, NY 11552
Tel. 516/485-0660, Ext. 21
    Arthur M. Rein, Sales Manager
    Product Sampling
    Customer profile: 85% female
    Can insert: 550,000 monthly
    Inserting charge: $15 M to $30 M
    Minimum test: 10,000

Grace Holmes Club Plan
Martin Street
Ashton, RI 02864
Tel. 401/723-9500, Ext. 213
    Ted Klein, Sales Prom. Mgr.
    General Merchandise Catalog
    Customer profile: 99% female
    Can insert: 25,000 monthly
    Inserting charge: $30.00 M
    Minimum test: 10,000

Greenland Studios
4500 Northwest 135th St.
Miami, FL 33054
Tel. 305/688-3531
    S. Kaplan, Vice-Pres.
    Gifts, novelties, needlework,
        fashions, books
    Customer profile: 80% female
    Can insert: 1,200,000 yearly
    Inserting charge: $30.00 M
    Minimum test: 10,000

Herrschner Pharmaceuticals
2200 E. Empire Ave.
Benton Harbor, MI 49022
Tel. 616/927-4461, Ext. 67
    Thomas C. Butcher, Adv. Coord.
    Health products
    Customer profile: 52% female
    Can insert: 200,000 yearly
    Inserting charge: $25.00 M
    Minimum test: 5,000

House of Wesley
2200 East Oakland Ave.
Bloomington, IL 61701
Tel. 309/662-3511
    James W. Owen, Pres.
    Horticultural Products
    Customer profile: 50% male
    Can insert: 1,000,000 yearly
    Inserting charge: $25.00 M
    Minimum test: 5,000

Hudson National, Inc.
89 Seventh Ave.
New York, NY 10011
Tel. 212/675-1320, Ext. 218
    Judy Breen, Mktg. Dept.
    Vitamins, drugs & toiletries
    Customer profile: 70% female
    Can insert: 300,000 yearly
    Inserting charge: $30.00 M
    Minimum test: 10,000

Jack Rabbit Company, Inc.
145 W. Kennedy St.
Spartanburgh, SC 29301
Tel. 803/585-4838, Ext. 36
    L.L. Larrabee, Mgr.
    Photofinishing
    Customer profile: 80% female
    Can insert: 600,000 yearly
    Inserting charge: Inquire
    Minimum test: 60,000

Jay Norris Corp.
31 Hanse Ave.
Freeport, NY 11520
Tel. 516/868-1600
    J. Jacobs, Pres.
    General Mdse.
    Customer profile: 60% male
    Can insert: 300,000 yearly
    Inserting charge: $35.00 M
    Minimum test: 5,000

Jim Dandy Film Service
Newberry, SC 29108
Tel. 802/276-1535

    J. Ted Pearson
    Film developing
    Customer profile: 75% female
    Can insert: Inquire
    Inserting charge: Inquire
    Minimum test: 1,000

Johnson Smith Co.
35075 Automation Dr.
Mount Clemens, MI 48043
Tel. 313/791-2800
    Paul Hoenle, Vice-Pres.
    Novelties, gifts & hobbies
    Customer profile: 85% male
    Can insert: 300,000 yearly
    Inserting charge: $30.00 M
    Minimum test: 5,000

J.W. Jung Seed Co.
Randolph, WI 53956
Tel. 414/326-3121

    John W. Jung, Gen. Mgr.
    Mail order seed & nursery
    Customer profile: 60% female
    Can insert: 140,000 Jan. 1 - June 1
    Inserting charge: $25.00 M
    Minimum test: 3,500

Kelly Brothers Nurseries, Inc.
Dansville, NY 14437
Tel. 716/987-2211

    John W. Kelly, Secy.-Treas.
    Nursery trees & plants
    Inquire for details

Lafayette Radio Electronics
111 Jericho Turnpike
Syosset, NY 11791
Tel. 516/921-7700, Ext. 321
    William D. Coale, Asst. Oper. Mgr.
    Radio Electronics
    Can insert: 25,000 monthly
    Inserting charge: $25.00 M
    Minimum test: 10,000

130

Lee Wards
1200 St. Charles
Elgin, IL 60120
Tel. 312/695-6000, Ext. 337

Mail Order
Customer profile: 90% female
Can insert: 2,200,000 yearly
Inserting charge: $25.00 M If
 by state selection: $30.00 M
Minimum test: 10,000

Meadowbrook Photo, Inc.
Box 490
Hornell, NY 14843
Tel. 607/324-0400
James I. Grimm, Pres.
Film processing
Write for information

Michigan Bulb Company
1950 Waldorf, N.W.
Grand Rapids, MI 49550
Tel. 616/453-5401
Horticultural products
Customer profile: 50% male
Can insert: 600,000 yearly
Inserting charge: $25.00 M
Minimum test: 5,000

National Bellas Hess, Inc.
715 Armour Rd.
Kansas City, MO 64116
Tel. 816/471-3080, Ext. 221
Ed Heim, List Mgr.
Mail Order Mdse.
Customer profile: 90% female
Can insert: 60,000 monthly to
 paid accts.
Inserting charge: $25.00 M
Minimum test: 5,000

National Photo Corp.
914 S. Detroit
Tulsa, OK 74120
Tel. 918/583-8127
Gerald E. Daugherty, Vice-Pres.
Photofinishing
Customer profile: 85% family
Can insert: 1,775,000 yearly
Inserting charge: $25.00 M
Minimum test: 5,000

Peoples Photo Center
221 S. Walnut St.
Muncie, IN 47305
Tel. 317/288-0247
Richard G. Handley, Owner
Film processing
Customer profile: 75% female
Can insert: 5,000 monthly
Inserting charge: $25.00 M
Minimum test: 5,000

R.P. Sales Company
160 Amherst St.
East Orange, NJ 07019
Tel. 201/673-1751
Robert Pinkus, Pres.
Coin values catalog
Customer profile: 60% male
Can insert: 10,000 monthly
Inserting charge: Inquire
Minimum test: 2,000

Raheb Color Corp.
5428 Hollywood Blvd.
Los Angeles, CA 90027
Tel. 213/462-6468
A.P. Raheb, Pres.
Photofinishing
Customer profile: 53% female
Can insert: 300,000 yearly
Inserting charge: $20-$25.00 M
Minimum test: 25,000

Schreiber Snapshot Service
31 W. Westfield Ave.
Roselle Park, NJ 07204
Tel. 201/241-0112
Byrant E. Schreiber, Pres.
Photo Service & Supplies
Can insert: 50,000 yearly
Inserting charge: $25.00 M
Minimum test: 5,000

Signet Club Plan
265 Third St.
Cambridge, MA 02142
Tel. 617/864-6600, Ext. 87
Robert Goldstein, Sales Prom. Mgr.
General Merchandise Catalog
Customer profile: 100% female
Can insert: 400,000 yearly
Inserting charge: $25.00 M
Minimum test: 5,000

Sleepy Hollow Gifts
6651 Arlington Blvd.
Falls Church, VA 22042
Tel. 703/534-0921
M.O. Michelsen
Quality gifts
Customer profile: 80% female
Can insert: Approx. 90,000 yearly
Inserting charge: $25.00 M
Minimum test: 5,000

Spectra Color Lab, Inc.
4302 W. Victory Blvd.
Burbank, CA 91504
Tel. 213/843-3232
Jim Sullivan, Pres.
Prof. photo service
Customer profile: 85% male
Can insert: 250,000 yearly
Inserting charge: Negotiate
Minimum test: 10,000

Stern's Nurseries, Inc.
404 William St.
Geneva, NY 14456
Tel. 315/789-1922
Robert E. Thompson, Mgr.
Nursery stock
Customer profile: 55% male
Can insert: 125,000 yearly
Inserting charge: $27.00 M
Minimum test: 5,000

Stickley-Siver, Inc.
200 Plaza Drive
Binghamton, NY 13902
Tel. 607/729-9311, Ext. 31
Karl B. Stickley, Jr., Exec. V.P.
Photofinishing
Can insert: 360,000 yearly
Inserting charge: $22.50 M
Minimum test: 10,000

Suburbia, Inc.
366 Wacouta
St. Paul, MN 55101
Tel. 612/225-7873
T.B. Westbee, Pres.
General Gift Mdse.
Customer profile: 67% female
Can insert: 2,000,000 yearly
Inserting charge: $25.00 M
Minimum test: 5,000

Thomas, Smith & Butterfield
3170 N.W. 36th St.
Miami, FL 33142
Tel. 305/633-0531
Alton W. Thomas, Pres.
Photofinishing
Customer profile: 65% female
Can insert: 50,000 monthly
Inserting charge: $25.00 M
Minimum test: Inquire

Two Brothers, Inc.
808 Washington Ave.
St. Louis, MO 63101
Tel. 314/421-0026
Personalized labels & mdse.
Customer profile: 75% female
Can insert: 25,000 monthly
Inserting charge: $25.00 M
Minimum test: 5,000

U.S. General Supply Co.
100 General Place
Jericho, NY 11753
Tel. 516/333-5000
Tom Bauer, Adv. Mgr.
Tools & hardware
Customer profile: 99% male
Can insert: 15,000 monthly
Inserting charge: $25.00 M
Minimum test: 5,000

U.S. Health Club, Inc.
25 North Broadway
Yonkers, NY 10701
Tel. 212/584-9686
  Peter Small, Pres.
  Vitamins
  Customer profile: 50% female
  Can insert: 5,000 monthly
  Inserting charge: $27.50 M
  Minimum test: 2,500

The Waltz Camera Man, Inc.
438 Sixth St. N.W.
Canton, OH 44701
Tel. 216/455-9421, Ext. 48
  Jim A. Arnold, Mgr. Adv. Dept.
  Photofinishing
  Customer profile: 60% female
  Can insert: 10,000 - 50,000 monthly
  Inserting charge: Inquire
  Minimum test: 5,000

Warshawsky & Co.
1104 S. Wabash Ave.
Chicago, IL 60605
Tel. 312/225-6800, Ext. 301
  L.B. Patterson, Sales Prom. Mgr.
  Auto Parts & Accessories
  Customer profile: 98% male
  Can insert: 100,000 monthly
  Exchange basis only: write for details
  details

Wayne's Photo Finishing, Inc.
111 National Ave.
Chehalis, WA 98532
Tel. 206/748-8891, Ext. 35
  Charles M. Lidberg, Vice-Pres.
  Photo processing wholesale
  Customer profile: 60% female
  Can insert: 100,000 monthly
  Inserting charge: $25.00 M
  Minimum test: 10,000

The Writewell Co.
108 Massachusetts Ave.
Boston, MA 02115
Tel. 617/536-2625
  Stephen F. Harris, Pres.
  DeLuxe name & address labels
  Customer profile: 65% female
  Can insert: 2,000 weekly
  Inserting charge: $25.00 M
  Minimum test: None

Zercher Photo, Inc.
P.O. Box 59
Topeka, KS 66601
Tel. 913/235-2341
  Photofinishing
  Customer profile: 70% female
  Can insert: 25,000 monthly
  Inserting charge: $25.00 M
  Minimum test: 5,000

Mail Co-Op Costs Enticing

On the basis of economy alone, mail co-ops are enticing. It can almost be said there's a rate for every budget. And, as in print and broadcast, many of the rates are "negotiable."

To give some approximate rates, the North American Publishing Co.'s post card mailing to 67,000 grade schools costs approximately $695 complete, including preparation, printing, and postage. It costs approximately $1,900 complete for the 210,000 circulation guaranteed for the Thomas Publishing Co.'s post card mailing.

Donnelley's co-ops vary between approximately $10 and $18 per thousand, plus printing, depending on volume and frequency. Many co-ops going to specialized markets run $25 to $35 per thousand, plus printing. Then there are PI (per inquiry) deals offered by some co-ops. For the most part, such co-ops negotiate a per inquiry charge or per order charge against a minimum guarantee.

Any way it's figured, distribution cost for a co-op mailing comes in at about a fourth or less of the cost of a solo mailing. Few expect to get the same percent of response on a co-op as on mailing solo, but the arithmetic does not require it.

Newspaper Co-Ops

A truly imaginative approach to co-ops is a newspaper co-op developed by Consumers Communication Corporation of Shawnee Mission, Kansas. This particular co-op is known as the *Flagwaver*, from the fact that this four-page insert, appearing in Sunday newspapers, contains a number of perforated coupons which may be removed by the consumer for in-store redemption or, in the case of direct response advertisers, for mailing directly to the advertiser.

Ted Isaac, President of Consumers Communication Corporation, stresses the high readership of the *Flagwaver* when used as a Sunday newspaper insert. Starch figures substantiate his claim. Here is what Starch figures showed for one particular release of the *Flagwaver*.

	Noting Scores, *Flagwaver*	Women Only Sunday Magazines
Front cover	97%	95%
All 4-color ad pages	89%	63%
All food 4-color ad pages	89%	67%
Food 4-color half-pages	73%	49%
Coupons as a class	72%	———

132

Front of four-page full-color "Flagwaver" newspaper insert. Insert includes a total of six different coupons.

While *Flagwaver* inserts compare very favorably with Sunday magazines, it should be noted that the *Flagwaver* contains only four pages, while the Sunday supplement magazines run to 48 pages and more.

While the *Flagwaver* is generally distributed as a Sunday insert, there is a weekday version now available which is of special interest for in-store coupon redemption. Over 100 newspapers have agreed to insert the *Flagwaver* on the best food day of the week.

A derivation of the *Flagwaver* newspaper supplement co-op is the envelope newspaper co-op, also developed by Ted Isaac. The envelope newspaper co-op is a takeoff of the Donnelley mail co-op. A common envelope is developed and loose inserts are enclosed in it, so that when the newspaper reader receives his or her newspaper an envelope full of coupons and direct response offers falls out.

Other Co-Ops

While special interest, package insert, and newspaper co-ops offer mass distribution opportunities to direct marketers at low cost, there are also several offbeat co-ops available. For instance, many giant mail order firms have turned to accepting post card inserts in their catalogs. Lee Wards, for example, which mails its catalog in the millions, offers a limited number of card inserts in each catalog. Similarly, some catalogs offer page ads to selected advertisers.

Not to be outdone are paperback book publishers, who offer card insert availability to direct response advertisers. Circulation can run into the millions. Direct response advertisers can select distribution by title. Thus the advertiser can pretty well guess the readers' demographics by the type of book they are buying. *Gone with the Wind* would probably be a good distribution channel for a female offer; *The Day of the Jackal,* for a male offer; and so forth.

Perhaps the largest single source for offbeat co-ops is Leonard G. Holland of Woodmere, Long Island. He has offered co-op distribution through the media of egg cartons and milk cartons, just to mention two. Still another offbeat medium is the "take one" bulletin board in supermarkets.

Compiled vs. Direct Response Lists

While compiled lists are ideal for in-store coupon redemption, such as the top 300 *Sales Management* markets offered by Donnelley, direct marketers have had a thirst for co-ops which go totally to direct response lists—lists of people and firms who have previously responded by mail.

One such co-op is the *Business Buyer's Guide,* of Plainfield, New Jersey. This firm offers a guaranteed circulation of 200,000 mail order buyers in the business field. The publisher states that all 200,000 have spent at least $50 within the past six months.

While the *Business Buyer's Guide* goes to businessmen, there is nothing to compare in size with a consumer co-op which is called The Big List. It is a conglomerate, unduplicated list of 20 million names of consumers who have responded by mail.

Some Sobering Thoughts about Co-Ops

While co-ops offer tremendous distribution opportunities at low cost, it should be recognized that co-ops are not for everyone. One of the multimillion direct response lists available for co-ops is that of Film Corporation of America. Mort Adler of FCA provides some sobering thoughts about co-ops. He states, "Participants should know their response will not be as good as a solo mailing. Therefore, a judgment must be made as to

134

whether cheaper cost in mail is worth lower positive results. In my experience, most national advertisers think it is."

He cautions, "Many companies are offering co-op mailings as a means of covering their postage and thereby getting their own piece mailed free. If postage is not covered, mailing is canceled. Therefore, prospective co-op participants should get a positive guarantee before agreeing to go into the deal."

As Adler aptly states, co-ops are not for everyone. But used correctly, they can offer additional circulation at reasonable cost. Co-ops are not likely for selling a $400 calculator, but co-ops are likely for getting inquiries about a $400 calculator. Co-ops are *very* likely for in-store coupon redemption. Co-ops are *very* likely for scores of direct response offers requiring a minimum of information for a targeted audience.

Self-Quiz

1. Two of the major misconceptions about co-ops are:

    1. _____

    2. _____

    _____

    _____

2. Typical redemption percentages for cents-off coupons are _____% to _____%.
3. Define a special interest co-op.

    _____

    _____

    _____

4. Define a post card co-op.

    _____

    _____

    _____

5. What is the primary advantage of package inserts?

    _____

    _____

    _____

6. The average cost of co-ops going to specialized markets runs $_____ to $_____ per thousand.
7. Define *Flagwaver.*

    _____

8. Name three types of offbeat co-ops available to direct marketers.

   1. _____

   2. _____

   3. _____

9. Many co-ops never see the light of day for lack of participation. What safeguard should a direct marketer take to avoid the loss of cost of material prepared in anticipation of circulation?

   _____

   _____

   _____

   _____

Pilot Project

You are looking for ways and means to beat the high cost of mailing. Co-ops have been suggested to you.

Your product is a digital AM/FM clock/radio selling for $49.95. You have always sold via solo mailings. But now your costs have got out of line. Hence your desire to see if you can make co-ops work.

You decide to make two tests in a post card publication called *Business Market Place,* mailed four times yearly to a cross-section of 100,000 businessmen. The publisher will allow a split-run. Therefore your assignment is:

1. Prepare copy for a single post card, size $5\frac{7}{8} \times 3\frac{3}{4}$ — designed to produce inquiries.
2. Prepare copy for a double card, size $5\frac{7}{8} \times 7\frac{1}{2}$ — designed to produce direct orders.

In addition to these two tests in a post card publication, review the list of firms accepting package inserts starting on page 129 and select six that you believe to be likely for your particular product. Give your reasons for each selection.

Chapter 7 Telephone Marketing

The telephone has been around for about 100 years, yet only in the last decade has it been adopted as a marketing medium and only during the last few years has its full potential begun to be recognized and exploited.

The material in this chapter has been provided by Murray Roman, who has played a major role in developing the telephone as a marketing medium. He was a pioneer in the use of the telephone—his first program in the '60s for the Ford Motor Co. placed more than 20 million calls to produce two leads per day for 23,000 salesmen in more than 7,000 U.S. dealerships. This was the first use of the telephone as a mass marketing tool. He is now the chairman of Campaign Communications Institute of America, Inc. in New York, an organization that specializes in developing and implementing telephone marketing programs for business and industrial clients, political campaigns, and fund-raising associations. His company is the largest of its type. It is credited with creating the concepts and setting the standards for what has become a multimillion dollar industry. Campaign Communications Institute of America, Inc. provides marketing services for some of the largest corporations in the world.

Why the upsurge in the use of the telephone? Saturation of much of the mass media, for one thing. But there have also been extreme changes in life style among consumers in the United States.

The consumer has changed and has caused business to change products, services, and marketing techniques. Ask the automobile designers in Detroit. Question the food companies and the fashion people.

The consumer has moved away from much of the glossy, toward a more *natural* approach both in products and services.

Perhaps a backlash to such things as super promotions, extra giant packaging, and fantabulous product claims has brought the consumer in America today to a saturation point. And the result can be seen in organic foods, unit pricing, consumer advocates, no-bra looks, and minicars which transport a person to his destination at a fraction of the cost of cars having sex-symbol fenders ornamented with triple chrome strips.

The consumers of the 1970s are striving to be unprogrammed . . . reaching for individual identity. Their rebellion is spreading throughout the consumer populace and manifesting itself in many different ways.

One thing is sure. It has had a powerful and dynamic effect on the corporate community. The message is loud and clear: "Listen to me—do something about my complaints—I want to talk to someone!" Among the prime beneficiaries of this revolt has been telephone marketing, for as a direct marketing medium it is compatible with what is happening in this country. It is a person-to-person medium. Telephone communication is the closest thing to eyeball-to-eyeball selling that is economically feasible.

The Telephone Is a Mass Medium

The telephone is a way of life in the United States.

On an average day throughout the year, approximately 400 million telephone calls are completed. Each year, in this country, more than 150 billion telephone conversations are held.

Now, with technological breakthroughs which have broadened the ways it can be applied and the scope of its effect, telephone marketing can accurately be classified as a mass medium. It is the only person-to-person mass medium that exists today.

The telephone is compatible with all other media, and today there is hardly a direct response campaign in which the telephone is not in some way used as an integral facet to complement others.

The telephone is used with other media as a door-opener or a follow-up for direct mail or a personal sales call. It is also used as an efficient means of advertising and prospecting, and for research, credit, and direct sales. The multimedia revolution heralded for so long is happening today. Now!

Other media, including direct mail and personal sales calls, are beset by skyrocketing costs. Each year, however, advances in equipment and other technological applications have either lowered the cost of using the telephone or resulted in improved operations at only slightly higher prices.

In 1950, a station-to-station, three-minute telephone call from New York to Philadelphia during the daytime cost 45¢. Today the cost is only 55¢.

In 1952, a call to San Francisco from New York was $2.50. Now it's only $1.35, and if you wait until after 5:00 P.M., which is 2:00 P.M. in California, the cost per station-to-station call drops to 85¢ for the first three minutes.

Also fostering the growth of telephone as a direct response medium is more sophisticated computerization.

Almost everything is being put on computer tapes, including census data that assure marketers of virtually unlimited availability of the lists needed to implement a program for any consumer bloc.

Varied Uses

There are many uses for the telephone, both in concert with other media and as a viable alternative.

1. *Sales*
   Direct application of telephone communication to solicit orders from prospects who have indicated prior interest (inquiries, etc.) or those who are reasonably defined as being in your potential audience.
2. *Sales Appointments*
   Telephone communication in order to screen and qualify prospects for interest and set a specific appointment for a personal sales visit.
3. *Lead Generation*
   The telephone as a prospecting tool, pinpointing individuals or groups with high sales potential to be followed up by a specific offering.
4. *Renewals*
   Maximizing repeat sales from present customers. Usually the telephone is used on an incremental basis after regular renewal efforts have achieved their maximal return.
5. *Marginal Account Coverage*
   Using telephone contact to cover those accounts too small in volume or too dispersed to be efficiently handled by a salesman.
6. *Conversions*
   Follow-up by telephone to convert and upgrade "trial" or marginal sale into a regular, profitable customer.

| | | FULL TIME | | | | | | | MEASURED TIME | | | | | | | | | | | |
| Service Area → | A1 | A2 | A3 | A4 | A5 | A6 | A1 | A2 | A3 | A4 | A5 | A6 | A1 | A2 | A3 | A4 | A5 | A6 |
							FIRST 10 HOURS						*EACH ADDITIONAL HOUR					
ALABAMA	$ 765	$1,070	$1,275	$1,480	$1,580	$1,835	$185	$215	$235	$255	$275	$310	$13.80	$16.10	$17.60	$19.20	$20.60	$23.30
ARIZONA	970	1,275	1,480	1,685	1,785	1,885	205	235	255	295	305	315	15.30	17.60	19.20	22.00	22.80	23.70
ARKANSAS	765	1,070	1,275	1,480	1,580	1,735	185	215	235	255	275	300	13.80	16.10	17.60	19.20	20.60	22.40
CALIFORNIA-NO.	1,070	1,375	1,685	1,785	1,885	1,940	215	245	295	305	315	320	16.10	18.50	22.00	22.80	23.70	24.10
CALIFORNIA-SO.	1,175	1,480	1,685	1,785	1,885	1,940	225	255	295	305	315	320	16.80	19.20	22.00	22.80	23.70	24.10
COLORADO	1,070	1,175	1,275	1,480	1,685	1,735	215	225	235	255	295	300	16.10	16.80	17.60	19.20	22.00	22.40
CONNECTICUT	510	765	1,375	1,630	1,785	1,990	135	185	245	285	305	325	10.20	13.80	18.50	21.30	22.80	24.50
DELAWARE	510	765	1,175	1,530	1,735	1,940	135	185	225	265	300	320	10.20	13.80	16.80	19.90	22.40	24.10
DISTRICT OF COLUMBIA	510	765	1,070	1,480	1,685	1,940	135	185	215	255	295	320	10.20	13.80	16.10	19.20	22.00	24.10
FLORIDA	1,070	1,375	1,480	1,580	1,685	1,940	215	245	255	275	295	320	16.10	18.50	19.20	20.60	22.00	24.10
GEORGIA	765	1,070	1,275	1,480	1,630	1,885	185	215	235	255	285	315	13.80	16.10	17.60	19.20	21.30	23.70
IDAHO	865	1,175	1,480	1,685	1,785	1,885	195	225	255	295	305	315	14.50	16.80	19.20	22.00	22.80	23.70
ILLINOIS-NO.	665	865	1,175	1,375	1,480	1,735	175	195	225	245	255	300	13.10	14.50	16.80	18.50	19.20	22.40
ILLINOIS-SO.	665	970	1,175	1,375	1,480	1,735	175	205	225	245	255	300	13.10	15.30	16.80	18.50	19.20	22.40
INDIANA	665	865	1,070	1,275	1,530	1,785	175	195	215	235	265	305	13.10	14.50	16.10	17.60	19.90	22.80
IOWA	765	1,070	1,175	1,480	1,580	1,685	185	215	225	255	275	295	13.80	16.10	16.80	19.20	20.60	22.00
KANSAS	865	1,070	1,175	1,480	1,630	1,685	195	215	225	255	285	295	14.50	16.10	16.80	19.20	21.30	22.00
KENTUCKY	665	865	1,070	1,275	1,530	1,835	175	195	215	235	265	310	13.10	14.50	16.10	17.60	19.90	23.30
LOUISIANA	865	1,175	1,375	1,530	1,685	1,785	195	225	245	265	295	305	14.50	16.80	18.50	19.90	22.00	22.80
MAINE	865	1,175	1,530	1,685	1,785	1,990	195	225	265	295	305	325	14.50	16.80	19.90	22.00	22.80	24.50
MARYLAND	510	765	1,175	1,530	1,735	1,940	135	185	225	265	300	320	10.20	13.80	16.80	19.90	22.40	24.10
MASSACHUSETTS	510	865	1,375	1,630	1,785	1,990	135	195	245	285	305	325	10.20	14.50	18.50	21.30	22.80	24.50
MICHIGAN-NO.	865	1,175	1,275	1,375	1,630	1,785	195	225	235	245	285	305	14.50	16.80	17.60	18.50	21.30	22.80
MICHIGAN-SO.	765	1,070	1,175	1,375	1,630	1,785	185	215	225	245	285	305	13.80	16.10	16.80	18.50	21.30	22.80
MINNESOTA	765	1,070	1,375	1,530	1,580	1,685	185	215	245	265	275	295	13.80	16.10	18.50	19.90	20.60	22.00
MISSISSIPPI	865	1,070	1,275	1,480	1,580	1,785	195	215	235	255	275	305	14.50	16.10	17.60	19.20	20.60	22.80
MISSOURI	865	970	1,175	1,375	1,530	1,735	195	205	225	245	265	300	14.50	15.30	16.80	18.50	19.90	22.40
MONTANA	1,070	1,275	1,480	1,630	1,735	1,785	215	235	255	285	300	305	16.10	17.60	19.20	21.30	22.40	22.80
NEBRASKA	865	1,070	1,275	1,480	1,630	1,685	195	215	235	255	285	295	14.50	16.10	17.60	19.20	21.30	22.00
NEVADA	765	1,175	1,530	1,735	1,835	1,885	185	225	265	300	310	315	13.80	16.80	19.90	22.40	23.30	23.70
NEW HAMPSHIRE	610	970	1,375	1,630	1,785	1,990	165	205	245	285	305	325	12.20	15.30	18.50	21.30	22.80	24.50
NEW JERSEY	510	665	1,275	1,580	1,735	1,940	135	175	235	275	300	320	10.20	13.10	17.60	20.60	22.40	24.10
NEW MEXICO	970	1,175	1,375	1,580	1,685	1,785	205	225	245	275	295	305	15.30	16.80	18.50	20.60	22.00	22.80
NEW YORK-N.E.	665	1,070	1,275	1,580	1,735	1,940	175	215	235	275	300	320	13.10	16.10	17.60	20.60	22.40	24.10
NEW YORK-S.E.	510	970	1,275	1,580	1,735	1,940	135	205	235	275	300	320	10.20	15.30	17.60	20.60	22.40	24.10
NEW YORK-WEST	665	865	1,275	1,580	1,735	1,940	175	195	235	275	300	320	13.10	14.50	17.60	20.60	22.40	24.10
NORTH CAROLINA	765	970	1,175	1,480	1,685	1,885	185	205	225	255	295	315	13.80	15.30	16.80	19.20	22.00	23.70
NORTH DAKOTA	865	1,275	1,480	1,580	1,630	1,685	195	235	255	275	285	295	14.50	17.60	19.20	20.60	21.30	22.00
OHIO-NO.	665	865	1,070	1,275	1,630	1,835	175	195	215	235	285	310	13.10	14.50	16.10	17.60	21.30	23.30
OHIO-SO.	665	865	1,070	1,275	1,630	1,835	175	195	215	235	285	310	13.10	14.50	16.10	17.60	21.30	23.30
OKLAHOMA	865	1,070	1,275	1,480	1,630	1,685	195	215	235	255	285	295	14.50	16.10	17.60	19.20	21.30	22.00
OREGON	865	1,275	1,630	1,735	1,885	1,940	195	235	285	300	315	320	14.50	17.60	21.30	22.40	23.70	24.10
PENNSYLVANIA-E.	510	765	1,175	1,480	1,685	1,885	135	185	225	255	295	315	10.20	13.80	16.80	19.20	22.00	23.70
PENNSYLVANIA-W.	665	765	1,175	1,480	1,685	1,885	175	185	225	255	295	315	13.10	13.80	16.80	19.20	22.00	23.70
RHODE ISLAND	510	865	1,375	1,630	1,785	1,990	135	195	245	285	305	325	10.20	14.50	18.50	21.30	22.80	24.50
SOUTH CAROLINA	765	1,070	1,275	1,480	1,685	1,885	185	215	235	255	285	315	13.80	16.10	17.60	19.20	21.30	23.70
SOUTH DAKOTA	865	1,175	1,275	1,530	1,630	1,685	195	225	235	265	285	295	14.50	16.80	17.60	19.90	21.30	22.00
TENNESSEE	865	970	1,175	1,375	1,530	1,835	195	205	225	245	265	310	14.50	15.30	16.80	18.50	19.90	23.30
TEXAS-E.	970	1,275	1,480	1,580	1,685	1,735	205	235	255	275	295	300	15.30	17.60	19.20	20.60	22.00	22.40
TEXAS-S.	1,175	1,375	1,480	1,580	1,685	1,735	225	245	255	275	295	300	16.80	18.50	19.20	20.60	22.00	22.40
TEXAS-W.	1,070	1,275	1,480	1,580	1,685	1,735	215	235	255	275	295	300	16.10	17.60	19.20	20.60	22.00	22.40
UTAH	970	1,070	1,375	1,630	1,735	1,835	205	215	245	285	300	310	15.30	16.10	18.50	21.30	22.40	23.30
VERMONT	610	970	1,375	1,630	1,735	1,990	165	205	245	285	300	325	12.20	15.30	18.50	21.30	22.40	24.50
VIRGINIA	665	765	1,070	1,480	1,685	1,885	175	185	215	255	295	315	13.10	13.80	16.10	19.20	22.00	23.70
WASHINGTON	1,175	1,480	1,685	1,785	1,835	1,940	225	255	295	305	310	320	16.80	19.20	22.00	22.80	23.30	24.10
WEST VIRGINIA	610	765	1,070	1,375	1,685	1,885	165	185	215	245	295	315	12.20	13.80	16.10	18.50	22.00	23.70
WISCONSIN	665	1,070	1,275	1,480	1,530	1,735	175	215	235	255	275	300	13.10	16.10	17.60	19.20	19.90	22.40
WYOMING	865	1,175	1,375	1,530	1,685	1,785	195	225	245	265	295	305	14.50	16.80	18.50	19.90	22.00	22.80

*Fractional parts of an hour beyond the first 10 hours are measured in tenths of an hour or major fraction thereof. The charge per tenth of an hour is one-tenth of the additional hour charge.

7. *Customer Service*

Through a schedule of periodic telephone contacts to present customers or by establishing a customer call-in service, to accept new orders and handle any billing, shipping, or other fulfillment problems. The growth of the recently available "800" *Wide Area Telephone Service* (WATS) has opened a whole new vista for customer communications.

8. *Credit Jogging/Credit Establishment*

Using the telephone to spur payments of delinquent accounts or screen credit acceptance of new customers.

9. *Surveys*

Telephone as a traditional market research tool is used as an effective cost-efficient alternative to the personal interview in many research projects.

10. *Validations*

To insure the validity of a sale before fulfillment; in this role the telephone can "police" other types of direct sales efforts and help a sale to "stick."

Each of these categories describes a general sales objective. Their adaptation to a specific goal will refine and, in many cases, combine elements of several objectives into an integrated marketing plan.

Planning and Implementation

In deciding how best to realize the marketing potential of telephone communication, we must consider the qualities and limitations of the product or service being offered. While it may not be productive to attempt direct telephone sales to a prospect who has never seen or heard of an expensive, difficult to conceptualize offer, telephone follow-up of direct mail or coupon inquiries or setting a sales appointment for this same offer may be highly successful. In the same way, cost efficiencies would probably not allow for validation of a $5 or $10 sale—while telephone conversion or upgrading of this same customer could be very profitable.

The variances in possible calling lists also determine how effective a telephone offering will be. When testing a program, the best lists—inquiries, past and present customers, and prospects within a target group having a high response to other direct selling approaches for the same or similar offers—should be tested first, on the premise that if the best list doesn't produce, there is small likelihood that lesser lists will.

Telephone's flexibility not only enables the marketer to choose from a number of alternative objectives; it also allows him to be wrong and still succeed in the end. Once a telephone marketing plan is implemented, necessary modifications can be injected almost as soon as problem areas surface. Offers can be modified, sales approaches changed, and a nonproductive calling list exchanged for one generating an acceptable response—without waiting until all the returns are in and all the dollars have been spent. Once a telephone marketing plan has been established, a decision must be made how best to achieve its goal.

Do-It-Yourself or Buy

The first and most basic question is: Do you handle the telephone sales function internally or contract to use the services of a professional telephone marketing agency?

Before you decide to do it yourself, consider the requirements: Is there an internal base of experience and expertise in telephone marketing you can draw upon? Do you have personnel available who can design a specific telephone sales approach to maximize the impact of your sales message, train, supervise, and motivate telephone sales people to deliver it in the best possible way, and coordinate all support media needed for the campaign? Whether your plan calls for pre- or post-mailings, cooperating advertisements, follow-up contacts by salesmen, credit screening, order fulfillment, or invoicing, careful preparation is necessary to insure returns.

Do you have to recruit telephone sales people? Anyone who represents your company by telephone to customers or potential customers should be trained, supervised, and experienced in both what you're offering and how best to use the telephone as your communication device. And how are they to be paid—by salary, commissions, incentives, or bonuses? Professional agencies know the advantages and pitfalls of each compensation method; you may not.

What types of telephone equipment can most efficiently reach your market? Here the range of services now placed in your hands by the telephone company can become a bewildering and expensive set of tools unless you know the advantages and limitations of each. Should calls be placed directly or is the extra impact of person-to-person contact worth the cost? Is *Wide Area Telephone Service* (WATS) feasible? If it is, what type of coverage do you need, national or partial, full time or measured time? Would an 800 number (inbound WATS) or collect calls better serve a call-in campaign? How many phone lines do you need? Should only one type of service be used, or is a mix of different calling modes better suited to your specific needs?

140

What length of time will the campaign run? Is it better to call your prospects during the day, in the evening, at their offices, or in their homes? Do you have their phone numbers?

And finally, are there any legal requirements affecting your campaign? Many states require licensing for real estate, insurance, and brokerage telephone solicitors. Before you place the first call, it's best to check with your company lawyer and state licensing board if you have any doubts.

Many marketers find the services of professional telephone sales agencies preferable to internal operations. The professional telephone marketer can help implement a campaign and assist in structuring initial goals in the same way an advertising agency applies its experience to guide a client.

An outside telephone sales operation should be considered the same way you'd consider the services of the advertising agency, direct mail supplier, or media consultant. Ask the same questions and set the same standards for *its* personnel as you would apply to your own people. Has this company shown a creative talent and expertise in telephone selling? How much help are they willing to give? Do they only pick up the phone and say what you tell them to say, or do they come up with suggestions for maximizing the investment that telephone selling implies?

A list of past clients is always a good indication of just how effective any telephone marketing agency will be. Is their experience broad? Have they completed projects for well-known, reputable clients? Do they know *your business* and how best to reach *your audience?*

What are the limitations of their call capacity? Will they be able to meet time, location, and volume requirements? Does the service this agency offers meet your needs effectively but at a cost-efficient level? Many professional telephone marketing companies use a network of housewives and other part-time personnel calling from their home phones. While this type of operation can be less expensive, fully staffed central workshops with local service and/or WATS often produce higher response rates that offset incremental costs.

Telephone Case Histories

The following two case histories, based on actual programs conducted by Murray Roman's organization, CCI, illustrate the telephone's flexibility and uniqueness as a two-way communicative medium. The first demonstrates that the telephone can often prove to be a viable, cost-effective medium, but when it is used in combination with other media the results will be even more impressive. The second portrays the telephone's making full use of being a two-way medium. The caller listens to the person being called and is properly equipped to deal with any problems that may arise.

Case History 1

Problem
Use of telephone to sell listings in a new directory being published by the Sweet's division of McGraw-Hill.

Background
The Sweet's division of McGraw-Hill publishes five multivolume catalog files each year that are distributed at no charge to major businesses and organizations in appropriate industries.

Revenue is produced for Sweet's through the sale of listings in the various directories contained in each catalog file.

141

The largest is *Sweet's Architectural ("A") Catalog,* a massive 12-volume file that is distributed each year to more than 20,000 architectural firms, engineering firms, general contractors, government agencies, and other major users in the $26 billion general construction industry.

Published first in 1906, the "A" file had been restricted in past years solely to listings of manufacturers of architectural products. For 1972, the decision was made to increase revenue by expanding listings to include a special consultants and professional services directory.

A telephone marketing program was devised by CCI for McGraw-Hill—initially on a test basis and then for a more extensive program—to follow up a direct mail promotion piece to 5,000 prospects with telephone calls designed to sell listings in the proposed directory.

Program

The telephone program was concerned with two areas: (1) "cold" calls—timed to occur shortly after the prospect should have received the direct mail piece; and (2) "reactive" calls—in response to inquiries for additional information received from recipients of the direct mail piece.

All CCI telephone operators were thoroughly briefed beforehand, and as part of their training received copies of the direct mail piece for which they would be providing follow-up. A key point incorporated into the scripts used by all operators was that the Sweet's *Architectural Catalog* is the architect's prime source for information, and during the preceding year subscribers referred to their Sweet's catalogs nearly 60 million times.

The minimum charge for a listing in the new directory was $165, and in order to be cost-effective a conversion rate in excess of 5% of completed calls would be necessary.

Results

The telephone program accounted for more than 75% of the 500 listings in the 1972 *Consultants and Professional Services Directory* published by Sweet's.

The results obtained from the list of cold prospects exceeded the minimum requirements and generated a conversion of 7% for completed calls.

Reactive calls, to people who had expressed interest but had not submitted orders for listings, resulted in a conversion rate of 35% for completed calls.

Conclusion

Many of the prospects called as cold either had not seen the direct mail piece or had discarded it. The 7% conversion rate obtained via the telephone program indicates that telephone in many instances can be used as an alternative to direct mail. Telephone is even more effective—as shown by the 35% conversion rate achieved with people who had acknowledged receipt of the direct mail piece—when used in concert with direct mail and other media.

Case History 2

Problem
Credit jogging and reactivation of accounts.
Client
CRM/Heritage Book Club.
Background
When CRM, the publishers of *Psychology Today* magazine, took over the Heritage Book Club, they inherited what publisher John Suhler termed "an atrocious mess."

Faced with 25,000 inactive accounts whose names and individual account statements were on computer tapes that had not been kept up to date, CRM retained CCI to develop a telephone program aimed at reactivating as many accounts as possible as members of the Heritage Book Club or other CRM clubs.

The contact by telephone would also be used to straighten out the individual accounts and as a "credit jogging" mechanism to generate payment of past due balances.

Program

Realizing that the 25,000 Heritage Book Club members had been written off as totally inactive and had not been communicated with for several months, all CCI telephone operators were instructed to completely familiarize themselves with each individual member's statement, as a means of refreshing the customer's memory and indicating personal knowledge about each account.

Prior to calling any customer, operators were instructed to check: (1) amount due; (2) all "open" unpaid accounts listed on statement; (3) names of the books marked "open," so that the customer's memory could be refreshed; and (4) dates when books were supposed to have been sent.

CCI's instructions to operators emphasized that no customer be pressured. Many club members had undoubtedly forgotten the amount of money they owed, and it was quite possible our statements did not accurately reflect the current status of accounts.

In developing an effective operator's script, we adopted a completely honest and forthright approach in which we admitted the computer tapes were fouled up and requested each member's assistance in straightening out his or her own account.

The introduction read as follows:

"Hello, Mr(s). _____, this is Mr(s). _____ calling long distance for the Heritage Book Club.

"Mr(s). _____, you haven't heard from us for a while, because frankly we've had a real mess on our hands trying to straighten out our computer.

"First, I'd like to tell you that the Heritage Book Club has been taken over by the publishers of *Psychology Today* magazine, who are very much interested in keeping you as a customer. There have been so many problems — with billing, with people not having received books or having sent books back — that we thought the best thing to do was to call you directly and see if we couldn't get your help in straightening out your account."

Operators were prepared to cope with any response. If there was an unusual response, such as anger, operators were instructed to find out why and make appropriate notations to enable CRM to take special action. If the customer had not received the books that had been ordered, the title and order dates were recorded. If books had been returned, the titles and dates were also recorded. In cases where customers claimed they had already paid, operators requested the date of payment, the amount paid, and, whenever possible, the number of the check.

If applicable, operators then proceeded to the credit jogging phase of the script:

"Tell me, Mr(s). _____, if the record I have is correct. It indicates that there is still a balance of $_____ due, since _____ (date). Did you know that?"

If the amount already had been paid, operators were instructed to obtain the date and check number.

If the amount was incorrect, operators continued:

"What do you think the correct amount should be? When do you think we might expect to receive your check in that amount?"

If customer requested bill, operators responded:

"We'll be happy to send you a copy of your account record, so that you can check it against the books you did receive."

After operators received the pertinent information relating to amount due, books that had or had not been received, and any specific complaints, they proceeded to the reactivation phase:

"Mr(s). _____, we're going to really do our best to straighten out your account, because we do value you as a customer. This is one way of our giving you some personal service, so that we can continue sending you new books, if you wish.

"Mr(s). _____, would you like to have me reactivate your account, and send you the material on the latest exciting series of Heritage Books?"

The customer's response was noted and the operator concluded by thanking him or her for cooperating in resolving the service problems.

CRM followed up each call with a personalized letter to each customer who chose to reactivate membership.

Results

The program was enormously successful. The "bad debt" amount which was outstanding was reduced considerably. More important, however, the telephone program realized a conversion rate of nearly 50% in reactivating accounts that had been written off the books by CRM. These accounts thus became viable, revenue producing customers, ordering new books and in many cases joining additional CRM clubs.

Conclusion

The telephone proved itself to be truly unique, a person-to-person medium capable of generating a direct response when all other media are ineffective.

Telephone Training

Oral communication is an art that few people ever take the time to master.

You may think that just because a person is a supersalesman, he is obviously adept at oral communication. This is not necessarily so.

A person who is an absolute whiz at face-to-face, eyeball-to-eyeball selling may actually fizz out when it comes to using the telephone.

The simple reason is that when it comes to face-to-face selling, about 70% of the communication is the result of nonverbal factors—a frown, a look of surprise or pleasure, a sincere handshake, or a wink.

And if you doubt for a minute the validity of this claim, think of a recent direct personal encounter with someone. Can you remember everything that was said? Or do you more or less remember the encounter in emotional terms? "We had a good meeting." "He was pleased when I left." "I was satisfied."

When you rely on telephone as the medium, it is therefore highly important that you utilize our oral communications skills better. Things like *tone of voice* cannot be offset by a wink. And you cannot be really sure how the other person is reacting.

We tell our operators, "Smile when you dial." You'd be surprised. It really works.

Speed is another important factor. In normal face-to-face selling, the person to whom you are talking will often be able to anticipate what you are going to say by observing your facial expressions. In addition, we all do a little lipreading without realizing it. Your talking too fast on the telephone will often lead to distrust on the other end of the line. It may appear that you are attempting to double-talk so that your audience cannot follow the conversation.

On the other hand, if you talk too slowly the other person may become impatient. After all, a look of deep, pensive thought without any verbal support is nothing but emptiness on a telephone line.

We have found that the best rate of speech is 150 words a minute. You can practice your speed yourself at home. Find a 750-word article. Read it aloud. It should take you five minutes. Just continue practicing until your rate of speed is normally adjusted to this.

144

Once you've got it all down pat, there's nothing worse than not *getting through to the right person* — the one who decides whether or not to buy whatever it is you are selling. Too often salesmen are willing to settle for the assistant manager, instead of the real buying authority. You can expect any good secretary to challenge you on the telephone. Don't be afraid to identify yourself and ask to speak to the boss, but don't bother going through an entire sales talk for a secretary who has no bearing whatsoever on the outcome of the sale.

If the person you are seeking is not available, ask what time he will be. Call him back and remind the secretary that you telephoned once before and were asked to call back.

And when you do get to talk to the person you are seeking, don't beat around the bush. Do use a little common courtesy and ask if he has a couple of minutes to learn about a product or service that can cut costs or be of real value to his company. If he's too busy at that time, ask when a more opportune time may be.

Telephone can be a very effective medium for selling products or services that require a simple buying decision. Don't try to use it for complicated proposals or for selling something requiring extensive visual support, such as blueprints, charts, or graphs. If you are selling a complex service or product, telephone may best serve you in setting up an appointment. That foot in the door can be as important as the item you are actually selling.

Telephone can be used to qualify an advertising lead. If someone writes in for information, a telephone call can pinpoint what exactly the prospect is seeking, and with the same telephone call an appointment can be arranged.

As a person-to-person medium, telephone must be used properly if you are going to realize its potential fully.

You must listen to the person on the other end of the line and hear what that person is saying. And after you've listened and heard, the key to successful telephone selling is the way in which you respond to that other person's needs.

Be prepared to answer obvious questions, and make sure you understand correctly what the other person is saying. Take notes. Read back the details to a buyer who places an order or sets up an appointment. And don't assume that the person on the other end of the line always understands everything you've said. Every once in a while, slip in a "Do you follow me?" or "Does this make sense to you?"

Communication is a two-way thing, and in any selling situation it's also the name of the game.

There are a lot of variables in telephone selling, and each of them can influence the degree of success.

One recent development in telephone selling has eliminated many variables. With taped messages, you only have to get it right once. Then it can be played over and over again.

Taped Messages

Taking a cue from political campaign strategists, marketing professionals are turning increasingly to the use of taped telephone messages as a direct response technique that achieves controlled, effective sales presentations.

Such notables as Gloria Steinem, Charlton Heston, Betty Furness, Norman Cousins, and Wall Street's Gustave Levy all have become voices on tape in support of either commercial products they endorse or worthwhile social causes.

Tape is increasing the effectiveness and accountability of the telephone. Also, the use of famous people can provide added dimension to a wide range of telephone programs, often reinforcing product credibility through third-person endorsement.

145

The burgeoning use of taped messages started in 1972, with the telephone program developed by CCI to launch Norman Cousins' *World Magazine.*

Today this program, which exceeded 300,000 calls, stands as a milestone in telephone marketing. While tape had been used previously in political campaigns, the program for Norman Cousins marked the first sophisticated commercial program using cost-effective methods and accountability.

In the past, political taped telephone messages rarely had exceeded 60 seconds in length, but for *World Magazine* the taped message needed to tell the story was longer. The *World* program started as a test to determine the feasibility of publishing the magazine. Because the publication was still in the concept stage, CCI decided to use Norman Cousins' voice on tape. Nobody else knew anything about the publication, and it took Norman Cousins more than two minutes to tell his story.

As the program for *World Magazine* progressed, techniques in the use of tape matured quickly and different messages were recorded, depending on the select list being called. The complete text for one tape follows:

Hello, this is Norman Cousins. I hope you will forgive the intrusion, but this is the most direct way available to me to tell you that my colleagues and I have decided to start a new magazine.

Ever since I resigned as Editor of the *Saturday Review,* for reasons I think you may know about, I have been thinking and dreaming about putting out another magazine, and I have been encouraged in this by letters from many readers. These letters have been most heartening and indeed nourishing. But starting a new magazine these days, as I'm sure I don't have to tell you, is a precarious and expensive undertaking. There is however one way it can be done. It can be done if enough readers are willing to take a chance on us, and to commit themselves to long term subscriptions.

For example, if we can obtain enough subscriptions at the special charter rate of $25.00 for 3 years, we can avoid the costly and perilous business of starting up with short term introductory offers. In this way, the magazine will be owned, quite literally, by its readers and editors. Readers who subscribe now need not pay all at once. They can pay later. What is important now, is that we know that people are willing to stand behind us. Incidentally, there is a lifetime subscription rate of $200.00.

We intend to publish every two weeks. Our aim is to put out what we hope will be the finest magazine in the world. We want to write about the things that excite the human mind, about the great issues and ideas of our time, about worthwhile books and films, plays, music and art. But we want to do this not just on a national scale, we want to review and report on a world scale.

Well, whether for one year, three years or a lifetime I want you to know how excited we are at the prospect of putting out a magazine again, putting it out with and for many of the same people who have been with us in the past.

Thank you.

The *World* telephone program is credited with much of the initial success in launching the publication. And while telephone did much for *World Magazine,* the program also greatly benefited the business of telephone marketing.

Since the *World* program, hundreds of telephone programs using taped personal messages have been created.

Dr. Franklyn Barry, president of the American Management Association's Extension Institute, went on to reach business executives, while J. Oppenheimer, publisher of Standard & Poor's *Outlook*, found the medium an effective way to reach subscribers.

Telephone tape messages are important new tools for industrial marketers like Bell & Howell, U.S. Steel, and Leasco; for insurance companies, correspondence schools, book publishing companies, and the AAA.

Gustave Levy, senior partner at Goldman, Sachs & Co., provided his endorsement on tape to *New York Affairs Magazine*. At the other end of the publishing spectrum, fashion czar John Fairchild extolled through taped telephone messages the virtues of subscribing to *Women's Wear Daily,* which he publishes.

Educator Robert Hutchins raised funds for the Center for the Study of Democratic Institutions, which he heads. For the National Organization for Women (NOW), the voice of Betty Furness effectively raised money.

D. Van Nostrand Co.

Hello, this is *Ben Plummer* of *Trinity College* in San Antonio, Texas . . . this is the most direct way available to me to bring my new book on organic chemistry to your attention and reach you before decisions are made for the second semester. . . .

Behavioral Research Laboratories

Hello, this is *Ann Fugate* . . . as teaching consultant I've worked closely with other Behavioral Research Laboratories' staff members to develop and produce materials and programs which are adaptable to the specific needs of each student. . . . Our telephone communicator will be coming back on the line to tell you how you may acquire . . . Behavioral Research Laboratories Programs for your school and to answer any questions you may have.

Encyclopaedia Britannica

Hello, this is *William Benton.* I am publisher of the *Encyclopaedia Britannica* . . . as a former United States Senator and as Ambassador to UNESCO, I've found we live in a highly competitive age — vast new fields of interest and knowledge have become vital. . . . I would like to suggest that one of my colleagues — a *Britannica* representative in your community — call on you — at home. Our telephone communicator will be happy to make an appointment — at a time convenient for you.

Amsterdam News

This is *Clarence Jones.* I'm editor and publisher of the *New York Amsterdam News.* . . . I'm convinced that you need the *Amsterdam News* to keep you and your colleagues informed about what's really going on in America's black community. Many executives . . . have sent me subscription orders for themselves and their associates. I think you should certainly join them by subscribing to the *Amsterdam News* for your people. . . .

Dodge Bulletin

I'm *Bill Dowling* of the *F. W. Dodge Company* . . . publishers of *The Dodge Bulletin*. . . . Whether your firm is involved in both public and privately owned construction or specializes in only one sector – you will find projects listed in *Dodge Bulletin* when they are in the early planning stages – while you still have plenty of time to pick and choose . . . and then go after the jobs you want most. . . . Our telephone communicator will be happy to enter a special, cost-saving subscription for you.

Dreyfus Publications

This is *Jerome Hardy,* President of the *Dreyfus Corporation.* . . . I've called you today – not to discuss mutual funds – but to tell you about another Dreyfus company: Dreyfus Publications, Ltd. and its new *Dreyfus Family Money Management Service* – designed to help you make your hard earned money work harder for you.

New York Law Journal

I'm *Jerry Finkelstein*, Vice Chairman of the Board of the *New York Law Journal*. . . . Because you've been reading your own personal copy of the *Law Journal* for the past month with our compliments, I'm sure you now know the *Law Journal* gives you information daily you can't get anywhere else. . . . When our telephone communicator comes back on the line he'll be happy to take your subscription order and answer any questions you may have.

Standard & Poor's Outlook

Hello, I'm *Joseph Oppenheimer,* publisher of *The Outlook*. . . . Every day I hear from people who are concerned about their investments . . . all the problems you probably worry about also . . . your *Outlook* will keep you continuously informed on just what action we think you should take. So that you will not miss out on the important opportunities that are developing, our telephone communicator has a special offer to extend your subscription now on a most attractive basis.

Hearst Magazines – Book Division

Hello, this is *William Campbell,* Vice President of *Hearst Magazines*. . . . We are especially excited about two very special book series now available to our readers – that bring together the knowledge and experience of *Popular Mechanics* and *Good Housekeeping* editorial experts into lasting libraries for your home. . . . We will be happy to send Volume I of the *Popular Mechanics Do-It-Yourself Encyclopaedia* and Volume I of the *Good Housekeeping Illustrated Encyclopaedia of Gardening* to you free and without obligation. For any additional volumes you then decide to take, you would be billed only.

Reader's Digest

Hello, this is *Geri Gantman* for *Reader's Digest* to announce the grand prize winning number in our current sweepstakes. If you have it, you win $2,000 a month for one

148

year, and if you don't win the grand prize, you may still win one of 2,000 other prizes. . . . You must, of course, return your sweepstakes blank to be eligible for any prize. And, to get your free mystery gift plus 12 months of *Reader's Digest* at our reduced, introductory price, simply check the "yes" box on your reply envelope and mail today.

Sweet's Architectural File (McGraw-Hill Information Systems)

Hello, this is *Robert Nichols,* new chairman of the *Professional Engineers in Private Practice* section of NSPE. . . . I learned of an ethical and professional communications medium now available to our members . . . This year, *Sweet's Architectural File* is cooperating with PEPP to maximize our members' participation in the *Directory of Consultants and Professional Services* . . . bound into Volume I of the *Architectural File.* . . . Listing in the *Sweet's Directory* is recognized by PEPP as an effective medium to reach the more than 120,000 key professionals who use the file. Through our cooperative agreement with *Sweet's,* all PEPP members . . . will receive at least a 5% discount off the listing rates . . . and, it could be higher, depending on the number of members who list.

Direct Marketing Magazine (Hoke Communications)

This is *Pete Hoke,* publisher of *Direct Marketing Magazine* . . . to personally tell you why I think our magazine is a useful and informative tool for your business. . . . We'd like to hear from you and involve your company in our future issues. . . .

An important advantage that taped messages have is that they maintain quality control. No matter how well trained telephone operators are, there will always be variations in effectiveness. With taped messages, the telephone sales message is delivered the same way every time, and operators are used in a service capacity.

How do people respond to rushing to the telephone for a message from Gloria Steinem or Betty Furness, only to find they are getting the voice and not the person?

Surprisingly, people understand that well-known personalities or business executives can't spend their whole day calling people personally, and they still would rather hear from a famous person or someone with whom they can identify in a peer relationship and who tells a totally authentic sales story, rather than a caller whose voice and name are unfamiliar to them.

A key ingredient of the programs has been the initial use of live telephone operators to determine if a person is willing to listen to a taped message.

People called rarely hang up. The operator's screening questions qualify the listener. Her response following the taped message answers questions, requests the order, and records the response.

A combined tape-live operator call can be especially effective for industrial marketers. Here, the combination serves as a "personal" sales presentation and is well suited to any campaign targeted to marginal prospects and accounts or offers too low-priced to support a salesman's visit.

Summary

There are numerous factors which must be considered when planning to implement any telephone program. The following basic outline includes some of the most important ones and will serve to summarize the major facets of telephone marketing.

1. *The Do-It-Yourself or Buy Decision.* Any company intending to implement its own telephone program must possess the necessary creativity and expertise. Proper implementation of a telephone program requires careful preplanning and constant monitoring to insure maximum results.

   There must be labor intensiveness to enable a company to shift into high gear quickly on completing the pretesting phase, and the appropriate telephone equipment should be used to maximize production at minimum costs.

   There are also certain legal requirements, especially at the state level. These can be particularly restrictive in such businesses as insurance, real estate, and mutual funds.

   A company deciding to retain an external organization for a telephone program should carefully review the capabilities and experience of the agency being considered. Certain organizations specialize in such areas as market research and validations and are not necessarily equipped to implement telephone as a medium for selling. Ask for the names of other clients represented by the organization, and make sure there are control mechanisms that will reflect at any given time the status of the ongoing program.

2. *Organizational Responsibilities/Assignments.* As with any facet of a total marketing program, the positioning and implementation are better accomplished with reinforcement by senior executive support. The telephone, more than certain other media, requires a well-conceived plan of coordination because of the speed with which the program is conducted.

   A squad of five telephone operators working an eight-hour day will quickly bring measurable results and must be monitored daily to insure proper results and best list utilization.

   Lead time factors must be determined concerning telephone's relationship to other media. Are you calling before or after a mail drop? Are cold prospects being called? Did coupon response cream the market first?

3. *Lists and Reporting Systems.* A telephone program is only as good as the universe to which it is directed, and in telephone marketing that universe is determined by the list of names which is compiled, rented, or purchased.

   It is rare to obtain a list on which more than 85% of the names are current. On most lists, one-quarter of the names cannot be reached. They have either unlisted or unpublished numbers. When businessmen are involved, an even larger percentage have either left the company or have changed positions.

   When acquiring lists, you must consider the manner in which telephone numbers will be obtained. When you hire someone to look up the telephone numbers, the normal charges can range from 10¢ to 20¢ per name, and you are billed for a name whether or not the telephone number is obtainable. The telephone company at one time provided a free look-up service on a time availability basis, but it is trying to eliminate this service. Without ZIP Codes, look-up costs are higher, and every list should be pretested before being implemented.

   The best lists should always be used at the beginning of the program, on the theory that if the best will not work the program is destined to fail. Some computer lists are now available that provide phone numbers for an additional charge.

4. *The Message.* The first consideration in developing the telephone message is whether a live telephone operator is to be used alone or in a service capacity as a control mechanism to introduce a tape.

The use of tape alone, without live telephone operators, has limited applications and is recommended only for call-in programs in instances where the person will not be offended.

In many programs, tape used with live telephone operators is preferable to using operators alone. The relevance of the voice on tape to the list being called is the key. Norman Cousins to his prospects, Alistair Cooke to watchers of Masterpiece Theatre, are better, more effective, and more personal than any operator could possibly be.

Tapes provide a uniform standard of quality that can be measured and controlled through program modifications. This uniform standard is impossible to achieve when live operators are used to deliver the sales message. There are, however, certain controls that can be implemented to maximize quality by formulating highly structured parameters for programs in which live operators are used exclusively.

Operators should be thoroughly briefed before implementing any telephone program, and an easy to present script should be provided that clearly outlines the purpose of the call.

Key questions should be anticipated, as well as objections to whatever it is the operator is selling. Suitable answers and explanations should be provided beforehand.

A checklist system for categorizing calls will simplify the operator's task. This will minimize time spent doing paper work and maximize time spent on the telephone.

The most common form of checklist, where a simple buy/no buy decision is involved, will normally include : (a) orders; (b) literature/information requests; (c) not interested; (d) request call back; (e) not available (particularly in business); and (f) didn't answer/busy (try four or five times).

5. *Fulfillment.* A verbal "yes" on the telephone is often speedily forgotten unless written verification is received by the prospect within a few days. Telephone operators should always reinforce the prospect's affirmative response by repeating whatever it is the person has agreed to.

Self-Quiz

1. Name the ten uses for telephone most widely applied by direct marketers.

1. _____ 2. _____

3. _____ 4. _____

5. _____ 6. _____

7. _____ 8. _____

9. _____ 10. _____

2. Direct telephone sales are usually not feasible when the offer is _____

3. When a telephone program is tested, which types of lists should be tested first?

_____

_____

4. What are the disadvantages of a do-it-yourself telephone sales function?

_____

_____

_____

_____

5. What are the advantages of using a professional telephone sales agency?

_____

_____

_____

_____

6. What is the best rate of speech for a telephone communication?

_____ words per minute.

7. If the right person is not available when you call, what should you do?

_____ Ask that he call back

_____ Talk to the next in command

_____ Call the right person back

8. What is the number-one advantage of a taped telephone message?

_____

9. How does the disadvantage of a taped message from a well-known personality outweigh the advantage of a live message from an unknown personality?

_____

_____

10. The most common form of checklist where a simple buy/no buy decision is involved will normally include

1. _____   2. _____

3. _____   4. _____

5. _____   6. _____

Pilot Project

You have just been given a most exciting project. You are working for a recording company with exclusive rights to an album by Frank Sinatra titled "The Years of Frank Sinatra."

This three-record album contains 21 songs for which Sinatra is famous. Selling price for the album is $19.95. Sinatra has agreed to do a taped phone sales message for you. But you must write the script for him.

The project is truly exciting in that the marketing director has agreed to provide you with a prime list of "nostalgia" record buyers, all of whom have bought and paid for similar record albums. You may offer "The Years of Frank Sinatra" on a 15-day free trial basis.

Time limit for the taped message is two minutes. Use your imagination!

SECTION ⫼ DEVELOPING THE RIGHT PROPOSITIONS FOR DIRECT MARKETING

Chapter 8 Importance of the Proposition

There are probably almost as many techniques for producing responses by mail and phone as there are direct response advertisers. At least it seems that way. But most professionals agree that the *proposition* is a major factor in the degree of success achieved.

To use a current phrase, it boggles the mind when one contemplates the variety of propositions possible. Differences in response rate, depending on the proposition or propositions, can be dramatic. Differences of 25%, 50% 100%, and more are commonplace.

Examples of Dramatic Differences

The following case history illustrates the dramatically different results that can be obtained from two propositions offering the same product to the same audience.

The "product" was a series of 12 sales bulletins by Harry Simmons, a nationally known sales consultant. The market was sales managers. The objective was to sell the series of bulletins in quantity for distribution to sales forces. Two different propositions were devised and tested.

Proposition A asked the sales manager to send for one complete set of the 12 sales bulletins for personal review. He was told that, upon receipt, he would have the following options: (1) 15 days' free review; (2) the right to return the bulletins at the end of the trial period, at which time the memo invoice in the amount of $3.75 would be cancelled; (3) the right to keep the set and honor the memo invoice; or (4) the right to keep the set and order additional sets for the sales force.

Proposition B involved sending the sales manager one sample bulletin with a letter of solicitation. The offer was, "Tell us how many salesmen you employ? We'll send you a free copy of the enclosed bulletin for every member of your sales force. Then, every two weeks thereafter, we'll send you an equal quantity until all 12 bulletins are received. If there are any bulletins you don't like, you can return them for full credit."

Here are the comparative results. Proposition A produced an average order of $5.25 for a single set and multiple set orders combined. Proposition B pulled a third more response than proposition A. And the average order was $27.50 compared to an average order of $5.25 for proposition A. The same "product" was offered to the same market, and it must be said that the quality of copy was the same. But proposition B pulled a third more response and an average order which was almost five times larger! Why the difference?

Under proposition A, the sales manager had to read all 12 bulletins to decide whether he wished his salesmen to receive them. Human inertia got in the way; obviously, a very large percentage of sales managers never got around to the chore. Under proposition B, the decision to become involved depended on reading just one bulletin instead of 12. No wonder B did so much better than A.

154

The Key: Overcoming Human Inertia

No matter which medium or media may be employed to make the proposition, the objective is to overcome *human inertia* — the natural resistance to becoming involved with the proposition. And since hundreds of propositions are proffered through every available medium daily, there is a strong, strong resistance out there! Theoretically, the more attractive the proposition, the less resistance there is likely to be and therefore the more response. Parlaying several propositions into one can produce an offer which is *almost* irresistible. Let us consider the melding of all the following propositions into one giant offer: *(a)* a sweepstakes contest (nothing to buy to enter), all prizes awarded! *(b)* a free merchandise gift for *trying* the product; *(c)* free S & H Green Stamps; *(d)* 30-day free trial; *(e)* one or more additional gifts for keeping the product; *(f)* cash discount for payment within 30 days; *(g)* installment terms available — 12 "easy" payments; and *(h)* full refund any time within 12 months if customer is not completely satisfied.

Wow — eight propositions all rolled into one "irresistible" offer! Would it overcome human inertia? Probably. Would it be good business? Maybe.

Danger of Overkill

There's such a thing as too much of a good thing: propositions which sound too good to be true or which produce a great front end response but make for poor pay-ups or poor repeat customers. Here are two sobering examples.

A comprehensive test was structured for a fund-raising organization to determine whether response would best be maximized by *(a)* offering a free gift as an incentive for an order; *(b)* offering a combination of free gift plus a cash bonus for completing a sale; or *(c)* offering a cash bonus only. The combination of free gift plus cash bonus pulled the lowest response by far; the free-gift proposition far outpulled the cash bonus proposition.

The other example: A $200 piece of electronic equipment was offered for 15 days' free trial. This was the basic proposition. But half of the people on the list were also invited to enter a sweepstakes contest. The portion of the list who were not invited to enter the sweepstakes responded 25% better than the portion who were invited to enter.

In both of these examples, the more generous proposition proved to be "too much." One must be most careful not to make the proposition so overwhelming that it overshadows the product or services being offered.

Another truly important consideration in structuring propositions is the axiom, "As you make your bed, so shall you lie in it." Here's what we mean.

If you obtain thousands of new customers by offering free gifts as incentives, don't expect a maximum degree of repeat business unless you continue to offer free gifts. Likewise, if you build a large list of installment credit buyers, don't expect these buyers to respond well to cash offers — and vice versa.

Given propositions attract given types of customers. Make sure that these are the types you really want. Here is an example of our axiom. A firm selling to businesses built a large customer list based on a series of soft sell propositions. They then went into another product line, offering these products to their customers and to cold prospect lists. Three propositions were tested: (1) a free gift for ordering; (2) a discount for ordering; and (3) no incentive. Below are the results of the three propositions against cold lists and against the customer list.

	Cold Lists	*Customer List*
Free gift	2.2%	3.2%
Discount	5.2%	3.1%
No incentive	2.5%	3.9%

Note the dramatic differences in response between cold lists and the customer list. The discount offer was more than twice as attractive to cold lists. But to the customer list, not nurtured in this manner, the discount offer was the least attractive. Note also that the proposition with no extra incentive was the most attractive to the customer list.

The "Unique" Proposition

It behooves each marketer to strive constantly for the *unique proposition* which best fits his product or service. The payoff can be astronomical.

One of the most unique propositions of the past decade has been that developed by the Franklin Mint and similar firms. They have offered *limited* series of medals with a guaranteed full price buy-back proposition—an almost "irresistible" proposition which has created a multimillion dollar market in a short period of time. A unique proposition, to say the least, one which would fit few other product categories. But a proposition which has melted away human inertia for the Franklin Mint as no other proposition possibly could.

Effect of Terms on Propositions

Where merchandise or services are offered for direct sales, the terms of payment become an integral part of the proposition. And what a difference terms of payment can make!

There are five general categories of payment terms which may be offered:

1. Cash with order
2. C.O.D.
3. Open account
4. Installment terms
5. Revolving credit

If a five-way split test were made among these categories, it is almost a certainty that response would be in inverse ratio to the listing of the five categories—revolving credit being the most attractive and cash with order being the least attractive terms. In a four-way split test on a merchandise offer, here's how four terms actually ranked. (The least appealing terms have a 100% ranking.)

> Cash with order 100%
> Cash with order and free gift for trying 144%
> Bill me offer (open account) 177%
> Bill me offer (open account) and free gift . . . 233%

As the figures disclose, the most attractive terms (bill me offer and free gift) were almost 2½ times more appealing than the least attractive terms (cash with order).

While C.O.D. terms are generally more attractive than cash with order requirements, the hazard of C.O.D. terms is refusal on delivery. It isn't unusual to sustain 8% refusal when C.O.D. terms are offered. (Many a C.O.D. order is placed emotionally, and emotion cools off when the postman calls and requests payment.)

When merchandise or services are offered on open account, payment is customarily requested in 15 or 30 days. Such terms are naturally more appealing than cash with order or C.O.D. Open account terms are customary when selling to business firms. When used in selling to the consumer, however, such terms, while appealing, can result in a high percentage of bad debts, unless carefully selected credit checked lists are used.

156

The ultimate in appeal are installment terms and revolving credit terms. Both types require substantial financing facilities and a sophisticated credit collection system. Installment selling in the consumer field is practically essential for the successful sale of "big ticket" merchandise—selling for $69.95 and up.

There is a way to have the best of two worlds—most appealing terms and no credit risk. This can be accomplished by making credit arrangements through a sales finance firm or through commercial credit card operations such as American Express, Diners Club, Carte Blanche, or one of the bank cards—BankAmericard or Master Charge.

When arrangements are made through commercial credit card operations, any member may charge his purchase to his credit card. Credit of all members in good standing is assured by the respective credit card operation. The advertiser is paid by the credit card operation for the total sales charged less a discount charge, usually in the range of 3% for bank cards and 7% for travel and entertainment cards.

Most marketers who have offered the alternative of either cash with order or charge through a commercial credit card have experienced a response of 10% to 15% of the total charging through the credit card. A plus advantage, over and above eliminating credit risks, is usually a larger average order on credit card purchases, particularly in the catalog field. It isn't unusual, for instance, for a firm that normally sells for cash via the catalog method to experience a 25% to 50% larger order on charge purchases. This more than makes up for the cost of financing.

Importance of the Guarantee

No matter what the terms or what the basic proposition may be, a strong guarantee is essential when selling products or services direct. For more than 86 years, Sears, Roebuck & Co. have guaranteed satisfaction for every article offered. And over all these years, no one else has ever succeeded in mail order without duplicating the Sears guarantee or using a derivation thereof.

SEARS
GUARANTEE

*Your satisfaction is guaranteed
or your money back*

We guarantee that every article in this catalog is accurately described and illustrated.

If for any reason whatever you are not satisfied with any article purchased from us, we want you to return it to us at our expense.

We will exchange it for exactly what you want, or will return your money, including any transportation charges you have paid.

SEARS, ROEBUCK & CO.

The importance of the guarantee is perhaps best understood by realizing a negative fact of life. It is this. Eighty-six years after Sears first established their ironclad guarantee, it is still a fact of human nature that one is hesitant to send for merchandise unless one knows that, should it not come up to expectation, it may be returned for full credit. Guaranteed satisfaction should be part and parcel of any and all propositions soliciting a direct sale.

Many marketers have developed unique guarantees which go well beyond the trial period. (We mentioned the Franklin Mint one earlier.) Madison House, for instance, advertised a new fishing lure in a March issue of *Family Weekly*. They knew, of course, that up North lakes were frozen over and that there would be no opportunity to test and use this lure before spring. They overcame the problem beautifully by urging the fishing buff to send for the lure *now,* with the proviso that the lure could be returned any time within six months for a full cash refund. This guarantee had two advantages: (1) it assured the fishing buff that even though he was ordering the lure out of season he could return it after he tried it in season; and (2) it enabled Madison House to advertise and get business out of season.

One of the most successful manuals ever produced at National Research Bureau was the 428-page *Retail Advertising and Sales Promotion Manual.* It was offered on a ten-day free trial basis with the guarantee: "If this manual isn't all we say it is, you may return it any time within twelve months for full refund." National Research Bureau sold over 20,000 manuals at $19.95 each with this guarantee. It is significant to note that, after several years, no one has ever asked for a refund!

Many marketers reinforce their own guarantees with a "third-party" guarantee. "Approved by Underwriters Laboratory" can mean a great deal where electrical appliances are involved. The *Good Housekeeping* Seal of Approval has long been accepted as a guarantee of validity of claim.

Publishers Clearing House makes this statement: "In addition to the publisher's own warranties, Publishers Clearing House makes you this unconditional guarantee: you may have a full cash refund at any time, or for any reason, on the unused part of any subscription ordered through the clearing house. This guarantee has no time limit. It is your assurance that you can order from Publishers Clearing House with complete confidence."

In direct sales, the right proposition and the right terms of payment are only two-thirds of the impetus. A clear, strong guarantee completes the equation.

Short- and Long-Term Effects of Propositions

A major consideration in structuring propositions is the effect a given proposition will have on your objectives.

- Is your objective to get a *maximum* number of new customers for a given product or service as quickly as possible?
- Is your objective to determine the *repeat business factor* as quickly as possible?
- Is your objective to break even or make a profit in the shortest possible period?

So the key question to ask when designing a proposition is, "How will this proposition help to accomplish my objective?"

Propositions Relate to Objectives

For example, say you are introducing a new hobby magazine. You have the choice of making a short-term offer (three months, for instance) or a long-term offer (12 months, for instance). Since you want to learn acceptances as quickly as possible (your objective), you would rightly decide on a short-term offer. Under the short-term offer, after three months you will be getting a picture of renewal percentages. If you made an initial offer of 12 months, you would have to wait for a full year to determine how well the publication renews. In the interim, it would be dangerous to go after additional subscriptions.

If the three-month trial subscriptions are renewed at a satisfactory rate, you could then safely proceed to develop propositions designed to get initial long-term subscriptions. It is axiomatic in the publishing field that the longer the initial term of subscription, the higher the renewal rate is likely to be. Professional circulation men know from experience that if they are getting, say, a 35% conversion on three-month trial, they can expect a conversion of 50% or more on 12-month initial subscriptions. So this knowledge can be extrapolated from the short-term objective to the long-term objective.

Looking at another side of the coin, Sol Blumenfeld, senior vice president of the New York office of Rapp, Collins, Stone & Adler, made some pertinent remarks about the dangers of looking only at the front end response when addressing a recent Direct Mail/Marketing Association convention.

Blumenfeld stated, "Many people still cling to the C.P.A. (cost per application) or C.P.I. (cost per inquiry) response syndromes. In their eagerness to sell now, they frequently foul up their chances to sell later."

He then proceeds to ask, "Can the practice of those who concern themselves only with front end response, at least partially explain book club conversions of only 50 to 60%? Magazine renewal rates of only 30%? Correspondence school attrition factors of as much as 40%?"

Blumenfeld gives us a case in point. A control for the Britannica Home Study Library Service, a division of Encyclopaedia Britannica, was run against several test ads developed by the agency. Control ads offered the first volume of *Compton's Encyclopedia* FREE. Major emphasis was placed on sending for the free volume, small emphasis was placed on the idea of ultimately purchasing the balance of the 24-volume set. Front end response was excellent; the rate of conversion to full 24-volume sets was poor. Profitability was unacceptable.

Against the control ad, the agency tested several new ads which offered Volume I free but also revealed the cost of the complete set—right in the headline. Here's what happened: The cost per coupon for the new ads was 20% higher than the control ad, but conversions to full sets improved a full 350%!

Effect on Bad Debts

Earlier we pointed out the danger of overkill—making the proposition too generous and therefore reducing believability. It is rarely mentioned that a misleading proposition can have a devastating effect on bad debts. A misleading offer causes the consumer, without consciously thinking about it, to feel that he has been rooked and often leads him to conclude, "They can whistle for their money." The justice, if it may be called that, is that those who would mislead usually end up paying dearly for their misdeeds.

The fact that it is poor business to make misleading propositions is underscored by this true story. For many years two large publishers exchanged mailing lists—each making noncompeting offers to the list of the other. These two publishers exchanged bad debt lists. Time after time the publisher known for its misleading propositions would send the other publisher a list of customers with whom it had bad debt experience. When the names were compared, it was found that, in over 80% of the cases where both publishers had the same customers, the publisher who practiced forthrightness had no bad debt experience with the identical customers. Honesty does pay.

Types of Propositions

So far in this section, we have covered the importance of the proposition, the effect of terms on propositions, and the short- and long-term effects of propositions. With all of this as a preamble, we now delve into the exciting alternatives open to us in structuring our propositions.

159

The checklist which follows lists and briefly describes 22 basic propositions which
may be used singly or in various combinations, depending on the marketer's objectives.
In succeeding pages we illustrate, through response forms, examples of most of the propositions in use. Certain propositions require additional commentary.

Checklist of Basic Propositions

1. Free information
   Often the most effective proposition, particularly when *(a)* leads for salesmen are
   the prime objective, or *(b)* nonprospects must be screened out at low cost before
   expensive literature is sent to prime prospects.
2. Samples
   A sample of a product or service is often the most effective sales tool. If a sample
   can be enclosed in a mailing package, results often more than warrant the extra
   cost. Consideration should be given to charging a nominal price for a sample. An
   investment in a sample promotes trying and usually results in a substantial increase in sales.
3. Free trial
   Bellwether of mail order. Melts away human inertia. Consider fitting length of trial
   period to nature of product or service, rather than standard 15 days.
4. Conditional sale
   Prearranges the possibility of long-term acceptance, based on sample. Example:
   "YES, please send me the current issue of *Psychology Today* and enter my name as
   a trial subscriber at the special introductory rate of $6 for 12 issues (half the regu-
   lar price). However, if not delighted with the first issue, I will simply write 'cancel'
   on the bill and return it without paying or owing anything, keeping the first issue
   as a complimentary copy."
5. Till forbid
   Prearranges for continuing shipments on a specified basis, the customer having the
   option to forbid future shipments at any specified time. Works well for business
   services offers and continuity book programs.
6. Yes-no
   An involvement proposition. Prospect is asked to respond, usually through a token
   or stamp, indicating whether he accepts or rejects the proposition. Historically,
   more favorable responses are received with this proposition than when no rejection
   device is provided.
7. Time limit
   Setting a time limit on a given offer *forces* action, either positive or negative. Usually it is more effective to name a specific date rather than a time period. Important
   to test for most effective time limit: A short period may not allow sufficient time for
   deliberation; a long period may promote inertia.
8. Get-a-friend
   Based on the axiom that the best source for new customers is present satisfied customers, many get-a-friend propositions get new customers in large volume at low
   acquisition cost. Best response for a get-a-friend propositions usually results from
   (a) limiting the number of friends' names requested; and *(b)* offering a reward for
   providing names and/or securing new customers.
9. Contests
   Contests create attention and excitement. Stringent FTC rules apply. Highly effective in conjunction with magazine subscription offers and popular merchandise offers.

160

10. Discounts

    A discount is a never ending lure to consumers as well as businessmen. Discounts are particularly effective where the value of a product or service is well established. Three types of discounts are widely offered: *(a)* for cash; *(b)* for an introductory order; and *(c)* for volume purchase.

11. Negative option

    Prearranges for shipment if customer doesn't abort shipment by mailing rejection form prior to deadline date. In popular use by book and record clubs. New FTC guidelines must be followed carefully.

12. Positive option

    Every shipment is based on a *direct action* by the club member, rather than a *non-action,* as exemplified by the negative option feature of most book and record clubs. Front end response to a positive option proposition is likely to be less, but long pull sales are likely to be greater.

13. Lifetime membership

    Under this, the member pays one fee, $5 for instance, at the time of becoming a member. In return the member is guaranteed substantial savings from established retail prices. There is no requirement to make any specified number of purchases, but the safeguard to the marketer is that the member is more likely to make purchases because of his front end investment.

14. Load-ups

    This proposition is a favorite of publishers of continuity series. Example: Publisher offers set of 12 books – one released each month. After purchaser has received and paid for first three books, publisher invites him to receive remaining nine – all in one shipment, with the understanding that payments can continue to be made monthly. Load-up proposition invariably results in more *complete sets* of books being sold.

15. Free gift

    Most direct response advertisers have increased response through free gift offers. For best results, test several gifts to determine the most appealing. There's no set criterion for the cost of a gift in relation to selling cost. Most important criteria are: *(a)* appropriateness of the gift; *(b)* its effect on repeat business; and *(c)* net profit per thousand circulation or distribution, including cost of the gift.

16. Deluxe alternatives

    Related to the famous Sears tradition of *good, better, best* are propositions which offer deluxe alternatives. A classic example would be a dictionary offered in regular edition or in a thumb-indexed edition for $2 more. By giving the prospect the choice, the advertiser often increases total response and total dollars.

17. Charters

    A charter proposition, by its very nature, denotes something special. The proposition plays on the human trait that most people want to be among the first to see, try, use something new. Most successful charter propositions include special rewards or concessions for early support.

18. Guaranteed buy-back

    "Satisfaction guaranteed" is the heart of mail order. But the guaranteed buy-back proposition goes much further. This guarantee pledges to buy back – if the customer so requests – at original cost, a number of years after original purchase.

19. Multiproduct

    Multiproduct propositions may take the form of a series of post cards, bound or unbound, or a collection of individual sheets, each with a separate order form. Each product presentation is structured to stand on its own feet.

20. Piggybacks

Piggybacks are "add on" offers which ride along with major offers at no additional postage cost. Unit of sale is usually much smaller than the major offer. Testing is advocated to determine whether piggybacks add to or steal from sales of major offer.

21. Bounce backs

Bounce back propositions succeed on the premise "the best time to sell a person is right after you have sold him." Bounce back order forms are usually included in shipments or with invoices or statements. Bounce backs may offer *(a)* more of the same; *(b)* related items; or *(c)* totally different items than originally purchased.

22. Good-better-best

The basis of the proposition is to give the prospect a choice between something and something. Example: for their State of the Union series, the Franklin Mint gives the prospect three choices: 24K gold on sterling at $72.50 monthly, solid sterling silver at $43.75 monthly, and solid bronze at $17.50 monthly.

Yes-No

Yes-no propositions add an extra dimension to other propositions — the free trial offer, for instance. The yes-no alternative *involves* the reader, it encourages him to make a conscious decision and express that decision with a yes or no response. With the basic free trial offer, it's easier to say "no" by simply taking no action. But the yes-no device, with its added dimension, plays on a basic human trait. It's probably true that most people dislike saying "no." Therefore they are more likely to say "yes," if confronted with making a yes-no decision.

Businessmen's Record Club conducted many tests involving the yes-no proposition in conjunction with the free trial offer. It was found generally that lists which would pull 1% without the yes-no involvement would pull close to 1½% in free trial orders with the yes-no involvement.

There were also interesting results as related to the percentages of yeses and of noes on given lists. Generally, there was little difference in total response between lists. A well-performing list which produced 1½% in free trial orders would produce about 2½% noes. A poorly performing list which brought 1% in trial orders would produce 3% noes. In both cases, the total response was about 4%.

When it comes to sweepstakes contests, of course, the yes-no feature is a legal necessity. The standard language is, "Yes, I am ordering. Let me know if I have won (or what I've won)." "No, I am not ordering at this time. But let me know if I've won (or what I've won)." In sweepstakes, too, there are wide variances between yes-no response percentages. It isn't unusual at all to get 10 to 15 no responses for every yes response when mailing to prospect lists. On the other hand, a sweepstakes offer to an active customer list often produces one or more yes responses for each no response.

Free Gift

Giving free gifts for inquiring, for trying, and for buying has got to be as old an incentive as trading stamps. And the incentive rarely fails to work. It is not unusual at all for the right gift to increase response by 25% and more. On the other hand, a free gift offer can actually reduce response or have no favorable effect on the basic proposition, as previously illustrated. Joan Manley, publisher of Time-Life Books, states they have been consistently unsuccessful with free gifts in conjunction with their Time-Life continuity book offers.

What's more, there is a tremendous variance in appeal of free gifts. For example, Airline Passengers Association tested two free gifts in conjunction with a membership offer: (1) an airline guide; and (2) a carry-on suit bag. The suit bag did 50% better than the guide.

A fund-raising organization selling to schools tested three different gifts: (1) a set of children's books; (2) a camera; and (3) a 30-cup coffee maker. The coffee maker won by a wide margin; the children's books came in a poor third.

Testing for the most appealing gifts is essential, because of the wide differences in pull. In selecting gifts for testing purposes, follow this good rule of thumb: Gifts which lend themselves to personal use tend to have considerably more appeal than those which don't.

There is still another consideration about free gifts: Is it more effective to offer a selection of free gifts of comparable value than just to offer one gift? The answer is that, more often than not, offering a selection of gifts of comparable value reduces response. This is perhaps explained by the inability of many people to make a choice.

The advisability of settling on one gift (after testing for the one with the most appeal) should not be confused with offering gifts with varying value for orders of varying amounts. This is quite a different situation. A multiple gift proposition could be: free travel clock for orders up to $15; free transistor radio for orders from $15 to $30; and free Polaroid camera for orders over $30.

A proposition that offers gifts of varying value for orders of varying amounts is logical to the consumer. And the advertiser can afford a more expensive gift in conjunction with a larger order. And his prime objective is accomplished by increasing his average order over and above what it would be if there were no extra incentive.

The multiple gift plan works for many, but it can also boomerang. This usually happens when the top gift calls for a purchase over and above what most people can use or afford. And the effect can also be negative if the gift offered for the price point most people can use and afford is of little value or consequence. The multiple gift plan tied to order value has good potential, but careful tests must be conducted. An adaptation of the multiple gift plan is a gift, often called a "keeper," for trying (free trial), plus a gift for keeping (paying for the purchase). Under this plan the prospect is told he can keep the gift offered for trying—even if he returns the product or service being offered for sale. But if the product or service being offered is retained, then the prospect also keeps a second gift of greater value than the first. Columbia House, to name one big mass marketer, has successfully applied the gift for trying and the gift for buying technique many times.

Still another possibility with gift propositions is the giving of more than one gift for either trying or buying. If the budget for the incentive is $1, for example, the advertiser has the alternative of one gift costing $1, two gifts costing $1 combined, or even three gifts totaling $1. From a sales strategy standpoint, some advertisers spell out what one or two of the gifts are and offer an additional "mystery gift" for prompt response. Fingerhut Manufacturing Co. of Minneapolis is a prime proponent of multiple gifts and "mystery" gifts.

Free gifts are tricky business, to be sure. Gift selection and gift tie-ins to propositions require careful testing for best results. The $64 question always is, "How much can I afford to spend for a gift?" Aaron Adler, executive vice president of the Chicago office of Rapp, Collins, Stone & Adler, maintains most marketers make an erroneous arbitrary decision in advance such as, "I can afford to spend 5% of selling price." He maintains that a far more logical approach is to select the most appealing gift possible, without being restricted by an arbitrary cost figure, than to be guided by the net profit figures resulting from tests. For example, let's take a gift costing $1 versus a gift costing $2 on a $29.95 offer and compare net profit, with a 50% better pull with the $2 premium.

$1 Premium Offer Produces 1% Net Pull			$2 Premium Offer Produces 1½% Net Pull		
Sales per M		$299.95	Sales per M		$449.25
Costs:			Costs:		
Mailing cost	$120.00		Mailing cost	$120.00	
Merchandise cost			Merchandise cost		
(45%)	134.98		(45%)	202.16	
Administrative cost			Administrative cost		
(10%)	30.00		(10%)	44.93	
Premium cost	10.00		Premium cost	30.00	
	$294.98	$294.98		$397.09	$397.09
Profit per M		$ 4.97	Profit per M		$ 52.16

It's interesting to note in this example that, when the $1 gift was offered, the mailing just about broke even. But when the cost of the gift was doubled, profit jumped from $4.97 to $52.16 per thousand mailed.

Another possibility of more attractive gifts — which naturally cost more — is to offer gifts of substantial value tied to cumulative purchases. This plan can prove particularly effective when the products or services being offered lend themselves to consistent repeat orders. A typical offer under a cumulative purchase plan could be: "When your total purchases of our custom-made cigars reach $150, you receive a power saw absolutely free."

Load-Ups

Load-up propositions are peculiar to continuity bookselling programs. However, the technique should interest all direct marketers, in that it shows how to attract customers with one proposition and change the arithmetic favorably through a subsequent proposition. The load-up technique came into vogue early in the 1960s and is still enjoying great success today. The director of administration of Britannica Home Library Service describes load-ups as follows:

The subscriber sends in an order card requesting the first volume in a set of books. Usually, the first volume is offered free, but it could also involve a token payment, the most common being a 10¢ or 25¢ offer.

If the subscriber does not cancel after receiving the first book, volumes 2 and 3 will be shipped separately at approximately monthly intervals. And then all remaining volumes are sent in one shipment. It is important to note that a subscriber can cancel at any time and the return of any book constitutes automatic cancellation.

The success of the mailing depends not only on front-end response, but also on the shipment retention factor, or "load factor" as it is commonly called. No mailer, to my knowledge, will release 12 volumes in a set without receiving at least one payment. In some cases two (or more) payments are required before the final volumes are released.

It is the end result of the load-up technique which makes the method attractive to book publishers. Under the one-book-a-month plan with no load-up, attrition is more likely to occur after four or five books are received in a 12-book series, for example.

But under the load-up technique, the subscriber receives the balance of 12 books after he has received and paid for the first two or three in a series. Even though the subscriber need pay for only one book a month and even though he may return the load-up shipment if he wishes, statistics prove a higher percentage of complete sets are sold under this method.

Get-a-Friend

Perhaps one of the most overlooked and yet most profitable of all propositions is the get-a-friend offer. If you have a list of satisfied customers, it's quite natural for them to want to let their friends in on a good thing.

Basic technique for get-a-friend propositions is to offer an incentive in appreciation for a favor. Nominal gifts are often given to a customer for the simple act of providing friends' names, with more substantial gifts being awarded for friends who become customers.

Here, based on experience, is what you can expect in using the get-a-friend approach:

You will get a larger number of friends' names if the customer is guaranteed his name will not be used in soliciting his friends.

However, response from friends will be consistently better if you are allowed to refer to the party who supplied their names.

Therefore, to get the best of two worlds, allow the customer to indicate whether his name may be used in solicitating his friends. For example:

"You may use my name when writing my friends."
"Do not use my name when writing my friends."

Response from friends becomes progressively less in relation to the number of names provided by an individual. One can expect the response from three names provided by one individual to be greater than the total response from six names provided by another individual. The reason for this is that it is natural to list the names in order of likelihood of interest.

There are two safeguards which may be applied to getting the maximum response from friends' names: (1) limit the number of names to be provided—for example, to three or four; and (2) promote names provided in order of listing, such as all names provided first as one group, all names provided second as another group, and so forth.

Those who have mastered the technique of getting friends' names from satisfied customers have found, with the rarest of exceptions, that such lists are more responsive than most lists they can rent or buy.

Developing the right proposition, as we have pointed out, is one of the six big keys to direct marketing success.

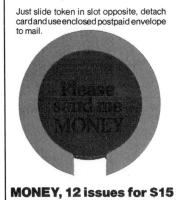

Just slide token in slot opposite, detach card and use enclosed postpaid envelope to mail.

MONEY, 12 issues for $15

Use enclosed envelope to mail the card at right today.

MONEY, Time-Life Building, Chicago, Ill. 60611

MONEY'S SUBSCRIBER BENEFITS

1 The annual subscription rate saves you $3 over the newsstand cost of 12 issues.

2 But MONEY can also save you big money—month after month.

3 To prove it, we'll send your first issue without obligation.

Money

TIME and LIFE's new monthly magazine of money management.

Without cost, obligation or commitment, send me the most recent issue of MONEY—and start my subscription now.

```
ROBERT STONE          M8L205
bDb LAUREL
WILMETTE IL bDD9L
```

12 issues for only $15. If, after examining the first issue, I like MONEY, I'll send my check or money order for my subscription (11 additional issues) when you bill me If not, I may keep the first issue you send me and return the bill marked "cancel"—with no further obligation or cost.

CONDITIONAL SALE

165

Market Survey For AMERICAN HIGHWAY ATLAS

Mail Today to:

The National Research Bureau, Inc.
National Research Building
415 North Dearborn Street
Chicago 10, Illinois

Gentlemen:

In return for my opinion and tentative order, please send me the AMERICAN HIGHWAY ATLAS . . . free of all cost—at once. This Atlas is to come to me in a life-time simulated leather cover, with my name embossed in 24 kt. gold.

Emboss My Name As Follows_____

(please print)

Enter my tentative Christmas order for _____ AMERICAN HIGHWAY ATLASES. I re-

(6 minimum)

serve the right to cancel my order 10 days after receipt of my free Atlas. I keep the free Atlas, regard-less of my decision.

PRICE SCHEDULE	
6 to 12 . . . . $4.25 each	51 to 100 . . . . $3.69 each
13 to 24 . . . . 3.98 each	101 to 250 . . . . 3.46 each
25 to 50 . . . . 3.78 each	251 to 500 . . . . 2.96 each

NOTE: Above prices include your firm name and address embossed in 24 kt. gold on simulated leather cover.

☐ (✓) Check here if you wish individual names embossed on front cover at additional cost of 35¢ each. (List names on back of this sheet.) All shipments F.O.B. Printing Plant.

My Name_____ Signature_____

(please print)

Firm_____

Address_____

City_____ Zone_____ State_____

TENTATIVE ORDER

166

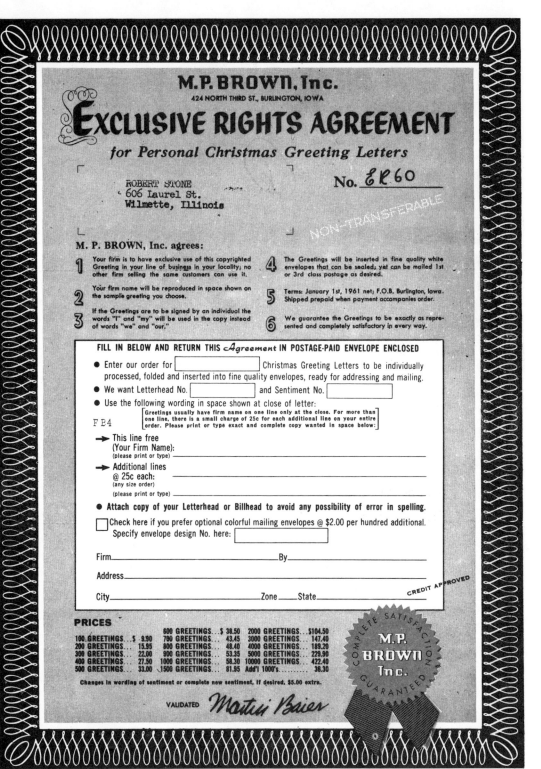

M. P. BROWN, Inc.
424 NORTH THIRD ST., BURLINGTON, IOWA

EXCLUSIVE RIGHTS AGREEMENT
for Personal Christmas Greeting Letters

ROBERT STONE
606 Laurel St.
Wilmette, Illinois

No. ER 60

NON-TRANSFERABLE

M. P. BROWN, Inc. agrees:

1 Your firm is to have exclusive use of this copyrighted Greeting in your line of business in your locality; no other firm selling the same customers can use it.

2 Your firm name will be reproduced in space shown on the sample greeting you choose.

3 If the Greetings are to be signed by an individual the words "I" and "my" will be used in the copy instead of words "we" and "our."

4 The Greetings will be inserted in fine quality white envelopes that can be sealed; yet can be mailed 1st or 3rd class postage as desired.

5 Terms: January 1st, 1961 net; F.O.B. Burlington, Iowa. Shipped prepaid when payment accompanies order.

6 We guarantee the Greetings to be exactly as represented and completely satisfactory in every way.

FILL IN BELOW AND RETURN THIS *Agreement* IN POSTAGE-PAID ENVELOPE ENCLOSED

● Enter our order for [_____] Christmas Greeting Letters to be individually processed, folded and inserted into fine quality envelopes, ready for addressing and mailing.

● We want Letterhead No. [_____] and Sentiment No. [_____]

● Use the following wording in space shown at close of letter:

F B4

> Greetings usually have firm name on one line only at the close. For more than one line, there is a small charge of 25c for each additional line on your entire order. Please print or type exact and complete copy wanted in space below:

➤ This line free
(Your Firm Name):
(please print or type) _____

➤ Additional lines
@ 25c each:
(any size order)
(please print or type) _____

● **Attach copy of your Letterhead or Billhead to avoid any possibility of error in spelling.**

[ ] Check here if you prefer optional colorful mailing envelopes @ $2.00 per hundred additional.
Specify envelope design No. here: [_____]

Firm _____ By _____

Address _____

City _____ Zone _____ State _____

CREDIT APPROVED

PRICES

	600 GREETINGS... $ 38.50	2000 GREETINGS...$104.50
100 GREETINGS... $ 9.90	700 GREETINGS... 43.45	3000 GREETINGS... 147.40
200 GREETINGS... 15.95	800 GREETINGS... 48.40	4000 GREETINGS... 189.20
300 GREETINGS... 22.00	900 GREETINGS... 53.35	5000 GREETINGS... 229.90
400 GREETINGS... 27.50	1000 GREETINGS... 58.30	10000 GREETINGS... 422.40
500 GREETINGS... 33.00	1500 GREETINGS... 81.95	Add'l 1000's...... 36.30

Changes in wording of sentiment or complete new sentiment, if desired, $5.00 extra.

VALIDATED *Martin Baier*

COMPLETE SATISFACTION
M. P. BROWN Inc.
GUARANTEED

EXCLUSIVE RIGHTS

Mail stamp to find out how Medicare makes possible benefits for people of all ages . . . INCLUDING FOLKS UNDER 65!

UNDER 65?
FIND OUT HOW YOU CAN GET PAID FOR STAYING WELL!

OVER 65?
FIND OUT HOW TO FILL THE GAPS IN MEDICARE

Paste your stamp on card and mail today for free facts!

FREE INFORMATION CERTIFICATE

Bankers Life and Casualty Co.
Chicago, Illinois 60630
Please send me free information on the new tax savings made possible by Medicare, and on your new money-saving plans for folks in my age group, as shown by this stamp. I understand there is no cost or obligation to me for this service.

Series: 01-0140 "6" 5028

Validated:

AFFIX
STAMP
HERE

8113   9   C

MR ROBERT STONE
606 LAUREL AV
WILMETTE IL   60091

PLACE STAMP ON CERTIFICATE—MAIL CERTIFICATE
TODAY IN POSTAGE-FREE ENVELOPE

FREE INFORMATION

Enjoy "NO TIME LIMIT" Membership
Take any 4 books for $1
when you join the Literary Guild

223-2

PASTE 4 STAMPS IN THESE SPACES

The enclosed offer was once reserved for Literary Guild members of long standing, Mr. Stone. But now we can extend this generous book club proposal to a number of readers in Wilmette and other selected cities, also. To learn why you've been included, read on...

Please accept my application for membership in the Guild—send me the 4 books indicated by stamps. (Bill me $1, plus a modest charge for shipping and handling.) Send me *The Literary Guild Magazine*, describing all books in advance every month. I'll use the easy form provided to notify you whenever I don't wish to receive a coming selection. For each book I take, you may bill me the Guild's low price (plus shipping and handling): **Guild prices average 30% below publishers'-edition prices.** I agree to remain a member for as long as it takes me to buy 4 selections or alternates, but

"No Time Limit" membership means *I may take as long as I want to buy 4 books.* Afterward I may resign with a note, or remain a member *without obligation* for as long as I wish. BONUS PLAN: With every book I buy at the Guild price, I'll receive at least one Bonus Coupon redeemable for big savings on *another* book I choose from a special catalog. (Most cost only $1 or $2 with these valuable Coupons.)

Mr.
Mrs.
Miss_____
(please sign here)

LIQ04

SPECIAL NO-RISK GUARAN-TEE: If you're not delighted, return all 4 books in 10 days to cancel membership; you'll owe nothing!

PLEASE DON'T RETURN THIS CARD
52 IF YOU'RE ALREADY A GUILD MEMBER.

Mr. Robert Stone
606 Laurel Avenue
Wilmette, Ill. 60091

— — — — — — SEPARATE ON THIS LINE AND MAIL ORDER CARD IN POSTPAID ENVELOPE TODAY! — — — — —

NO TIME LIMIT

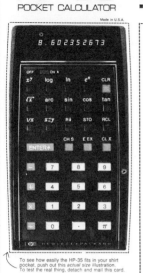

HP-35
POCKET CALCULATOR

Made in U.S.A.

8. 602352673

To see how easily the HP-35 fits in your shirt pocket, push out this *actual size* illustration. To test the real thing, detach and mail this card.

15-DAY TRIAL;
MULTIPLE CHOICE PAYMENT PLAN

The first electronic "answer machine" that gives you
- The portability and convenience of the slide rule . . .
- The problem-solving power of a small computer . . .
- And is priced so you can have this advanced mathematical capability in your shirt pocket!

HEWLETT **hp** PACKARD

Advanced Products Department SDM
10900 Wolfe Road
Cupertino, California 95014

IMPORTANT: When using your purchase order, please include this dept. number

I'd like to "shirt-pocket-test" your HP-35 on the job for 15 days.

Please ship me the HP-35 Pocket Calculator, complete with leather carrying case and recharger, at $395.00. I have checked below the payment option I prefer . . . but I understand that if I'm not completely satisfied, I may return the unit and accessories within 15 days for full credit.

CHECK ONE PAYMENT OPTION:

☐ BILL MY COMPANY for $395.00 plus $4.95 shipping and handling charge and any applicable state or local taxes. Please indicate bank information below.

BANK NAME   BRANCH LOCATION OR PHONE NO.

☐ BILL MY CREDIT CARD for $395.00 plus $4.95 shipping and handling charge and any applicable state or local taxes, if desired. I can use deferred payment plans as available thru my charge card.

CHARGE TO: ☐ American Express ☐ BankAmericard ☐ Master Charge

MY COMPLETE
CARD NO. IS:

If using MASTER CHARGE, please include 4-digit bank number appearing on card just above your name

If your name and address on charge card do not correspond to that shown below, indicate changes:

NAME APPEARING ON CREDIT CARD

STREET ADDRESS   CITY, STATE, ZIP

☐ CASH PAYMENT: Check is enclosed for $395.00 plus applicable state and local taxes. Hewlett-Packard pays shipping and handling. Same 15-day return privilege applies.

If this is not correct ship address, please necessary c[...]

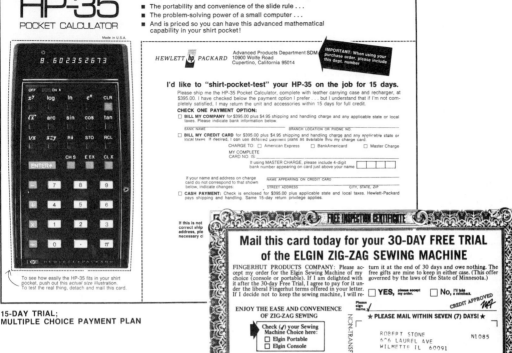

FREE INSPECTION CERTIFICATE

Mail this card today for your 30-DAY FREE TRIAL
of the ELGIN ZIG-ZAG SEWING MACHINE

FINGERHUT PRODUCTS COMPANY: Please accept my order for the Elgin Sewing Machine of my choice (console or portable). If I am delighted with it after the 30-day Free Trial, I agree to pay for it under the liberal Fingerhut terms offered in your letter. If I decide not to keep the sewing machine, I will return it at the end of 30 days and owe nothing. The free gifts are mine to keep in either case. (This offer governed by the laws of the State of Minnesota.)

ENJOY THE EASE AND CONVENIENCE OF ZIG-ZAG SEWING

Check (✓) your Sewing Machine Choice here . . .
☐ Elgin Portable
☐ Elgin Console

Your Free Gifts! Mail your "YES" answer today, get the Master Craft Portable Electric Handmixer AND a Surprise Bonus Gift, FREE TO KEEP . . . just for accepting this Free Trial.

☐ YES, please accept my order.   ☐ No, I'll take a raincheck.

CREDIT APPROVED

Please sign name

★ PLEASE MAIL WITHIN SEVEN (7) DAYS! ★

ROBERT STONE   N1085
606 LAUREL AVE
WILMETTE IL 60091

If address is wrong, please correct it. Do not obliterate old address.

BONUS GIFT! Don't forget the extra Surprise Gift added to your regular gift.

FOR OFFICE USE ONLY

OP-1514

30-DAY TRIAL;
FREE GIFTS; YES - NO

SUBSCRIBE NOW to the Kiplinger Washington Letter...

. . . with the understanding that the unused portion of your payment will be returned to you promptly, any time you feel this service is not worth far more to you than it costs. You'll use the Letter every Monday morning to interpret, analyze, weigh and evaluate all developments pertinent to your job or your business. You'll find decision-making easier, your work week smoother, and your business and personal planning more effective and profitable.

Since 1923 men of affairs have read and used the Kiplinger Letter to their personal profit. Regular readers pay $28 a year for this service . . . and renew their subscriptions year after year . . . proof that they find the Letter a valuable investment.

Check and return this form promptly

THE KIPLINGER WASHINGTON EDITORS, INC.
1729 H Street, Northwest, Washington, D.C. 20006

Please send me the weekly Kiplinger Washington Letter for 4 months . . . only $4.

This special trial offer is open only to new subscribers.

ROBERT STONE
RAPP COLLINS STONE ADLER
222 S RIVERSIDE PLAZA
CHICAGO, ILL.   60606

Check may be made payable to KIPLINGER

☐ bill company   ☐ bill me   ☐ payment enclosed
Entitles you to an extra bonus FREE

Check he[...]   ☐ 1 year

Mail today in the postage-paid reply envelope enclosed

INTRODUCTORY OFFER; GUARANTEE;
BILLING CHOICE; GIFT FOR ADVANCE PAYMENT

Free "Inflation" Letter For Sending Payment Now

Send payment for your new subscription along with your order, and we will rush you FREE our special Letter: "How to Deal with Inflation & Controls."

This revealing report forecasts continuing gov't controls and inflation far into the future. Then it tells how to adjust to them. On your costs. Profits. Business planning. And how to hedge on investments...personal and business.

Thousands of our readers found this report extremely helpful, and it's yours FREE...if you send payment with your order.

THE KIPLINGER WASHINGTON LETTER · 1729 H St., N.W., Washington, D.C. 20006

YES - NO WITH TOKEN
WITH REQUEST FOR PROSPECT NAMES

Here's your chance to get a MASTER CHARGE CARD
PLUS
a special $3 coupon

REMOVE CARD AND PASTE IN SPACE OPPOSITE

master charge
Town & Country Charge

Paste your answer here

mas **YES** arge
THE INTERBANK CARD

I'd like you to send me a free Master Charge card as soon as possible.

☐ NO THANKS
THE INTERBANK CARD

No. I want to pass up your free offer at this time.

YES - NO; FREE OFFER;
GIFT FOR ACCEPTANCE

MAKE YOUR
YES OR NO
SELECTION
OF FINE CIGARS
NOW!

Place cigar box in slots above.

Press out "CIGAR BOX" Put in slot

YOUR OPPORTUNITY TO SAMPLE THE FINEST CIGARS MADE IN THIS COUNTRY SINCE 1963!

YES Here is my vote to try the Thompson Variety Cabinet on a no-risk-to-me basis.

SEE BACK OF THIS CARD FOR NAMES OF CIGAR SMOKING FRIENDS

NO But I am recommending the names of some cigar connoisseurs on the back of this card.

HERE IS MY SELECTION: TOM TIMMINS

TO: Tom Timmins, Thompson & Co., P. O. Box 1839, Tampa, Fla.
Please send me postpaid your Thompson Variety Cabinet of 48 mild factory fresh cigars. I understand that this places me under no obligation to buy; that if I send payment now, it will be refunded in full if I am not satisfied; that if I return the unused portion of the Cabinet, you will pay the return parcel post charges.

☐ $6.95 Enclosed   ☐ Bill me. I'll remit in 10 days or return the remainder of the cigars.

SIGN HERE ►

R   STONE
606 LAUREL
WILMETTE   IL 60091

169

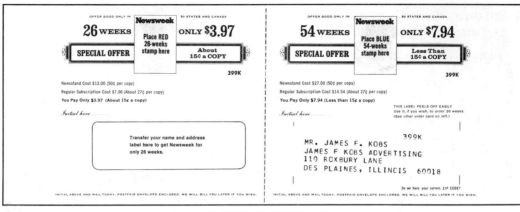

DUAL OFFER WITH ATERNATE CHOICE

SWEEPSTAKES OFFER WITH MULTIPLE ENTRIES

Self-Quiz

1. All direct marketing professionals agree: the _____ is a major factor in the degree of success achieved.

2. Define human inertia.

   _____

   _____

3. Name four propositions which could be parlayed into one offer.

   1. _____

   2. _____

   3. _____

   4. _____

4. What is meant by "danger of overkill"?

   _____

   _____

   _____

   _____

5. If you attract new customers by offering free gifts, what rule must you follow in seeking repeat business?

   _____

   _____

6. Define a unique proposition.

   _____

   _____

   _____

7. Name the five general categories of payment terms.

   1. _____ 2. _____

   3. _____ 4. _____

   5. _____

171

8. Rate the five general categories of payment terms on a basis of attractiveness to the prospect, listing the most attractive first.

1. _____ 2. _____

3. _____ 4. _____

5. _____

9. What is the hazard of C.O.D. terms?

_____

_____

10. What is the hazard of open terms to the consumer?

_____

_____

_____

_____

11. What are the two safe ways to make credit available to the consumer?

1. _____

2. _____

12. Name five commercial credit cards through which consumer sales may be charged.

1. _____ 2. _____

3. _____ 4. _____

5. _____

13. What is the approximate interest charge for bank cards? _____%; for travel and entertainment cards? _____%.

14. Where the prospect is offered the alternative of cash or charge through a commercial card, what percentage are likely to charge their purchase? _____% to _____%

15. In the catalog field, if a customer charges his purchase rather than paying cash, one can expect the average order to be _____% to _____% larger.

16. Why is a guarantee essential in mail order?

_____

_____

_____

17. What is meant by a "third-party" guarantee?

_____

_____

18. Name three possible objectives which may affect the structuring of a proposition.

   1. _____

      _____

   2. _____

      _____

   3. _____

      _____

19. When is it advisable to structure a short-term offer for a publication?

_____

_____

20. What does "C.P.A." stand for?

_____

21. What does "C.P.I." stand for?

_____

22. What is the danger of being concerned with "front end" response only?

_____

_____

_____

_____

23. What is the danger of a misleading proposition?

_____

_____

24. What is the basic advantage of the "yes-no" proposition?

_____

_____

_____

173

25. When you select gifts for testing purposes, a good rule of thumb to follow is this: Gifts which lend themselves to _____ _____ _____ _____ _____ _____ _____ _____ _____.

26. Is it more effective to offer a selection of free gifts of comparable value than just one gift? _____ Yes _____ No

27. Under what condition are multiple gift selections advisable?

_____

_____

28. What is the difference between a "keeper" gift and a gift for keeping?

_____

_____

29. What is the most logical approach to deciding how much a direct marketer can afford for a free gift?

_____

_____

_____

30. What is the advantage of substantial gifts tied to cumulative purchases?

_____

_____

_____

31. How does a load-up plan work?

_____

_____

_____

32. When using get-a-friend propositions, the basic technique is to offer _____ in appreciation.

33. If you are after maximum quantity of friends' names, you guarantee

_____

34. If maximum response from friends' names is the objective, response will be better if

_____

35. The best of two worlds between maximum quantity of friends' names and maximum response from them is _____

_____

36. Response from friends' names becomes progressively less in relation to _____

_____

Pilot Project

You are the advertising manager of a business service organization. Your firm has developed a series of 24 training booklets for salesmen. Your assignment is to develop three different propositions designed to get maximum sales.

1. Develop three basic propositions for testing purposes.
2. Decide on your terms of payment for each of the three basic propositions.
3. What will your guarantee be for each of the three propositions?

SECTION IV CREATING AND PRODUCING DIRECT MARKETING

Chapter 9 Techniques of Creating Direct Mail Packages*

Copywriting is an art, especially when it involves direct marketing. It takes good copy — and usually fairly long copy — to get a reader to order something by mail, sight unseen. Or, for that matter, to take some other specific action.

Through the years, the writer has played a more important role in the direct mail creative process than the artist. In the last few years, graphics have become more important . . . as we see a growing trend toward modern design and dramatic four-color printing.

But in most creative shops, the copywriter is still the key man. He not only writes the copy for a direct mail package, he also normally does the rough layouts for the envelope, brochure, and other enclosures that establish the physical format of the mailing. And he often is involved in creating the offer or suggesting what should be tested.

A good copywriter is a unique person. Or, to put it more accurately, a combination of persons. He's a psychologist who understands human nature and basic desires. He's a communicator who knows how to present his story in a dramatic, yet believable, way. He's a motivator who is willing to put his typewriter where his mouth is and use it to invite action. And most important of all, he's a salesman who is not afraid to ask for the order.

Benefit/Price/Value Equation

A good salesman knows that he can get a sale only when the customer considers something a value. This is often expressed in a simple equation: BENEFIT divided by PRICE equals VALUE.

Don Kanter, vice president and senior account executive of RCS&A (Chicago), used this formula when he headed a staff of more than 100 copywriters at Montgomery Ward. And here's how he describes it: "Every time a person is confronted with a buying decision, he will subconsciously assign a worth to the benefits he perceives. At the same time, he assigns a worth to the price he has to pay. And very subjectively, very subconsciously, he divides one into the other to reach his buying decision.

"If in his mind, the benefits outweigh the price . . . he will buy. If in his mind, the price outweighs the benefits . . . he will not buy."

The writer's job, then, is to come up with enough strong and relevant benefits to make the product more attractive than the price. And to present them clearly and forcefully to the prospect.

How does he accomplish this? By using the same tools every other direct mail writer has at his disposal — the 26 letters of the alphabet, plus a handful of punctuation marks. The secret, of course, is what he does with those tools, how he forms them into words and strings them together to make sentences and paragraphs. Equally important is how much "homework" he's done before he puts the first word on the paper.

*Jim Kobs, vice president — general manager of the Chicago office of RCS&A, provided the major input for this chapter.

176

Preparation Pays Off

Too many people "sit down to write a sales letter" without preparation. Their copy shows it. Selling points are written as they occur. Thoughts are disjointed. The letter lacks direction. The writer fails to incite action.

The person hasn't been born who can sit down and dash off a great piece of direct mail copy. It is hard work. There are no shortcuts. Almost without exception, the success of any direct mail letter is in direct ratio to the time spent on its preparation. In my book, figuring out *what* to say is just as important as *how* you say it.

There are three mental exercises that are very important in the copy preparation stage: 1. Think about your objective. 2. Think about your offer. 3. Think about your market.

The first point seems obvious. But do it anyway. If your objective is too complicated or has too many parts, then you know you are in trouble. Try to crystallize your objective and reduce it to one central goal. Do you want somebody to place an order? Request a sales call? Ask for more information? Remember that you are going to try to influence thinking. The clearer your own thinking, the easier it is to influence the thinking of others.

In Chapter 8 we reviewed more than 20 offers. Decide which one you'll use. Get your offer down on paper *before* you start to write your mailing piece. The offer you decide on will influence the amount and kind of emphasis you should give it in your copy. A particularly strong or attractive offer should be featured prominently in your headlines and other display copy.

Now start thinking about your market—the type of people you want to sell. Some writers like to think about a person they know who fits the market profile. Others try to write a description of their typical prospect. The better you know your prospect, the better job you can do of appealing to him. Naturally, your copy style should fit the audience. If you are writing for doctors, you will not write copy the same way you would for mechanics. Your copy for top executives will vary drastically from copy for housewives.

Translate Product Features into Benefits

The next preparatory exercise is also important. It involves the subtle but important distinction between a product feature and a product benefit. A product feature or selling point is something the product has or does. It belongs to the product.

A product benefit, on the other hand, is what that feature means to the reader. It belongs or applies to the customer. Let's look at some examples. Suppose you're writing copy for a portable counter-top dishwasher. Here are a few common features, and alongside each is the benefit that feature provides:

Product Feature	*Product Benefit*
1. Has a ten-minute operating cycle.	1. Does complete load of dishes in only ten minutes.
2. Measures 18 inches in diameter.	2. Small enough to fit on a counter-top.
3. White base with clear plastic top.	3. See-through top lets you watch washing cycle, know when dishes are done.
4. Has universal hose coupling.	4. Fits any standard kitchen faucet.

After you list your product features, jot down the appropriate benefit next to each one. Then try to list these benefits in order of importance so you can put the proper emphasis on the most important. Once you cultivate the habit of thinking benefits, you'll be surprised how much easier it is to write good direct mail copy.

The Right Copy Strategy

With your benefits down on paper, you now have to decide on the copy strategy or appeals that will do the best selling job. Creative types refer to this in different ways. Some talk about how you "position" the product in the prospect's mind. Others refer to "coming up with the big idea" behind the copy.

What is it about your offer and benefit story that is *most* appealing? When you stop to think about it, people respond to any given proposition for either one of two reasons: To gain something they do not have, or to avoid losing something they now possess.

As you can see from the accompanying chart, basic human wants can be neatly divided into these two categories. The professional copywriter carefully sifts and weighs the list of basic human wants against his proposition to come up with the main appeal. (In Chapter 11 you'll see how the same product can be slanted for many different appeals just by changing your headline.)

BASIC HUMAN WANTS

The desire to gain:
*To make money.
*To save time.
*To avoid effort.
*To achieve comfort.
*To have health.
*To be popular.
*Enjoyment.
*Cleanliness.
*Praise.
*To be in style.
*To gratify curiosity.
*To satisfy appetite.
*To have beautiful possessions.
*To attract the opposite sex.
*To be an individual.
*To emulate others.
*To take advantage of opportunities.

The desire to avoid loss:
*Avoid criticism.
*Loss of possessions.
*Physical pain.
*Reputation.
*Danger in buying.
*Loss of money.
*Trouble.

Does your proposition offer the promise of saving time, avoiding hard or disagreeable work? Most people like to avoid work. Saving time is a fetish of the American people. Appeal to this basic want, if you can.

Does your proposition help people to feel important? People like to keep up with the Joneses. People like to be made to feel that they are part of a select group. A tremendous number of people are susceptible to snob appeal.

178

Perhaps you can offer a terrific bargain by mail and capitalize on the appeal of saving money. The desire to "get it wholesale" is a strong one.

The writer's job is to determine which appeal or appeals come closest to hitting the "hot button" of the prospect. And the decision can have a lot to do with results you get. To illustrate the point, Jim Kobs uses the example of two letters American Peoples Press tested to sell an electric home organ.

Letter A points out how easily you can learn to play the organ and how it can make you more popular — "Do you wish you were the creator of all that happiness and beauty . . . the center of attraction?"

Letter B appeals to the family enjoyment an organ can provide — "There's just something warm and wonderful about a home that's filled with good music." It goes on to show how each member of the family would benefit from this family music center.

What happened when they were split-tested? Letter B did 34% better! And it's important to realize that this letter was not *written* any better than the other one. It's the big idea behind the copy — the family appeal — that made it more successful.

Selecting the Format To Do the Job

As we said, the copywriter usually plays a key role in developing the physical format of the mailing package. And that's only fitting, because the format should present the copy in the most attractive manner.

It's been said that a direct mail copywriter often starts the creative process by folding and unfolding a piece of paper to come up with the right format — before he ever begins writing. In thinking about the format, you'll want to consider how much copy and how many illustrations you'll need to present your story adequately.

The format should also be suitable for your audience. Do you want a package that will stand out among the many other mailings on a businessman's desk, or is it something designed for leisurely reading by the consumer at home? Very often the budget for a mailing will help determine the format you use. And, of course, the format must physically conform to postal requirements.

The Classic Mailing Package

Because direct mail offers almost unlimited creative freedom, there are dozens of formats and variations to choose from. The choice can be a difficult one. When in doubt, go with the format that's been so popular through the years it's become a classic.

It consists of a mailing envelope . . . letter . . . circular . . . and order or reply form. Very often a gift slip or a reply envelope is used with it. This format has proved to be effective for a wide variety of products, services, and audiences.

Even with this classic format, there are plenty of variations possible. The letter, for example, can be all typewritten; it can be illustrated, personalized by computer, or have a built-in order form as a reply device. It can be one page, two pages, four pages, or even more. And a multipage letter can be printed on both sides of a sheet or on separate pages. Use the letter format that seems most appropriate for your copy story and audience, and, if possible, test variations. One other word of advice about the letter: it should *look* like a letter. That means sticking with a typewriter face which has the look and feel of a personal letter.

The same kind of variety is possible for another element of the classic mailing package — the circular. It's sometimes referred to as a brochure. There are three main types of circulars or brochures:

A *folder* is usually an inexpensive, flexible format. It often is simply an 8½ × 11 sheet folded in thirds. But it can vary considerably in size, shape, and how it's folded.

A booklet is normally used when you have a longer story to tell. There is no limitation on size or number of pages, and it can be stapled or glued. It has more permanence than a folder. On the other hand, booklets do not suggest urgency, so you run the risk that the prospect will put it aside for later reading . . . and never get back to it.

A broadside is an oversize sheet, like that commonly found in consumer book and merchandise mailings. It's often printed in full color, and may be 17×22 or larger. A broadside may be designed so each side of the sheet tells a complete story, like a poster. Or it may present the sales story piece by piece, as the broadside is unfolded. In addition to plenty of copy room, you have the room to include a number of illustrations or photographs.

Which one should you use for a given promotion? That's up to you. But try to pick the circular format that best fits your selling story. Does your copy message lend itself best to a series of small panels (folder or booklet) or to the larger sheet (broadside)? How much copy room do you need? And how important are illustrations of the product or service you're selling? Will one large picture be better than a series of smaller ones?

Self-Mailers — An Inexpensive Favorite

Any mailing piece that's sent out without an envelope is considered a self-mailer. And next to the classic mailing package, it's probably one of the most widely used formats, especially by retailers. It can range in size from a simple card to a giant folder.

From a cost standpoint it's certainly attractive, because there are economies in printing, addressing, and mailing a single piece. But in terms of results, it will usually not do so well as the envelope/letter/circular/reply format. I've seen exceptions, but not too many. If you want to use a self-mailer, I suggest two things. First, choose a large-size format. Then, build in as many elements of the classic mailing package as you can. Use one panel for a letter-type message and another area to do the job of a circular . . . and include a detachable order form. Some self-mailers even include a preformed envelope, which is a good idea for a cash offer.

Specialized Formats

Because of the creative freedom that direct mail offers, there are dozens of specialized formats. They include giant letters, die-cut shapes, tip-on gadgets, and pop-ups. Three of the most widely used for direct response are the illustrated letter, the invitation, and the simulated telegram.

The illustrated letter has one big thing going for it: A picture can quickly grab the reader's interest before he makes that split-second decision to read on or pitch it! Research has shown that three out of four people will open and at least glance at direct mail. When they come to the letter, the right illustration can capture that glance and attract favorable attention to your message. Illustrations can be photographs, line art, or cartoon drawings. They can include a product, people, a free booklet that's being offered, a simulated check, a certificate, or dozens of other possibilities. But the illustration should be relevant to the product and help dramatize the key benefit you are trying to get across. That means, save the picture of your building for the annual report — and use one that will help you win that split-second decision.

The invitation format is as old as the hills, but it still works very effectively. Especially for publishers, memberships, and credit card solicitations. It's designed to simulate a formal invitation: "You are cordially invited to accept . . . " The inside of the invitation normally carries a letter explaining the offer. And naturally, it includes an R.S.V.P. — a call for action.

While the simulated telegram is less formal, it has much more urgency to it. Scores of magazines use it somewhere in their renewal series. And it fits in well with many types of follow-up mailings. It's usually reproduced on yellow stock, and has a masthead that ties in with the product or service being offered. A physical fitness magazine, for instance, could send a renewal notice called a "Health-O-Gram."

One important point to remember is that the best format is not always the most expensive one. A simpler format not only costs less to mail; it will sometimes outpull a

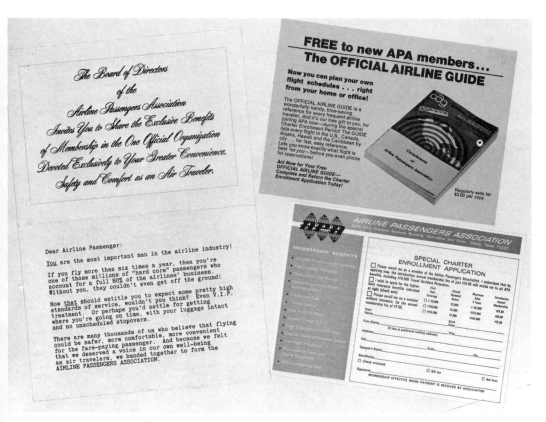

Invitation package, with a simple four-page folder, outpulled a more expensive package with a separate letter and illustrated brochure. The same gift slip and application were used in both packages.

more elaborate package. A dramatic example of this is the invitation format used by Airline Passengers Association. The four-page folder combined an invitation with the message. It was tested against a more expensive package, consisting of a separate letter and an illustrated brochure, and the invitation consistently pulled a higher response.

On the other hand, when you have a product with a big ticket price, a more expensive package is often called for. The purchase becomes less of an impulse — and you may need lots of illustrations and copy to get that order. Fortunately, you usually have a larger profit margin with an expensive product. So you can afford a higher in-the-mail cost for your package without raising your break-even response to an unrealistic level.

Involvement Increases Response

Regardless of the kind of format you use, reader involvement can make it dramatically more effective. If you get the reader involved with your offer and message, you're well on your way to a sale.

Typically effective involvement devices are gummed stamps and token order cards. Publishers Clearing House has long used a sheet of gummed stamps to dramatize the variety of magazine subscriptions they offer. Book offers very often include a token on the order card that's to be punched out and returned to get the first selection in the series.

In building up the excitement of a sweepstakes or free gift offer, many mailers have good success with rub-off devices, mystery envelopes, or perforated panels that have to be opened. Just getting the reader involved in checking a list of winning sweepstakes numbers pays off.

Award-winning Polaroid mailing used a 2-piece brochure to involve the reader and simulate how the camera produces instant pictures.

A classic involvement format is the Polaroid mailing package that was a top award-winner a few years ago. The two-part brochure was designed so that you pulled out the inner part, just as you would pull the film tab out of the camera after taking a Polaroid picture.

The ultimate way to get the reader involved is by including a product sample or swatch in the mailing. Obviously it's not suitable for all types of merchandise. But nothing beats letting somebody touch, feel, and try what you're selling. Whether your offer is men's shoes or ladies' car coats, a swatch of the material can be worth a lot of words.

Creating the Classic Mailing Package

Now that we've looked at some of the wealth of available formats, let's go back to the classic mailing package mentioned earlier. And before we get to the letter, let's talk about the other parts of the package.

The Envelope. Its job is simply to get attention—whet the reader's appetite and make him open the package to see what's inside. Some creative experts prefer a blank white envelope, feeling that curiosity will get it opened.

Others believe that if you have a strong offer—like "10 Records for 98¢" or "Volume 1 Free"—the place for it is right on the envelope. And the offer itself will get people inside.

A third school of thought feels that, to put it rather bluntly, you shouldn't spill your guts on the envelope. Just use teaser copy to arouse the reader's interest. In other words, promise a benefit or make some intriguing statement about the subject.

One word of caution: You want the reader to open the envelope in a positive, receptive frame of mind. So don't mislead him with your envelope copy. To use a somewhat farfetched example, an envelope that says "$10 Bill Enclosed" is a surefire bet to get opened. But if you don't have a $10 bill inside, the reader won't be very receptive to your selling story.

The Brochure. As noted, most mailing packages require a good brochure or circular in addition to a letter. It can be a small, two-color affair. Or a beautiful, giant circular that's almost as big as a tablecloth. But the job it has to do is the same, and it deserves your best creative effort.

In a talk at Chicago Direct Mail Day, Kobs outlined these four requirements for a good circular:

1. *Capture the product excitement on paper.* If a copywriter is enthused about what he's selling, he has to transfer that enthusiasm to the reader with words and graphics, ink and paper. You can use an unusual brochure format to dramatize the product, such as die-cuts or a novel fold. And you can sometimes capture a product's excitement with strong headlines or illustrations.

2. *Guide the reader step by step.* Just as a good salesman skillfully leads a prospect through his sales presentation, a brochure should be organized to present your sales story in the most logical sequence. That means deciding which part of the story should strike the reader first, what should come next, and so on. Even the headlines and subheads should be written to tell a fairly complete story. Many prospects will skim through a circular before they decide whether to read it, and this gives you a great chance to catch their interest.

3. *Explain product benefits thoroughly.* The circular's function is to provide a detailed, self-contained selling story. It should contain all the nuts-and-bolts

NOW—Collect Past Due Accounts With the NEW Deluxe M. P. Brown Collection Stickers

<u>You've got money coming</u> . . .

. . . from past due accounts. And here is a simple, <u>proved-effective</u> way to collect it in cash . . . <u>at practically no collection cost</u>!

These attention-getting collection stickers are the <u>ten best producers</u> among scores tested over two decades by 116,483 business firms we serve. They <u>bring back the cash</u>. Yet -- these stickers will keep the friendship and good will of your customers.

And the cost of these cash-producing collection stickers? Less than 1¢ each in quantity. It's hard to believe that so much cash could be collected at practically no collection cost. But here are the comments of just a few typical users.

Gets results!

"We have never used anything where we got the results we have with these stickers."
-- American Printers, San Antonio, Texas

$309.30

"We collected $309.30 on two different accounts. Both were about one year old."
-- Tuttle & Wittig, Hicksville, Ohio

$1,632.95

"Cold cash, amounting to $1,632.95, was delivered in person within four days after we used the sticker."
-- Stutzenburger, North Bergen, New York

You can expect to bring in the cash with these stickers, too. They're so easy to use. Just affix the collection sticker of your choice to your statement and mail. The message flags the attention of the debtor ... jogs him to action. And back comes the cash!

But the proof of the pudding is in the eating. Therefore -- <u>we will guarantee results</u>. If you don't collect more cash than you expected within 30 days -- return the unused portion and receive a cash refund.

So with cash to collect and with tested collection stickers to help you speed your money your way . . . we urge you to order your supply <u>today</u>. We'll pack your stickers in a durable, easy-to-use box.

Stickers will be equally assorted. Or, you may order a special selection. Either way -- <u>you get the results you expect</u>, or you receive a cash refund.

Postage-free envelope enclosed.

Norman Seligman

Norman Seligman, for
M. P. BROWN, INC.

Samples of actual collection stickers at the top of the letter provide maximum involvement, and help boost results for M. P. Brown.

facts—size, specifications, colors, offer, and guarantee. And don't worry about repeating some of the same points that are covered in the letter—it gives you a great chance to emphasize them.

4. *Answer questions in advance.* In some respects, selling in print is much more difficult than selling in person. A good salesman is experienced in answering objections. He can watch facial expressions, see what benefits spark the prospect's interest, and skillfully field any questions that come up. But there's no salesman standing over the prospect's shoulder when he reads your mailing piece. And any important question that's left unanswered can cost you the sale. So you have to anticipate the most common questions that might come up and make sure they're covered by your copy. Many insurance mailings even include a question and answer section to accomplish this.

One way or another your circular has to do a complete selling job. To give yourself every chance for success, review the appearance, content, and preparation of your circulars. "20 Ways to Improve Circulars" is a handy checklist for this purpose.

20 Ways to Improve Circulars

Appearance

1. Is the circular in character with the market you are reaching?
2. Is the presentation in character with the product or service you are offering?
3. Is the circular in harmony with the rest of the mailing package?

Content

4. Is there a big idea behind your circular?
5. Do your headlines stick to the key offer?
6. Is your product or service dramatized to its best advantage by format and/or presentation?
7. Are good quality drawings or photographs used to portray the product?
8. Do you show widely adaptable examples of your product or service in use?
9. Is your copy believable?
10. Is your copy easy to read—short words, sentences, and paragraphs?
11. Are your statements backed up by proofs and endorsements?
12. Does your entire circular presentation follow a logical sequence and tell a complete story—including price, offer, and guarantee?
13. Does your entire circular presentation build toward inducing the reader to take specific action?

Preparation

14. Does the layout have the feel of a good direct response circular?
15. Will the circular cut out of stock size paper?
16. Is the quality of paper stock in keeping with the presentation?
17. Is color employed judiciously to show the product or service in its best light?
18. Are typography, photography, and art in keeping with the market and the proposition?
19. Has art been prepared in the best manner for the printing process to be employed?
20. Have color proofs been approved by the artist or art studio before going to press?

The Order Form. If Ernest Hemingway had been a direct response writer, he probably would have dubbed the order form "the moment of truth." Many prospects make a final decision on whether or not to respond after reading it. Some even read the order form before anything else in the envelope, because they know it's the easiest way to find out what's being offered at what price.

The best advice I can give on order forms comes from Henry Cowen of Publishers Clearing House. He says: "There are direct mail manuals around that recommend simple, easy-to-read order forms. But my experience indicates the mailer is far better off with a busy, rather jumbled appearance and plenty of copy. Formal and legal looking forms that appear valuable, too valuable to throw away, are good."

The key words in Cowen's statement are *too valuable to throw away.* The order form or reply form that appears valuable induces readership. It impels the reader to do some-

Montage of gift slips shows variety of sizes, colors, and graphic treatments from simple, all-type one to elaborate 4-color slip.

thing with it, to take advantage of the offer. High on the list of devices and techniques which make order forms look valuable are certificate borders, safety paper backgrounds, simulated rubber stamps, eagles, blue handwriting, seals, serial numbers, receipt stubs, and so on. And sheer size alone can greatly add to the valuable appearance of a response form. (You've seen examples of many of these techniques on the order forms shown in Chapter 8.)

By all means don't call your reply device an order form. Call it a Reservation Certificate, Free Gift Check, Trial Membership Application, or some other benefit heading . . . and it automatically seems more valuable to the reader.

Getting more inquiry and order forms back starts with making them appear too valuable to throw away. But, to put frosting on the cake, add the dimension of personal involvement. Give the reader something to do with the order form. Ask him to put a token in a "yes" or "no" slot. Get him to affix a gummed stamp. Have him tear off a stub that has your guarantee on it. Once you have prodded the prospect into action, there is a good chance you will receive an order.

Finally, the order form should restate your offer and benefits. If a prospect loses the letter or circular, a good order form should be able to stand alone and do a complete selling job. And if it's designed to be mailed back on its own (without an envelope), it's usually worthwhile to prepay the postage.

Gift Slips and Other Enclosures. In addition to the letter, brochure, and order form, one of the most common enclosures is a free gift slip. If you have a free gift offer, you'll normally get much better results by putting it in a separate slip, rather than building it into your circular.

You want any extra enclosure to stand out from the rest of the mailing and get attention. You can often accomplish this by printing the enclosure on a color stock and making it a different size than the other mailing components. Most free gifts, for example, can be adequately played up on a small slip that's $3\frac{1}{2} \times 8\frac{1}{2}$ or $5\frac{1}{2} \times 8\frac{1}{2}$.

Another enclosure that's often used is a business reply envelope. It isn't essential if the order form can be designed for mailing back without an envelope. But if you have an offer that the reader may consider to be of a private nature, an envelope is usually better. Buying a self-improvement book, for example. Or applying for an insurance policy, where the application asks some personal questions. And the extra expense of a reply envelope is often justified if you want to encourage more cash with order replies.

Good Typography

Just as good layout is important in making direct mail easy to read, so is good typography. It's been said with some authority: "A type book in the hands of the uninitiated is a dangerous instrument!"

Type, used right, can "talk" convincingly for any advertiser. Type sets moods, expresses character. Type can scream or whisper, attract or detract, build confidence or suspicion, express dignity or crudeness, be masculine or feminine, bold or refined. Type can motivate or repel. Type makes an image—good or bad—every time.

Virgil D. Angerman, sales promotion manager of Boise Cascade Envelopes, has investigated the subject of typefaces in depth. In the course of his research, he has selected 20 representative typefaces, each of which expresses a basic image.

In direct mail, the advertiser enjoys the luxury of plenty of space to play with. So the opportunities to make type talk favorably are great. But this very freedom of space often results in atrocities—a multiplicity of typefaces and sizes not in the image of the advertiser or his proposition.

187

Antiquity INLAND COPPERPLATE	Delicate BERNHARD MODERN	Firmness CENTURY NOVA	*Oriental* REINER SCRIPT
Boldness FRANKLIN GOTHIC	Dependability GARAMOND BOLD	Gaiety P. T. BARNUM	**PATRIOTIC** SAPHIR
Character CRAW MODERN	Dignity MELIOR	Luxury CASLON OPEN FACE	Progressive AMERICANA BOLD
Conservatism EUROSTYLE	Ecclesiastical OLD ENGLISH	**Masculinity** FORTUNE EXTRA BOLD	Reliable GOUDY OLD STYLE
Continental BERNHARD TANGO	Femininity FUTURA LIGHT	Movement BRUSH	**Strength** COOPER BLACK

ACME FAST FREIGHT, Inc.
525 WEST 47TH STREET
CHICAGO, ILLINOIS 60609
Italic type indicates movement

MOSER
Secretarial School
308 NORTH MICHIGAN AVENUE
CHICAGO, ILL. 60601 • PHONE 329-0954
Feminity reflected in typeface

J. C. JEWELERS
7566 MILWAUKEE AVENUE
NILES, ILLINOIS 60648
Hand-tooled type
signifies luxury

FRUEHAUF
CORPORATION
P. O. BOX 8170
DETROIT, MICHIGAN 48213
Forceful type suggests strength

COMPUTER BUSINESS
SERVICES, INC.
6400 N. CENTRAL EXPRESSWAY, DALLAS, TEXAS 75206
Discloses type of business

CONTINENTAL ILLINOIS NATIONAL BANK
AND TRUST COMPANY OF CHICAGO
231 S. LA SALLE STREET
CHICAGO, ILLINOIS 60690
Conservatism expressed in type

A-B-C Business Forms, Inc.
5481 MILWAUKEE AVE. — CHICAGO, ILLINOIS 60630
Type used implies progressive firm

Allstate
Allstate Plaza
Northbrook, Ill. 60062

GraybaR
ELECTRIC COMPANY, INC.
2045 North Cornell Avenue
MELROSE PARK, ILL. 60160

FORWARDING COMPANY
1601 S. Western Avenue
CHICAGO, ILLINOIS 60608

Mobil
150 EAST 42ND STREET
NEW YORK, NEW YORK 10017

Sunset
Lane Magazine & Book Company
Menlo Park, California 94025

5000 WEST ROOSEVELT ROAD
CHICAGO, ILLINOIS 60607

The Swiss Colony
MONROE WISCONSIN
53566

Intext
Scranton, Pennsylvania 18515

20 basic images or feelings expressed in typefaces.

Chad Jefferson, a Chicago commercial artist of stature, makes these pertinent comments about typography:

One of the essential ingredients of good mail order advertising is good typography. While trends in typography change from time to time, the fundamentals remain constant and the "far out" and "gimmicky" soon pass away.

Regardless of design or illustrative treatment, the real guts of any advertisement is the "word." Thus, skillful selection and use of typography are essential to an effective presentation. The many new designs in type offer the inventive designer a wide range of possibilities.

Large areas of text overprinting bright colors such as red will discourage even the most interested reader. Exceptionally long lines with too little line leading will interrupt normal eye movement and discourage readership. Unusually narrow margins will again interfere with the normal tracking pattern of the eye.

The ideal would be relatively narrow columns of perhaps 45 to 60 characters with ample margins and adequate line leading. The background should provide as much contrast as possible with the type itself. The eye movement patterns of the reader are well established and every effort should be made to stay within these. The advertiser who assumes his prospect will "struggle" to read his message is courting disaster.

Anatomy of a Successful Mailing

As we have just seen, each component of a classic mailing package has to do its part of the total selling job. But it's equally important that the anatomy of that mailing be carefully tailored to the audience you're trying to reach.

A good example, I think, is the mailing package offering Dartnell's *Advertising Manager's Handbook*. It was designed to sell this four-pound volume of advertising information with a $24 price tag. And it was mailed to advertising managers throughout the country. The mailing package consisted of a 6 × 9 envelope, letter, two-collor brochure, and order card. The classic mailing package. (See page 190.)

This mailing is taken out of the ordinary class, in my opinion, by the creative strategy and the strong use of graphics throughout the package. Dartnell realized that handbooks like this are bought primarily for reference. As an executive security blanket, if you will, that can be consulted at a moment's notice when a problem or question pops up.

So the creative strategy was simply to emphasize the size, scope, and completeness of the book. Unusual photography angles were used to make the point visually. The copy emphasized "the most complete storehouse of advertising know-how ever published." And the whole concept was dramatized with a "friendly challenge" right on the envelope.

The result was a highly successful mailing package. And while books aren't normally sold by the pound, in this case the right package sold a few tons' worth.

Writing a Winning Letter

Now we're ready to write a letter, one of the key elements in any successful mailing package. As suggested earlier, we've thought about the objective. We've decided on our offer. We know the market—the people we're writing to. We have a complete list of product benefits. And we've chosen the right copy strategy.

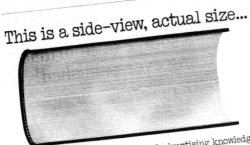
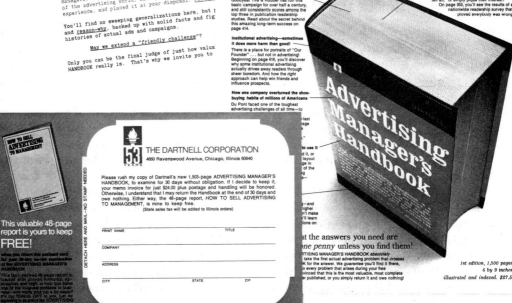

Dartnell mailing employs unusual photography angles and strong copy theme to portray the size and scope of this reference handbook.

Our first task is to decide on the lead for our letter. Nothing is more important than the lead. Just as a salesman's opening remarks set the stage for a successful or unsuccessful interview, so the lead sets the stage for a successful or unsuccessful letter. It's important to start with your best foot forward, and numerous tests have shown that one letter lead can pull substantially better than another.

Let's look at six of the most common types of leads used in sales letters. And to help you compare them, let's take a sample product and write six different leads for that same product. The product we'll use is a self-improvement book for businessmen, which includes biographical sketches of a dozen prominent business leaders.

1. *News.* If you have a product or service which is really news, then you have the makings of an effective lead. For there is nothing more effective than news. If you have a product or service that's been around a while, perhaps you can zero in on one aspect of it that's timely or newsworthy.

    Example: Now . . . you can discover the same success secrets that helped a dozen famous business leaders reach the top!

2. *How/What/Why.* Any beginning newspaperman is taught that a good story should start out by answering the main questions that go through a reader's mind—who, what, when, where, why, and how. You can build an effective lead by promising to answer one of these questions and then immediately enlarging on it in your opening paragraphs.

    Examples: How successful men really get ahead;
        or
    What it takes to survive in the executive jungle;
        or
    Why some men always get singled out for promotions and salary increases.

3. *Numbered Ways.* This is often an effective lead because it sets the stage for an organized selling story. If you use a specific number, it will attract curiosity and usually make the reader want to find out what they are.

    Example: 17 little-known ways to improve your on-the-job performance—and one big way to make it pay off!

4. *Command.* If you can use a lead which will command, without offense and with authority, you have taken a big step toward getting the reader to do what you want him to do.

    Example: Don't let the lack of education hold you back any longer!

5. *Narrative.* This is one of the most difficult types of leads to write, but it can prove to be one of the most effective, for it capitalizes on people's interest in stories. A narrative lead, to be effective, must lead into the sales story in a natural way and still hold the reader's interest. Ideally, it should also give the reader some clue to where the story is going to lead or why he should be interested.

    Example: When he started in the stock room at IBM, nobody ever thought Tom Jones would some day be president of this multimillion dollar corporation.

6. *Question.* If you can start with the right type of question, you can immediately put your reader in the proper frame of mind for your sales message. But be sure the question is provocative. Make sure it's a specific question, promising benefits. And one that's certain to be answered in the affirmative.

    Example: If I can show you a proved way to get a better job, without any obligation on your part—will you give me a few minutes of your time?

It is impossible to put too much emphasis on the importance of working on your leads. The lead is the first thing your reader sees. Usually he makes his decision to read or not read at this point. I always write out at least three or four different leads, then choose the one I think will do the best job of appealing to the reader's basic wants.

Pros and Cons of Writing to Formula

Of course, it's not enough to just write an effective lead for your letter. From this starting point, you have to weave a selling story that will present your product or service in its best light and move the reader to ACTION!

One way to do so is by following a formula. I should warn you that some direct mail writers are antiformula. They feel a formula is a straitjacket that inhibits creativity. Other writers, myself included, feel that a formula is simply a road map that helps you follow a logical copy route and get to your destination. Used wisely, it *can be* a valuable creative tool instead of a straitjacket.

Perhaps the best known of all letter-writing formulas is the one commonly referred to as AIDA: Attention – Interest – Desire – Action. Let's examine it more closely:

The writer is told to start the letter with a lead or first paragraph that will attract the *favorable attention* of the reader. Then, get the reader's *interest* by telling him what your product or service will do for him. Next, transform that interest into his *desire* to have what is offered or do what is proposed. Finally, get *action* now. It's a good, logical formula. The only trouble is that it tells you what to do, not how to do it.

Seven-Step Formula

Here's a letter-writing formula which has served me well over the years. I feel it follows a more detailed route than most formulas. And used wisely, it should not shackle your creativity.

1. *Promise a benefit in your headline or first paragraph – your most important benefit.* You just can't go wrong by putting your best foot forward and attracting favorable attention by leading off with the most important benefit *to the reader.* There are those who believe in the slow buildup. But most professional writers I know advocate hitting the bull's-eye fast.
2. *Immediately enlarge upon your most important benefit.* This step is vital. Many writers come up with a great lead, but then fail to follow through. Or they catch attention with their heading, but then take two or three paragraphs to warm up to their subject – and the attention is gone! Try hard to enlarge on your most important benefit immediately, and you'll build up interest fast.
3. *Tell the reader specifically what he is going to get.* It's amazing how many letters lack specifics on such basic things as size, color, weight, and sales terms. Perhaps the writer is so close to his proposition, he assumes the reader knows all about it. A dangerous assumption! And when you tell the reader what he's going to get, don't overlook the intangibles that go along with your product or service. He's getting smart appearance in addition to a pair of slacks; knowledge in addition to a 340-page book; and so on.
4. *Back up your statements with proof and endorsements.* Most prospects are somewhat skeptical about advertising. They know it sometimes is a little overenthusiastic about a product. So they accept it with a grain of salt. If you can back up your own statements with third-party testimonials or a list of satisfied users, then everything you say becomes more believable.

192

5. *Tell the reader what he may lose if he doesn't act.* As noted, people respond affirmatively either to gain something they do not possess *or* to avoid losing something they already have. Here's a good spot in your letter to overcome human inertia. To imply what may be lost if action is postponed. People don't like to be left out. And a skillful writer can use this fact as a powerful and effective device.

6. *Rephrase your prominent benefits in your closing offer.* Like a good salesman, sum up the benefits to the prospect in your closing offer. This is the proper prelude to asking for action. This is where you intensify the desire to have. The more strong benefits you can get the reader to recall, the easier it will be for him mentally to justify an affirmative decision.

7. *Incite action* — NOW. This is the spot where you win or lose the battle with human inertia. We all know that once a letter is put aside or tossed in that file, you're out of luck. So wind up with a call for action and a *logical reason* for acting now. Too many letters close with a statement like "supplies are limited." That's an unbelievable argument. Today's consumer knows you probably have a warehouse full of merchandise. So make your reason a believable one. For example, "It may be many months before we go back to press on this book." Or "Orders are shipped on a first-come basis. The sooner yours is received, the sooner you can be enjoying your new widget."

Classic Sales Letter Fits the Formula

To illustrate how the seven-step formula can be applied, let's take a second look at the classic Kiplinger "boom or bust" letter, which was illustrated in the very first chapter.

I frankly don't know whether or not the writer used a formula in creating this letter. But note how closely the letter (see page 194) fits the seven-step formula.

One final word about formulas: Any formula, no matter how good, is practically worthless in the hands of an unskilled writer. For the truth of the matter is, no one ever learned to write copy by memorizing a formula. Only good creative writers make letter-writing formulas hit pay dirt!

Techniques the Pros Use To Improve Letter Copy

In my years of trying to write better letters, it has been my privilege to rub shoulders with many of the real pros in the business. I'd like to pass along some of the techniques they use for writing and editing copy. Whether you do some writing yourself or just evaluate copy others have written, I think you'll find them helpful.

Bucket Brigade. The best suggestion I ever received for improving my own copy came to me from Maxwell C. Ross, a noted direct mail consultant. He recommended the use of connecting links — words and phrases that connect one paragraph with the next. They help carry the reader along from one thought to another (hence the term "bucket brigade"). Used properly, these links help your copy flow smoothly, give it continuity, and make even a long letter very readable. Here are a few examples:

> "But that is not all . . ."
> "And in addition . . ."
> "So that is why . . ."
> "But please remember . . ."
> "As I mentioned . . ."

193

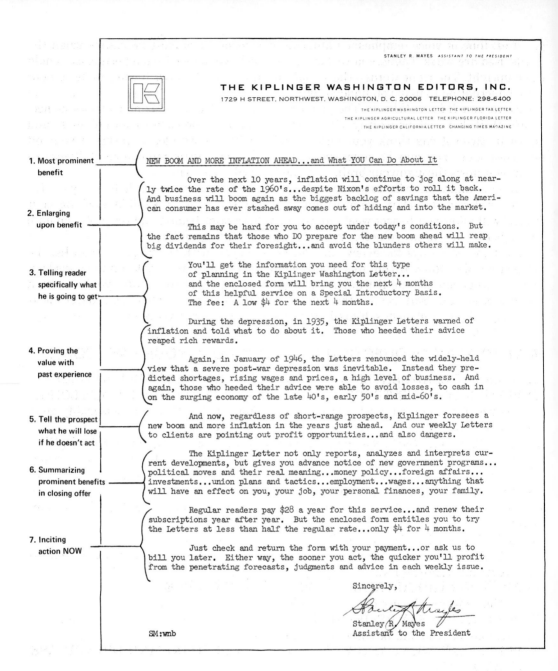

STANLEY R. MAYES *ASSISTANT TO THE PRESIDENT*

THE KIPLINGER WASHINGTON EDITORS, INC.

1729 H STREET, NORTHWEST, WASHINGTON, D. C. 20006   TELEPHONE: 298-6400

THE KIPLINGER WASHINGTON LETTER   THE KIPLINGER TAX LETTER
THE KIPLINGER AGRICULTURAL LETTER   THE KIPLINGER FLORIDA LETTER
THE KIPLINGER CALIFORNIA LETTER   CHANGING TIMES MAGAZINE

1. Most prominent benefit

NEW BOOM AND MORE INFLATION AHEAD...and What YOU Can Do About It

Over the next 10 years, inflation will continue to jog along at nearly twice the rate of the 1960's...despite Nixon's efforts to roll it back.
And business will boom again as the biggest backlog of savings that the American consumer has ever stashed away comes out of hiding and into the market.

2. Enlarging upon benefit

This may be hard for you to accept under today's conditions. But
the fact remains that those who DO prepare for the new boom ahead will reap
big dividends for their foresight...and avoid the blunders others will make.

3. Telling reader specifically what he is going to get

You'll get the information you need for this type
of planning in the Kiplinger Washington Letter...
and the enclosed form will bring you the next 4 months
of this helpful service on a Special Introductory Basis.
The fee: A low $4 for the next 4 months.

4. Proving the value with past experience

During the depression, in 1935, the Kiplinger Letters warned of
inflation and told what to do about it. Those who heeded their advice
reaped rich rewards.

Again, in January of 1946, the Letters renounced the widely-held
view that a severe post-war depression was inevitable. Instead they predicted shortages, rising wages and prices, a high level of business. And
again, those who heeded their advice were able to avoid losses, to cash in
on the surging economy of the late 40's, early 50's and mid-60's.

5. Tell the prospect what he will lose if he doesn't act

And now, regardless of short-range prospects, Kiplinger foresees a
new boom and more inflation in the years just ahead. And our weekly Letters
to clients are pointing out profit opportunities...and also dangers.

6. Summarizing prominent benefits in closing offer

The Kiplinger Letter not only reports, analyzes and interprets current developments, but gives you advance notice of new government programs...
political moves and their real meaning...money policy...foreign affairs...
investments...union plans and tactics...employment...wages...anything that
will have an effect on you, your job, your personal finances, your family.

Regular readers pay $28 a year for this service...and renew their
subscriptions year after year. But the enclosed form entitles you to try
the Letters at less than half the regular rate...only $4 for 4 months.

7. Inciting action NOW

Just check and return the form with your payment...or ask us to
bill you later. Either way, the sooner you act, the quicker you'll profit
from the penetrating forecasts, judgments and advice in each weekly issue.

Sincerely,

Stanley R. Mayes
Assistant to the President

SM:wnb

Short Words and Sentences. Make sure you don't slow your reader down with too many long words. You can apply a simple adaptation of Rudolf Flesch's famous formula: For every 100 words you write, make sure that at least 75% of them have five letters or fewer.

Sentences that average more than 17 words can also slow down reading. Short sentences are punchy. Mix them in with longer ones to give your copy better rhythm.

Grammar and Punctuation. Most professional writers I know are more concerned with communicating than with rules for grammar and punctuation. If you had an English teacher who rated grammar next to cleanliness, she may not be happy with your direct mail copy. But as Paul Bringe has said: "Punctuation is a writer's substitute for

194

gestures, tone of voice, emphasis and facial expression. It is most necessary when the words used are weak, vague and without color. Such words need strong crutches to hold them upright. The right words—those that jar, jump and shout with energy—need very little punctuation to help you understand."

Rewrite and Edit Ruthlessly. The pros rewrite their letter copy as many times as necessary until they feel it's worthy of their own signature. And each time they revise and polish it. Even if you think your letter is all set, it's a good idea to retype it yourself one more time. You may be surprised to see how many "little improvements" you can make as it flows through your brain . . . and from the typewriter.

If time permits, it's wise to set your completed copy aside for a while before you give it that final review. Let it age overnight. Or for a few days, if possible. Looking at it "fresh" will allow you to spot weak areas you didn't notice before, and probably come up with a better way to say something you struggled with originally.

One of the best ways to review and edit your copy is with the 20-point checklist developed by Max Ross. It contains a lifetime of experience and a gold mine of wisdom. Ross suggests you use the list to play 20 questions with your copy. After you've written the first or second draft, review the questions one by one to see where your letter needs strengthening. Out of such self-discipline comes greatly improved copy!

HOW TO PLAY 20 QUESTIONS—AND IMPROVE YOUR OWN COPY!

1) DOES THE LEAD SENTENCE GET IN STEP WITH THE READER AT ONCE?
2) IS YOUR LEAD SENTENCE NO MORE THAN TWO OR THREE LINES LONG?
   (Although many successful letters have longer leads, this is a reasonably good rule of thumb.)
3) DO YOUR OPENING PARAGRAPHS PROMISE A BENEFIT TO THE READER?
   (Did you waste too much time "introducing"? Could you strip away a paragraph or two and have a better lead?)
4) HAVE YOU FIRED YOUR BIGGEST GUN FIRST?
   (Don't hold back. If you save the best till last, your reader may have left you by then.)
5) IS THERE A BIG IDEA BEHIND YOUR PROPOSITION?
   (The Big Idea is important for every company. Its absence is often the reason direct mail ventures fail.)
6) ARE YOUR THOUGHTS ARRANGED IN LOGICAL ORDER?
   (This is where the use of a set formula helps.)
7) IS WHAT YOU SAY BELIEVABLE?
   (It may be true, but not necessarily believable.)
8) IS IT CLEAR WHAT YOU WANT THE READER TO DO, AND DID YOU ASK HIM TO DO IT?
   (An extremely important point.)
9) IF THERE IS AN ORDER FORM INVOLVED, DOES THE COPY TIE IN WITH IT, AND HAVE YOU DIRECTED ATTENTION TO THE ORDER FORM IN THE LETTER?
10) DOES THE LETTER HAVE "YOU ATTITUDE" ALL THE WAY THROUGH?
11) DOES THE LETTER HAVE A CONVERSATIONAL TONE?
    (Try to write as easily as you talk—or to put it another way, write as you would talk if you could edit what you are going to say.)
12) HAVE YOU FORMED A BUCKET BRIGADE THROUGH YOUR COPY?
    (Subtly connect one paragraph with the next and lead your reader through the copy gently.)

13) DOES YOUR COPY SCORE BETWEEN 70 AND 80 WORDS OF FIVE LETTERS OR FEWER FOR EACH 100 WORDS YOU WRITE?
14) ARE THERE ANY SENTENCES WHERE YOU COULD HAVE AVOIDED BEGINNING WITH AN ARTICLE – "A," "AN," OR "THE"?
15) ARE THERE ANY PLACES WHERE YOU HAVE STRUNG TOGETHER TOO MANY PREPOSITIONAL PHRASES?
    (An important point to watch because this can rob your copy of power.)
16) HAVE YOU KEPT OUT "WANDERING VERBS"?
    (Where the verb strays too far away from its subject.)
17) HAVE YOU USED ACTION VERBS INSTEAD OF NOUN CONSTRUCTION?
    ("We will gladly bill you later" instead of "We will be glad to send you a bill at a later time.")
18) ARE THERE ANY "THAT'S" YOU DON'T NEED?
19) HOW DOES THE COPY RATE ON SUCH LETTER-CRAFTSMANSHIP POINTS AS: (a) USING ACTIVE VOICE INSTEAD OF PASSIVE, (b) PERIODIC SENTENCES INSTEAD OF LOOSE, (c) TOO MANY PARTICIPLES, (d) TOO MANY SPLIT INFINITIVES, (e) REPEATING COMPANY NAME TOO OFTEN?
20) DOES YOUR LETTER LOOK THE WAY YOU WANT IT TO INSOFAR AS THESE ITEMS ARE CONCERNED? (a) PLACEMENT ON PAGE, (b) NO PARAGRAPHS OVER SIX LINES, (c) INDENTATION AND NUMBERED PARAGRAPHS FOR EMPHASIS, (d) UNDERSCORING AND CAPITALIZATION USED SPARINGLY, (e) PUNCTUATION FOR READING EASE.

Make a Letter Look Inviting. Here's one final, very important tip from the pros. They try to make their letters look attractive, inviting, and easy to read. They keep paragraphs to a maximum of six or seven lines. They use subheads and indented paragraphs to break up long copy and emphasize pertinent thoughts, knowing that many readers will scan indented paragraphs before they decide whether to read a letter clear through. They use *underscoring,* CAPITAL LETTERS, and a second ink color to make key words and sentences stand out. And they skillfully use leader dots and dashes to break up long sentences.

Note how much more inviting to read the Amoco Torch Club letter is in the mailed version compared to the original typewritten version. Same copy, but one encourages reading and the other doesn't.

Letter Lengths and the P.S.

One of the questions that invariably seems to pop up at a Direct Mail Day or seminar is: "Do people read long copy?" The answer is a simple one: Yes!

People will read something for as long as it interests them. An uninteresting one-page letter can seem too long, while a skillfully woven four-pager can hold the reader until the bitter end. So a letter should be long enough to cover the subject adequately and short enough to maintain interest.

The product or service being sold and the prospect's prior knowledge of it will help determine the copy length. *Time,* for example, has had some success with short, one-page, memo-size letters. Virtually everyone knows what the magazine is, so a brief message and a strong offer are enough to do the job. On the other hand, if you're promoting a brand new or little-known magazine, it may take three or four pages to explain and romance what the publication is all about.

Don't fear long copy. If you have something to say – and say it well – it will probably do better than short copy. After all, the longer you can hold a prospect's interest, the more sales points you can get across and the more likely you are to win an order.

196

Amoco Torch Club
International Credit Card

P.O. BOX 2182 · OAK PARK, ILLINOIS 60303

Special Two Month Trial Memberships — Please read this letter for details!

Dear Credit Card Holder:

I am delighted to inform you that your name has been suggested for membership in The American Torch Club.

The American Torch Club is not, frankly, for everybody. First, only Standard Oil credit card holders are eligible.

But even this is not enough. In addition, you must have an exemplary credit standing and history with Standard Oil. We estimate that less than one per cent of the population is eligible to join The American Torch Club.

As a member, you will carry the most unique credit card in America. It combines the credit privileges of your Standard Oil credit card with the world-wide charge power of the Diners Club.

At first glance, the American Torch Club card may seem much like an American Express or Carte Blanche credit card. This is natural, because the American Torch Club card gives you instant credit throughout the world. You can use it at airlines, hotels, and motels, fine restaurants, car rentals, specialty shops and service organizations.

But an American Torch Club card has these exclusive features:

1) It is the only major travel and entertainment card that is also honored at 30,000 American Oil Company service stations throughout the United States. Our service stations generally do not accept "outside" credit cards . . . but they will honor your American Torch Club card.

2) It is the only major travel and entertainment card that lets you budget virtually everything you charge.

    (Except for airline tickets bought on "extended charge," the other travel and entertainment cards request full payment in 30 days.)

Amoco Torch Club
International Credit Card

P.O. BOX 2182 · OAK PARK, ILLINOIS 60303

Special Two Month Trial Membership
Please read this letter for details!

Dear Credit Card Holder:

I am delighted to inform you that your name has been suggested for membership in the American Torch Club.

The American Torch Club is not, frankly, for everybody. First, only Standard Oil credit card holders are eligible.

But even this is not enough. In addition, you must have an exemplary credit standing and history with Standard Oil. We estimate that less than one per cent of the population is eligible to join the American Torch Club.

As a member, you will carry the most unique credit card in America. It combines the credit privileges of your Standard Oil credit card with the world-wide charge power of the Diners Club.

At first glance, the American Torch Club card may seem much like an American Express or Carte Blanche credit card. This is natural, because the American Torch Club card gives you instant credit throughout the world. You can use it at airlines, hotels and motels, fine restaurants, car rentals, specialty shops and service organizations.

But an American Torch card has these exclusive features:

It is the only major travel and entertainment card that is also honored at 30,000 American Oil Company service stations throughout the United States. Our service stations generally do not accept "outside" credit cards, but they will honor your American Torch Club card.

It is the only major travel and entertainment card that lets you budget virtually everything you charge.

(Except for airline tickets bought on "extended charge," the other travel and entertainment cards request full payment in 30 days.)

Regardless of letter length, however, it usually pays to tack on a P.S. The P.S. is one of the most read parts of any letter. Many prospects will glance at a letter first. The eye will pick up an indented paragraph here, stop on an underlined statement there, and finally come to rest on the P.S. If you can get across an important thought or benefit in the P.S., they may go back and read the whole letter.

This makes the P.S. worthy of your best efforts. Use it to restate a key benefit. Or to cover an added inducement, like a free gift. Even when somebody has read the rest of the letter, the P.S. can make the difference between whether or not he orders. So use it to close on a strong note, to sign off with the strongest appeal you have.

Developing a Copy Style

Everyone, whether he realizes it or not, has a copy style. In my opinion, there are only two important things to say about the subject. First, a writer should strive to improve and make his style as professional as possible. Second, he then must become competent enough to vary his style to fit the particular offer or audience he's selling.

Let's start with improving your basic writing style. A good, professional writer should be able to paint pictures with his words. To go beyond the nuts-and-bolts details he gets from a product fact sheet and weave a benefit-packed story. To translate a common mattress into a heavenly night's sleep. Witness these two examples of copy selling a piece of luggage:

"The big 2-suiter has dome-shaped construction, with 3 handy side pockets. Sturdily built. Has 3-ply frame . . . nickel-plated steel locks . . . and unbreakable plastic handle. Made of new Vin-Tuf fabric that's water-repellent and scuff-resistant."

"This roomy 2-suiter has a unique dome-shaped construction that provides plenty of wrinkle-free space for your suits . . . plus shirts, slacks, underwear, shoes, and toilet kit. Three handy side pockets keep socks and other small items at your fingertips. Made to stand up under rough, jet-age travel with crush-proof 3-ply frame . . . nickel-plated steel locks that won't tarnish . . . and unbreakable plastic handle that is contoured to comfortably fit your hand. The smart-looking new Vin-Tuf fabric shrugs off scuffs. And just a swish of a damp cloth wipes away most travel grime, leaving your luggage as fresh-looking as the wardrobe inside!"

While the second paragraph is certainly longer than the first, it covers the same basic product features. But notice how many more product benefits the second writer has conveyed, and how he's painted a word picture of that suitcase and how it will be used.

A good writer must also be able to vary his style to fit the particular product he's selling and audience he's trying to reach. Let's look at some more examples.

For Time-Life's book series on *The Old West*, notice how this copy builds excitement and momentum to give you a perfect preview of what you'll be reading about:

"Its volumes are crackling with the excitement of men and women pushing out beyond the frontier, raising children and Cain, busting sod and staking out ranches in a land as wild and rugged as the open sea, hunting buffalo and bear, and finally becoming that marvelous blend of fact, legend and myth that has fascinated us since two men named Lewis and Clark first crossed the country. Sound like the kind of great adventure you'd want to take with us?"

For *Newsweek*, here's a refreshing, low-key copy style aimed at people who have received many other magazine offers:

"You've undoubtedly 'heard everything' by now in the way of promises and premiums. I won't try to top any of them. If you subscribe to Newsweek, you won't get rich quick. You won't bowl over friends and business associates with clever remarks and sage comments after your first copy of Newsweek arrives. (Your conversation *will* benefit from a better understanding of the events and forces of our era, but that's all. Wit and wisdom are gifts no magazine can bestow.)"

For Thompson & Co., a mail order cigar firm, narrative copy is skillfully used to lead into their product story:

"If you like fine cigars and if you recall with mouth-watering nostalgia that wonderful tobacco we used to enjoy B.C. (before Castro), then you'll be interested in a true story that has all the elements of a cloak-and-dagger novel . . . and beats James Bond 007 right off the map!

"The incredible story begins in 1963 when the Castro embargo hit the cigar industry like an atomic bomb, wiping out our supply of this choice tobacco. Not a pound of this choice tobacco has arrived in this country since.

"A daring group of ex-patriate Cubans, unsympathetic to Castro and the Communists, banded together and made a pact that would cost them their lives if discovered.

"One dark night, under the cover of a storm, they put to sea in a small boat and ran the bristling gauntlet of Castro's gunboats. Their small craft, tossed and driven by giant waves, carried a precious cargo—tobacco seeds bound for Tegucigalpa, Honduras."

Three very different copy styles. Each taken from a very successful letter. A versatile writer must be able to change the mood and style of his copy, just as a good actor changes his voice and mannerisms to play different roles.

Special Types of Letter Copy

The suggestions we have just reviewed apply to the most common types of direct mail letters — those selling a specific product to the consumer market. Do they also fit special situations, like selling a service instead of a product? Or selling to businessmen? Or raising funds by mail? Let's look at these special areas.

Selling Services or Intangibles. As we pointed out in the first chapter, among the most successful exponents of direct marketing are those who sell intangibles.

They recognize that people don't buy a magazine because of its size, or a book because of its number of pages. They buy it because of the information and knowledge they can get from it. And going a step further — how they can use that information to become a better cook, improve their photography, or make investments more profitable.

A good example are the stock market services sold by mail. Many investors gladly pay $100 a year or more for such a service, even though they can easily get accurate and factual information on the market from their daily newspaper.

So in writing letters for services like these, you should dress up and romance your selling story. Recognize the importance of the reader and play up to his ego. Talk about what your product can do for him. And relieve his doubts by using testimonials or examples of how others have benefited.

Our agency had an assignment to sell a travel and entertainment charge card to blue-collar workers. Most of the other cards on the market at the time were carried by white-collar executives. The creative strategy that evolved was to play up our prospect's importance — to explain how he could use this card to dine at the better restaurants and never worry about the embarrassing problem of not having enough cash on hand. In other words, to show how he could be just as important as Mr. Big. And it worked.

Selling to Businessmen. There seems to be a strong conviction that when a man goes to work in the morning and sits behind a desk, he has to be sold differently than when he's sitting in an easy chair at home. To some extent, that's true. He needs nuts-and-bolts facts to make an intelligent buying decision for his company.

But he also buys for many of the same emotional reasons and appeals we examined earlier in this chapter. So your copy should do more than cover the same dull facts the competition talks about. It should give him the emotional ammunition that will permit him to buy.

One of the most experienced writers in this area is Paul Bringe, a well-known direct mail consultant. In a Direct Mail Day speech, he outlined these tips for selling to businessmen or industrial buyers:

1) Give your buyer a chance to be a hero in his daily work. He gets so few opportunities to prove he is just as smart as the big boss. Give him a really good opportunity and he will snatch it.

2) Give him a chance to be ahead of the crowd — to be modern and progressive. He loves to brag even if it is the silent kind of bragging you can do with the latest piece of office equipment on your desk.

3) Give him the arguments he will need to convince others. Don't expect him to find them himself. Tell him exactly the things he is going to tell to others to justify his purchase. Even if he is the boss, he needs those reasons because the boss must justify himself to employees.

4) Give him enough facts about your product to help him rationalize to himself, so that he does not need to admit his emotional reasons for buying.

199

Raising Funds by Mail. Whether you are raising funds for a welfare organization, a national health fund, a religious organization, or an educational institution, the problem is the same. There is a great deal of competition for the donor's dollar. And you are asking him to give it up to help others rather than to get something specific for himself.

Your job as a writer is to tug at the heartstrings. To capture on paper the feeling of satisfaction and happiness we all get from helping the underdog.

In their book, *Tested Methods of Raising Money* (New York: Harper & Row, 1959), Margaret M. Fellows and M. H. Koenig suggest:

The instinct to give of oneself, one's time and money, is present to some degree in all persons and needs only to be stirred to become active. Obviously it is to this instinct, this emotion of kindliness and willingness to help others, that you must appeal if you are to touch your prospect's pocketbook. And if you are to touch his pocketbook, you must first touch his heart.

We know that man's heart is easier to reach than his head; that his dreams and hopes are very much like our own. Our job is to appeal to his highest and most human qualities, to recount a human situation in simple terms, so that he can feel "there but for the grace of God go I," or my son or my daughter. And we know that he will feel this, for it would be a response common to all people.

Select then that part of your work which has the most human appeal and which will, therefore, create in your prospect's heart a desire to contribute. Best calculated to do this is an appeal to love, pity, patriotism, security, pride, duty, responsibility, self-interest, and self-preservation. These are the springboards of all human action.

One other good bit of advice: Regardless of how big your fund-raising goal is, bring it down to amounts the prospect can understand and appreciate. Show him what different contributions accomplish. For example, "$2 will feed a growing boy three square meals for one day . . . $25 will send a boy to camp for a week," and so on.

The Value of Versioned Copy

Suppose, just suppose, that instead of sending exactly the same letter copy to all your prospects, you could create a number of versions for each major segment of the market. And instead of talking about *all* the advantages and benefits of the product, you could just zero in on the ones that fit each market segment. Sounds like a logical idea that should increase response, doesn't it?

Yet my own experience with versioned or segmented copy has been rather mixed. Sometimes I've seen it work very effectively; other times it's been a bomb. So all I can suggest is that you test it for yourself. If your product story is substantially different for certain audience segments — and you can identify and select them on the lists you're using — develop a special version of your regular copy and give it a try.

One type of versioned copy that generally does pay off is special copy slanted to your previous buyers. Customers like to think a firm remembers them and will give them special treatment. And in going back to your satisfied buyers, there's not so much need to resell the company — you can concentrate on the product or the service that is being offered them.

200

Writing Computer-Personalized Letters

Back in 1967, I devoted an *Advertising Age* column to a *Reader's Digest* mailing that represented a dramatic new approach to personalized mailings. The prospect's name and address was mentioned twice at the top of the letter. His name was in the salutation. The body of the letter mentioned his town and even several neighboring towns.

The technique was new. But the idea was not. Personalization has always been an effective direct mail tool to hypo response. But the cost had become prohibitive for mass mailings. That is, until the computer came along to personalize millions of letters at high speed and low cost.

Today, computer letters have come of age as an effective creative tool. Many mailers are even using computer-personalized booklets and order forms. And copywriters are using much more sophisticated personalization to get their story across. Here are a few guidelines to follow:

1. Don't overdo the number of personalized references. Three or four times in the body of a letter are usually ideal. More than that and the letter becomes unnatural.
2. Vary the personalization. Don't just repeat somebody's name over and over. Use the name, address, and any other personal information you can extract from the computerized list you're using.
3. Computer letters should be written in a personal style. The form letter approach with the addition of a few personalized references usually doesn't come off very well.

As an example, note the first page of a computer letter from New Process Co., illustrated on the next page. It uses the prospect's street address and town name, both effectively woven into the letter message.

How To Improve a Good Mailing Package

Until now we've been talking about how to create a new mailing package. Let's suppose you've done that . . . and you want to make it better. Or you've got a successful mailing package you've been using for a couple of years (your control) and you want to beat it. How do you go about it?

One of the best ways I know is to come up with an entirely different appeal for your letter. For instance, suppose you're selling an income tax guide and your present letter is built around saving money. That's probably a tough appeal to beat. But to develop a new approach you could write a letter around a negative appeal—something people want to avoid.

Experience with many propositions has proved that a negative appeal is often stronger than a positive one, yet it's frequently overlooked by copywriters. An appropriate negative copy appeal for our example could be something like "How to avoid costly mistakes that can get you in trouble with the Internal Revenue Service." Or "Are you taking advantage of these six commonly overlooked tax deductions?"

Another good technique is to change the type of lead on your letter. Review the examples of six common types of leads given earlier. If you're using a news lead, try one built around the narrative approach. Or develop a provocative question as the lead. Usually a new lead will require you to rewrite the first few paragraphs of copy to fit the lead, but then you can often pick up the balance of the letter from your control.

One top creative man who has a well-organized approach for coming up with new ideas is Sol Blumenfeld, senior vice president of RCS&A (New York). Here's how he does it:

JOHN L. BLAIR
PRESIDENT

NEW PROCESS COMPANY
WARREN, PENNSYLVANIA 16365

Mr. James N. Kobs
110 Roxbury Ln
Des Plaines, Ill. 60018

Dear Mr. Kobs:

Suppose I knocked on your Des Plaines door
and told you my new Tropical Slacks are the most
comfortable Slacks you ever wore --

Suppose I promised you'll <u>never</u> spend a penny
to have them dry-cleaned or pressed; and, <u>uncondi-
tionally guaranteed</u> they'll keep their sharp crease
even if you get caught in one of those Illinois
rainstorms --

Suppose I went even further and told you
that even though my Slacks look like $20
a pair, they can be yours for UNDER
$8 a pair!

You wouldn't believe me, would you?

That's why I'm sending 2 pairs to your
Roxbury Ln address to wear a full week
FREE -- to <u>prove,</u> at <u>my</u> expense, you don't have to
spend a bundle of cash to be one of the best dressed
men in Des Plaines.

Feel the fabric samples, Mr. Kobs.
This is the big reason these Tropical Slacks <u>are</u>
so terrific. It's an air-cooled weave of 65%
Dacron polyester and 35% rayon with "Blair-Press"
Permanent Press added to keep slacks looking neat.
So neat, in fact, I'll give you new Slacks free if these
ever lose their sharp crease through rough/tough wear,
muggy summer days or repeated machine washing.

... and, Mr. Kobs, your "JB"

over, please

*Effective computer letter employs prospect's name, city, state, and street address as per-
sonalization.*

"Sometimes an idea for beating your control mailing comes with a clap of thunder and the blaring of trumpets. But more often, it is a matter of probing, hypothesizing, synthesizing. And for this, I go through a simple routine. I use my present control package as a sort of jumping-off point and proceed along several channels."

Here are some of the approaches Blumenfeld uses:

The Additive Approach. This means adding something to a control package that can increase its efficiency more than the extra cost involved. Usually, it involves inserts. A classic example is the "Publisher's Letter" developed by Greystone Press. The message is directed to "those who do *not* plan to take advantage of this offer" and has increased results for many publishers up to 30%.

Inserts that can be used to heighten response include testimonial slips, extra discounts, a free gift for cash with order, and a news flash or bulletin. Other additive ideas include building stamps or tokens into the response device. And, if you have a logical reason to justify it, adding an expiration date to your offer.

The Extractive Approach. This copy exercise involves a careful review of your existing mailing package copy. Very often, you can find a potential winning lead buried somewhere in the body copy. As an example, Blumenfeld cites an experience with the *National Observer,* where the body copy mentioned the social success a subscriber could enjoy from this unusual news weekly. He extracted it from the body copy and built it into the winning heading, "Now My Friends Listen When I Talk."

The Innovative Approach. Unlike the extractive approach, this is designed to come up with completely new ideas. If you are testing three or four new copy approaches, at least one of them should represent a potential breakthrough. Something that's highly original, perhaps even considered a little wild.

I agree with encouraging writers to let themselves go, because I've seen them produce real breakthroughs this way. Dramatic new formats, copy approaches, and offers that have really shellacked the old control!

One approach that has worked for me is simply saving mailing packages that I particularly like. Then when I'm stuck for an idea, I glance through them. Looking at one strong approach after another really puts an electric charge into the brain and never fails to give me a few good ideas.

In Review—How To Create Mailing Packages That Sell

In direct mail, copy is still king. What you say, how you phrase it, the appeals you use, and your copy style all affect the results you achieve.

The successful writer doesn't write a word until he's thought about the objective, the offer, and the market. He then translates product features into benefits and develops the right copy strategy. The strategy that will sell the most people.

From a copy standpoint, the lead is the most important part of every letter. Test your leads. Take advantage of the letter-writing techniques the pros use to make their copy more readable. And don't be afraid of long copy.

When you come to circulars, envelopes, and order forms, don't neglect the importance of graphics and typography. All these pieces should be inviting to the eye and should visually support your selling copy. Use color to advantage. Stick with typefaces that are easy to read and avoid using too many different ones on the same piece.

To keep your mailing packages on target, see the 28-point creative checklist developed by Tom Collins. (See page 205.) It will help you put your thinking in focus and eliminate the weak areas that can often make the difference between a success and failure.

203

The best way to improve your copywriting is by continual writing and testing. But if your market is too small to test, or you're just getting started in direct mail, here are some safe bets. These basic principles work for most mailers most of the time . . . and, if applied by a good copywriter, will produce better than average results.

Mailing Format:
- The letter ranks first in importance.
- The most effective mailing package consists of outside envelope, letter, circular, response form, and business reply envelope.

Letters:
- Form letters using indented paragraphs will usually outpull those in which indented paragraphs are not used.
- Underlining pertinent phrases and sentences usually increases results slightly.
- A separate letter with a separate circular will generally do better than a combination letter and circular.
- A form letter with an effective running headline will ordinarily do as well as a filled-in letter.
- Authentic testimonials in a sales letter ordinarily increase the pull.
- A two-page letter ordinarily outpulls a one-page letter.
- Computer letters ordinarily outpull printed letters, providing personalization is meaningful and the tone of the letter is low key.

Circulars:
- A circular which deals specifically with the proposition presented in the letter will be more effective than a circular of an institutional nature.
- A combination of art and photography will usually result in a better circular than one employing either art or photography alone.
- A circular usually proves ineffective in the sale of news magazines and news services.
- In the sale of big ticket products, deluxe large-size, color circulars most always warrant the extra cost over circulars of 11 × 17 or smaller.

Outside Envelopes:
- Illustrated envelopes increase response if tied into the offer.
- Variety in types and sizes of envelopes pays, particularly in a series of mailings.

Reply Forms:
- Reply cards with receipt stubs will usually increase response over cards with no stub.
- "Busy" order and/or request forms which look important will usually produce more response than neat, clean-looking forms.
- Postage-free business reply cards will generally bring more responses than those to which the respondent must affix postage.

Reply Envelopes:
- A reply envelope increases cash with order response.
- A reply envelope increases responses to collection letters.
- An airmail reply envelope usually increases responses to "impulse" offers.

Color:
- Two-color letters usually outpull one-color letters.
- An order and/or reply form printed in colored ink or on colored stock usually outpulls one printed in black ink on white stock.
- A two-color circular generally proves more effective than a one-color circular.
- Full color is warranted in the promotion of food items, apparel, and merchandise faithfully depicted in full color.

Postage:
- Third-class mail ordinarily pulls as well as first-class mail.
- Postage meter usually pulls better than postage stamps.
- A "designed" printed permit usually does as well as a postage meter.
- Outgoing airmail postage seldom warrants the extra cost over first class.

Creative Checklist for Direct Mail

1. Do you have a good proposition?
2. Do you have a good offer?
3. Does your outside envelope select the prospect?
4. Does your outside envelope put your best foot forward?
5. Does your outside envelope provide reading motivation?
6. Does your copy provide instant orientation?
7. Does your mailing visually reinforce the message?
8. Does it employ readable typography?
9. Is it written in readable, concrete language?
10. Is it personal?
11. Does it strike a responsive chord?
12. Is it dramatic?
13. Does it talk in the language of life, not "advertise at?"
14. Is it credible?
15. Is it structured?
16. Does it leave no stone unturned?
17. Does it present an ultimate benefit?
18. Are details presented as advantages?
19. Does it use, if possible, the power of disinterestedness?
20. Does it use, if possible, the power of negative selling?
21. Does it touch on the reader's deepest relevant daydreams?
22. Does it use subtle flattery?
23. Does it prove and dramatize the value?
24. Does it provide strong assurance of satisfaction?
25. Does it repeat key points?
26. Is it backed by authority?
27. Does it give a reason for immediate response?
28. Do you make it easy to order?

Self-Quiz

1. Complete this equation for making a sale:
   BENEFIT divided by _____ equals _____.
2. What are the three mental exercises one should do before writing direct mail copy?

   1. _____

   2. _____

   3. _____

3. What is the difference between a product *feature* and a product *benefit?*

_____

_____

_____

4. What are some of the basic wants inherent in most people?

1. _____   2. _____

3. _____   4. _____

5. _____   6. _____

7. _____   8. _____

9. _____ 10. _____

5. What do most people desire to avoid?

1. _____   2. _____

3. _____   4. _____

5. _____   6. _____

6. What is the number-one rule in selecting the right format to do the job?

_____

_____

7. What are the components of the classic mailing package?

1. _____   2. _____

3. _____   4. _____

8. What are the four requirements for a good circular?

1. _____

2. _____

3. _____

4. _____

9. What is the key objective in preparing an order form?

Make order forms look _____   _____   _____   _____

_____   _____.

206

10. Name four typical *involvement* devices.

1. _____ 2. _____

3. _____ 4. _____

11. Name the six most common types of leads used in sales letters.

1. _____ 2. _____

3. _____ 4. _____

5. _____ 6. _____

12. Complete this letter-writing formula:

A _ _ _ _ _ _ _

I _ _ _ _ _ _

D _ _ _ _ _

A _ _ _ _ _

13. List the points in the seven-step letter-writing formula in sequence:

1. _____

   _____

2. _____

3. _____

4. _____

5. _____

6. _____

7. _____

14. What is the definition of "connecting links"?

_____

_____

15. Name some techniques which can be used to make letters look attractive, inviting, and easy to read.

1. Keep paragraphs to minimum of _____ or _____ lines.

2. Use _____ and _____ paragraphs to break up long copy.

207

3. Use _____.

4. Use _____ letters.

5. Use _____ and _____ to break up long sentences.

16. What are the two best applications of a P.S.?

1. To restate _____. 2. To offer an added _____.

17. Why is a person likely to buy a magazine by mail?

_____

_____

_____

18. When selling to businessmen by mail you've got to give them facts, but you've also

got to help them to _____ their buying decision.

19. When attempting to raise funds by mail you should appeal to one or more of the following emotions:

1. _____ 2. _____ 3. _____

4. _____ 5. _____ 6. _____

7. _____ 8. _____ 9. _____

20. When writing computer letters, copywriters should keep one rule in mind—what is it?

_____

_____

21. Define each of these approaches for improving a good mailing package:

1. The additive approach: _____

_____

_____

2. The extractive approach: _____

_____

_____

3. The innovative approach: _____

_____

_____

Pilot Project

The pilot project for this chapter consists of a series of checklists guiding the would-be writer through a multiplicity of decisions he will have to make in constructing a direct mail package.

MARKETING FACTS:

You are advertising manager of a company that has just developed the Carocelle Counter-Top Dishwasher. Your boss has asked you to prepare a test package to determine if the product can be successfully sold to the consumer market by direct mail. The product will sell for $39.95, and your firm is prepared to offer it on a free trial basis.

PRODUCT FACTS:

The product works on water pressure and is easily hooked up to any faucet by a flexible connector hose. It requires no special plumbing, installation, or electricity. The Carocelle washes a complete service for four in ten minutes, without prerinsing or scraping of dishes. The unit measures $19\frac{1}{4}''$ in diameter and $16''$ high, and is lightweight enough to be easily portable. It is the only product of its kind on the market, and is backed by a full year's guarantee.

1. Which of the following do you think is the *main appeal* of the product (CHECK ONE):
   - ( ) No installation like a normal dishwasher
   - ( ) Costs less to operate because no electricity needed
   - ( ) Saves time and bother of washing dishes by hand
   - ( ) Small enough to carry from room to room
   - ( ) Gets dishes cleaner than handwashing
   - ( ) Price is at least 50% less than a standard dishwasher
2. What would be the most effective *copy strategy* to dramatize the time-saving aspect of the product (CHECK ONE):
   - ( ) Figure out how many dishes the average woman washes in a year
   - ( ) Get a famous movie star to endorse the product and explain how much time it saves her
   - ( ) Show how many minutes would be spent in a typical day doing the breakfast, lunch, and supper dishes
   - ( ) Point out the other chores a woman could do in the kitchen while the Carocelle is washing her dishes
3. Below are listed a number of *copy phrases* about the product. Next to each one, indicate whether it is a product feature or benefit.

	Feature	Benefit
Has a ten-minute operating cycle	( )	( )
Unit is small enough to fit on a counter-top	( )	( )
Works on water pressure instead of electricity	( )	( )
White base with clear plastic top	( )	( )
Fits any standard kitchen faucet	( )	( )
Uses water hotter than your hands can stand	( )	( )

4. Now use the product facts to jot down at least one additional product benefit:

_____

_____

5. How long should your *letter copy* be (CHECK ONE):
  ( ) One page   ( ) Four pages
  ( ) Two pages   ( ) As long as necessary to tell your story adequately
6. Which of the following should *increase readership and results* from your letter copy (CHECK ONE or MORE):
  ( ) Using underscoring and indented paragraphs
  ( ) Employing good transitions between paragraphs
  ( ) Using a modern magazine typeface instead of typewriter type
  ( ) Putting some of the copy in a second color
  ( ) Using small words and short sentences
7. Where would you work the *price and payment terms* into your letter (CHECK ONE or MORE):
  ( ) First paragraph   ( ) Near the end of the letter
  ( ) About the middle of the letter   ( ) The P.S.
8. Which of the following do you think would be the most effective way to *close your letter* (CHECK ONE):
  ( ) Send for it today—you'll be glad you did!
  ( ) Take advantage of this free trial offer today and I guarantee you'll never go back to doing dishes the old-fashioned way.
  ( ) Discuss it with your husband tonight and see if he doesn't feel it would be a real time-saver.
  ( ) Supplies are limited—act NOW.
9. The *P.S. on the letter* should be used (CHECK ONE):
  ( ) To explain any copy points you forgot in the rest of the letter
  ( ) To mention the price
  ( ) Only when you have something extra to say
  ( ) To reemphasize a strong benefit
10. Which of the following do you think would make the *strongest headline* for the brochure (CHECK ONE):
  ( ) World's First Completely Automatic Counter-Top Dishwasher
  ( ) Send Your Dishpan to the Smithsonian!
  ( ) Enjoy a Free Vacation from Dishes for 2 Full Weeks
  ( ) Imagine Doing Your Dishes in 10 Minutes Flat
  ( ) Enjoy an Automatic Dishwasher with No Plumbing or Installation
11. A good direct mail package has to answer all the reader's questions in advance. Where would you include *technical copy points,* like the size and weight of the unit (CHECK ONE):
  ( ) Letter   ( ) Envelope
  ( ) Brochure   ( ) Order card
12. If you had a *premium offer,* how would you work it into the mailing package (CHECK ONE or MORE):
  ( ) Illustrate it on the outer envelope   ( ) Mention it in the letter
  ( ) Work it into the main brochure   ( ) Prepare a separate
  ( ) Include it on the order form   premium slip

Chapter 10 Techniques of Creating Catalogs

America has carried on a long love affair with catalogs. According to an A. C. Nielsen survey, nearly eight out of ten consumers (77%) have nothing against catalogs generally, and six out of ten like to receive them.

Readership of catalogs is tremendous: more than three out of four consumers open and read through or at least thumb through them. Thorough readership is very high — 64%. But the real payoff is that, of those receiving catalogs, 66% make purchases at least some of the time. How much business is being done by the catalog method? Exact figures are not available, but an educated guess is that catalog sales are at an annual volume of about $4 billion. In 1957, the estimated volume was $1.5 billion.

Continued growth of catalogs boggles the minds of many marketers when they consider that shopping centers continue to spring up like mushrooms. Leisure time continues to expand, allowing more time for personal shopping. Yet, all the while, more and more business and consumer catalogs emerge. And more and more people buy by mail and phone.

Why?

Catalogs Offer Six Consumer Benefits

Here are six prime reasons why the American consumer continues his love affair with catalogs. The catalog (1) saves time; (2) offers better selection; (3) saves money (usually); (4) makes credit available (for big ticket items); (5) describes product features better; and (6) guarantees satisfaction.

In combination, the six consumer benefits are difficult to match at the retail store level. Then there's the fact the American consumer really enjoys catalog shopping. It's fun. Let's take a closer look at just two of the consumer benefits: Better selection and better description of product features.

A case can be made that in metro areas in particular, you can see, touch, and feel practically every model at every price for any given product category which may strike your fancy. True. But to complete the task of comparison shopping, one might have to visit a number of stores and spend several hours in the process.

Consider comparison shopping in retail stores as contrasted to comparison shopping through the general catalog. Let's take the Americana/John Plain merchandise catalog. In this 480-page catalog, you can compare to your heart's content in the comfort of your living room. To dramatize this possibility, let's consider just one merchandise category — watches.

Watches

Jules Jurgensen	24 different watches	$51.95 to	$298.00
Hamilton or Elgin (ladies')	15 " "	50.00 to	470.00
Gruen	21 " "	32.50 to	73.50
Waltham	45 " "	15.45 to	79.90
Clinton	38 " "	16.95 to	45.00
Helbros	21 " "	19.50 to	59.95
Benrus	46 " "	9.95 to	109.90
Seven national brands	210 " "	$ 9.95 to	$470.00

We find 19 consecutive pages of brand name watches, all beautifully illustrated in full color and clearly described.

Just imagine: Seven national brands; 210 different models; a price range of $9.95 to $470. No wonder the American consumer holds the catalog in such high regard.

For the most part, better selection is a consumer benefit of specialty as well as general catalogs. What nursery can match the selection to be found in a Henry Field catalog? What retail store can match the selection of sportswear and equipment in an Eddie Bauer catalog? What automotive supply store can match the parts and accessories in a J. C. Whitney catalog?

Precise Description Is Catalog Forte

I've always enjoyed the gag about the lady who stepped up to the camera counter in a leading department store. She asked the clerk, "What's the difference between this $69.95 Polaroid camera and the $99.95 model?" The clerk replied, "The difference is $30, madam."

Those who sell via the catalog method can't afford the luxury of descriptions which leave voids in selling points. Illustrations must be true. Descriptions must be precise. And the consumer benefits thereby.

For example, note the description of just two of the 210 watches offered in the Americana/John Plain catalog:

DIAMOND SCEPTRE. 21-jewel, four genuine diamonds set in a 14K, white gold, faceted case. Unbreakable mainspring. Shock absorbing movement. Gold-filled mesh bracelet, lock adjustment.
. . . . Only $79.90

DIAMOND QUEEN. 21-jewel, 10 genuine diamonds set in a white 14K solid gold case. Faceted crystal. Unbreakable mainspring. Shock absorbing movement. Gold-filled bracelet, slide lock.
. . . . Only $109.90

A minimum of words (plus full color photography) enables the shopper readily to see why one watch sells for $79.90 and the other for $109.90. The reason for the $30 difference is obvious.

Classic Route to Building Successful Catalogs

The first lesson about building a successful catalog operation is that *most catalog operations did not start with a catalog.* Bankruptcy files are cluttered with distressing stories of firms who attempted to start in the catalog business from scratch. Of the many reasons for failure, certainly the prime one has got to be *lack of an existing customer list.* A catalog operation has a much greater chance for success when it *emerges* from the careful building of a customer list.

Many a firm has grown into a catalog operation from small-space ads in the *New York Times* mail order section, the Sunday supplements like *Parade,* and other mail order sections — shelter books in particular. Many of the ads one sees in the mail order sections of Sunday newspapers week after week fail to turn a profit. But by featuring leader items, advertisers build customer lists quickly. In recent years both radio and TV have emerged as strong media for single item mail order sales.

A Look at Specialty Mail Order Firms

Several steps down the ladder from the mail order giants—Sears, Ward, Spiegel, Aldens, and J. C. Penney—are the discount catalog operations and the specialty mail order houses. The growth of the specialty mail order field, particularly in the past two decades, has been phenomenal. And there's a Horatio Alger fascination about specialty mail order firms, because many have been started on the proverbial shoestring. Their size and number of customers are something to behold.

Customer-list counts for five of the largest gift and gadget specialty merchandise firms follow:

Firm	Total Customers	Period
Foster & Gallagher	2,404,000	(Jan. 1972–June 1973)
Hanover House..................	1,448,000	(1971–73)
Miles Kimball	2,000,000	(1971–73)
Spencer Gifts	4,500,000	(1971–73)
Sunset House	6,500,000	(1971–73)
Grand total	16,852,000	

The granddaddies of special interest catalogs are unquestionably the seed and nursery catalogs. Many a gardener keeps happy during the cold winter months thumbing through his nursery catalog, anticipating "The flowers that bloom in the spring."

W. Atlee Burpee Co.—one of the old-timers—has been issuing catalogs for over 95 years. There were over 2.5 million 184-page Burpee catalogs distributed free in 1971. Of the 184 pages, 40 were full color pages offering flowers, vegetables, trees, shrubs, house plants, and garden aids such as mole killers, bulb planters, and a flying disk to scare birds away.

Another pioneer in the field of nursery catalogs is Henry Field Seeds & Nursery Co. of Shenandoah, Iowa.

A recent development in catalog selling has seen the emergence of the catalog showroom. Under the catalog showroom method, the consumer receives the catalog in the mail or through house-to-house distribution. But instead of mailing his order, the consumer selects the items he wants from the catalog and then goes to the catalog showroom where he may see them on display. He makes his purchase and then takes it home. Catalog showrooms aim to combine the atmosphere and quick service of fine department stores with catalog convenience and the savings to be had at discount stores.

Changing Times, the Kiplinger magazine, points out that by 1971 approximately 1,800 catalog showrooms sold an estimated $1 billion worth of goods. They expect that the volume may be tripled by 1975 as more sellers—including big discounters and retailers like Grand Union, May Stores, Supermarkets, General, even premium stamp companies—get into the business.

The Basics of a Successful Catalog

It is an understatement to say that "successful catalogs don't happen by accident." Successful catalogs develop as a result of living by the basics. The basics require considerable thought and much expertise. To turn out a successful catalog the first time around is nothing short of a miracle. Following the basics gets one to a successful catalog lots faster.

Basic Number 1: Right Reason for Being

To say "Let's put out a miniature Sears catalog" is the sure road to failure. Every catalog must have a reason for being: Every catalog must justify its existence on its own. When Len Carlson, founder of Sunset House, started his mail order operation on the West Coast, he determined through small-space advertising that there was a big market out there for gifts and gadgets—particularly if he assembled hundreds of them in one interesting catalog. He offered a convenient way for the consumer, particularly the housewife, to shop for gifts and gadgets at home. There were few—if any—retail stores offering such a wide assortment of items all in one department. The wisdom of Carlson's thinking is proved by the fact that, 15 years after the launching of Sunset House, sales volume was pushing $30 million.

A careful study of successful catalogs will verify that each has an underlying theme. "Everything in Office Supplies," "Maintenance Supplies at Direct-To-You Prices," "Useful and Entertaining Hobbies," "Executive Gift Guide," "Wholesale Auto Parts for All Makes"—these are but a smattering of expressed purposes and themes for catalogs destined to do the complete selling job. Prime connotations of a catalog are economy, selection, ease of ordering. Themes which play on these connotations operate within a favorable climate.

Basic Number 2: Right Merchandise Selection

The theme, the reason for being, dictates the type of merchandise to be offered in a catalog. But there is good merchandise and bad merchandise. The right merchandise selection is essential to success. The established mail order catalog operation determines the proper merchandise for its market through a process of evolution. For a firm starting cold, the right merchandise selection is particularly difficult.

There are several guidelines which should be followed by the beginner in selecting merchandise for his catalog.

1. Obtain copies of all catalogs which may in any way be considered competitive. Cut out descriptions and illustrations of any and all items which you feel may fit within the theme of your catalog.
2. Note carefully when the same items are carried in more than one catalog. This indicates the item has better than average sales appeal.
3. Obtain copies of all publications offering merchandise which fits your merchandise categories.
4. Using a directory like *Thomas Register,* look up and list available manufacturers for each of the merchandise categories you have selected for your catalog.
5. Write a letter to every manufacturer, spelling out the theme of your catalog. Each manufacturer could be asked, for example, to specify the three most popular items in his line which fit the quality image to be established.
6. Ask each manufacturer to specify the following:
   a. What is their discount (should have 50% or better)?
   b. Do they drop ship and what is the charge?
   c. What is the policy on returned goods (any refurbishing charge?)?
   d. What is the minimum order to get maximum discount?
   e. How fast and in what quantities can they fill repeat orders?
   f. Can a special model be developed which is not available in retail stores?
7. Have the merchandise buyer attend all major consumer and dealer merchandise shows which display the categories of merchandise being sought for the catalog.

214

These are some of the courses which should be followed in selecting merchandise for a catalog. The process requires digging, organization, ingenuity, determination . . . plain hard work!

When a mail order operator "grows" into a catalog operation, his process of merchandise selection is easier and safer. For example, a mail order operator who is constantly running small-space ads on a variety of items automatically selects an audience interested in like items. The winners in space become featured items in the catalog. Then it simply becomes a case of expanding the line.

Many a mail order operation has built a very large customer list through the medium of solo mailings. It becomes a simple process to convert the winning solo mailings into a catalog. For example, here is a list of solo offerings later combined into a successful catalog:

AM/FM radio

Sewing machine

Color TV set

Power saw

Ladies' and men's wristwatches

Socket wrench set

When one has *proved* sellers to offer a customer list through a catalog, one can hardly miss. The item which sells best through a solo mailing will almost always be the biggest seller when converted to a catalog presentation. The success of the technique of using nothing but proved winners in a catalog is explained by the fact that, if you are offering 15 proved items, it is a cinch that no one on the customer list has purchased all 15 items—but they have been satisfied with one or more of the items. This is a technique which hasn't been used by too many mail order firms, but it offers a vast profit potential if developed correctly.

Basic Number 3: Right Positioning and Grouping of Merchandise

The merchandise has been selected. How do you decide what goes where? How much space do you allot to each item? Tough questions, particularly when you are producing a maiden catalog. Easier to answer when you have done several catalogs.

For the beginner especially, it's important to know what most professionals in catalog selling have experienced. They've found, with rare exceptions, that the logical way to position merchandise is by popularity of the category—starting a catalog with the most popular and working back.

An example of the wisdom of leading with your best is what was divulged by analyzing a large nursery catalog. Sales analysis showed the best-selling category in nursery stock was featured in the back of the catalog. In the following season, this category was moved to the front of the catalog—and not only did sales in it increase over the previous season's but all other categories benefited as well. (The theory here is that, if you can attract readership in the front of the catalog with your most popular items, a higher percentage will shop the balance of the catalog.)

There are those in the catalog field who arrange their catalogs by groupings of merchandise categories or in categories such as "party games," "kitchen aids," "space savers," and so forth.

And then there are those who disregard categories completely, "mixing" items throughout the catalog. (The theory here is that the reader will go through the entire catalog to find items of particular interest.) Roy Hedberg, president of Sunset House, is against arranging catalogs by categories. His opposition is based on careful tests conducted by his firm. He feels his readers are more likely to shop the entire book if they are not "turned off" by specific category sections which they do not judge interesting.

Allotting space for individual items of merchandise is a tricky business, especially where previous sales data do not exist. However, there are certain guidelines which can be followed.

1. When you select items which are carried in other catalogs, pattern your space allotment after theirs.
2. When you have a firm cost estimate for your entire catalog in the mail, determine your advertising cost per catalog page and per unit of space per page. Then determine how many of the given items you must sell for the space you plan to allocate in order to break even. If this sales quota seems too high to you, reduce the allotted space.
3. If you have great confidence in an item but a considerable amount of space must be used for illustrating it to describe it properly, don't cut the space. Either use sufficient space or drop the item.
4. When you are offering more than one model of the same item, feature the model which you feel offers the greatest sales potential and sublist the additional model or models. For example, say you have two digital clock radios, one AM and the other AM/FM. You could list the AM digital clock radio and describe it, listing the price next to the item number. Under this item number, you would show the price and item number for the AM/FM digital clock radio. Just one line gives you an opportunity to offer another item for sale.

These guidelines certainly aren't foolproof. But they are a track to run on until results from a maiden catalog are computed.

Basic Number 4: Right Graphics

A catalog which must sell on its own can ride or fall on graphics. Graphics start with the cover. Covers register positive or negative impressions. Positive impressions encourage the prospect to get into the catalog; negative impressions turn the reader off.

So how does one decide what one's catalog cover should look like? Here's where having a theme gives direction. Let's say we are producing a sporting goods catalog with top-of-the-line equipment and apparel. The theme of the catalog could be: "The Finest in Accessories and Apparel for Major Participation Sports." The theme almost automatically dictates a sport scene in deluxe surroundings.

For example, if the catalog is released prior to the skiing season, a shot of two attractive people—male and female—coming down a slope at a fashionable resort would certainly seem to mesh with the catalog theme. And it goes without saying that it would be appropriate to have the models use equipment and clothing offered in the catalog.

Let's turn now from such a catalog to other aspects of catalog covers. The decision must always be made whether products should be offered for sale on the front and back covers of a catalog. Most professionals agree—practically always on the back cover, almost always *not* on the front cover. Back covers are choice selling space, an excellent location for hot items. But the front cover must carry the theme of the catalog. Trying to sell off the front cover tends to steal from the opportunity to set the theme. (Displaying merchandise in use on the front cover, referring to page numbers for full information, is not to be confused with attempting to sell off the front cover.)

Since the theme is so important, the cover of a *sale catalog* can be extremely appropriate for the direct sale of merchandise. The sale becomes the theme, especially for established customers. And the catalog cover brings the big news into immediate focus.

216

Setting the theme with the cover is just the first step, of course. Putting the book together graphically is really the big job. There are some art studios in major metropolitan areas that specialize in putting catalogs together. There are a few direct marketing agencies that have had extensive experience in producing catalogs.

The most serious mistake made by most neophytes who produce their own catalog is believing that stock photos of merchandise from manufacturers will do the job. They will save money, but they will rarely do the job. The number-one problem of using stock photos is that the catalog will almost certainly end up a hodgepodge, with a multiplicity of photo techniques, varying degrees of sharpness, straight product shots, and in-use photos. And many photos won't shoot down right for the space allotted.

An art studio experienced in catalog production will gang-shoot many items, shooting in proper perspective and showing items in their best light. Most important, a house experienced in catalog production will put human interest into a catalog, putting sell into photography with lots of in-use shots.

Good photography is but one facet of good graphics. There are layout, design, and typography to be considered — all integral parts of good graphics. So many catalogs become sterile and monotonous, with page after page laid out the same way.

Good graphics are the opposite of monotony. Each page is interesting, a new adventure. A variety of layouts are employed for the same size units. Note the two facing pages from a Sunset House catalog. There are a total of eighteen units on the two pages. Fourteen items are each given one unit of space and two items are each given two units of space. The two double units serve as "stoppers" and win attention for the balance of each page.

This is but one layout arrangement within the 94-page Sunset House catalog. Other layouts include six-unit pages of equal size, facing six-unit pages with four units of equal size and one double unit, six-unit pages of equal size facing six-unit pages with three units of equal size and one triple unit. Interspersed are some one- and two-item pages.

Working with unit spaces offers a tremendous economic advantage not apparent to the neophyte. Take the nine-item right-hand page as an example. Let's assume that six of these nine items were profitable. Following good catalog principles, Sunset House would want to drop the three losing items and repeat the six winning items for the next catalog. With unit spaces, they don't need to make up a new page. They simply remove the losing items from their negatives and drop in three new items in the same units of space.

Right paper stock is part and parcel of right graphics. The finest of art and photography will be ruined by the wrong paper. Here it is important to check with your printer and see examples of what the finished product will look like.

Basic Number 5: Right Use of Color

When to use one color, when to use two colors, when to use four colors? These are agonizing questions, particularly when there are no result figures as guidelines. Usually, the big question is between one color and four colors. Cost of photography and engravings is substantial where four colors are used.

There are certain guidelines which may be considered in deciding between one color and four colors:

1. When a catalog is divided between one- and two-color pages and four-color pages, it is most always true the four-color pages will "steal" some of the business which would have come from the one- and two-color pages if they weren't competing with four-color pages. Therefore, a proper analysis must consider the *total* pull of the book rather than separately computing the business secured from the four-color pages.

2. If any four-color is used in the book, it makes good common sense to set the theme by using it on the front and back cover.

3. Four-color work increases sales of some items tremendously and has little or no effect on sale of others. A good question to ask is, "Is it essential to use four colors really to show the merchandise?" Full color is an obvious advantage when showing apparel, home furnishings, and food. On the other hand, a beautiful one-color photo of sterling silver may do more for the display of the merchandise than adding other colors for background purposes.

4. Finally, the use of full color must be related to the total production run, as a practical matter. Since full color photography and plates constitute a major cost item, there is a real possibility that increased sales can never sop up increased cost if the production run is too small. For instance, if full color work for a catalog comes to $20,000 and the run is only 100,000 copies, then the cost of color figures out at $200 additional for each 1,000 catalogs. Obviously a prohibitive amount. The same cost—$20,000—amortized over one million catalogs brings the cost down to only $20 additional per thousand catalogs, and this is a very realistic additional cost.

218

Basic Number 6: Right Size

Another major consideration in producing a catalog is deciding on the right size—not only page size, but number of pages. First, let's consider some fundamentals of right page size:

1. Economics dictates that page size, whatever it may be, should cut out of standard sized sheets or rolls and should print most economically on high-speed presses.
2. If a catalog is to be an industrial catalog, major consideration should be given to producing a standard sized catalog which fits into catalog files maintained by most manufacturing firms.
3. Most statisticians in the catalog field can prove the thickness of a catalog does have a relationship to sales. If a catalog is too thin, it takes on the complexion of a "flyer" to be scanned and tossed away rather than kept for future reference. Therefore, when the total number of items to be offered through a catalog is scant, wisdom dictates a smaller page size—such as $5^{1}/_{2} \times 8^{1}/_{2}$ instead of $8^{1}/_{2} \times$ 11. Twelve pages of $8^{1}/_{2} \times 11$ turns into 24 pages of $5^{1}/_{2} \times 8^{1}/_{2}$.
4. Another consideration is the actual merchandise being offered for sale. Some items, such as a complete cookware set or a complete tool set, require a great deal more display than other items, such as kitchen utensils, vitamins, and so forth.
5. Many catalog professionals have found that change of pace in catalog size is an aid to increased sales. Two of the leading firms in the specialty merchandise field—Spencer Gifts of Atlantic City, New Jersey, and Sunset House of Los Angeles, California—customarily produce several editions of a small-size catalog throughout the year until the time of their Christmas catalog. They then switch to an $8^{1}/_{2} \times 11$ catalog.

Finally, many professionals will tell you that, as you increase the total number of pages in a given catalog, the total response from that catalog will increase. An example would be going from 86 pages to 94 pages. (The theory is that, as you increase the number of offerings, you increase the opportunity for attracting more customers.)

Naturally there is a point of no return for this theory. Just adding "any old items" won't do it. Items added must be of equal appeal to the overall book. And naturally, one must take the additional cost into consideration.

Basic Number 7: Right Copy

Since a mail order catalog must *sell on its own,* copy is a major factor in the success or failure of any given catalog. You can have the best of themes, excellent product selection, good graphics—but if your copy is dull, sales will suffer. Maxwell C. Ross, a direct mail consultant, points out that there are not enough action verbs used in headlines in catalogs. Too many catalogs simply apply labels like "peach trees," "apple trees," and so forth—instead of saying "You Can Grow Peaches Like These in Only Three Years."

Precise description is vital in mail order selling—size, weight, color selection, materials, and so forth. But the pro uses a mixture of specifications and selling copy.

Sunset House is a master at using end-use selling headlines under their in-use photographs. Consider some of these headlines:

Dust High Spots Easily!   No-Slip Ironing!
Chase Away Silverfish One Wipe Cleans Your Iron!
Hang Your Ironing Board

219

Still another technique is that of headlines which are labels in conjunction with sub-heads which are selling headlines. WinCraft of Winona, Minnesota, a firm that sells fund-raising and school promotional items to schools, follows the technique of labels plus selling headlines throughout their catalog. Here are a few examples:

MINI-PEP POM POMS
Ideal for Pep Clubs, Drill Teams, Marching Units of All Kinds!

ECOLOGY BUTTONS
Help Fight Pollution!

MASCOT BUTTONS
Add "Booster Power" to Your School's Spirit!

One of the most important pieces of copy in any catalog is the *guarantee*. A review of guarantees in hundreds of catalogs discloses that, while there is general recognition that guarantees are essential, there is little recognition of the fact that they should be clear and simple. Many guarantees are garbled, with confusing legal terms.

A good example of a simple and clear guarantee is that of Spring Hill Nursery. Spring Hill guarantees that high-quality plants exactly as represented, government inspected, true to name, will arrive safe and healthy in living growing condition. Any plants that reach you otherwise will be replaced free, if the nursery is notified within one month after delivery of your order. The basic guarantee, relating to safe and healthy arrival, is reinforced by a replacement guarantee. Here is the exact wording of that guarantee:

REPLACEMENTS—Spring Hill will replace any plants that fail to grow at half the original purchase price if notified within SIX MONTHS after delivery of your order. Please be sure to return your original order form for prompt adjustment of claims. Our liability in all cases is limited to the purchase price.

While a clear-cut guarantee is essential to every good mail order catalog and, indeed, provides an incentive for ordering, an equal or even stronger incentive is knowing that your peers like what they buy. There is one best way to provide this assurance: Spread *testimonials* throughout the catalog. It is surprising—amazing—how few firms who sell via the catalog method make good use of testimonials. More often than not, the president of the company keeps testimonials securely locked in his desk, a secret from his prospects and customers.

WinCraft consistently uses testimonials in their catalog. A page from the WinCraft catalog graphically illustrates this.

Basic Number 8: Right Sales Stimulators

It can't be said too often: A catalog must sell on its own. Most catalogs just arrive and lie there. Other catalogs are live, vibrant, exciting. Careful analysis will usually indicate that sale stimulators make the difference. The key question is—how do you stimulate readership and action? There are many great techniques. Here are some of the basics.

220

WinCraft
Experience Exceeding A Century

CHEERLEADER POM POMS
ADD EXCITEMENT TO YOUR EVENTS!

PREFERRED BY CHEERLEADERS ALL OVER THE WORLD!

Everywhere you go, across the nation and around the world, you'll find stadiums and gymnasiums ablaze with the color and excitement of WinCraft Cheerleader Pom Poms! The most obvious reason for this popularity is the **extraordinary size and fullness** of WinCraft Pom Poms . . . but another reason, equally important, is **quality craftsmanship.**

WinCraft Pom Poms, you see, are made from only the finest, most colorful tissue. So they're light and fluffy . . . yet, durable enough to hold their shape game after game!

What's more, you won't find a Cheerleader Pom Pom that's more maneuverable or easier to handle. That's because of WinCraft's exclusive "Easy-Spin," "Sure-Grip" and "Sta-Put" handles. They're light, comfortable . . . designed to fit your hand perfectly!

CHOOSE FROM THESE EXCITING POM POM STYLES IN YOUR CHOICE OF COLORS!

- WHIRLERETTE
- JUMBO PEP
- SUPER PEP
- CHEERLEADER PEP
- JUMBO WHIRLERETTE
- THE SPINNER
- TWIN WHIRLERETTE
- Plus many, many more!

BIG NEWS FOR CHEERLEADERS:
WinCraft's NEW VINYL POM POM!

Here's the big, beautiful pom pom you've been waiting for! Now . . . lead cheers from the gym floor without shedding . . . cheer in the rain without staining your hands or uniform . . . boost school spirit a full season with one pair of good-looking, long-lasting pom poms! For the full story on WinCraft's new Plasti-Pep Pom Pom, see page 19.

Thanks again for your wonderful service, and for such fabulous pom poms!

Conra Weber, Cheerleader
Green River High School
Green River, Utah

WinCraft is a name that stands for good quality and fast service in our school. We love dealing with you.

Devlyn Akiona
Cheerleader Captain
St. Joseph High School
Hilo, Hawaii

We were delighted with the size of the pom poms . . . and your speedy delivery!

Mary M. Krasin
Cheerleader Sponsor
Strassburg Junior High
Sauk Village, Illinois

221

1. *Overwraps*. Perhaps the greatest spur to catalog readership over the past decade has been the development of the overwrap. Traditionally, scores of firms marketing through mail order have carried a printed letter on the first inside page of the catalog. Research has shown that, almost without exception, that letter is the least read piece of copy in the catalog. But when the letters are carried as an overwrap, readership has increased dramatically. There is something about a printed letter on top of the catalog which induces the prospect to read it to determine what the catalog is all about.

   The overwrap is the ideal device for featuring special incentives to order. It has additional advantages. For example, you can develop specific pieces of copy for the overwrap, to allude to specific customer and prospect categories, without needing to alter your basic catalog.

   For instance, you can address a letter for your best customers as "Dear Preferred Customer." You can make a special effort toward customers about to be taken off your mailing list by specifically stating that is the last catalog which will be sent unless an order is received.

   Another example of the flexibility of the overwrap: say you are sending a school catalog to many categories within a school. Through overwrap letters, you can allude to the special interest of each of the following:

   Principal   Director of mathematics department
   Parent-Teacher Association   Director of science department
   Director of language department

   Because all overwraps are four pages, there are additional opportunities. Traditionally, the overwrap runs two pages for the letter — first outside page and first inside page. This leaves space for offering merchandise on the back inside page that often more than pays for the full cost of the overwrap. There is still another opportunity for page 3. It enables the marketer to test new items at low cost without making basic changes in his catalog.

   Finally, there is page 4, which is best used as an additional order form. Since the order form is also used for addressing purposes, the label appears directly above the order form. This helps tremendously in processing, since the label with the list key is right on the order form. Statistics show that, more often than not, the order form which becomes page 4 of the overwrap is the first order form used.

   There is little question that overwraps for catalogs are here to stay. This excellent idea has time and again resulted in order increases of 50% and more.
2. *Incentives for Early Orders*. Because so many catalogs are seasonal in nature, it is to the advantage of the mail order firm to get as many early orders as possible. In order to do this, it must provide incentives to the customer.

   Sunset House faced this problem by designing a sweepstakes with a built-in incentive to order early. Daily drawings gave the customer 30 opportunities to win if he or she responded immediately. If a prospect responded three days after the first deadline, for instance, he had 27 opportunities to win; if he responded ten days later, he had 20 opportunities to win; and so forth.
3. *Telephone Orders*. IN-WATS telephone service has proved a boom to catalog merchandisers. Major catalog firms like Sears have for years done a very substantial portion of their business by telephone. But it is only in the last several years that other catalog merchandisers have latched onto the tremendous appeal of offering phone-in orders.

   The ease of toll-free telephone service is a strong appeal in itself. But particularly exciting to the mail order firm is the opportunity to increase the average

Examples of flexibility of catalog overwraps.

order. Time after time we have seen an average order increase from 20% to 30% when phone-in order privileges are offered. The well-disciplined telephone ordering operation will take the basic order a customer phones in and then suggest add-ons.

4. *Bank Cards.* Offering bank card charge privileges is similar in effect to offering phone-in order privileges. The average order is larger. Offering bank card privileges is particularly attractive to firms who normally sell for cash. Bank card privileges give the marketer the opportunity to charge without any accounts receivable problems.

Ambassador Leather Goods offers the opportunity of phone-in orders and bank charge privileges in this manner:

"If you have a Master Charge or BankAmericard account, you don't even need pen and check book. Just pick up your telephone and call your order in to us, toll free!"

5. *Free Trial Periods.* In a way it's ironic—direct marketers who offer a 15-day trial period in solo mailings offer no free trial period when selling via the catalog method. Yet the chances for increased sales with a free trial period are well known.

Where practical, consideration should be given to this technique. It's hard to beat the appeal of this headline: "Everything in This Catalog Offered for 15 Days' Free Trial!"

6. *Free Gifts, or Discounts Tied to Size of Order.* Increasing the size of the average order can mean the difference between profit and loss, especially for specialty catalog operations where the average order is traditionally small.

One catalog offers a free purse with orders of $4.95 or more. Spencer Gifts offers a 10% discount certificate with orders for $3.95 or more. Swiss Colony has special Value Shop pages to encourage the customer to order for himself as well as for gifts.

Many catalogs which cater to business offer free gifts, of varying value tied to the dollar amount of the total order. An example could be: "Free coffee mug for any order between $10 and $25. Free transistor radio for any order $25 to $50. Free digital clock radio for any order for $50 or more."

Many specialty merchandise firms increase the average order by grouping merchandise and applying discounts based on the number of items purchased from a given page, a given spread, or a given number of pages. For instance, if a customer buys ten or more $1 items, he pays only 88¢ each.

These are some of the basic sales stimulators used by profitable catalog operations.

Basic Number 9: Right Order Forms

In the final analysis, the one thing you want to get back from your catalog is the order form. No one can possibly compute the amount of business lost annually as a result of confusing order forms, but the figure must be staggering. Nothing can be left to chance where the order form is concerned.

What are the basics of an effective order form?

1. Is there space to indicate how many, item number or style number, name of item, color if there is a choice, size if there is a choice, imprinting if offered, and the dollar amount?

224

HOW TO PLACE YOUR WinCraft ORDER
SO IT COMES TO YOU RIGHT & ON TIME!

1. **Start with a WinCraft Order Form** — Double check your figures and make sure you haven't left out any important information that'll delay your order. On imprinted orders, supply the imprint copy you want (neatly printed, please) and a rough sketch of your imprint design.

2. **Watch for our acknowledgement** — As soon as we receive your order, we'll acknowledge receipt by sending you a copy. If you find an error, **notify us immediately!** Most WinCraft products are custom-made to individual specifications and, for this reason, cannot be cancelled once in production.

3. **Allow for production and shipping time** — Chances are, the WinCraft items you order will be custom-made for you. So . . . to help you allow for this time in your planning, we've listed the **approximate production time** in the price box for each item. Please try to give us at least this much time to complete your order (and preferably a little more in the Fall, when we're busiest). Also, don't forget to allow for the time it takes to ship your merchandise from our plants to your school! The delivery map below shows **normal shipping time** to help you in your planning.

4. **FOR FASTER SERVICE, PHONE TOLL FREE TODAY!** Just dial 800-533-0380 (In Minnesota, call collect 507-454-5510) and ask for the "Order Department". You'll find the telephone a fast, convenient way to place your WinCraft order, especially when you collect all the facts you'll need **before** you place your call. (One easy way to have all this information at your fingertips is simply to fill out a WinCraft Order Form . . . and use it as a guide when you call!)

5. **How about shipping costs?** In most cases, rather than ask you to pay shipping, handling and insurance charges upon delivery, we add them to your 30-day invoice. The most economical method of shipment available will be used, unless otherwise specified. However, you must include **full payment, plus $1.25 postage and handling, if your order totals $10 or less.**

6. **Your credit's good with us** — We're happy to extend credit to any official school group or organization. This is only possible, however, when your order is signed by your group's faculty advisor or school principal. Terms are net, 30 days.

7. **Return policy** — Of course, we'll stand behind our guarantee and make good any orders proven defective in materials or workmanship . . . but, we cannot accept returns on unsold and/or custom-imprinted products.

8. **Prices** — All prices in this catalog are FOB Factory and subject to change without notice.

DELIVERY TIME CHART

IF YOU ARE LOCATED IN GROUP:

1. 2-3 days shipping time. (UPS)

2. 3-4 days shipping time. (UPS)

3. 4-5 days shipping time. (UPS)

4. 5-7 days shipping time. (UPS)

5. 10-14 days shipping time. (By Mail)

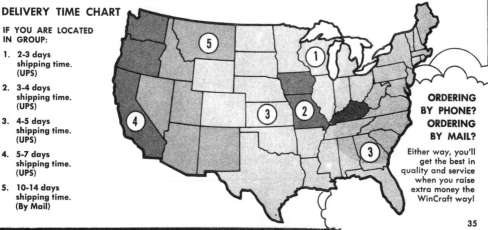

ORDERING BY PHONE? ORDERING BY MAIL?

Either way, you'll get the best in quality and service when you raise extra money the WinCraft way!

35

2. Consistent with the total number of items called for on the average order, is there sufficient number of lines for listing the items desired? (It is always desirable to leave space for more than the average as an incentive for ordering more items.)

3. Are the terms perfectly clear? If postage, insurance, and handling charges are extra, is the chart clear? If there are taxes to be added, is the percentage specified? If charge card privileges are offered, is there space to give the required identification numbers? If interest charges are applied to installment accounts, does the explanation comply with the Truth in Lending Law?

4. If drop shipments are solicited, is space allocated to provide for instructions?

5. If a discount is offered for exceeding a minimum order requirement, is it clearly spelled out?

The Ambassador Leather Goods order form illustrated here is a good example of a well-structured catalog order form. It takes the prospect through all the necessary steps in logical sequence. A key question to be asked when developing a mail order cat-

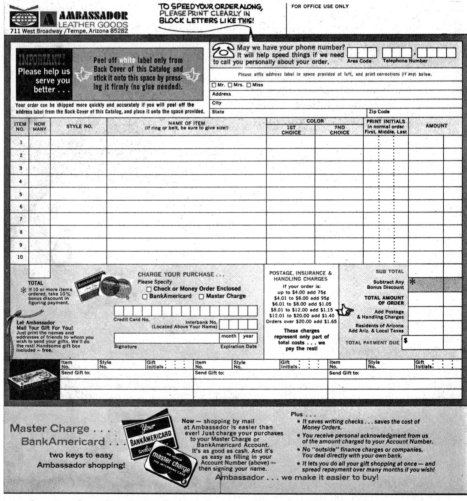

Ambassador Leather Goods bind-in order form covers all the necessary steps in logical sequence. Not shown is the attached envelope with additional merchandise featured on the other side.

alog is: Should we use a bind-in order form, or should we print an order form as a page, requiring the prospect to tear out the page and mail it in his own envelope? The overwhelming vote among the pros is for a bind-in order form with an attached reply envelope. This is based on carefully controlled test results. Not only does the bind-in order form increase results in most cases; it also affords an opportunity to feature one or more additional items on the flap. In many, many cases the additional business secured with this added exposure of items more than pays for the cost of the bind-in combination order form and reply envelope.

Basic Number 10: Right Analysis

Every catalog sales manager worth his salt is in reality a financial analyst. If he is good, he is a ruthless analyst. The professional catalog sales manager is never satisfied simply to learn that the total catalog distribution was profitable. He wants to know which items were the winners, which the losers—he wants all the facts and figures.

The Bible is undoubtedly the most purchased book ever published. But to every catalog sales manager, the second most valuable book is a marked up copy of his last catalog. This was brought home to me recently when I had a meeting with the catalog sales manager of one of the world's largest mail order firms. He had one book on his desk. It was his latest catalog, in excess of 800 pages. Written in grease pencil on every single page was the total sales of that page! There is no more dramatic way to see visually how products moved or didn't move.

The catalog sales manager looks at item exposure in a catalog the same way an advertising manager looks at space advertising in print media. Every inch of space you use in a catalog costs a specific amount of money. The cost of space is charged to the item being advertised.

To illustrate the importance of analysis by item, by page, we are going to review an analysis of four pages out of a 76-page catalog. Statistics for these four pages follow:

Page No.	Item No.	Space Allocation	Dollar Volume	Advertising Cost	Product Cost	Total Advertising & Prod. Cost	Profit	Loss	Profit for Page	Loss for Page
23	#1618	½ pg.	$6,699	$ 968	$1,608	$2,576	$4,123			
	#1619	¼ pg.	556	484	133	617		$ 61		
	#1620	¼ pg.	1,004	484	241	725	279			
TOTALS FOR PAGE			$8,259	$1,936	$1,982	$3,918	$4,402	$ 61	$4,341	---------
47	#2612	⅔ pg.	$8,592	$1,291	$3,007	$4,298	$4,294			
	#2613	⅙ pg.	386	323	135	458		72		
	#2614	⅙ pg.	193	323	68	391		198		
TOTALS FOR PAGE			$9,171	$1,937	$3,210	$5,147	$4,294	$ 270	$4,024	---------
67	#3499	½ pg.	$ 817	$ 968	$ 531	$1,499		$ 682		
	#3500	¼ pg.	925	484	426	910	$ 15			
	#3501	¼ pg.	316	484	205	689		373		
TOTALS FOR PAGE			$2,058	$1,936	$1,162	$3,098	$ 15	$1,055	———	$1,040
69	#4621	¾ pg.	$3,226	$1,452	$1,484	$2,936	$ 290			
	#4622	¼ pg.	1,689	484	777	1,261	428			
TOTAL FOR PAGE			$4,915	$1,936	$2,261	$4,197	$ 718		$ 718	---------

Now let's look at these pages, starting with page 23. Note three items are offered, one getting a space allocation of half of a page and the other two each getting one-fourth page. Note the half-page allocation has an advertising cost of $968 as compared to an advertising cost of $484 for the quarter-page units.

It is significant that Item #1618, with a space allocation of one-half page, did $6,699 in sales, over 80% of the total sales for the page. Item #1619 lost a small amount of money. Item #1620 made a minimum profit. If profits were calculated for the total page, ignoring the contribution of each item, then Item #1619 would not show up as a loser and Item #1620 would not show up as a minimum profit item.

Page 47 is also a profit maker, but note that only Item #2612 is at a profit, whereas the other two items are losers.

Page 67 is a bad page. Two of the items lost money and the other just about broke even. Total loss for the page — $1,040.

Finally let's look at page 69. Both items were profitable. But take specific note of the fact that the item which was allocated three-fourths of a page produced $290 in profit, whereas Item #4622, which was allocated only one-fourth of the page, produced $428 in profit.

Now let's take a deeper look at these figures through the eyes of the catalog sales manager. The first thing he will do is to look at his big winners. Out of the four pages he has two big winners: Item #1618 and Item #2612. He allocated one-half page to Item #1618. For the next edition of his catalog, he well may consider increasing the space to three-fourths of a page or even possibly a full page. He allocated two-thirds of a page to Item #2612. For the next edition, he may consider going to one full page.

Now let's look at his losers. Item #1619 was a small loser. He may consider dropping this to one-sixth of a page or eliminating it entirely. On page 47 he had two losers: Item #2613 and Item #2614. Since he only allocated one-sixth of a page, he can go one of two ways — eliminate the items entirely or give them more space with the hope that additional space will put them in the profit column.

On page 67 he also had two losers: Item #3499 and Item #3501. He gave one-half page to Item #3499. Now he has to decide whether he thinks this item can make it in less space, or whether it should be eliminated entirely. Since he only gave one-fourth page to Item #3501, it is a moot question whether he can put it in the profit column by reducing the space further. These are difficult decisions to make.

One factor which will influence a catalog sales manager's decision one way or the other is whether the theme of the book is *full line selection* or not. The general merchandise house with full line selections must often live with losers, whereas the specialty merchandise house — like Miles Kimball, Foster & Gallagher, and Sunset House — is rarely confronted with the problem.

The sophisticated catalog sales manager sees things in figures the neophyte never sees. For the sake of illustration, let's assume Item #1618, a big winner, was a sport sweater. The catalog sales manager follows this reasoning. If sport sweaters sell so well, why shouldn't we test sport jackets, sweatshirts, and jacket emblems? Thus, he builds on a winner.

A few final comments on the importance of space allocation. The amount of space allocated is first determined by the minimum amount of space required to describe and illustrate an item properly. Beyond this, increasing a one-half page to one page will not necessarily double sales — although in some cases it will more than double sales. Conversely, decreasing space allocation from a half-page to a quarter-page, for instance, will not necessarily cut sales in half. Of all of the means of communication now existing — and even considering those to come — it is a safe bet the catalog will continue to enjoy a love affair with its public.

228

Self-Quiz

1. Name the six consumer benefits offered by catalogs.

   1. _____ 2. _____

   3. _____ 4. _____

   5. _____ 6. _____

2. How do catalog descriptions differ from those of retail sales clerks?

   _____

   _____

   _____

3. What is the classic route to building a successful catalog operation?

   _____

   _____

   _____

   _____

4. Who are the leading specialty mail order firms?

   1. _____ 2. _____

   3. _____ 4. _____

   5. _____

5. Name the ten basics of a successful catalog.

   1. _____ 2. _____

   3. _____ 4. _____

   5. _____ 6. _____

   7. _____ 8. _____

   9. _____ 10. _____

6. Why is a theme for a catalog important?

   _____

   _____

   _____

7. Name four guidelines for selecting catalog merchandise.

1. _____

2. _____

3. _____

4. _____

8. What is the number-one rule for positioning merchandise in a catalog?

_____

_____

9. What are the advantages of grouping merchandise?

_____

_____

10. What are the advantages of "mixing" merchandise, regardless of category?

_____

_____

11. Name four guidelines for space allotment.

1. _____

2. _____

3. _____

4. _____

12. When should merchandise be featured on a catalog cover?

_____

_____

13. What is the advantage of working with unit spaces?

_____

_____

14. What is the number-one criterion for determining whether merchandise should be shown in full color?

_____

_____

_____

15. Under what conditions is a 5½ × 8½ page size preferable to an 8½ × 11 page size?

_____

_____

_____

16. What type of headlines do best under product illustrations?

_____

_____

17. Clear-cut guarantees are essential for successful catalogs. What other techniques should be employed to help the prospect anticipate satisfaction?

_____

_____

18. Name six sales stimulators for increasing catalog response.

1. _____ 2. _____

3. _____ 4. _____

5. _____ 6. _____

19. Are bind-in order form/envelopes usually worth the additional cost?
    ☐ Yes   ☐ No

20. What technique can be used to absorb the added cost of a bind-in order form/envelope combination?

_____

_____

21. What is the most graphic way to observe how each item in a catalog performed?

_____

22. When should space allotment be increased?

_____

23. When should space allotment be decreased?

_____

Pilot Project

Develop a marketing plan for a catalog catering to those interested in the subject of ecology. Your plan should answer the following questions:

1. What is your catalog theme?
2. What do you consider to be your prime markets? (Examples: Municipalities, schools, industrial firms.)

3. What categories of merchandise could you select? (Examples: Books on the sub-ject, slogan buttons, ashtrays, glassware.)
4. What sales stimulators would you develop to hypo sales?
5. What would your guarantee be?
5. From whom would you seek testimonials?
7. What size catalog would you produce?

Chapter 11   Techniques of Creating Print Advertising*

Many of the creative techniques involved in creating a successful direct mail package (Chapter 9) are also involved in creating productive direct response ads in magazines and newspapers. But the space available for words and pictures is much more severely limited, and most of the gimmicks, gadgets, showmanship, and personal tone of direct mail do not apply here. This throws a heavy load of responsibility for the success of the ad on a carefully worded headline, a compelling opening, tightly structured copy, and appropriate visual emphasis.

But before the actual work of creating an ad begins, two important questions should be answered: (1) Who is the prospect? and (2) What are the outstanding product advantages and/or customer benefits?

Often there is no single clear answer but, rather, several distinct possibilities. Then the profitable course of action is to prepare ads embodying all of your most promising hypotheses and then split-test as many of them as your budget permits.

Visualizing the Prospect

Every good mail order or direct mail piece should attract the most attention from the likeliest prospects, and every good creator of direct response advertising visualizes his prospect with varying degrees of precision when he sits down at his typewriter or drawing board.

Good response advertising makes its strongest appeal to its best prospects and then gathers in as many additional prospects as possible.

And who are the best prospects? They are the ones with the strongest predilection for what you're selling. You must look for the common denominators.

For instance, let's say you are selling a book on the American Revolution. Here are some of the relevant common denominators that would be shared by many people in your total audience.

1. An interest in the American Revolution in particular.
2. An interest in American history in general.
3. A patriotic interest in America.
4. An interest in history.
5. An interest in big, beautiful coffee table books.
6. An interest in impressing friends with historical lore.
7. A love of bargains.
8. An interest in seeing children in the family become adults with high achievement.

And so on. I am sure the list could easily be doubled.

Now out of the total audience of 1,000, some readers would possess all eight denominators, some would possess some combination of six, some a different combination of six, some just one of the eight, and so on.

If you could know the secret hearts of all 1,000 people and rank them on a scale of predilection, you would place at the very top of the list those who possessed all eight denominators, then just below them those who possessed just seven, and so on down to the bottom of the scale, where you would place people who possess none.

---

*Tom Collins, executive vice president of RCS & A (New York), one of America's most renowned direct response writers, provided the major input for this chapter.

Obviously, you should make as many sales as possible among your hottest prospects first, for that is where your sales will be easiest. Then you want to reach down the scale to sell as many of the others as you can. By the time you get down to the people possessing only one of the denominators, you will probably find interest so faint that it would almost be impossible to make your sales effort pay unless it were fantastically appealing.

Obvious? Yes, to mail order professionals who learned the hard way. But to the tenderfoot, it is not so obvious. In his eagerness to sell everybody, he may muff his easiest sales by using a curiosity-only appeal which conceals what is really being offered.

On the other hand, the veteran but uninspired pro may gather up all the easy sales lying on the surface but, through lack of creative imagination, fail to reach deeper into the market.

For instance, let's say that out of 1,000 readers, 50 possess all eight denominators. A crude omnibus appeal which could scoop up many of them would be something like "At last—for every liberty-loving American family, especially those with children, whose friends are amazed by their understanding of American history, here is a big, beautiful book about the American Revolution you will display with pride—yours for only ⅕ of what you'd expect to pay!" A terrible headline, but at least one that those possessing the eight denominators of interest would stop to look at and consider. You may get only 5% readership, but it will be the right 5%.

Now suppose, on the other hand, you want to do something Terribly Creative in order to reach a wider market. So you do a beautiful essay advertising message headed "The Impossible Dream," in which you somehow work your way from that starting point around to what it is you're selling. Again, you may get only 5% readership, but these readers will be scattered along the entire length of your scale of interest. Out of the 50 people who stopped to read your message, only two or three may be prime prospects possessing all eight denominators. Many people really interested in books on the American Revolution, in inspiring their children with patriotic sentiments, and in acquiring big impressive books at big savings will have hurried past unaware.

The point: Don't let prime prospects get away. In mail order you can't afford to. Some people out there don't have to be sold; they already want what you have, and if you tell them that you have it, they will buy it. By themselves they may not constitute enough of a market to make your selling effort pay, but without them you haven't got a chance. So through your clarity and directness, you gather in these prime prospects; then through your creative imagination you reach beyond them to awaken and excite mild prospects as well.

Once the prospect is clearly visualized, a good headline almost writes itself. For example, here is an effective and apparently successful headline from an ad by Quadrangle/The New York Times Book Co. It simply defines the prospect so clearly and accurately that the reader who fits feels an instant tug:

FOR PEOPLE WHO ARE ALMOST (BUT NOT QUITE) SATISFIED
WITH THEIR HOUSE PLANTS . . . AND CAN'T FIGURE OUT
WHAT THEY'RE DOING WRONG

Our most successful ad for Washington School of Art, a correspondence course, resulted from our finally bringing the psychographic profile of our prime prospect into sharp focus. We began to confront the fact that the prospect was someone who had been drawing pictures better than the rest of us since the first grade. Such people are filled with a rare combination of pride in their talent and shame at their lack of perfection. And their goal is not necessarily fame or fortune, but simply to become a "real artist," a

234

phrase that has different meanings to different people. So the winning headline simply reached out to the right people and offered them the right benefit:

> IF YOU CAN DRAW FAIRLY WELL
> (BUT STILL NOT GOOD ENOUGH)
> WE'LL TURN YOU INTO A REAL ARTIST

Of course a good headline does not necessarily present an explicit definition of the prospect, but it is always implied. Here are some classic headlines and the prospects whom the writer undoubtedly visualized:

> CAN A MAN OR A WOMAN MY AGE
> BECOME A HOTEL EXECUTIVE?

The prospect is a — probably — middle-aged man or woman who needs, for whatever reason, an interesting, pleasant, not too technically demanding occupational skill, such as hotel management, and is eager for reassurance that you CAN teach an old dog new tricks. Note, however, how wide the net is cast. No one is excluded. Even a person fearing he may be too young to be a hotel executive can theoretically read himself into this headline.

> DON'T ENVY THE PLUMBER—BE ONE

The prospect is a poorly paid worker, probably blue collar, who is looking for a way to improve his lot and who has looked with both indignation and envy at the plumber, who appears not much more skilled but earns several times as much per hour.

> HOW TO STUMBLE UPON
> A FORTUNE IN GEMS

The prospect is everybody, all of us, who all our lives have daydreamed of gaining sudden wealth without extreme sacrifice.

> IS YOUR HOME PICTURE-POOR?

The prospect is someone, probably a woman, with a home, who has a number of bare or inadequately decorated walls, and who feels not only a personal lack but also, perhaps more important, a vague underlying sense of social shame at this conspicuous cultural "poverty." She recognizes, whether she appreciates it or not, that art, books, and music are considered part of "the good life" and are supposed to add a certain richness to life.

> BE A "NON-DEGREE ENGINEER"

This is really a modern version of "Don't envy the plumber." The prospect is an unskilled or semiskilled factory worker who looks with a mixture of resentment and grudging envy on the aristocracy in his midst, the fair-haired boys who can earn much more, dress better, and enjoy special privileges because they are graduate engineers. The prospect would like to enjoy at least some of their job status, but is unwilling or unable to go to college and get an engineering degree.

235

"Can he really play?" a girl whispered. "Heavens, no!" Arthur exclaimed. "He never played a note in his life."

They Laughed When I Sat Down
At the Piano
But When I Started to Play!—

ARTHUR had just played "The Rosary." The room rang with applause. I decided that this would be a dramatic moment for me to make my debut. To the amazement of all my friends I strode confidently over to the piano and sat down.

"Jack is up to his old tricks," somebody chuckled. The crowd laughed. They were all certain that I couldn't play a single note.

"Can he really play?" I heard a girl whisper to Arthur. "Heavens, no!" Arthur exclaimed. "He never played a note in all his life... But just you watch him. This is going to be good."

I decided to make the most of the situation. With mock dignity I drew out a silk handkerchief and lightly dusted off the keys. Then I rose and gave the revolving piano stool a quarter of a turn, just as I had seen an imitator of Paderewski do in a vaudeville sketch.

"What do you think of his execution?" called a voice from the rear.

"We're in favor of it!" came back the answer, and the crowd rocked with laughter.

Then I Started to Play

Instantly a tense silence fell on the guests. The laughter died on their lips as if by magic. I played through the first bars of Liszt's immortal Liebesträume. I heard gasps of amazement. My friends sat breathless—spellbound.

I played on and as I played I forgot the people around me. I forgot the hour, the place, the breathless listeners. The little world I lived in seemed to fade—seemed to grow dim—unreal. Only the music was real. Only the music and the visions it brought me. Visions as beautiful and as changing as the wind-blown clouds and drifting moonlight, that long ago inspired the master composer. It seemed as if the master musician himself were speaking to me—speaking through the medium of music—not in words but in chords. Not in sentences but in exquisite melodies.

A Complete Triumph!

As the last notes of the Liebesträume died away, the room resounded with a sudden roar of applause. I found myself surrounded by excited faces. How my friends carried on! Men shook my hand—wildly congratulated me—pounded me on the back in their enthusiasm! Everybody was exclaiming with delight—plying me with rapid questions ... "Jack! Why didn't you tell us you could play like that?"..."Where *did* you learn?"—"How long have you studied?"—"Who *was* your teacher?"

"I have never even *seen* my teacher," I replied. "And just a short while ago I couldn't play a note."

"Quit your kidding," laughed Arthur, himself an accomplished pianist. "You've been studying for years. I can tell."

"I have been studying only a short while," I insisted. "I decided to keep it a secret so that I could surprise all you folks."

Then I told them the whole story.

"Have you ever heard of the U. S. School of Music?" I asked. A few of my friends nodded. "That's a correspondence school, isn't it?" they exclaimed.

"Exactly," I replied. "They have a new simplified method that can teach you to play any instrument *by note* in just a few months."

How I Learned to Play Without a Teacher

And then I explained how for years I had longed to play the piano.

"It seems just a short while ago," I continued, "that I saw an interesting ad of the U. S. School of Music mentioning a new method of learning to play which only cost a few cents a day! The ad told how a woman had mastered the piano in her spare time at home—and *without a teacher!* Best of all, the wonderful new method she used required no laborious scales—no heartless exercises—no tiresome practising. It sounded so convincing that I filled out the coupon requesting the Free Demonstration Lesson.

"The free book arrived promptly and I started in that very night to study the Demonstration Lesson. I was amazed to see how easy it was to play this new way. Then I sent for the course.

"When the course arrived I found it was just as the ad said—as easy as A. B. C.! And as the lessons continued they got easier and easier. Before I knew it I was playing all the pieces I liked best. Nothing stopped me. I could play ballads or classical numbers or jazz, all with equal ease. And I never did have any special talent for music."

Play Any Instrument

You, too, can now *teach yourself* to be an accomplished musician—right at home—in half the usual time. You can't go wrong with this simple new method which has already shown almost half a million people how to play their favorite instruments *by note*. Forget that old-fashioned idea that you need special 'talent.' Just read the list of instruments in the panel, decide which one you want to play and the U. S. School will do the rest. And bear in mind no matter which instrument you choose, the cost in each case will be the same—just a few cents a day. No matter whether you are a mere beginner or already a good performer, you will be interested in learning about this new and wonderful method.

Send for Our Free Booklet and Demonstration Lesson

Thousands of successful students never dreamed they possessed musical ability until it was revealed to them by a remarkable "Musical Ability Test" which we send entirely without cost with our interesting free booklet.

If you are in earnest about wanting to play your favorite instrument—if you really want to gain happiness and increase your popularity—send at once for the free booklet and Demonstration Lesson. No cost—no obligation. Sign and send the convenient coupon now. Instruments supplied when needed, cash or credit. **U. S. School of Music, 812 Brunswick Bldg., New York City.**

Classic ad from the past, written by the great direct response writer John Caples, appealed to a broad spectrum of prospects with a fervent desire to impress their friends.

ARE YOU TIRED OF COOKING
WITH ODDS AND ENDS?

The prospect is Everywoman who has accumulated, over the years, an enameled pan here, an aluminum pot there, an iron skillet elsewhere, and to whom a matched set of anything represents neatness, order, and elegance.

CAN YOU CALL A MAN
A FAILURE AT 30?

The prospect is a young white-collar worker between 25 and 32 who is deeply concerned that life isn't turning out the way he dreamed and that he is on the verge of failing to "make it" — permanently.

Selecting Advantages and Benefits

Advantages belong to the product. Benefits belong to the consumer. If the product or service is unique or unfamiliar to the prospect, then stressing benefits is important. But if it is simply a new, improved model in a highly competitive field where there already is an established demand, then the product advantage or advantages become important.

Thus when pocket electronic calculators were first introduced, such benefits as PRIDE, POWER, and PROFIT were important attributes. But then, as the market became flooded with competing types and brands, product advantages such as the floating decimal became more important.

There are two kinds of benefits, the immediate or obvious benefit and the not so obvious ultimate benefit — the real potential meaning in the customer's life of the product or service being sold. The ultimate benefit often proves to have a greater effect, for it reaches deeper into the prospect's feelings.

For a girl who is a prospect for a course in Speedwriting shorthand, the obvious benefit is "a good job with more pay." But a strong possible ultimate benefit was expressed in the headline:

CATCH YOURSELF A NEW BOSS, ETC.

(Needless to say, the "etc." could easily be interpreted to mean "husband.")

Victor Schwab, one of the great mail order pioneers, was fond of quoting Dr. Samuel Johnson's approach to auctioning off the contents of a brewery: "We are not here to sell boilers and vats, but the potentiality of growing rich beyond the dreams of avarice."

It pays to ask yourself over and over again, "What am I selling? Yes, I know it's a book, or a steak knife, or a home study course in upholstering — but what am I *really* selling? What human values are at stake?"

237

For example, suppose you have the job of selling a correspondence course in advertising. Here is a list of ultimate benefits and the way they may be expressed in headlines for the course. Some of the headlines are patently absurd, but they illustrate the mind-stretching process involved in looking for the ultimate benefit in your product or service.

HEALTH: "Successful ad men are healthier and happier than you think – and now you can be one of them."

MONEY: "What's your best chance of earning $50,000 a year by the time you are 30?"

SECURITY: "You are always in demand when you can write advertising that sells."

PRIDE: "Imagine your pride when you can coin a slogan repeated by 50 million people."

APPROVAL: "Did you write that ad? Why I've seen it everywhere!"

ENJOYMENT: "Get more fun out of your daily job. Become a successful ad man!"

EXCITEMENT: "Imagine working until 4:00 A.M. – and loving every minute of it!"

POWER: "The heads of giant corporations will listen to your advice – when you've mastered the secrets of advertising that works." (Just a wee bit of exaggeration there, perhaps.)

FULFILLMENT: "Are you wasting a natural talent for advertising?"

FREEDOM: "People who can get million-dollar advertising ideas don't have to worry about punching a time clock."

IDENTITY: "Join the top advertising professionals who keep the wheels of our economy turning."

RELAXATION: "How some men succeed in advertising without getting ulcers."

ESCAPE: "Hate going to work in the morning? Get a job you'll love – in advertising!"

CURIOSITY: "Now go behind the scenes of America's top advertising agencies – and find out how multimillion dollar campaigns are born!"

POSSESSIONS: "I took your course five years ago – today I own two homes, two cars, and a Chris-Craft."

SEX: "Join the guys and the gals who've made good in the swinging advertising scene."

HUNGER: "A really good ad man always knows where his next meal is coming from."

Harnessing the Powers of Semantics

A single word is a whole bundle – a nucleus, you could say – of thoughts and feelings. And when different nuclei are joined together, the result is nuclear fusion, generating enough power to move the earth.

A whole new semiscience, semantics, has been founded on this unique property of words. The newspaper columnist Sydney Harris has popularized it with his occasional feature, "Antics with Semantics." A typical antic goes something like this: "I am sensible in the face of danger. You are a bit overcautious. He is a coward." The factual content may be the same, but the semantic implications vary widely.

Semantics is the hydrogen bomb of persuasion. In politics, for example, entire election campaigns sometimes hinge on the single word "boss." If one side manages to convince the public that the other side is controlled by a boss or bosses, but that the first side has only "party leaders," it will probably win the election.

In direct marketing, clear understanding and skillful use of semantics can make a powerful contribution to ad headlines. Here are a few examples.

What do you think when you read the word "Europe"? Perhaps there are certain negative connotations – constant military squabbles, lack of Yankee know-how, and so on. But far more important in the psyche of most Americans are the romantic implications – castles, colorful peasants, awesome relics of the past, charming sidewalk cafes, all merging into the lifelong dream of making the Grand Tour of Europe.

238

Another semantically rich word is "shoestring." A man is a fool to start a business of his own with inadequate capital. But if he succeeds, he is a "wizard," and his inadequate capital is seen in retrospect as a "shoestring." Harian Publications got the idea of linking these two words with a couple of modest connectives and achieved verbal nuclear fusion that sold thousands of books on low-cost travel: *Europe on a Shoestring.*

Since there is no copyright on semantic discoveries, Simon & Schuster could capitalize on Harian's discovery and publish their $1 *Complete Guide to Florida.* In fact, they were so successful they broke the mail order "rule" that a product selling for only $1 cannot be profitably sold in print ads.

For the word "Europe" they simply substituted another semantically rich word, "Florida," and came up with another powerful winner. A one-inch advertisement using this headline drew thousands of responses at a profitable cost per order, even when this tiny ad appeared completely lost on a 2,400-line page filled with larger ads screaming for attention.

The fascinating thing about this kind of verbal nuclear fusion is that once it has been achieved it can be repeated almost endlessly—not only in the same form but in other forms as well.

For example, a real breakthrough in selling *Motor's Auto Repair Manual* was achieved many years ago with the headline, "Now You Can Lick Any Auto Repair Job." Every single word made a contribution to the power of the headline, as indeed each word always does in a long-lived headline. "Now" made the ad a news event, even after it had been running for years. "You," perhaps the sweetest word ever sounded to the ears, made it clear that the benefit included the reader and not just professional auto mechanics. "Can," another great word, promises power, achievement. "Lick" promises not only sure mastery but sweet triumph. Notice how much richer it is than "do." "Any" increases the breadth of the promise to the outermost limit. "Auto" selects the prospect and defines the field of interest. "Repair" defines the proposition, and "Job" emphasizes the completeness of its scope.

Once this breakthrough had been achieved, it was possible to make the same statement in many different ways with equal success. "Now Any Auto Repair Job Can Be 'Duck Soup' for You," "Now Any Auto Repair Job Can Be Your 'Meat,'" and so on.

"Engineer" is a rich, many-faceted word. To an artist or a writer, the word may connote a literal-minded square. To an engineer's prospective mother-in-law, it may connote a good provider. To an engineer, it means a degree in engineering and professional standing earned by hard study at college.

But to the manual and semiskilled workers in an electronics plant, our agency reasoned in developing appeals for the Cleveland Institute of Electronics, the word "engineer" suggests the college-educated wise guy who is the fair-haired boy in the plant—an object both of envy on the part of the workers and of secret derision born of envy. We couldn't promise "You too can be an engineer," because "engineer" all by itself is taken to mean a graduate engineer, and completion of CIE courses doesn't provide college credits or a college degree. However, many of the job titles, such as "broadcast engineer," "field engineer," or "sales engineer," have the word "engineer" in them without requiring a college degree. So we were legitimately able to promise prospective enrollees the prestige and other rewards of being an engineer in an ad headed, "Be a Non-Degree Engineer."

Semantic considerations like these cause mail order people to spend hours discussing and tinkering with a single headline or even a single word in the headline. It will pay you to study the mail order headlines you see used over and over again and try to analyze and apply the semantic secret of their success.

At 4½ she's reading 3rd grade books

a child prodigy? not at all! your child, too can be reading one, two or three years beyond his present age level...even if he's a "poor" reader now

Prove it to yourself...with this 10 day free trial!

Reading is fun for Sarah—as it *should be* for every child. At age four and a half, she's already choosing her own books at the San Diego, Cal. library. She reads books many third graders find "hard going." Yet she won't enter first grade for another year.

Sarah is typical of thousands of children who learned to read with "Listen and Learn with Phonics"—a reading kit that actually makes reading fun.

"Listen and Learn with Phonics" was developed by a reading expert. It has been endorsed, after extensive testing by teachers, schools, and educators.

This practical (and inexpensive) home-learning kit *fascinates* eager young minds from three to ten. The child *hears* the letters or sounds on the phonograph record, *sees* them in his book and repeats them himself. This makes an absorbing *game* of better reading—with amazing results!

FOR EXAMPLE:

- Slow or average readers show sudden, often spectacular improvement in reading, in spelling, in understanding.
- Older children often advance their reading skills several years beyond their age levels.
- Young "pre-schoolers" actually *teach themselves to read* by this simple but startlingly effective phonics method of words, pictures, and records.

6 TEACHING GAMES INCLUDED FREE
Set includes six separate "word building" games. All six are sent with your Listen and Learn Phonics Set FREE of charge!

TEACHERS & PARENTS ACCLAIM RESULTS
"I received your Combination Teaching Set and am positively delighted with it! . . . your marvelous approach to reading is just what we need."
Mrs. Rogavin, Central High School, Snyder, N.Y.

"We purchased 'Listen and Learn With Phonics' . . . for our nine year old son...within two weeks his reading had improved 100%."
Mrs. Gregory Knight, San Leandro, Cal.

4-MONTH UNCONDITIONAL GUARANTEE
If not delighted with the progress shown by your child—just return the set for complete refund.

These "Learning Tools" Simple to Use!
You don't need special teaching skills to use this program. Nor do you need any special knowledge of phonics.

In fact, your child needs no special supervision on your part. This set is so simple, so fascinating, he can learn "on his own" *without help*.

10-DAY FREE TRIAL—PLUS 4-MONTH MONEY-BACK GUARANTEE!
Results are so dramatic, the publishers will make the complete kit available to your child with an equally dramatic FREE trial and guarantee.

Under the terms of this unusual offer you can test the kit free of charge for ten days. Moreover you may use the kit for four months and then return it for *full refund* if you're not completely satisfied with your child's progress!

See for yourself how fast your child can learn to read. Just fill out and mail the coupon below. There's no obligation, and six teaching games are included free—yours to keep whether you buy or not. Americana Interstate, a division of Grolier, Inc., publishers of Book of Knowledge, Mundelein, Ill.

A classic ad. *This ad, appearing in scores of publications over a period of years, has consistently outpulled all ads tested against it. Its continuing success may well be attributed to the strong appeal to parental pride in the major headline.*

240

How to Become a "Non-Degree" Engineer in the Booming World of Electronics

Thousands of real engineering jobs are being filled by men without engineering degrees. The pay is good, the future bright. Here's how to qualify...

By G. O. ALLEN

President, Cleveland Institute of Electronics

THE BIG BOOM IN ELECTRONICS—and the resulting shortage of graduate engineers—has created a new breed of professional man: the "non-degree" engineer. He has an income and prestige few men achieve without going to college. Depending on the branch of electronics he's in, he may "ride herd" over a flock of computers, run a powerful TV transmitter, supervise a service department, or work side by side with distinguished scientists designing and testing new electronic miracles.

According to one recent survey, in military-connected work alone 80% of the civilian field engineers are not college graduates. Yet they enjoy officer status and get generous *per diem* allowances in addition to their excellent salaries.

In TV and radio, you qualify for the key job of Broadcast Engineer if you have an FCC License, whether you've gone to college or not.

Now You Can Learn at Home

To qualify, however, you do need to know more than soldering, testing circuits, and replacing components. You need to really know your electronics theory—and to prove it by getting an FCC Commercial License.

Now you can master electronics theory at home, in your spare time. Over the last 30 years, here at Cleveland Institute of Electronics, we've perfected AUTO-PROGRAMMED™ lessons that make learning at home easy, even if you once had trouble studying. To help you even more, your instructor gives the homework you send in his undivided personal attention—it's like being the only student in his "class." He even mails back his corrections and comments the same day he gets your work, so you hear from him while everything is still fresh in your mind.

Does it work? I'll say! Better than 9 out of 10 CIE men who take the U.S. Government's tough FCC licensing exam *pass it on their very first try*. (Among non-CIE men, 2 out of 3 who take the exam *fail*.) That's why we can promise in writing to refund your tuition in full if you complete one of our FCC courses and fail to pass the licensing exam.

Students who have taken other courses often comment on how much more they learn from us. Says Mark E. Newland of Santa Maria, Calif.:

"Of 11 different correspondence courses I've taken, CIE's was the best prepared, most interesting, and easiest to understand. I passed my 1st Class FCC exam after completing my course, and have increased my earnings by $120 a month."

Mail Coupon for 2 Free Books

Thousands of today's "non-degree" engineers started by reading our 2 free books: (1) Our school catalog "How to Succeed in Electronics," describing opportunities in electronics, our teaching methods, and our courses, and (2) our special booklet, "How to Get a Commercial FCC License." To receive both without cost or obligation, mail coupon below.

CIE Cleveland Institute of Electronics
1776 E. 17th St. Dept. PS-6, Cleveland, Ohio 44114

Cleveland Institute of Electronics
1776 East 17th Street, Dept. PS-6, Cleveland, Ohio 44114

Please send me without cost or obligation:

1. Your 40-page booklet describing the job opportunities in Electronics today, how your courses can prepare me for them, your methods of instruction, and your special student services.
2. Your booklet on "How to Get a Commercial FCC License."

I am especially interested in:

- ☐ Electronics Technology
- ☐ First Class FCC License
- ☐ Broadcast Engineering
- ☐ Electronic Communications
- ☐ Industrial Electronics
- ☐ Advanced Engineering

Name .... Age ......
(Please print)

Address ....

City .... State .... Zip ....

Present Job Title ....

Accredited Member National Home Study Council
A Leader in Electronics Training...Since 1934

The power of semantics is shown in this strong headline. It incorporates many favorable connotations in the promise to become a "Non-Degree Engineer."

Building in the "Hook"

A successful direct marketing ad must compete fiercely for the reader's time and attention. No matter how great the copy is, it will be wasted if the headline does not compel reading. So most successful headlines have a "hook" to catch the reader and pull him in. The most common hooks are such words as WHY – HOW – NEW – NOW – THIS – WHAT. They make the reader want to know the answer. *Why* is it? *How* does it? *What* is it?

Consider the flat statement:

> INCREASING YOUR VOCABULARY CAN HELP YOU
> GET AHEAD IN LIFE.

This is merely an argumentative, pontifical claim. It doesn't lead anywhere. But notice how the addition of just one word changes the whole meaning and the mood;

> HOW INCREASING YOUR VOCABULARY CAN HELP YOU
> GET AHEAD IN LIFE.

This unstylish, uncreative headline, and the copy that followed, sold hundreds of thousands of copies of a vocabulary book. It selected the prospect (people who were interested in larger vocabularies), it promised an ultimate benefit (SUCCESS), and it built in a hook (HOW).

Of course, the hook can be merely implied. There is no hook word in the headline, "Be a Non-Degree Engineer." But there is a clear implication that the copy is going to tell you how to achieve this.

Writing the Lead

Perhaps the most troublesome and important part of any piece of mail order copy is the lead, or opening. A lead that "grabs" the reader doesn't guarantee that he will read the rest of the copy. But one that fails to grab him does practically guarantee that he *won't* read the rest.

You should always remember, in writing or judging a lead, that your reader has better things to do than sit around and read your advertising. He doesn't really want to read your copy – until you make him want to. And your lead has got to make him want to.

A common error in writing leads is failure to get to the point immediately – or at least to *point* to the point. Haven't you had the experience of listening to a friend or associate or public speaker who is trying to tell you something but not able to get to the point? Remember how impatient you felt as you fumed inwardly, "Get to the point!" Your readers feel that same way about copy – and can very easily yawn and turn away. A good roundabout lead is not impossible, but it takes a brilliant writer.

A good principle to follow is that the copy should proceed from the headline. That is, if your headline announces what you are there to talk about, then you should get down to business and talk about it. Although it is true that some successful advertising merely *continues* the message started by the headline or display copy, there is far less danger of confusion if the copy *repeats* and *expands* the headline message, exactly the way a good news item does.

Notice how marvelously these leads from the *Wall Street Journal* news columns form a bridge between the headlines and the rest of the stories:

242

NEW POSTAGE-STAMP INK
TO SPEED MAIL PROCESSING

NEW YORK – U.S. postage stamps will soon be tagged with a special luminescent ink that will permit automatic locating and cancelling of the stamps to speed processing of the mail.

AFFLUENT AMERICANS AWASH IN
DOCUMENTS SNAP UP HOME SAFES

NEW YORK – There's a popular new home appliance that won't wash a dish, dry a diaper, or keep a steak on ice. It's a safe. And it's being propelled into prominence by a paper work explosion.

Notice, too, that although the lead restates the thought of the headline, it does it in a different way, recapping the thought but also advancing the story.

Classic Copy Structure

In a classic mail order copy argument, a good lead should be visualized as the first step in a straight path of feeling and logic from the headline or display theme to the concluding call for action. In that all-important first step, the reader should be able to see clearly where the path is taking him. Otherwise he may not want to go. (This is the huge error of ads that seek to pique your curiosity with something irrelevant and then make a tie-in to the real point. Who's got time for satisfying that much curiosity these days?)

The sections of a classic copy argument may be labeled PROBLEM – PROMISE OF SOLUTION – EXPLANATION OF PROMISE – PROOF – CALL TO ACTION. However, if you're going to start with the problem, it seems like a good idea at least to hint right away at the forthcoming solution. Then the reader won't mind your not getting to the point right away, as long as he knows where you're going. A generation ago, when the pace of life was slower, a brilliant copywriter could get away with spending the first third of his copy leisurely outlining the problem before finally getting around to the solution. But in today's more hectic times, it's riskier.

Here is an ad seeking Duraclean dealers in which the problem lead contains the promise of solution.

I FOUND THE EASY WAY TO ESCAPE FROM BEING A "WAGE SLAVE"

I kept my job while my customer list grew . . . then found myself in a high-profit business. Five years ago, I wouldn't have believed that I could be where I am today.

I was deeply in debt. My self-confidence had been shaken by a disastrous business setback. Having nobody behind me, I had floundered and failed for lack of experience, help, and guidance.

Now the copy could have simply started out, "Five years ago, I was deeply in debt," etc. But the promise of happier days to come provides a carrot on a stick, drawing us down the garden path. You could argue that the headline had already announced the promise. But in most cases, good copy should be able to stand alone and make a complete argument even if all the display type were removed.

Here, from an ad for isometric exercises, is an example of the flashback technique referred to above:

243

[Starts with the promise]

Imagine a 6-second exercise that helps you keep fit better than 24 push-ups. Or another that's capable of doubling muscular strength in 3 weeks!

Both of these "quickie" exercises are part of a fantastically simple body-building method developed by Alabama Doctor of Education, fitness expert and coach, Donald J. Salls. His own trim physique, his family's vigorous health and the nail-hard brawn of his teams are dramatic proof of the results he gets—not to mention the steady stream of reports from housewives, athletes, even school children who have discovered Dr. Salls' remarkable exercises.

[Flashback to problem]

Most Americans find exercise a tedious chore. Yet we all recognize the urgent personal and social needs for keeping our bodies strong, shapely, and healthy. What man wouldn't take secret pride in displaying a more muscular figure? What woman doesn't long to trade in those flabby spots for a slimmer, more attractive figure?

The endless time and trouble required to get such results has been a major, if not impossible hurdle for so many of us. But now [return to the promise] doctors, trainers, and physical educators are beginning to recommend the easy new approach to body fitness and contour control that Dr. Salls has distilled down to his wonderfully simple set of 10 exercises.

Of course a really strong, exciting promise doesn't necessarily need statement of the problem at all. If you're selling a "New Tree that Grows a Foot a Month," it could be argued that you don't actually have to spell out how frustrating it is to spend years waiting for ordinary trees to grow up—this is well known and implied.

Other Ways To Structure Copy

There are as many different ways to structure a piece of advertising copy as there are to build a house.

But response advertising, whether in publication or direct mail, has special requirements. The general advertiser is satisfied with making an impression, but the response advertiser must stimulate immediate action. Your copy must pile up, in your reader's mind, argument after argument, sales point after sales point, until his resistance collapses under the sheer weight of your persuasiveness and he does what you ask.

One of the greatest faults in the copy of writers who are not wise in the ways of response is failure to apply this steadily increasing pressure.

This may sound like old-fashioned hard sell, but ideally the impression your copy makes should be just the opposite. The best copy, like the best salesman, does not appear to be selling at all, but simply to be sharing information or proposals of mutual benefit to the buyer and seller.

Of course, in selling certain kinds of staple merchandise, copy structuring may not be important. There the advertising may be compared to a painting in that the aim is to convey as much as possible at first glance, and then convey more and more with each repeated look. You wouldn't sell a 35-piece electric drill set with a 1,000-word essay but, rather, by spreading out the set in glowing full color illustration richly studded with "feature call-outs."

But where you are involved in selling intangibles, an idea or ideas instead of familiar merchandise, the way you structure your copy can be vitally important.

In addition to the classic form mentioned above, here are some other ways to structure copy.

The Cluster-of-Diamonds assembles a great many precious details of what you are selling and presents them to the reader in an appropriate setting. The "67 Reasons

244

Why" subscription advertising of *U.S. News & World Report,* listing 67 capsule descriptions of typical recent news articles in the magazine, is a good example. Note that the "setting"—the surrounding copy containing general information and argumentation—is as important as the specific jewels in the cluster. Neither would be sufficiently attractive without the other.

The String-of-Pearls is similar but not quite the same. Each "pearl" is a complete little gem of selling, and a number of them are simply strung together in almost any sequence to make a chain. David Ogilvy's "Surprising Amsterdam" series of ads is like this. Each surprising fact about Amsterdam is like a small-space ad for the city, but only when all these little ads are strung together do you feel impelled to get up from your easy chair and send for those KLM brochures.

This technique is especially useful, by the way, when you have a vast subject like an encyclopedia to discuss. You have not one but many stories to tell, and if you simply ramble on and on, most readers won't stay with you. So make a little list of the stories you want to tell, write a tight little one-paragraph essay on each point, announce the subject of each essay in a boldface subhead, and then string them all together like pearls, with an appropriate beginning and ending.

The Fan Dancers is a line of chorus girls equipped with Sally Rand fans. They are always about to reveal their secret charms, but they never quite do. You've seen this kind of copy many times. One of the best examples is the circular received in answer to an irresistible classified ad in *Popular Mechanics.* The ad simply said "505 odd, successful enterprises. Expect something odd." The circular described the entire contents of a book of money-making ideas in maddening fashion. Something like: "No. 24. Here's an idea that requires nothing but old coat hangers. A retired couple on a Kansas farm net $240 weekly with this one." "No. 25. All you need is a telephone—and you don't call them, they call you to give their orders. A bedridden woman in Montpelier nets $70 a week this way." And so on.

The Machine Gun simply sprays facts and arguments in the general direction of the reader, in the hope that at least some of them will hit. This may be called the no-structure structure, and it is the first refuge of the amateur. If you have a great product and manage to convey your enthusiasm for it through the sheer exuberance of your copy, you may be able to get away with this technique. But the chances are that your copy will succeed not because of your technique but despite it. And the higher the levels of taste and education of your readers, the less chance you will have.

Establishing the Uniqueness of Your Product or Service

What is the unique claim to fame of the product or service you are selling? This could be one of your strongest selling points.

The word "only" is one of the greatest advertising words.

If what you offer is "better" or "best," this is merely a claim in support of your argument that the reader *should* come to you for the product or services offered.

But if what you are offering is the "only" one of its kind, then the reader *must* come to you if he wants the benefits that only you can offer.

Here are some of the ways in which you may be able to stake out a unique position in the marketplace for the product or service you are selling:

"We're the largest." People respect bigness in a company or a sales total—they reason that, if a product leads the others in its field, it must be good. Thus "No. 1 Best-Seller" is always a potent phrase, for it is not just an airy claim but a hard fact that proves some kind of merit.

But what if you're *not* the largest? Perhaps you can still establish some unique position. . . .

"We're the largest of our kind." By simply defining your identity more sharply, you may still be able to claim some kind of size superiority. For example, there was the Trenton merchant who used to boast that he had "the largest clothing store in the world in a garage!"

A mail order photo finisher decided that one benefit it had to sell was the sheer bigness of its operation. It wasn't the biggest — that distinction belonged, of course, to Eastman Kodak. But it was second. And Eastman Kodak were involved in selling a lot of other things too, such as film and cameras and chemicals. Their photo finishing service was only one of many divisions. So the advertiser was able to fashion a unique claim: "America's Largest *Independent* Photo Finisher."

"We're the fastest-growing." If you're on the way to *becoming* the largest, that's about as impressive a proof of merit as being the largest — in fact, it may be even *more* impressive, because it adds the excitement of the underdog coming up fast. *U.S. News & World Report* used this to good effect during the 1950s while its circulation was growing from approximately 400,000 to around three times that figure: "America's Fastest-Growing Newsmagazine." More recently the same claim was used effectively for Capitol Record Club, "America's Fastest-Growing Record Club."

"We offer a unique combination of advantages." It may be that no one claim you can make is unique, but that none of your competitors is able to equal your claim that you have *all* of a certain number of advantages.

In the early 1960s, the Literary Guild began to compete in earnest with the Book-of-the-Month Club. They started offering books that compared very favorably with those offered by BOMC. But the latter had a couple of unique claims which the Guild couldn't match — BOMC's distinguished board of judges and its book-dividend system, with a history of having distributed $375 million worth of books to members.

How to compete? The Guild couldn't claim the greatest savings — one of Doubleday's other clubs actually saved you more off the publisher's price. It couldn't claim that it had books offered by no other club — some of Doubleday's other clubs were offering some of the same books, and even BOMC would sometimes make special arrangements to offer a book being featured by the Guild.

But the Guild was able to feature a unique *set* of advantages which undoubtedly played a big part in the success it has enjoyed: "Only the Literary Guild saves you 40% to 60% on books like these as soon as they are published." Other clubs could make either of these two claims, but only the Guild could claim both.

"We have a uniquely advantageous location." A classic example of this was James Webb Young's great ad for "Old Jim Young's Mountain Grown Apples — Every Bite Crackles, and the Juice Runs Down Your Lips." In it Jim Young, trader, tells how the natives snickered when his pappy bought himself an abandoned homestead in a little valley high up in the Jemes Mountains. But "Pappy" Young, one of the slickest farmers ever to come out of Madison Avenue, knew that "this little mountain valley is just a natural apple spot — like they say some hillsides are in France for certain wine grapes. The summer sun beats down into this valley all day, to color and ripen apples perfectly; but the cold mountain air drains down through it at night to make them crisp and firm. Then it turns out that the soil there is full of volcanic ash, and for some reason that seems to produce apples with a flavor that is really something."

Haband Ties used to make a big thing out of being located in Paterson, New Jersey, the silk center of the nation. Even though most of their ties and other apparel were made of synthetic fibers, somehow the idea of buying ties from the silk center made the reader feel he was buying ties at the very source. In the same way, maple syrup from Vermont should be a lot easier to sell than maple syrup from Arizona.

Finally, suppose you feel that you have something unique to sell but you hesitate to start an argument with your competitors by making a flat claim that they may challenge. In that case you can . . .

Imply your uniqueness . . . by the way in which you word the claim. "Here's one mouth wash that keeps your mouth sweet and fresh all day long" doesn't flatly claim that it's the only one, it simply says, "at least *we've* got this desirable quality, whether any other product does or not." *Newsweek* identified itself as "the news magazine that separates fact from opinion"—a powerful use of that innocent word "the" which devastates the competition.

Effective Use of Testimonials

If you have a great product or service, you have an almost inexhaustible source of great copy practically free—written by your own customers.

They are the best writers you can possibly find. They will come up with selling phrases straight from the heart that no copywriter, no matter how brilliant, would ever think of. They will write with a depth of conviction that the best copywriters will find hard to equal.

The value of testimonials in mail order advertising has been recognized for nearly 100 years, is generally taken for granted—and is nonetheless frequently overlooked. If a survey were conducted of companies dependent on responses by mail, it would undoubtedly reveal that a shockingly high percentage have no regular, methodical system of soliciting, filing, and using good testimonials.

Yet a direct marketing enterprise may often stand or fall on whether or not it makes good use of testimonials.

Many years ago the Merlite Co. was founded to sell the Presto midget fire extinguisher, entirely through agents. The advertising job was to pull inquiries from prospective agents, who were then converted to active salesmen by the follow-up direct mail package.

One of the first efforts for Merlite was the creation of a testimonial-soliciting letter. From this, which was mailed to a fair number of their best agents, came the story which formed the basis for a successful small-space ad which ran for years and resulted in the sale of thousands of units. The headline: "I'm Making $1,000 a Month—and Haven't Touched Bottom Yet!"

In those days, $1,000 a month was big money—it represented just about the top limit of the wildest dreams of people of modest means. If the ad had claimed, "Make $1,000 a month selling this amazing little device," it would have sounded like a hard-to-believe get-rich-quick scheme. But the fact that an actual agent said it (his name and picture appeared in every ad) made the possibility a fact, not a claim. And the "haven't touched bottom yet" was a homey additional promise that probably no city slicker copywriter would have thought of if he were creating a fictional testimonial.

Many U.S. Schools of Music ads in the past were built around testimonials. Being able to play a musical instrument has a deep meaning for people that could best be expressed by the students themselves.

One ad bore a headline extracted from an ecstatic student's comments: "I Can't Believe My Ears—I'm Playing Music! My friends all think it's me, but I keep telling them it's your wonderful course."

One of the most appealing and effective stories used in art school advertising was that of a Florida mother who enrolled in the course and became one of the state's best-known painters. Her story was filled with more joy of fulfillment, credible praise for the course, and identification for other women than could be used in the ad.

247

For instance, the day her textbooks arrived, she felt like "a child with a new toy." Her instructors were "just wonderful. I actually came to feel they were my friends." But what if you're a housewife tied down with housework and babies? Isn't it hard to find time to paint? "It's not as hard as it sounds. When you have something exciting to look forward to, the housework flies. It's like when you're expecting a guest. You seem to get through the chores easily because you're looking forward to the visit."

But won't hubby and kids be resentful if Mom spends a lot of time painting? Not her family. "They're so enthusiastic. Every time I complete a painting, it's like a wonderful family party at our home." Isn't this reassuring? Isn't this what every creative woman would enjoy? And doesn't she make it all sound wonderfully possible and attainable?

You may have received some unsolicited testimonials which you have got permission to use and are already using. But if you expand this by setting up a methodical testimonial-soliciting program, you can increase tenfold your effective use of testimonials. Since the quality and usefulness of testimonials vary widely, the more testimonials you pull in, the more pure gold you should be able to pan from the ore.

Of course, it's important to get the testimonial donor's signature on some kind of release giving you permission to use his comments, name, and photo, if any. The wording of these releases varies. Some companies are content with a very simple "You have my permission" sentence; others use a more elaborately foolproof legal form. You should consult your attorney about the kind you choose to use.

Your testimonial-soliciting letter should drop a few gentle hints about your interest in hearing of actual benefits and improvements from your product. Otherwise you'll get too many customers writing similar lines of empty praise with "it's the greatest" and "it's the finest," etc.

Justifying the Price

"Why Such a Bargain? The Answer is Simple." These eight magic words constitute one of the most important building blocks in the mail order sale. They have been expressed hundreds of different ways in the past, and will appear in hundreds of new forms in the future. But whether in the mail order ads of magazines and direct mail yesterday and today, or the televised home-printed facsimile transmission of tomorrow, the *price justification argument* will undoubtedly always be with us. It does an important job of making the low price seem believable and the high price not really so high.

Here are a number of examples of price justification from the past. As you read through them, ask yourself if it isn't likely that similar arguments will still be used in the year 2000.

Doubleday Subscription Service: "How can the Doubleday Subscription Service offer these extremely low prices? The answer is really quite simple. Not everyone wants the same magazines. By getting all the publishers to allow us to make their offers in one mailing, each subscriber has a chance to pick and choose; each magazine gets its most interested readers at the lowest possible cost. The savings are passed on to you in the lowest possible prices for new, introductory subscriptions."

Reader's Digest (Music of the World's Great Composers): "How is this low price possible? Without the great resources of RCA and the large 'audience' of Reader's Digest, such a collection would have to cost about $60. This sum would be needed to cover royalties to musicians, the cost of recording, transferring sound from tape to records, manufacturing and packaging. But because a single large pressing of records brings down the cost of manufacturing, and because the entire edition is reserved in advance for Digest subscribers, you can have these luxury-class records now at a fraction of the usual price for records of such outstanding quality!"

248

Singer (socket wrench and tool set): "This set is not available in stores—but sets like these sell regularly in stores at a much higher price. You save the difference because—unlike the usual store which sells just a few sets at a time, we sell many hundreds, thus enabling us to purchase large quantities at big savings which we pass on to you."

American Heritage (History of the Civil War): "The post-publication price of the standard edition will be $19.95; it can be kept down to this level because of the exceptionally large first printing. But if you reserve a copy before publication (a great help with shipping, storage, inventory, etc.) we shall be glad to reduce the $19.95 price by 25 percent." (Notice the double whammy here. First the value of the postpublication edition is justified, and then the even greater value of the prepublication edition is justified.)

Book-of-the-Month Club (Pre-Publication Society): "Like the 'limited edition'—a very old custom in publishing—'pre-publication' offerings are designed to help *underwrite* the costs of any publishing project where there is an exceptionally high risk and heavy investment. Under modern printing conditions, if a publisher can be assured of a relatively large edition, the per-copy cost is reduced with almost every extra thousand copies printed. In recent years the usual procedure has been for the publisher, himself, to print an elaborate circular announcing the 'pre-publication offer' (similar to the one enclosed) and to permit booksellers, at a slight cost, to mail these announcements to selected good customers. Rarely, however, do more than a few hundred booksellers over the country participate in this kind of promotion, with the result that comparatively few book lovers ever learn of it, and usually only in large cities. The efforts of the Pre-Publication Society will be far more thorough and widespread."

Visual Reinforcement of Words and Ideas

All our powers of comprehension are built on our earliest sensations and associations. First comes touch, but that won't be much help to advertising till Aldous Huxley's "Feelyvision" is invented. Next, when we are several months old, comes image, as we learn to associate Mama's smiling face with getting fed, burped, and changed. Then comes the spoken word, when we learn to call Mama by name. This early experience with the image and the spoken word is what makes television such a potent advertising force.

Our earliest experience with the printed word is usually in our heavily illustrated first reader (or preschool picture book). It is printed in large clear serif type, in lower case—which is why serif body types seem more readable than sans serif, and lower case more comfortable than upper. And when the book says, "Oh! See the boy!" sure enough, there is usually a picture of a boy. This makes it less likely that we would stand up in class and read aloud, "Oh! See the doy!"

Advertising has seized on this fact of human development and evolved it into an astonishingly effective tool of communication. It has learned, probably far more than ever before in human history, to team words and pictures for greater impact than either alone can achieve.

Sometimes it's a *rebus,* in which a picture is substituted for some of the words. For instance, instead of saying "(A SUMMONS, A WILL, A DEED, A MORTGAGE, A LEASE) ARE A FEW OF THE REASONS WHY EVERY FAMILY SHOULD HAVE A LAWYER," an ad for New York Life Insurance Co. substituted a picture of a will, a mortgage, etc., for the words in parentheses.

Sometimes it's a *pantomine,* with the words providing only the necessary minimum of explanation. An Itkin Brothers office furniture ad showed in four pictures what the subhead promised: "In less than 45 minutes you can have four new offices without changing your address, increasing rent or interrupting work." The pictures were really the headline, and the four captions under the photos of the partitions being installed simply read: "8:45 . . . 8:50 . . . 9:15 . . . and 9:25."

Sometimes it's a *visual literalism*. For instance, our small-space ad for U.S. School of Music headed "Are You Missing Half the Fun of Playing the Guitar?" showed . . . half a guitar. The instrument was literally sawed in half.

Sometimes it's an *abstract picture*. How the devil can you picture the abstract concept "two," for instance? Avis made it literal with a photo of two fingers.

Also, the overall appearance of the ad provides visual reinforcement. Even if there are no illustrations—which is often true—the typography and overall design can convey a great deal about what kind of company is behind the advertising. For decades, most mail order advertising was notorious for being less attractive than general advertising; much of it still is. Whether this helps or hurts results is hotly debated. It could be that a certain homey or buckeye look adds an air of unsophisticated honesty and sincerity. But for any company involved in starting an *ongoing relationship with a customer,* the appearance of its direct marketing advertising should convey that it is a responsible, tasteful, orderly company to do business with.

The Response Device

Most direct response ads have a reply coupon or card for ease of responding. The significant exception is small-space ads. A two-inch ad would have to be about twice as big in order to accommodate a coupon. Many advertisers find that it does not produce twice as many results.

A black and white page with an insert card—a postpaid reply post card inserted by the magazine next to the ad—costs about 2.5 times more than a black and white page alone but usually pulls at least four times as much as a page with coupon. (Advantages of insert cards were explored in Chapter 3.)

There are many variations of the postpaid reply envelope, depending on cost and publication policy—oversize card insert, full page insert with detachable card, four-page card stock insert with detachable card, eight-page newspaper advertising supplement with bound-in or stuck-on card or envelope, loose envelope (such as for film processing) inserted in Sunday newspapers, and so on.

The creative problem in preparing coupon or card copy is to summarize the message from the advertiser to the prospect as clearly, succinctly, and attractively as possible. Many readers tear out a card or coupon and leave it in a pocket or drawer for days or even weeks before deciding to send it in. At that point, the reader wants to know what this minicontract involves. It is important to provide as much resell and reassurance as feasible.

If it is a club, the coupon copy should spell out terms of membership clearly.

Check boxes, numbers to be circled, and other aids to easy filling out should be provided wherever possible.

Any money back guarantee, whether already mentioned in the adjoining copy or not, should be clearly stated.

"Telescopic" Testing

It has been common in direct mail for many years to test as many as five or six or even ten or 12 different copy appeals, formats, or offers simultaneously. Giving each package equal exposure over a representative variety of lists is probably the most precise and scientific research method in advertising.

But this practice has *not* been so common in publication advertising. There, for a long time, advertisers were limited to the simple *A-B split-run* test, in which every other copy of a given issue of a publication would contain ad A and every other copy ad B (separately keyed, of course).

This, too, is very precise—the only thing is to make sure that the circulation purchased is large enough to provide a statistically significant variation in results between the two ads. But in terms of testing your way to a breakthrough, it can be *slow.*

If you test two ads, wait for the results, then test two more, and so on, a year or so may pass before you discover the "hot button."

On the other hand, if you test the control against one ad in publication A and another in publication B (we often do), it is useful—but it does introduce *another variable,* the difference in the two publications. And a truly scientific test has only one variable.

All our experience and common sense tell us that six or eight tests are far more likely to produce a hit than just two.

To solve this problem, direct marketing advertisers are turning increasingly to multiple ad testing. We call it "telescopic" testing because it permits the advertiser to telescope a year's testing experience into a single insertion.

Telescopic testing simply applies the direct mail principle of multiple testing to publication advertising. But it requires publications or formats with the *mechanical capability* to run such tests.

Probably the first magazine to offer this capability was *TV Guide.* Because television programs are different in each region, *TV Guide* publishes 84 different regional editions. Theoretically, you could do *84 different split-runs,* one in each regional edition, in a single week. (But you wouldn't, because the circulation for each test would be too small.) By testing ad A vs. ad B in the first region, ad A vs. ad C in the next region, and so on, it is possible to test as many as ten or 15 different ads or ad variations simultaneously. By assigning ad A results the numerical value of 100, we can give the other ad results proportionate numerical values and rank them accordingly.

Of course, an easier way to do multiple testing is by intermixed *card-stock inserts* in the centerfold. The only trouble is that these positions are reserved years in advance by repeat advertisers. They are also very costly.

So advertisers began testing new appeals and offers by doing A-B regional splits of *black and white pages* and even *half-pages* in the local program section of *TV Guide.* The following examples illustrate what can be done.

> A book series achieved a 252% improvement.
> A correspondence course inquiry ad was improved 209%.
> A name-getting giveaway program brought its advertising cost per coupon down to 19¢!

(The technique of applying telescopic testing is explored in Chapter 14.) Today there are three basic methods of running multiple tests:

1. *Simultaneous split-runs in regional editions* of a magazine which offers such a service, with one ad used as a control in all the splits.
2. *Free-standing stuffers* or loose newspaper preprints, intermixed at the printing plant before being supplied to the publication.
3. *Full page card inserts in magazines,* intermixed at the printing plant.

It's a rather expensive game to play, but major direct marketers today are playing for multimillion-dollar stakes. And all it takes is one breakthrough to pay for all the research in a very short time.

A dramatic example of the application of telescopic testing is a series of seven ads for *Psychology Today,* tested simultaneously in regional editions of *Time* . . . all the same issue date. Study the ads carefully and see if you can rate the ads A through G.

251

A

252

Psychology Today is not afraid

to talk about death

One issue's theme was what Editor T George Harris called "the zone of fear that psychologists have avoided as they would a dark cemetery." In it a lifelong student of suicides explored common attitudes toward death. A research questionnaire invited participation by readers. And the last comments received from the late, great Abraham Maslow spoke movingly of the joy of the "post-mortem life" after one has achieved a sense of completion and a willingness to die.

to take ESP seriously

"Parapsychology," research pioneer J. B. Rhine observes ruefully, "is treated like a ragged little urchin tagging along, an urchin Psychology doesn't want to be photographed with." But Psychology Today presented a long interview with Rhine, a do-it-yourself ESP research kit, and startling proof of ESP in sleeping subjects in the Dream Laboratory of Maimonides Medical Center.

to debunk popular notions

It's just plain common sense that pornography turns teen-agers into deviants. Or that heavy drinkers are trying to compensate for feelings of inadequacy. Or that living and working in crowded conditions is bad for people. But in these and many other instances, professional researchers who contribute to Psychology Today have

shown through controlled scientific experiments and statistical studies that—common sense is often *wrong*.

to play games with you

The latest thing is simulation games, in which the players recreate life experiences. Psychology Today has led the way with pull-out games bound right into the magazine as extra-value reader bonuses. For example, Man & Woman (later sold boxed at $7.95) and Blacks & Whites (later sold boxed at $6.95) gave players sharp insights through role reversal. Body Talk (later $5.95) made it fun for uptight people to loosen. More coming!

to talk about nude group therapy

Faddism? Quackery? Thrill-seeking? No, as serious clinical psychologist, Paul Bindrim described his startling new method, it can be a tender, beautiful mystical experience "which seemed to have a lasting effect on the post-marathon attitudes and behavior of many of the participants. An increased sense of inner worth, a sense of having completed a crucial psychic or spiritual cycle, helped some to a better understanding of their marriage partners."

to take sides

Our contributors speak as freely and frankly as they would in private discussions with their colleagues. One

bluntly advocated brainwashing criminals to make them law-abiding. Another showed that permitting petty thievery among employees is actually cheaper for a company than attempting total prevention. Another blasted therapists who seek to adjust their patients to an unsatisfactory status quo. Another criticized the practice of researchers fooling, frightening, and humiliating student guinea pigs in the name of science.

Can you take it? Does future shock leave you numb…or excited and invigorated? If you're the type who relishes rather than shrinks from the current explosion of knowledge about mankind and womankind, then you should join the company of some 600,000 kindred spirits—the readers of Psychology Today.

Every generation has its own magazine. This one is yours. Every month it will transport you to the frontiers of behavioral and humanist psychology, where laymen and professionals alike can share in explorations and discoveries as profoundly thrilling as the probes of outer space and the ocean depths.

And the breathtaking avant garde graphics will let you know you've really taken a trip.

You can discover Psychology Today without risking a penny. Just mail the coupon. We'll send you a copy to read free and enter your name as a trial subscriber at the special introductory rate for new subscribers as indicated in the coupon. However, if you're not delighted with the first issue, simply write "cancel" on the bill and return it without paying or owing anything, keeping the first issue with our compliments.

Are you?

B

253

Are you missing what's happening in Psychology Today?

A revolution is taking place just over the horizon. In campus behavioral labs. On the analyst's couch—if he still uses one. In groups of people sitting around in a circle, or floating around nude in a swimming pool. Even in executive conference rooms and employee meeting halls.

Psychology has progressed as far from Freud's id and Pavlov's salivating dogs as rockets have from kites and balloons. But many people still don't know what's happening.

Psychology Today is a monthly magazine devoted to bridging the gap between the laboratory and the living room, the pioneering professional and the educated layman. Here are some of the questions explored in its pages:

Instead of punishing criminals, why not brainwash them?

Does sports activity really build character?

What may be the group-decision secret of avoiding future Vietnams?

What are the characteristics of a successful investor?

Should we teach children to read the way pigeons are taught to play ping pong?

Why do fat people eat even when they're not hungry?

Can three people be happily married—to each other?

Does "the screaming cure" really work? What makes George Wallace followers mad?

How can income tax forms be made foolproof?

Is there really such a thing as hypnosis? Can a chimpanzee learn to read and write?

Is schizophrenia a breakdown—or sometimes a breakthrough?

Some of it is daring theory. Some is outrageous opinion. But much is startling fact and measured experiments which will rob you of some of your fondest pet notions—and provide you with powerful ammunition for the next time you get into an argument with friends.

And the prize-winning avant garde graphics help make adult learning the adventure it should be.

Isn't it about time you stopped missing out on Psychology Today?

To find out, just mail the coupon. We'll send you a copy to read free and enter your name as a trial subscriber at the special introductory rate for new subscribers you've indicated in the coupon. However, if you're not delighted with the first issue, simply write "cancel" on the bill and return it without paying or owing anything, keeping the first issue with our compliments.

C

15 Examples of Psychology Today

D

255

The year, 1930.
The place, Berlin. You are a practicing psychoanalyst confronting an interesting new patient. His name is Adolph Hitler. He is a professional politician regarded as one of the country's rising young men. Now he has come to you because...

...he is troubled by persistent anxieties.

He speaks confidently about his plans for Germany, yet he admits to fear of failure and therefore punishment by "lesser" beings.

Lately, however, when he considers some of the harsh deeds demanded by his grandiose plans, he has been bothered by feelings of guilt. Nevertheless, he is convinced that the ends he has in mind fully justify the means.

He is bothered only because his increasing anxieties and guilt feelings may impede him in the execution of his designs.

Hitler asks you to put an end to these disturbing feelings. *Can you help him?*

This was the disturbing question put to readers of Psychology Today by psychologist Marvin Frankel, in his article on "Morality in Psychotherapy."

In it he argued persuasively against the view which Freud developed—and which has profoundly influenced so many analysts—that the patient is not responsible for his actions but is at the mercy of his subconscious.

Instead of this traditional behavioral therapy, Frankel favors what is called integrity therapy. The analyst focuses on a patient's free choices—his motives and decisions.

In such treatment, Hitler would not have been encouraged to give up his guilt feelings. Instead, he would have been made aware of the risks he was taking with his mental health by choosing to pursue such grandiose and ruthless plans.

Many professionals among Psychology Today's readers and contributors would not necessarily agree with Frankel. But they would welcome his views as the kind of bold, challenging, often controversial presentation they have come to expect and appreciate in this unusual monthly magazine.

You don't have to be a professional, a psychologist, doctor, minister, educator, or social worker (although many of our readers are) to enjoy Psychology Today.

All it takes is a normal amount of curiosity about how and why people act as they do. And about how many of them (perhaps including you) are learning to feel and behave differently as a result of the discoveries being made and applied on the frontiers of psychology.

Today's exploration of the moonscape of the mind is as thrilling an adventure for mankind—and potentially as important—as the probes into outer space and the ocean depths.

But until Psychology Today came along, these fascinating findings were destined to remain buried for years in dry scholarly journals. Or occasionally, if an item were juicy and sexy enough, it might be picked up and sensationalized by the popular news media.

Now Psychology Today gives it to you straight and clear, neither jargoned over nor jazzed up, but visually enhanced with prize-winning breathtaking graphics. It's a monthly meeting ground where professionals and educated laymen can share in the excitement of discoveries about human behavior and new ways of shaping it. Such as:

Criminals Can Be Brainwashed—Now
How the American Boy Is Feminized
Games Babies Play
Why Hard-Hats Hate Hairs
A Little Larceny Can Do A Lot for Employee Morale
Adrenaline Makes the Heart Grow Fonder
Can Fingers See Color?
The Importance of Daydreaming
Psychology Across the Chessboard
Understanding Children's Art
Speaking in Tongues: Is It Really Supernatural?

Day Care Can Be Dangerous
How Groupthink Led to the Vietnam War
Why We Expect Beautiful People to Be Smarter
Characteristics of the Successful Investor
A Still, Small Voice Inside of You—Learning to Listen
Spare the Rod—Use Behavior Mod

Many of the most famous names in the behavioral sciences write for or are interviewed by Psychology Today—men and women like Carl Rogers, Margaret Mead, B. F. Skinner, Erich Fromm, Paul Goodman, Harvey Cox, John Lilly, Bruno Bettelheim. It took a generation for Freud's ideas to trickle out to the educated public. But you can learn immediately the current ideas and methods which will have as profound an influence on the world tomorrow.

You can discover Psychology Today without risking a penny. Just mail the coupon. We'll send you a copy to read free and enter your name as a trial subscriber at the special introductory rate for new subscribers you've indicated in the coupon. However, if you're not delighted with the first issue, simply write "cancel" on the bill and return it without paying or owing anything, keeping the first issue with our compliments.

Mail coupon for complimentary copy
and Half-Price Offer
to New Subscribers

E

Psychology Today is neither pop, pap, nor chicken

It's a magazine of authentic communiques from the frontier of discoveries about people and relationships...de-jargonized and visually enhanced.

Every intellectually curious person ought to be able to keep up with Psychology. For it touches on almost everything we do, think, and feel.

But until Psychology Today came along, you had your choice of roughly two kinds of psychology reportage.

There were stodgy professional journals and books where hair-raising discoveries were carefully concealed with an overlay of professional jargon and statistics...and where far-out probes into things like ESP, graphology, nude group therapy, and talking with dolphins were ignored or frowned on.

Then there was psychology for the masses, ranging from cute news items about the psychology of sex and marriage to self-help books on how to control yourself and others.

Meanwhile extraordinary, world-changing discoveries were being made in campus behavior labs, analysts' offices, and encounter-group workshops. Discoveries that could quite possibly lead to ending war, preventing crime, wiping out illiteracy and prejudice, saving marriages—as well as help you stop smoking, lose weight, and win at chess. But it was hard for you to find out.

Psychology Today was introduced to bridge the gap between the laboratory and the living room, the professional and the educated layman.

Each month it brings you the views and findings of pioneering professional researchers and thinkers, including leaders like Carl Rogers, Bruno Bettelheim, Margaret Mead, Erich Fromm, Harvey Cox, John Lilly, B. F. Skinner, Kenneth Keniston, Herbert Marcuse.

Not jazzed up. Not watered down. Not clouded over with professional jargon. Just straight and clear, in a way that both professionals and an interested general audience can enjoy and appreciate. And visually enhanced with colorful prize-winning avant garde graphics that reinforce the tingling feeling of high adventure.

Just a few examples:

Could Psychology Today have prevented Vietnam? "How could we have been so stupid?" President Kennedy asked after the Bay of Pigs. But stupidity was not the answer. The men who had participated in the decision were brilliant.

Irving L. Janis spent two years looking for the answer. He studied not only the Bay of Pigs but also Pearl Harbor, Vietnam, and other policy disasters. In each case he found that the decision-makers appeared to be the victims of certain clear laws of Groupthink that result in the distortion of sound collective judgment. And he made 9 recommendations for doing better, whether in the White House or your local P.T.A.

All the world loathes a loser. Why do we tend to hate martyrs? In a controlled experiment designed to find out, observers watched a 10-minute video tape of a person reacting with apparent pain and suffering to supposed electric shocks for incorrect responses. The observers were then asked to rate the attractiveness of the victim in terms of cooperativeness, maturity, kindness, etc. One startling finding: when the observers were powerless to alter the victim's fate and believed that they would have to watch the victim suffer again, they saw the victim as an undesirable, unattractive person.

Persuasion that persists. In just 40 minutes, using no coercion, a psychologist can alter your basic values and change your behavior. Students at one university showed changed behavior as long as 17 months after the experiment, says a social psychologist as he ponders the ethical emplications of his work.

Do you have what it takes to be a successful investor? 64 students were asked to manage imaginary stock portfolios. Later, psychological tests showed that the successful investors—those who did substantially better than the Dow Jones Industrial Average—had definite personality patterns. Then 60 stockbrokers were studied, and all 9 of the traits that identified successful student investors were found to be reliable predictors of actual career success.

Spare the Rod, Use Behavior Mod. Instead of spending years searching for the cause of troublesome behavior by a child, argue the behavior modification theorists, why not just change the behavior? Douglas was an 18-year-old who hadn't been able to sleep for two years. He consulted his mother about his worries 25 or 30 times a night. He had tried tranquilizers, a psychiatrist, a psychologist. After two weeks of behavior modification therapy, his bedtime visits ceased.

Is Psychology Today for you? You can find out without risking a penny. Just mail the coupon. We'll send you a copy to read free and enter your name as a trial subscriber at the special introductory rate for new subscribers indicated in the coupon. However, if you're not delighted with the first issue, simply write "cancel" on the bill and return it without paying or owing anything, keeping the first issue with our compliments.

Mail coupon for complimentary copy
and Half-Price Offer to New Subscribers

F

257

Psychology Today is not what you think it is

Forget Freud and Pavlov? Of course not. But we've come a long way since then.

Freud and Pavlov seemed to narrow down the human (and animal) condition to simple cause and effect—whether it was mother love and an Oedipus complex or a ringing gong and a salivating dog.

But current psychology is discovering a dazzling infinity of motives and possibilities.

Just browsing through one copy of Psychology Today, the monthly magazine devoted to conveying the excitement of what's really happening in the field, will open your eyes and mind to the galaxy of psychological potentials coming into view.

Psychology Today is into everything that people do (and don't do!). Such as—

Does sports activity really build character?

What is this thing called Love, and can it be studied in the laboratory? (The astonishing answer: yes, it can.)

Can a psychological test predict your success in business? In investing?

What makes George Wallace supporters mad?

Why do fat people eat even when they're not hungry?

Honestly, how effective are far-out therapy approaches like the Nude Group and the Primal Scream?

Should an analyst really refrain from making moral judgments about his patients?

How could psychology have prevented our Vietnam war?

Why do many bright, capable women in business have a will to fail?

Psychology Today is neither pop nor pap. Many of our readers as well as our contributors are psychologists and social scientists themselves. They demand authentic research findings and uncompromising views.

But the prose is de-jargonized and the ideas are illustrated with prize-winning breath-taking graphics. The result is an adventure in continuing education for the educated layman as well as the professional.

Many of the most famous names in the behavioral sciences write for or are interviewed by Psychology Today—men and women like Carl Rogers, Margaret Mead, B. F. Skinner, Erich Fromm, Paul Goodman, Harvey Cox, John Lilly, Bruno Bettelheim. You learn today the ideas and methods that will probably reshape the world tomorrow.

You can discover Psychology Today without risking a penny. Just mail the coupon. We'll send you a copy to read free and enter your name as a trial subscriber at the special introductory rate for new subscribers we've indicated in the coupon. However, if you're not delighted with the first issue, simply write "cancel" on the bill and return it without paying or owing anything, keeping the first issue with our compliments.

Mail coupon for complimentary copy
and Half-Price Offer to New Subscribers

G

Have you rated the ads? Okay — here's the way they ranked from the best to the poorest by actual coupon count.

Test Ad   D F G C B E A
Rank   1 2 3 4 5 6 7

If you didn't pick the winning ad, which pulled over 50% better than the poorest, don't be disheartened. This same series of ads was submitted to a panel of over 500 direct marketing "experts." Close to 50% of them picked ad **E** as the best. It came in a poor sixth!

Creating print advertising can be both frustrating and rewarding. But because your goal is direct response, you can measure your progress by coupons rather than by opinion.

Self-Quiz

1. Good direct response advertising should make its strongest appeal to _____

   _____

2. Who are the best prospects? _____

   _____

   _____

3. Advantages belong to the _____

   Benefits belong to the _____
4. When are benefits more important?

   _____

5. When are advantages more important?

   _____

6. Fill in this list of ultimate benefits.

1. _____	7. _____	13. _____
2. _____	8. _____	14. _____
3. _____	9. _____	15. _____
4. _____	10. _____	16. _____
5. _____	11. _____	17. _____
6. _____	12. _____	

7. Semantics is the hydrogen bomb of _____
8. Most successful headlines have a "hook" to catch the reader and pull him in. The most common hooks are such words as:

1. _____ 2. _____ 3. _____

4. _____ 5. _____ 6. _____

9. A common error in writing leads is that the writer _____

_____

10. A good writing principle is that body copy should _____

_____

11. What are the labels which may be applied to the sections of a classic copy argument?

    1. _____ 2. _____

    3. _____ 4. _____

    5. _____

12. Name four other ways to structure copy.

    1. _____

    2. _____

    3. _____

    4. _____

13. What four-letter word is one of the greatest advertising words? _____

14. Name five unique claims to fame which may prove to be one of the strongest selling points for a product or service.

    1. _____

    2. _____

    3. _____

    4. _____

    5. _____

15. What is the major advantage of using testimonials in direct response advertising?

_____

_____

16. Name one of the most important building blocks in the mail order sale.

_____

_____

17. Name four ways you can give visual reinforcement to words and ideas.

1. _____ 2. _____

3. _____ 4. _____

18. When is a coupon not indicated for a direct response ad?

_____

_____

19. What is the definition of "telescopic" testing?

_____

_____

20. What are the three basic methods of running multiple tests?

1. _____

2. _____

3. _____

Pilot Project

You are a copywriter by profession. You have just been employed by a direct response advertising agency. The agency has been appointed by a home study school offering a course in *accounting*. Your copy supervisor has asked you to come up with headlines designed to get inquiries. Develop one headline for each of these ultimate benefits.

HEALTH: _____

_____

MONEY: _____

_____

SECURITY: _____

_____

PRIDE: _____

_____

APPROVAL: _____

_____

ENJOYMENT: _____

_____

EXCITEMENT: _____

_____

POWER: _____

_____

FULFILLMENT: _____

_____

FREEDOM: _____

_____

IDENTITY: _____

_____

RELAXATION: _____

_____

ESCAPE: _____

_____

CURIOSITY: _____

_____

POSSESSIONS: _____

_____

SEX: _____

_____

HUNGER: _____

_____

Chapter 12 Production Techniques

In football, the quarterbacks and the halfbacks get the accolades. The defense—well, they're just doing the job they're supposed to do. So it is in direct marketing. The marketing director, the advertising manager, they get the cheers when the team wins. The production people—they are just doing the job they're supposed to do.

What top management rarely recognizes or acknowledges is the fact that, for every winning sales effort—with the rarest of exceptions—there is a winning production effort. Without teamwork between advertising and production, there is waste, ineffective advertising, and delay.

Probably the best-kept secret in all of advertising is the incredible amount of dollars which goes down the drain because of ineffective production planning and execution. Let's mention a few of the "typical" bloomers: spelling errors caught *after* the job is printed; engravings or offset reproduction which require corrections in color and tones at the proof stage; terrible production quality because of wrong paper stock; air express bills to cover late delivery of plates to publishers, shipments of mailing lists and envelopes etc., etc., etc.

And type bills—wow! Be there a bill from a typesetter without the tag line, "alterations and corrections"? Most typesetters I've talked to tell me alterations and corrections come to about 20% of the bill, on the average. The typesetter usually gets blamed, of course, but chances are someone in advertising said, "Let's set it and see how it looks." Then they started nit-picking at the copy.

These are just some of the standards. How about calls like these from the lettershop: "We're ready to insert your mailing pieces, but we can't machine-insert because you don't have a half-inch envelope clearance." Or, "The envelopes just arrived two weeks late. We'll have to go on overtime to meet your deadline." Or, "We're cleaning up your 300,000 mailing and we find we're 50,000 short on your four-color circular." Funny? Or tragic? It happens all the time.

When the mailing results or ad results are all in, somebody adds up the *total* costs. Ouch! The mailing that was supposed to come in at $120 per thousand totals out at $156 per thousand. The space ad billed by the publisher at $1,500 has a $900 production bill attached to it. The uncalled-for extra production costs more often than not have the effect of killing off future mailings and future ads.

Personnel and Planning the Answer

When costs go through the stratosphere, as they often do, one or more of these procedures is usually followed: (1) the extra costs are swept under the rug; (2) an overworked and harassed production manager is given hell; (3) one or more suppliers are beaten down. This solves practically nothing, of course, because the next job is destined to follow the same route!

Getting efficient and economical production is a team effort: knowledgeable production people working with knowledgeable advertising people—*planning* together. And the mark of an efficient production manager is that he insists upon a *reverse time schedule* for each and every job. The *reverse time schedule* illustrated on page 264 graphically shows the multitude of dates to be met to get just one job out on time. It is to be noted the time span for this particular mailing is from November 20 (layout due) to January 15 (projected drop date)—a time span which is a shock to most advertising departments. But every time you try to squeeze the time interval, extra unnecessary costs are likely to crop up.

Here is a rule of thumb time schedule for various components involved in typical mailings.

Mailing lists	—3 to 4 weeks
Rough layouts	—1 to 2 weeks
Finished art	—1 to 3 weeks
Typography	—3 to 7 days
Paper stock	—4 to 8 weeks
Envelopes	—3 to 5 weeks
Printed letters	—1 to 2 weeks
Computer letters	—4 to 8 weeks
Color separations	—2 to 3 weeks
4-color circulars	—2 to 3 weeks
2-color circulars	—1 to 2 weeks
4-color order forms	—2 to 3 weeks
2-color order forms	—1 to 2 weeks
Lettershop service	—1 to 2 weeks

The capable production manager wears many hats. He or she is a coordinator between the advertising department and the various suppliers involved. The knowledgeable production manager knows there is a *right source* or sources for each and every job and that there is no one source for all jobs. The production manager worth his salt is an expediter who lives by his reverse time schedule. He doesn't wait till due date to find out if a particular component is going to be on time: He checks before due date. And Lord help any culprits who are throwing the schedule out of kilter!

But there is more to an efficient production department than coordinating and expediting. The X factors are production knowledge and knowledge of the capabilities of suppliers.

TIME SCHEDULE FOR A TYPICAL PROMOTION MAILING

PROJECT: **ABC MAILING** REVERSE TIME SCHEDULE PROJECTED DROP DATE: **January 15th**

ELEMENT	Creative			Production			Mailing				
	LAYOUT DUE	COPY DUE	TYPE DUE	FINAL ART DUE	SEPARATIONS DUE	PRINTING DUE	DELIVERY TO MAILING SERVICE	LABELS TO BE AFFIXED BY MAIL SERV.	AFFIXING TIME	PRE-ADDRESSED MATERIAL	DROP DATE
CIRCULAR 17 x 11—4/c-2/s Fold to 8½ x 5½	11/20	11/25	11/29	12/5	12/19	1/4	1/5				J A
BONUS SHEET 8½ x 5½—2/c-1/s	12/1	12/7	12/10	12/8	12/26	1/4	1/5				N
LETTER 17 x 11—2/c-2/s Fold to 8½ x 5½	12/1	12/7	12/10	12/18		1/4	1/5				U A
ORDER CARD 11½ x 5½—2/c-2/s Die-cut fold to 8½ x 5½	12/1	12/5	12/8	12/14		1/4	1/5				R Y
OUTER ENVELOPE 9 x 6—2/c-1/s Open side die-cut perforated cellophane window	11/20	11/25	12/2	12/4		1/3	1/4				15
REPLY ENVELOPE 6¾ x ?—1/c-1/s	11/20	11/25	12/2	12/4		1/3	1/5				
ADDRESSING MATERIALS								12/30	1/5-1/7	1/5-1/7	

Production Knowledge Assures Efficiency

Most creative people have little concern for or understanding of production economies. And this is understandable. But a capable production person will often say, "If you can make this circular just one inch shorter, our printers can use a standard sized sheet." The advertiser saves a bundle and creativity suffers not. Another thing a capable production manager will do is develop a "working dummy." This dummy, with all specs, will go to everyone to be involved: artists, typesetters, mailing houses. The results: Any potential production snags are eliminated before the job reaches the production stage. And if a job is sent out for bids, everyone is bidding on the same job, the same weight and type of paper stock, the same everything.

Here are some safeguards the production manager applies to make sure a job starts right, proceeds right, and comes out right with good quality at the most economical cost.

- Paper dummies are made up to insure that the finished job will be within postal weight limits. (How many thousands of dollars go down the drain in extra postage because weight wasn't checked before printing?)
- Reader proofs are provided to copywriters and proofreaders before etch proofs are made. (The original copywriter is often the only person who can be certain of the correct spelling of unusual words peculiar to a given product or proposition.)
- Silver prints, brown lines, or ozalids are carefully checked before giving the approval to print one- and two-color jobs. (This is when to check whether halftones are clean, whether the job is in register, whether any pasted-down type has shifted or fallen off in camera.)
- Progressive proofs are carefully checked for all four-color printing jobs. (Many a pending color fiasco is prevented by the experienced eye of the production manager who has the wisdom to adjust color values at the plate stage.)

Insertion orders are coordinated between the media department or agency, the plate makers, and the publishers. (This prevents many a missed insertion date and saves on shipping costs.) Mailing schedules are provided to mailing services with dummy mailing pieces, mailing quantities, and a key number for each and every list. (This cuts down errors and enables the mailing service to return a schedule for each mailing, giving the count and mailing date.)

Knowledge of Suppliers Is Essential

And this same production knowledge carries over to knowledge of suppliers. Every well-run production department has a long list of suppliers in each service category. They know the strengths and limitations of each. Each is rated by the standards of price, quality, capacity, and service. Here are some guidelines for each category.

Art Studios

The production department should know the areas of specialization for each studio, as well as its limitations. Each studio should be measured against the requirements of each project. A studio known for fashion would be unlikely for a circular designed to sell socket wrenches. A studio expert in food ads would be unlikely for ads selling books. (There are a limited number of studios that work in many areas of specialization.) The production manager should know whether each studio is equipped to handle color photography and retouching. And—does it have a reputation for meeting deadline requirements?

Typographers

Some type houses just set type. Others have the ability to make type "talk." The type-setting rates run the gamut. Some typesetters, usually those with the lowest rates, put the proofreading burden on the client. Others, usually those with medium to higher rates, consistently deliver "readers" and etch proofs letter-perfect. Knowing type and type houses is essential whether the requirement be electronic typesetting or the most artistic hand-setting.

Envelope Manufacturers

The production department begins with envelope manufacturers at the inception of each job, starting with the working dummy. Each manufacturer is rated for capacity, creativity, price, quality, and performance. Such details as dies available and speciali-zation are carefully recorded.

Cost of envelopes, like any printing component, is related to the total press run. Many users of envelopes continually reorder the identical envelope many times during the year. In most instances this results in an excessive cost.

Many envelope manufacturers are willing to print a 12-month supply, warehouse the envelopes, and ship and bill quantities as needed. For example, say the total #10 enve-lopes required are 100,000 a year. The envelope manufacturer prints 100,000 envelopes at the 100,000 price. The user specifies that 25,000 envelopes are to be shipped and billed every three months. Instead of paying the 25,000 price each time, the user gets the advantage of the 100,000 price.

Still another way to save money on envelopes is to stick to standard sizes wherever possible. There are many from which to choose. Here's a chart of standard envelopes, all of which can be machine-inserted.

Size	No.	Style
$3^1/_2 \times 6$	$6^1/_4$	Commercial
$3^5/_8 \times 6^1/_2$	$6^3/_4$	Commercial
$3^3/_4 \times 6^3/_4$	7	Official
$3^7/_8 \times 7^1/_2$	$7^3/_4$	Official
$3^7/_8 \times 7^1/_2$	M	Monarch
$3^7/_8 \times 8^7/_8$	9	Official
$4^1/_8 \times 9^1/_2$	10	Official
$4^1/_2 \times 10^3/_8$	11	Official
$4^3/_4 \times 11$	12	Official
$5 \times 11^1/_2$	14	Official
$4^1/_2 \times 5^7/_8$	$2^1/_2$	Booklet
$4^3/_4 \times 6^1/_2$	3	Booklet
$5^3/_4 \times 8^7/_8$	6	Booklet
6×9	$6^1/_2$	Booklet
$6^1/_4 \times 9^5/_8$	7	Booklet
$8^3/_4 \times 11^1/_2$	9	Booklet
$9^1/_2 \times 12^5/_8$	10	Booklet

List Sources

List compilers and list brokers have attained a great deal of sophistication in the past decade. Since you can't have a mailing without a list, the list source is a key link in the

266

production chain. It behooves the production department to rate each list source for knowledge and reliability. Can the source be counted on to give an accurate estimate of the time required to fulfill each list order? Will the source make certain that test specifications are followed to the letter? Is addressing consistently of good quality? Are exclusive mailing dates honored consistently? Are mailing counts by ZIP Code and other criteria consistently accurate? Are list keys always assigned properly?

Printers

Human nature being what it is, there is a tendency, even among the largest of advertisers, consistently to use one printer for just about every job. It's a big, fat mistake. There's a right printer for every job, and no printer is the right printer for all jobs. The capable production manager can tell you what size and type presses each printer has. He'll know how many sheet-fed presses he has, and whether he has any web presses; he'll know whether he has one-color, two-color, three-color, and four-color presses. He'll be able to tell you which printers have perfectors, whether they can perforate on press, whether they can number consecutively, whether they do their own separating. And most of all—each printer will be rated for reliability and *consistent* quality.

A firm with the reputation of getting bids on every printing job is almost certain to enjoy lower printing costs consistently than firms who become "married" to given printers. I've seen many firms in direct marketing give printing orders of major size to their favorite printer without even requesting a bid. More often than not, it isn't until things get tough that a halt is called to such sloppy practices.

Still another sloppy practice which many direct response advertisers fall into is the practice of ordering all components in short runs—one piece at a time. Very often, with some ingenuity, the gang-run principle can be applied. Let us say your total run of a given mailing package comes to only 10,000 pieces consisting of the following:

> 8½ × 11 letter—2 pages
> 8½ × 11 circular
> 5½ × 8½ testimonial sheet
> 5½ × 8½ order form

Actually this job could all be run on one 17 × 22 sheet of paper. The illustration which follows shows how all the components would be laid out for one sheet of paper.

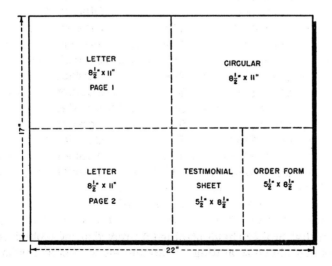

Let's check the savings from using this gang-run principle. If we use a 17×22 sheet of paper, the complete mailing unit will require just 10,000 impressions on the basis of a one-color job. If each of the four units were printed separately, there would be a total of 50,000 impressions. The gang-run principle isn't always practical, but it is one to keep in mind.

Major savings are possible where paper is concerned. Sometimes cutting down slightly on the weight of paper enables you to get in under minimum postage rates. By making a paper dummy of all of the components of the mailing before printing, you can determine the exact weight of the mailing package.

Major consideration should be given to preparing components which cut out of standard paper sizes. The amount of paper wasted through trimming is abominable. Many times a special run of paper is required because of oversize sheets. Waste, too, should be avoided if possible. To safeguard against wastage of paper in printing, know the standard sizes. A chart follows:

Sheet-Fed Offset Presses:	Web Offset:
17×22	38×23
23×29	38×50
25×38	
35×45	
38×50	
50×76	

Mass mailers, those who mail in very large quantities, can effect major savings by purchasing their own paper and having it shipped directly to the printer. Savings result, not because the mailer can purchase paper cheaper than the printer, but because the printer does not take a markup on paper owned by the mailer.

Many mass mailers who mail in the millions often split their purchases for the components of a mailing package among several printers, with all components being purchased at best prices. For instance, outside mailing envelopes may be purchased from one envelope house, reply envelopes from another. Letters may be produced by one printer, circulars by another, order cards by still another. Using a multiplicity of printers requires careful coordination on the part of the production department. But substantial savings usually justify the procedure.

Mailing Services

The lettershop is the last link between the mailer, Uncle Sam, and the prospect. And it is at this point that weeks of production planning can go right down the drain. The well-run lettershop is as efficient as the well-run production department. Being accurate and meeting deadlines are a creed. Here are some of the things the production department must know about each lettershop. How much automatic inserting equipment do they have? What is the maximum size they can machine-insert? Do they have special attachments (trailing arm) for inserting pieces with short folds? Can they automatically affix stamps or labels to mailing pieces? Do they maintain lists? Can they handle Cheshire labels? Do they systematically check on receipt of all outside mailing lists and components of a mailing package against the time schedule? Do they check counts of all material received? Do they accurately key response forms in accordance with the keying schedule? And do they consistently mail on time?

It's an understatement to say that the functions of a production manager are not for a boy scout. It's a complex, often frustrating, and always demanding position. But it's rewarding—rewarding in terms of accomplishment, money saved, and money made.

268

The Importance of Controls

I swear every production manager would be washed up at the same age as flight controllers if it weren't for one safeguard—the job number system. It's simple, but vital. Here's the way it works.

1. A master job number is assigned to every project.
2. A separate purchase order is issued for each component of the project, but the same job number is given in conjunction with each purchase order number.
3. The master job number is printed on all pieces of art work, all type proofs, etc.
4. A job envelope, bearing the master job number, is opened for each project.
5. Duplicate copies of all purchase orders are put in the job envelope.
6. As bills are received against the purchase orders, these are recorded on the front of the job envelope.
7. When all bills are received, the complete cost of the project is totaled.

Controlling production instead of having production control you is a difficult task, at best. There are certain basic forms which, when used religiously, will go a long way toward obtaining printing at the right prices, avoiding excess costs, and getting printing and mailing done on time.

Several of these forms, as used by an advertising agency, are shown on the following pages. They are easily adaptable to use by direct marketers who do their own production.

Competent production managers may never get the accolades of quarterbacks and halfbacks. But they should. They're the unsung heroes of a winning team.

RAPP, COLLINS, STONE & ADLER INC.
222 S. Riverside Plaza, Chicago, Ill. 60606 • 312/648-1199
Direct Response Advertising

Job Number _4508_
Client _R. Thomas, Inc._
Description _Layouts for_
catalog cover

LAYOUT ESTIMATE

Artist _Daniel Markell_
Markell & Assoc.

☒ Original Estimate
☐ 1st Revision
☐ 2nd Revision
☐ 3rd Revision

You are hereby authorized to prepare
for the job designated above.

✓ Pencil layouts

_____ Rough color layouts

_____ Comp. color layouts

at a cost not to exceed _$ 200.00_

Layouts due on _Dec. 1_

Approved by _S.E. Polachek_
Date _November 20_

WHITE — ARTIST'S COPY
GREEN — TRAFFIC COPY
YELLOW — BILLING COPY
PINK — ACCT. EXEC. COPY
GOLD — CREATIVE DIRECTOR'S COPY

NOTE: You may not bill Rapp, Collins, Stone & Adler for any part of this job other than layouts unless you have a signed estimate from us.

Layout estimate: *Form designed to be submitted to one or more art studios.*

PURCHASE ORDER

NRA Graphics
233 N. LaSalle St.
Chicago, Illinois
60606

order number — **13523**

date December 19

production number 4508

client R. Thomas, Inc.

time wanted May 12

please enter our order for:

1 set: 4 color positives per attached artwork
12 pages 8 3/8 x 10 7/8", 150 line screen.
Positives & Ozalids
Proofs due December 26
$540.00

Our order number must appear on all invoices. All invoices must be billed in TRIPLICATE. PER Anna Walf

Purchase order: *All purchase orders should have an order number and a production/job number. The same job number should appear on all purchase orders concerning the same job.*

JOB COST ESTIMATE

☒ Original Cost	
☐ 1st Revision	
☐ 2nd Revision	
☐ 3rd Revision	

Client **R. Thomas, Inc.**

Description **mid-year customer catalog mailing**

Date **11/19**

Our Job No. **4508**

ITEM	LAYOUT	PHOTOGRAPHY	KEYLINED ASSEMBLY	TYPE & LETTERING	PHOTOSTATS & PHOTOPRINTS	ILLUSTRATION	RETOUCHING	OTHER ITEMS Composition	TOTAL
CIRCULAR catalog	450.00	2000.00	740.00	60.00	50.00			2400.00	5,700.00
OUTER ENVELOPE	150.00	225.00	150.00	40.00	25.00			100.00	690.00
RETURN ENVELOPE									
ORDER CARD		75.00	100.00	25.00	20.00			110.00	330.00
LETTER		120.00			20.00			100.00	240.00
OTHER ITEMS	75.00	—	85.00	20.00	15.00	75.00		90.00	360.00
AD MATERIAL Premium Slip									
AGENCY COMMISSION									
TOTAL	675.00	2300.00	1195.00	145.00	130.00	75.00		2800.00	7320.00

COMMENTS: _____

Approved by: **S. E. Palachek**

Date **11/19**

Submitted by: **O. Markell**

Date **11/19**

Job cost estimate: *Job cost estimates are essential to keeping total costs under control. Note the ceiling of 10% on estimates as a safeguard against costs' getting out of control.*

RAPP, COLLINS, STONE & ADLER INC.
222 S. Riverside Plaza, Chicago, Ill. 60606 • 312/648-1199
Direct Response Advertising

JOB COST REVISION

Artist **Daniel Markell**
Markell & Assoc.

Job Number **# 4508**

Client **R. Thomas, Inc.**

Description **Mid-year Customer Catalog Mailing**

ELEMENTS	Catalog	Outer Envelope	Order card	Premium slip			
LAYOUTS	450.00	150.00		75.00			
ROUGHS							
FINISH							
PHOTOGRAPHY	2220.00	250.00	75.00				
MODELS							
PROPS							
SETS							
RETOUCHING	50.00						
ILLUSTRATION				75.00			
TYPE/LETTERING	60.00	40.00	25.00	20.00			
HAND LETTERING							
PHOTO-LETTERING							
COMPOSITION	2500.00	100.00	110.00	100.00			
PHOTOSTATS	50.00	25.00	20.00	15.00			
KEYLINE ASSEMBLY	740.00	150.00	100.00	85.00			
OTHER ITEMS							
TOTALS	6030.00	2965.00	330.00	370.00			

You are authorized to proceed with the above job at the prices shown.
You may not bill more than 10% over the above prices unless you have
a signed job cost revision form authorizing greater charges.

Approved by: **S. E. Palachek**

Date **December 8**

Job cost revision: *For various reasons, the nature of a job often changes in midstream.
When this occurs, a job cost revision should be prepared by the production department.*

RAPP, COLLINS, STONE & ADLER

PRINTING QUOTATION

CLIENT _R. Thomas_ JOB NO. _4508_

DESCRIPTION _Mid-Year Catalog_ ELEMENT _Catalog_

QUANTITIES _60,000_

DELIVERY DATE _1/1_

SIZE FLAT _8 3/8 x 10 7/8 "_ SIZE FOLDED _—_

NUMBER OF FOLDS _—_ BLEEDS _Yes_ INK COVERAGE _40%_

NUMBER OF PAGES _12_ BODY _8_ COVER _4_

INK COLORS _4/c Flat (Black, Red, Gold, & Black)_

PAPER STOCK: BODY _60# Matte_

COVER _80# c/1/s_

FILM FURNISHED _Yes_ ART FURNISHED _No_

PROOFS FURNISHED/REQUESTED: PROGS _Yes_ OZALIDS _No_

COLOR KEYS _No_ CHROMALIN _No_

SILVER PRINTS _No_

BINDING METHOD _Saddle Stich_

DELIVERY INFORMATION: IN CARTONS _X_ ON SKIDS _X_

AIR _____ SURFACE _____

SHIPPING INSTRUCTIONS: _Ship 5000 Catalogs to R. Thomas, Inc. 243 Scott, L.A., California_

SUPPLIER	Catalog	QUANTITIES		
Bronsen Mailing	55,000			

Printing quotation: *There are a multitude of details which apply to each printing quotation. The more specific the quotation request, the less likely are chances of error, or excess charges.*

JOB TICKET—SPACE AD

CLIENT _R. Thomas, Inc._

DESCRIPTION _"Is your VP doing his job?" (Headline)_
2 color, coupon in lower right
corner.

NO. ____

DATE _October 21_

AE _S.E. Polachek_

WRITER _A. Phillips_

ARTIST ____

PROD _M. Brune_

OFFER INFORMATION

ITEM ____
____ FREE TRIAL PERIOD ____

SELLING PRICE ____ POSTAGE & HANDLING ____ TOTAL ____

GIFT _Executive Calendar / Reminder_

____ KEEPER? ____

COMMENTS ____
____
____

MEDIA*

PUBLICATION _Executives In Action_ POSITION OR SECTION _Right page_

ISSUE DATE _1/20_ CLOSE DATE _1/2_ NATIONAL/REGIONAL ____
*If ad runs in more than one publication, list the one with the earliest closing.

MECHANICAL SPECIFICATIONS

SIZE: PAGE UNIT _1_ INCHES _7" X 10"_ BLEED? _Yes_

COLORS _Red, Black_ HT SCREEN ____ TYPE OF PRINTING ____

☐ INSERT. ☐ WILL ☐ WILL NOT BE PRINTED BY PUBLICATION.

☐ BIND-IN CARD. SIZE ____ COLORS ____

☐ BIND-IN ENVELOPE. SIZE ____ COLORS ____

TESTS

A) ____

B) ____

C) ____

D) ____

SCHEDULE

WRITER'S ROUGH _11/18_ FINISHED LAYOUTS _12/1_ COPY _12/7_ ART _12/18_

☐ ACCOUNT SUPERVISOR ☐ CREATIVE DIRECTOR ☐ ACCOUNT EXECUTIVE ☐ COPYWRITER ☐ MEDIA DIRECTOR ☐ PRODUCTION MANAGER ☐ PRODUCTION FILE

Job ticket—space ad: *Closing dates and mechanical specifications are vital where space advertising is concerned.*

Please complete and return 1 copy
of this form to each of the following

☐ CLIENT:

Grant Hudson Company

☐ AGENCY:

*Rapp, Collins, Stone
& Adler*

**ADDITIONAL INFORMATION REQUEST
FOR PRE-PRINTED ADVERTISING INSERT**

PUBLICATION NAME AND ADDRESS

*Chicago Tribune
Tribune Tower
Chicago, Illinois*

TODAY'S DATE: *March 25, 1973*   ADVERTISER: *Grant Hudson Company*

DESCRIPTION OF INSERT: *"Suddenly your floor is spotless"
4/colors x 2 sides 7 9/16" x 29 1/2"*

INSERTION DATE: *4/28/73* DAY OF WEEK: *Sunday*   MORNING   EVENING   <u>SUNDAY</u>

TO BE COMPLETED BY NEWSPAPER

DATE DUE AT PUBLICATION: EARLIEST— *26 days prior* LATEST— *2 week* LOGO REQUIRED? ☒ YES ☐ NO

CIRCULATION: *1,157,000*   PRESS RUN: *1,175,000* DATE LINE REQUIRED? ☐ YES ☒ NO

IS DUMMY INSERT REQUIRED? ☒ YES ☐ NO

SHIPPING ADDRESS AND SPECIAL INSTRUCTIONS

IMPORTANT: Shipping instructions should include any special information on receiving hours, person responsible, receiving address and telephone number, skid weight and size limitations, etc. Unless otherwise specified all shipments will be made in corrugated cartons on disposable skids. If logo is required send reproduction proofs to ☐ CLIENT: ☐ AGENCY:

Additional information request for preprinted advertising insert: *Printing and delivery requirements often vary considerably, especially among newspapers. This form, mailed to newspapers before printing and shipping, helps to avoid costly errors.*

PRODUCTION CHECKLIST

Job No. *4508*　　　Client *R. Thomas, Inc.*

Description *mid-year customer catalog mailing*

Date

___Basic idea of nature, scope and timing of job　　*October 21*

___Specific component specifications　　*October 28*

___Insertion order received　　*October 31*

___Estimates on printing, mailing, lettershop requested　　*November 1*

___Estimates on same furnished to AE　　*November 7*

___Finished art checked for size and specs　　*December 18*

___PACKAGE DUMMIED (window position, fit, inserting order checked)　　*November 1*

___ADVANCE POSTAGE REQUESTED FROM CLIENT　　*December 10*

___ADVANCE POSTAGE RECEIVED FROM CLIENT　　*January 8*

___Mailing Lists received　　*December 30*

___Components delivered　　*January 5*

___Counts and dates reported to AE　　*Daily ✱*

___Artwork sent back and filed　　*January 29*

Comments *✱ AE To receive daily drop counts from mailing service beginning January 15.*

Production checklist: *This production checklist enables the production department to keep track of the many components of any given job.*

276

MAILING PRODUCTION SCHEDULE

PROMOTION _Mid-Year_   MAILING NO. _4508_

                              TO BE MAILED _1/15_

QUANTITY _55 m_ LIST _House_   KEY _RT-8_

SPECIAL INSTRUCTIONS _NONE_

	NO. PAGES	STOCK	INK	SIZES	LEAD
1. Letter	2	60#	2/c	8½" x 11"	
2. ~~Circular~~ Catalog	12	60# Matte	4/c (Flat)	8⅞" x 10¾"	
3. Order Form	2	70# Bulk	2/c	8½" x 11"	
4. Gift Insert	1	60# Matte	2/c	4¼" x 5½"	
5. Sample					
6. Reply Envelope					
7. Outer Envelope		24# WW	2/c	9" x 12"	
8.					

SEQUENCE _Order Card, Gift Insert, Catalog, Letter_

COMPLETED AND MAILED ON _1/15/73_ ACTUAL QUANTITY MAILED _53,445_

                    MAILING CHECKED BY _MB_

LETTER SHOP CHARGES

Addressing: Addressing	Extension			Extension
$3.00/m	160.33	Metering		None
		Sorting Tie & Mail @ $2.00/m		106.90
Hand Gathering:	None	Folding		None
Machine Inserting: 2 pieces 2.00/m	636.00			
each additional piece 3 @ 1.00/m	159.00	TOTAL Per M		$20.05
Sub-total	955.33			

Charge to _____ Pieces @ $ _____ Per M - - - $ _____

Mailing schedule: _Where mailings are involved, a mailing schedule should be prepared for each list being mailed. Copies should be provided to the mailing house and advertising department._

MAILING PIECE ANALYSIS

Offer _Catalog Sales._

List _Executive Purchases_

Quantity used _10,000_ Date Mailed _1/16_ Balance Remaining

Key _1A_

DATE	NO.	QUAN.	$ SALES		DATE	NO.	QUAN.	$ SALES	
T 1/20	20		500	00	T				
T 1/21	25		650	00	T				
T 1/22	150		2200	00	T				
T 1/23	90		1100	00	T				
T 1/24	70		900	00	T				
T 1/25	45		820	00	T				
T 1/26	41		700	00	T				
T 1/28	23		560	00	T				
T 1/29	15		315	00	T				
T					T				
T					T				
T					T				
T					T				
T					T				
T					T				
T					T				
T					T				
T					T				
T					T				
T					T				
T					T				
TOTAL					TOTAL				

Response tally form: _The advertising department should be provided with a tally form for each and every list mailed and for all advertising insertion orders._

DATE STARTED: October 21	DATE DUE: 12/18		Stone & Adler Inc.	JOB NO: 4508		
DATE BILLED:	INV:	AMT.:		CLIENT: R. Thomas, Inc.		
SPECIAL INSTRUCTIONS:			IF AD. SPACE:	☐ B & W ☐ CLR C/D		
DESCRIPTION: Mid-Year Customer Catalog Mailing			PUBLICATIONS:			

DATE	PURCHASE ORDER	SUPPLIER	DESCRIPTION	INVOICE NO.	AMOUNT	CURRENT ENTRIES	INV. TO DATE
ART:							
12/18	11299	Daniel Markell	Layouts	22870	$190.90	IN 12/18	
STATS:							
12/3	12022	Art Suppliers	Finished Art	22012	35.00	IN 12/8	
PHOTO-RET:							
TYPE:							
12/15	12350	Typers	Type per Purchase Order	32033	121.65	IN 12/17	
ENGR:							
12/16	12441	Northern	Positives & Ozalids	5700	300.29	IN 12/18	
PRTG:							
MISC.:							

Job envelope: *A master job envelope is essential for keeping copies of all papers relating to each specific job in one place.*

Self-Quiz

1. What is a reverse time schedule?

2. What is a working dummy?

3. Outside of proofreaders, to whom should reader proofs be sent?

4. In selecting an art studio, the production department must know the areas of

5. At what point in a project should the production department start working with an envelope manufacturer?

6. How can a direct marketer save money by ordering envelopes on an annual basis?

_____

_____

_____

7. List compilers and list brokers should be rated primarily for their _____

knowledge and _____.

8. Why is it a big mistake to use one printer for just about every job?

_____

_____

9. What is the advantage of getting more than one bid on every printing job?

_____

_____

10. What is meant by gang-run printing?

_____

_____

_____

11. What is the best way to avoid wasting paper?

_____

_____

12. Lighter weights of paper cost less, but how else may lighter paper save money?

_____

_____

13. Name ten key things a production department should know about a mailing service (lettershop).

    1. _____

    2. _____

    3. _____

    4. _____

    5. _____

    6. _____

7. _____

8. _____

9. _____

10. _____

14. What are the essentials of a job number system?

1. _____

2. _____

_____

3. _____

_____

4. _____

_____

5. _____

_____

6. _____

_____

7. _____

_____

Pilot Project

You are the production manager of an advertising agency. An important client has asked your agency to take on *full responsibility* for a total mailing of one million direct mail pieces.

Responsibilities include writing copy, doing all layouts, being responsible for finished art—including typography—ordering mailing lists, paper, printing—including envelopes—and finally, arranging for the complete mailing of the one million pieces—all on the same date.

The account supervisor on the account has asked you, the production manager, to prepare a complete reverse time schedule, giving him the earliest date you can drop the complete mailing.

Prepare your reverse time schedule, starting with today's date.

Chapter 13 Mathematical Criteria Direct Marketers Live By

It is fitting and proper that the last section of this book be devoted to mathematics. For it has been evident in all sections that, to be truly successful in direct marketing, one must respect the importance of figures, apply mathematics properly, and have the ability to interpret the meaning of the mathematics developed.

Because direct marketing is the most *measurable* way of selling available to marketers, working with figures becomes intriguing and can be extremely rewarding. Successes are built on working effectively with figures; failures are built on a lack of understanding of how to use and apply mathematics.

Establishing the Break-Even Point

Wherever there is advertising, there is a product or service involved. So it isn't just the cost of getting an order, or an inquiry. It's the cost of getting the inquiry and/or the order, *plus* all costs involved in delivering the product or service. This leads to the key question: What is my break-even point?

It's right here that direct marketing mathematics often breaks down. Sloppy arithmetic calculates that break-even point equals selling price, less cost of product or service, less cost per order. Tain't so! There are many other costs involved.

The way to make certain you know your true break-even point is to use a work sheet like the one illustrated on page 283. Let's review its key points.

Price of Merchandise or Service

In this hypothetical example, a set of books is being offered for $25. This could be an arbitrary price established by the marketer, or it could be a firm price established by the publisher that the marketer must live with.

If the price is arbitrary (sort of taken out of the air), then there are a number of considerations. The $25 price is excellent from an arithmetic standpoint, since it gives a 5-to-1 markup, with a base cost of $5. But there are other considerations, such as: *(a)* Are there other sets of books on the market of similar quality at higher or lower prices? *(b)* Is the break-even point realistic? (Item 16 shows the break-even point to be nine orders per M, which is a realistic expectation); *(c)* Would the response per M at a lower selling price increase sufficiently to increase net profit over a higher price? *(d)* Conversely, would a higher selling price, which would lower the break-even point, produce the best net profit of all?

It's a fact that most products or services sold via mail order are "blind items" within limits. Therefore price testing, wherever allowable, is critical to success.

Cost of Filling the Order

There are six possible expense items under the cost of filling an order. Those who are careless about their arithmetic rarely concern themselves with more than one — cost of merchandise or service. But the other five often prove to be the straws which break the camel's back.

282

WORKSHEET FOR PLANNING PROFITABLE MAILINGS

Date: *Date*

PROPOSITION *Practical Mathematics*   KEY *64*

1 - Selling Price of Merchandise or Service _____ | $25.00

2 - Cost of Filling the Order

    a) Merchandise or Service _____ | 5.00

    b) Royalty _____ | —

    c) Handling Expense (Drop Shipping & Order Processing) _____ | .75

    d) Postage and Shipping Expense _____ | .60

    e) Premium, including Handling and Postage _____ | .30

    f) Use Tax, if any (1 x *3* %) _____ | .75

    TOTAL COST OF FILLING THE ORDER _____ | | 7.40

3 - Administrative Overhead

    a) Rent, Light, Heat, Maintenance, Credit Checking,
       Collections, etc. (*10* % of # 1) _____ | 2.50

    TOTAL ADMINISTRATIVE COST _____ | | 2.50

4 - Estimated Percentage of Returns, Refunds or Cancellations _____ | 10%

5 - Expense in Handling Returns

    a) Return Postage and Handling (2c plus 2d) _____ | 1.35

    b) Refurbishing Returned Merchandise (*10* % of # 2a) ____ | .50

    TOTAL COST OF HANDLING RETURNS _____ | 1.85

6 - Chargeable Cost of Returns (*10* % of $ *1.85*) _____ | | .19

7 - Estimated Bad Debt Percentage _____ | 10%

8 - Chargeable Cost of Bad Debts (# 1 x # 7) _____ | | 2.50

9 - Total Variable Costs (# 2 plus # 3, # 6, and # 8) _____ | | 12.59

10 - Unit Profit after Deducting Variable Costs (# 1 less # 9) _____ | | 12.41

11 - Return Factor (100% less # 4) _____ | 90% |

12 - Unit Profit Per Order (# 10 x # 11) _____ | | 11.17

13 - Credit for Returned Merchandise (*10* % of # 2a) _____ | | .50

14 - Net Profit Per Order (# 12 plus # 13) _____ | | 11.67

15 - Cost of Mailing per 1,000 _____ | 96.03 |

16 - NUMBER OF ORDERS PER 1,000 NEEDED TO BREAK EVEN _____ | | 8.2

For additional copies of this form, contact Marketing Services Manager,
Boise Cascade Envelopes Division, 313 Rohlwing Rd., Addison, IL 60101 - Tel. 312, 629-5000

Form No. 8-7

283

Let's look at our example. Cost of merchandise (books) is $5. But other costs – all necessary to filling the order – come to $2.40, almost 50% of the cost of merchandise. So the total cost isn't $5. It's $7.40.

In this day of high costs, even where computers are involved, 75¢ for handling an order which includes mail opening, crediting to keys, and processing is quite typical. And there's no way to get away from postage and shipping expense. What's more, if a premium is given, its cost should be included in the total cost of filling the order.

Administrative Overhead

An often overlooked cost in computing break-even is overhead. You can't operate a business without paying rent, light, heat, cost of equipment, credit checking, collection follow-up, office supplies, etc. These overhead costs can chew up an otherwise successful operation.

Administrative overhead costs vary tremendously between operations. The range is usually between 10% and 20%. Since so much of administrative overhead represents fixed costs, it's axiomatic that overhead tends to go down as volume of promotion goes up.

Estimated Returns and Expense of Handling

Returned goods can be a plague. And the percentage of a given item which will be returned under a free trial offer varies considerably. There are several factors which can push up the percentage of returned goods. Here are just a few: overselling the product or service; overpricing the product or service; offering a gift for trying which is appealing out of proportion to the product or service; offering a product which is difficult to assemble or to operate; offering a product which can easily be damaged in shipment. There are many instances of where mechanical products have been returned to the tune of 40% and better.

In our example we're figuring returned goods at 10% – a minimum estimate. But note that the cost of handling returns figures out at better than 35% of raw merchandise cost.

Unit Profit and Net Profit

It is interesting to note the total variable costs for our set of books came to $12.59 (items #2 plus #3, #6, and #8). When we deduct these costs from the selling price – $25 – it leaves a unit profit of $12.41. But then we have to take into account the return factor of 10% (item #4). After allowing for this, we come down to a net profit per order of $11.67.

So we started with a margin of $20 ($25 selling price less $5 raw product cost) but we ended up with an "honest" margin of $11.67 per order – after all costs were accounted for.

Establishing Break-Even Point

The bottom line of the work sheet is the one which tells the seasoned marketer whether or not he's got a feasible proposition.

Before discussing the number of orders needed per thousand to break even (item #16), let's discuss cost of mailing (item #15). This naturally has a great bearing on the number of orders necessary per thousand mailed to break even.

There's a management question to be asked every time a new test mailing or test ad is made. Should the full cost of creative art and production be charged to the test? The answer should almost always be NO. If all prep costs are charged against the test, break-

284

even point is certain to be distorted. The best rule to follow is—spread the prep cost over the *total* projected mail and/or print and broadcast schedule you will follow if the tests equal or exceed break-even.

In our example, raw cost of the mailing package is figured at $95.53 per M and a proportionate cost of 50¢ per M is added for prep costs, making the in-the-mail cost $96.03 per thousand. The break-even figure of nine orders per thousand is arrived at by dividing net profit per order of $10.67 (item #14) into $96.03, cost of mailing per M (item #15).

The Arithmetic of Two-Step Promotions

Up to now, we have assumed that a company uses individual mailings or ads to produce sales. Very often, it is more profitable to generate inquiries with various low-cost methods and then to convert these inquiries into sales through the use of special mailings or through salesman calls. We refer to this as a two-step or inquiry conversion program. Robert Kestnbaum, president of R. Kestnbaum & Co., Chicago, points out that, for bigger ticket items in particular, the two-step method is often the most profitable. He gives some interesting examples to prove his point.

Inquiries can be generated through any of the media available to the direct marketer. In each case, the cost of placing an advertisement, making a mailing, or taking any other action to produce inquiries should be related to the number of inquiries generated in order to determine cost per inquiry.

As an example, if $3,000 were spent to generate each 1,000 inquiries, the cost per inquiry would be $3. In addition, there would be a cost of perhaps $30 per thousand to process inquiries into a usable mailing list. The inquiry/conversion ratio needed to make a 15% profit would now look something like this if the average sale were $100, the profit objective $15, and the contribution to circularization cost $20 after allowance for profit:

Contribution to circularization cost after allowance for profit	$ 20
Total cost of obtaining and processing 1,000 inquiries	3,030
Cost of follow-up mailing ($175 less $25 list rental)	150
Total	$3,180
Required orders to break even (15.9)	159

Under these assumptions, the company must convert 15.9% of the inquiries costing $3 each in order to generate 15% pre-tax profits on sales.

Varying the media, kinds of advertisements, appeals, and offers will change the cost of generating inquiries. Typically, the more highly qualified an inquiry is, the more costly it will be to generate but the higher the conversion rate will be. The thoughtful direct marketer will experiment continuously with various ways to produce inquiries and various means of conversion in order to fine-tune his program to maximize profits.

Most companies also find their inquiry list will support repeated conversion mailings. There is, of course, a fall-off in response to each mailing, but it is profitable to continue making conversion mailings until the incremental cost of the last mailing is greater than the contribution it generates. In our example, the company could continue to make conversion mailings at a cost of approximately $150 per thousand until the last mailing generated fewer than $750 (7.5 orders averaging $100) in sales per thousand pieces mailed.

285

Contribution to circularization cost and profit			$ 35.00
Profit objective			$ (15.00)
Contribution to circularization cost			$ 20.00
Cost per M of conversion mailing			$150.00
Orders required to recover mailing costs			7.5

If a company were thus looking at a series of conversion mailings, each of which produced 40% of the orders produced by the preceding one, the arithmetic for its conversion series could look like this:

	Circularization Cost	No. Mailed	No. of Orders	Contribution
Contribution to circularization and profit				$ 35
Conversion mailing #1 including cost of generating and processing inquiries	$3,180	1,000	120	4,200
Conversion mailing #2 (A)	132	880	48	1,680
Conversion mailing #3 (A)	124	832	19.2	672
Conversion mailing #4 (A)	122	813	7.7	269
Total	$3,558	3,525	194.9	$6,821

(A) Mailing cost $150 per thousand

Thus the total conversions from this series of four mailings are just under 19.5% and the total sales at $100 each are $19,490. Total contribution would be $6,821. Pre-tax profit would be $3,263 after subtracting $3,558 selling cost, yielding profit of 16.7% to sales.

Improving the Figures

Developing an "honest" work sheet prior to test mailings or test ads just makes good sense. First of all, the work sheet will help to avoid making tests which just aren't in the cards. And where tests are made, a true reading will give direction for contemplating continuations. If the test is close to break-even or just makes it, a retest with changes of one or more of the elements would be indicated. The goal, once break-even is reached, is to increase response sufficiently to make the desired profit or to make other changes which will increase the profit potential.

Possibilities for dramatic increases in profits are ever present with a minimal increase in response. Stanley Rapp, president of RCS&A, gives a simple example of how a 10% increase in response can increase profit by 40%.

Taking as an example a product which sells for $15, he sets up the following typical costs and gross profit margins for 1,000 responses: product cost—$5; indirect cost—$2; advertising cost—$6; profit—$2. He then shows a comparison between 1,000 responses and 1,100 responses—a 10% increase.

286

	1,000 Responses	*1,100 Responses*
Product cost =	$ 5,000	$ 5,500
Indirect cost =	2,000	2,200
Advertising cost =	6,00υ	6,000
Total costs =	$13,000	$13,700

Now let's see what this 10% increase in response means to profits.

Sales of 1,000 units:	Sales of 1,100 units:
Total sales = $15,000	Total sales = $16,500
Less costs = 13,000	Less costs = 13,700
Profit = $ 2,000	Profit = $ 2,800

A 10% increase in response means a 40% increase in profit!

Knowing that a 10% increase in response can increase profit 40% is one thing. Making it happen is often quite another. But an astute direct marketer does make it happen. He looks at his figures and asks himself the key question: "What can I do to make these figures come out better?"

Walter Marshall, an account supervisor of RCS&A (New York), relates how a book club operation looked at their conversion figures and their sales per member and evolved a plan in conjunction with their agency to make the figures better.

On the subject of making bottom-line figures more attractive, Marshall says:

"During the past few years we have been involved with a number of clients in testing various approaches to order processing, fulfillment, and customer service across a wide range of marketing propositions. During this time I have been amazed over and over at the sizable effect that fulfillment has had on the bottom line—how sometimes minor changes in the back end bring dramatic improvements to profitability.

"One of the most remarkable results came in a test we conducted for one of our clients involved in a Club operation. Briefly, their offer involved an introductory up-front 'enrollment' package which was shipped to new Club members along with an invoice for approximately $4.00 plus shipping and handling charges.

"The average fulfillment time, from the day a new Club member mailed in the coupon until the day he received his initial enrollment package, was about six weeks. The reason for this considerable amount of time was the various steps through which the coupon went. First it went through editing and verification, key punching and entry into the data processing system, and in-file and outside credit checking. Then it was forwarded to a regional shipping center where the order was packed, and finally shipped out by fourth class mail. We questioned what the effect would be of getting the introductory shipment into the Club members' hands in dramatically less time.

"The test was conducted by taking a total of 5,000 new customers generated by a TV Guide insert and breaking them into two groups. The control group of 2,500 received standard fulfillment; the test group received what we called 'speed ship' service. Instead of being handled in the regular way, the 'speed ship' orders were handled as follows: The coupon was Xeroxed when it was received and without any editing or verification or credit checking the Xerox copy of the coupon was sent to the regional shipping center, where the order was packed and shipped to the new customer by parcel post special handling.

"We set up procedures to determine whether the increased cost of handling new orders this way, coupled with the expected rise in bad debts due to the lack of credit screening, would be offset by the improved performance of those customers who 'converted' and paid the initial invoice.

"The Club operation involved 13 four-week 'cycles.' At the end of the first 6 cycles an analysis was run by computer to determine the conversion rate (the percentage of both groups, paying the initial invoice), and the 'take' of each member (the number of units of merchandise purchased each cycle). The financial analysis, which follows, showed that the conversion rate of the 'speed ship' group, where fulfillment time averaged about 2½ weeks, was 17% higher than that of the control group, which received the standard fulfillment of about 5 weeks. And the 'take' of the 'speed ship' members was over 20% higher than the control group.

Comparison of Member Performance "Speed Ship" Fulfillment -VS-
Normal Handling   ACCEPTED & PAID UNITS PER MEMBER

	CYCLE 1	CYCLE 2	CYCLE 3	CYCLE 4	CYCLE 5	CYCLE 6	TOTAL UNITS
REGULAR FULFILLMENT (AVERAGE 5.3 WEEKS) CONVERSION RATE 52%	.417	.440	.373	.379	.404	.366	2.10
"SPEED SHIP" FULFILLMENT (AVERAGE 2.6 WEEKS) CONVERSION RATE 61%	.449	.411	.403	.420	.445	.476	2.54

"SPEED SHIP"   21% GREATER "TAKE" PER MEMBER   17% MORE CONVERTED MEMBERS

"After seven months had elapsed, and the initial analysis prepared, the test was repeated, this time using a total of 10,000 new members, 5,000 on each side of the test, selected from three different media sources—two publications and one direct mail campaign. While the second test showed some variation depending on the media source, it confirmed the earlier experience.

"What we learned from the test was enough incentive to completely revamp the fulfillment system and improve it to the point where new members received their introductory package in about 3½ weeks."

Still another way to make figures more favorable when engaged in mail order is to *acknowledge orders promptly.* The interminable wait after sending an order in before actually receiving the merchandise probably turns more people away from buying by mail than anything else. A most effective way to overcome this negative is to acknowledge orders promptly. Marshall cites what happened when a major book club sent an order acknowledgment mailing to "condition" new customers vs. the normal procedure of no acknowledgment between the time of receipt of application and actual first shipment. He states:

"In addition to containing a personalized thank-you letter, the order acknowledgment mailing also contained an 8-page booklet which described the Club. It took the new member on sort of a guided tour through Club headquarters, introduced him to a number of key Club officials, and previewed some of the selections planned for future months. The mailing did not contain an invoice and was sent in a stamped first-class envelope.

288

"The test group received the order acknowledgment mailing and regular fulfillment of the introductory shipment; the control group received the regular introductory shipment. There was no difference in the handling of the initial shipment—both groups received their shipment about 5 weeks after mailing the coupon. This time we measured three factors: the conversion rate, the bad debt rate, and the returned merchandise rate. The results showed that the new members who received the acknowledgment mailing converted better and had a substantially reduced returned merchandise rate.

"Of course, there are costs associated with this technique. In this case the total cost per new member was approximately 12¢—this included the printing and mailing by first-class mail and the additional EDP and fulfillment costs. (These costs were not based on the test quantities but projected for those of an ongoing promotion.) I think the results certainly justified the 12¢ investment made."

Comparison of New Member Performance—Regular Handling -VS- First-class Acknowledgement Mailing

	STANDARD FULFILLMENT	ORDER ACKNOWLEDGEMENT TEST
CONVERSION RATE	72.2%	79.7% (+ 10.4%)
BAD DEBT RATE	18.7%	15.2% (− 18.7%)
RETURN RATE	9.1%	5.1% (− 44%)

When one studies the foregoing chart, the dramatic differences in figures become quite apparent. Conversion rate increased 10.4%. Bad debt rate reduced 18.7%. Returned merchandise rate reduced 44%!

Better Markup as a Key

Better response is but one avenue to better profits. Better markup is an equally important avenue. And the astute direct marketer knows better response means little if markup is inadequate. The cost/sales computer chart which appears on page 290 enables the marketer to determine the revenue he needs per thousand at *(a)* various percentages of markup, and *(b)* various costs per thousand mailing pieces to break even.

The shaded example (70% markup, requires break-even revenue of $243 on a mailing costing $100 a thousand) underscores why many mail order offers are unprofitable. Seventy percent markup is too little for most mail order propositions. If an item cost $10, the selling price would be established at $17. Therefore break-even point would be almost 1.5%, not including indirect costs (15 orders × $17 = $255).

Contrast this high break-even point with an item costing $5 and selling for $15 (300% markup). At a mailing cost of $100 per thousand, the break-even point would be $133 per thousand, exclusive of indirect costs, vs. $243 per thousand at a 70% markup. Break-even point from a percent of response standpoint would be around nine orders per thousand vs. 15 in the other example. Quite a difference!

For those who regard a three-time markup as exorbitant, it should be pointed out such a markup compares favorably with classical markups between manufacturer's cost and retail selling price in retail stores.

It would be naïve, of course, to assume profits can be increased automatically simply by marking up all mail order items three times. Retail selling price must represent a good value and be truly competitive. Otherwise percent of response will surely decrease and returned goods increase.

The cost/sales computer chart

% Mark-up	$80	$100	$120	$140	$160	$180	$200	$220	$240	$260	$280	$300	$320	$340	$360	$380	$400	% Mark-up
15%	$640	$800	$960	$1120	$1280	$1440	$1600	$1760	$1920	$2080	$2240	$2400	$2560	$2720	$2880	$3040	$3200	15%
20	480	600	720	840	960	1080	1200	1320	1440	1560	1680	1800	1920	2040	2160	2280	.2400	20
25	400	500	600	700	800	900	1000	1100	1200	1300	1400	1500	1600	1700	1800	1900	2000	25
30	348	435	522	609	700	782	870	952	1043	1130	1217	1304	1391	1478	1565	1652	1739	30
35	308	385	461	538	615	693	770	846	962	1000	1077	1154	1231	1308	1384	1462	1538	35
40	280	350	420	490	560	630	700	770	840	910	980	1050	1120	1190	1260	1330	1400	40
45	258	323	387	452	516	580	645	710	774	839	900	968	1032	1097	1161	1226	1300	45
50	240	300	360	420	480	540	600	660	720	780	840	900	960	1020	1080	1140	1200	50
60	213	266	320	373	427	480	533	586	640	693	746	800	853	907	960	1013	1068	60
70	194	243	291	340	388	437	485	534	582	631	680	728	777	825	874	922	971	70
80	180	225	270	315	360	405	450	495	540	585	630	675	720	765	810	855	900	80
90	169	211	253	295	337	379	421	463	506	549	591	633	675	717	760	802	844	90
100	160	200	240	280	320	360	400	440	480	520	560	600	640	680	720	760	800	100
110	155	191	229	267	305	344	380	420	458	500	534	572	611	649	687	725	763	110
120	147	183	220	257	294	330	367	404	441	477	514	550	587	624	661	698	734	120
130	142	177	212	247	283	319	354	391	425	460	497	531	566	602	637	672	708	130
140	137	172	206	240	274	309	343	377	412	446	480	514	549	583	618	652	686	140
150	133	166	200	233	266	300	333	366	400	433	466	500	533	566	600	633	666	150
160	130	163	195	228	260	293	325	358	390	423	455	488	520	553	585	618	650	160
170	127	159	190	222	254	286	317	349	381	411	444	476	508	540	571	603	635	170
180	124	155	186	218	249	280	311	342	373	404	435	466	498	529	560	591	622	180
190	122	153	183	214	244	275	305	336	367	397	427	458	490	520	551	580	611	190
200	120	150	180	210	240	270	300	330	360	390	420	450	480	510	540	570	600	200
220	117	146	175	205	234	263	292	322	351	380	410	439	468	498	526	555	585	220
240	113	142	170	200	227	255	283	312	340	368	398	425	453	482	510	539	566	240
260	111	139	166	195	222	249	277	305	332	360	390	415	443	471	498	527	554	260
280	109	136	163	190	217	244	272	300	326	353	382	407	434	461	488	515	542	280
300	107	133	160	186	213	240	266	293	320	346	373	400	426	453	480	506	533	300
325	104	130	157	183	209	235	261	288	314	340	366	393	418	444	471	497	523	325
350	103	129	155	180	206	232	257	283	309	334	360	386	412	437	463	489	515	350
375	102	127	152	177	203	228	253	279	304	330	355	381	406	431	456	482	507	375
400	100	125	150	175	200	225	250	275	300	325	350	375	400	425	450	475	500	400
425	99	123	148	173	198	222	247	272	296	321	346	370	395	420	444	469	494	425
450	98	122	146	171	196	219	244	269	293	318	343	367	392	417	440	465	489	450
475	97	121	145	170	194	217	242	267	290	315	340	363	389	414	436	461	485	475
500	96	120	144	168	192	215	240	264	287	312	336	359	385	409	432	456	480	500
525	95	119	143	166	190	213	238	262	285	309	334	357	381	405	428	452	476	525
550	94	118	142	165	189	212	236	260	283	307	332	355	379	402	425	449	473	550
575	93	117	141	164	188	211	235	258	281	305	329	352	376	399	422	446	469	575
600	92	116	140	163	187	210	233	256	279	303	327	350	374	397	420	443	466	600
650	91	115	139	162	185	208	231	253	277	300	323	346	369	392	415	438	461	650
700	90	114	138	161	184	206	229	251	275	297	320	343	366	389	412	434	457	675
% Mark-up	$80	$100	$120	$140	$160	$180	$200	$220	$240	$260	$280	$300	$320	$340	$360	$380	$400	% Mark-up

Determining sales per thousand mailing pieces needed to break even is calculated by following the "% mark-up" column (first column at left) down to the mark-up percentage established for your product or service. Then proceed to the right to the point where per cent mark-up intersects with figure in box beneath established "Mailer Cost Per M." This figure indicates dollar sales per thousand needed to break even. (Copyright 1970—Henry A. Berg Direct Mail Printing Co., New York.)

Another way to make the break-even point more attainable is to reduce advertising cost. Increased response is one way to reduce *cost per order*. The other way is to reduce *cost per thousand mailing pieces* at the same response level. Or cost per thousand circulation in space. Or cost per thousand listeners or viewers in radio and TV.

Referring again to the example we cited in the cost/sales computer chart, let's note the break-even point per thousand mailed would be reduced by $49 per thousand — $194 instead of $243 — if the mailing cost were simply reduced by $20 per thousand — $80 instead of $100.

Projections

For the beginner in direct marketing, in particular, one of the most frustrating problems is knowing time patterns. At what point have I secured one-half of my inquiries, at what point two-thirds, at what point 90% or better? At what point do I have a "go" or

290

"no-go" situation? Once a history is established, decisions come easier. Bob Kestnbaum, the noted direct marketing authority, makes some interesting observations about projections in the following paragraphs:

Among the most important things for any direct marketer to understand are the basic time patterns that relate to his business. Each basic method of producing inquiries and orders has associated with it a pattern of receipt which usually remains fairly constant. In some cases, adjustments must be made for seasonal variations. Similarly, if returned goods are an important factor, a pattern can also be established for their receipt. In general, all these patterns take the approximate shape of the curve below.

Experience indicates that there can be a good deal of fluctuation during the early portion of this pattern, but that by the time about two-thirds of inquiries, orders, or returns are received the pattern smooths out and the balance becomes quite projectable. For this reason, the so-called half-life method of projection is not recommended, as it can yield significantly larger error.

Calculation of these patterns is not difficult. If cumulative inquiries, orders, or returns are recorded each week, the total "percent done" can be calculated by the week after the end of the program. By merging the results of several mailings or advertisements, you can determine an overall average pattern. For example, the table on page 292 shows the receipt of inquiries generated by advertisements in several different monthly publications.

Patterns for receipt of orders and returns can be calculated in the same manner.

Once these patterns have been established, it becomes possible to project the total number of inquiries, orders, or returns that will be generated after the first few weeks' receipts are known. The higher the percent done, of course, the safer the projection is.

Since all direct marketing expenditures and all revenues can be related in time to the actions necessary to generate inquiries or orders and to the consequences of these actions, knowledge of these essential patterns permits computation of cash flow. Once a cash flow is projected, a discounted cash flow can be calculated on the basis of predetermined objectives for ROI (return on investment). A simplified example is shown on page 293.

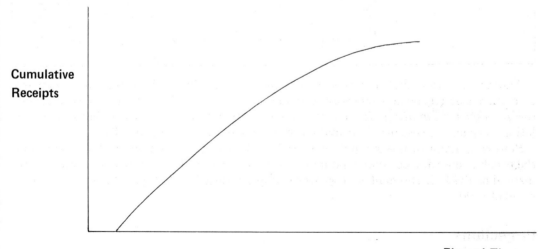

Cumulative Receipts

Elapsed Time

Week No.	Publi- cation A	Publi- cation B	Publi- cation C	Publi- cation D	Publi- cation E	Aver- age
1	7.6	13.2	10.6	11.8	8.3	11.0
2	24.7	33.8	36.7	31.1	48.3	35.0
3	41.4	41.8	52.2	43.8	63.3	47.6
4	53.6	48.9	59.0	51.1	68.9	54.9
5	62.4	56.9	63.3	60.1	71.4	61.9
6	65.8	66.2	78.5	75.5	74.1	72.2
7	73.0	72.0	81.0	80.1	80.0	77.3
8	80.6	76.0	84.0	82.7	82.8	80.9
9	85.4	80.1	86.2	85.6	86.9	84.4
10	88.2	84.2	88.4	87.9	90.1	87.4
11	90.1	87.8	90.6	90.8	93.7	90.4
12	93.2	90.3	92.4	94.9	96.9	93.5
13	95.7	93.5	94.7	96.9	98.4	95.9
14	96.8	95.7	96.8	98.5	98.8	97.4
15	98.9	99.2	98.9	100	100	99.5
16	100	100	100			100

Plot the line reflecting the contribution to circularization cost and profit of your product. For example, if the contribution per unit is $50, the sale of 2 units will contribute $100, sale of 4 units will contribute $200, etc.

Next, draw a horizontal line cutting the vertical scale at the point corresponding to your circularization cost. Then drop a vertical line to the bottom scale from the point where circularization cost intersects the slanting contribution line. The point where the vertical line crosses the bottom scale indicates the number of units that must be sold to break even. A direct mail package with complete in-the-mail cost of $200 per thousand requires sale of 4 units per thousand (.4%).

If actual sales achieved equal 6 units per thousand (.6%), a total contribution of $300 per thousand pieces mailed will be realized, of which $200 is required to pay for circularization, leaving $100 profit. On this basis, a mailing of 200,000 pieces would generate $200 \times \$100$, or $20,000 profit.

The major point that this chart dramatizes, however, is the rapidity with which profit grows with each additional unit sold as the slope of the contribution line (the amount of contribution per unit) increases.

Investing in New Customers

With a work sheet which reflects all costs, it's easy to establish the break-even point on a one-time sale. But most mail order operations are dependent on repeat business in order to realize a profit. Thus most first orders are taken at a loss, requiring an investment until such time as sufficient repeat business is received to turn the loss to a profit.

This brings up three vital questions:

1. What is the average amount of repeat business I can expect per new customer over a specified period of time (say, 12 months)?
2. At various levels of initial response (to acquire new customers), what is my required cash investment?
3. At what point will this investment be returned?

292

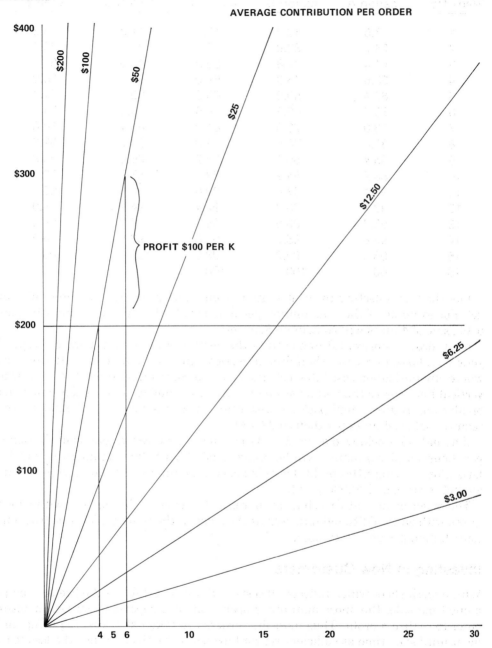

CIRCULARIZATION
COST PER THOUSAND

RELATIONSHIP BETWEEN CIRCULARIZATION
COST, CONTRIBUTION, AND BREAKEVEN

AVERAGE CONTRIBUTION PER ORDER

$400

$200 $100 $50 $25

$300

$12.50

PROFIT $100 PER K

$200

$6.25

$100

$3.00

4 5 6   10   15   20   25   30

NUMBER OF ORDERS
PER THOUSAND

These are toughies. And, sad to say, most neophytes *(a)* overestimate the amount of repeat business they have a right to expect; *(b)* underestimate the amount of cash investment required to reach break-even point; and *(c)* underestimate the length of time required to reach break-even. Many a bankruptcy takes place in the interim.

History records the amount of repeat business attained, of course. But more often than not, it's impractical to wait for a history to develop over 12 months or more. So predictions have to be made.

Business service publishers, who provide their services on a monthly basis, calculate repeat business on the basis of attrition (how many subscribers remain at the end of each month). Magazine publishers calculate on the same basis, only they calculate on the basis of subscription periods, such as three, six, and 12 months.

The attrition scale which follows is hypothetical but based on actual experience. The attrition rate (drop-off) is usually a great shocker to the enthusiast who lacks experience.

ATTRITION SCALE

Month	No. of Subscriptions	%
1st	3,000	100
2nd	2,700	65
3rd	2,250	55
4th	1,800	50
5th	1,500	48
6th	1,400	46
7th	1,300	44
8th	1,250	42
9th	1,200	40
10th	1,150	38
11th	1,100	36
12th	1,050	35

This attrition scale is based upon an original response of 3% on a 100,000 mailing. It is to be noted that at the end of four months, only 50% of the original 3,000 subscribers remain. At the end of 12 months, 35% of the original group are still "alive."

The attrition scale indicates the business service organization went into the second month of operation with repeat billing to 2,700 of the original 3,000 subscribers; by the fifth month, repeat business was coming from only 1,500 of the original 3,000; and by the twelfth month, there was repeat billing to only 1,050 of the original 3,000 subscribers.

Now the $64 questions are: How much cash is required to reach break-even point on a cash investment basis, and how long a period is required to turn red figures to black figures? Again — a shocker.

The accumulated cash flow chart which follows provides precise answers based on the repeat business factor as revealed by the attrition scale. It is important to note the following, which are included in the computations:

1. Cost of test mailing—100,000 pieces in October.
2. Cost of continuation mailing—one million pieces in January.
3. Cost of service, fulfillment, refurbishing, bad debts, and overhead.
4. All cash received from billings is computed at an average of 90 days from billing date.

100,000 Test Mailing Plus 1,000,000 Continuation Mailing 2%-8% Response

ACCUMULATED CASH FLOW CHART

Percentage of Response

Month	2%	3%	4%	5%	6%	7%	8%
October	*$(16,705)	$(16,705)	$(16,705)	$(16,705)	$(16,705)	$(16,705)	$(16,705)
November	(16,105)	(15,555)	(15,005)	(14,455)	(13,905)	(13,355)	(12,805)
December	(16,540)	(15,960)	(15,375)	(14,595)	(14,210)	(13,630)	(13,045)
January.......	(135,635)	(134,575)	(133,505)	(132,245)	(131,175)	(130,315)	(129,245)
February	(131,025)	(123,730)	(116,925)	(108,930)	(101,625)	(94,530)	(87,225)
March	(129,445)	(121,115)	(113,270)	(104,235)	(95,890)	(87,755)	(79,415)
April	(118,970)	(105,150)	(91,815)	(77,295)	(63,450)	(49,840)	(36,000)
May	(103,500)	(81,695)	(60,375)	(37,870)	(16,045)	5,555	27,375
June	(88,510)	(58,945)	(29,885)	370	29,935	59,285	88,855
July	(74,590)	(37,815)	(1,495)	35,920	72,795	109,255	146,135
August	(61,290)	(17,610)	25,595	69,925	113,690	157,060	200,815
September	(48,620)	1,745	51,485	102,450	152,755	202,755	253,100
October	(36,520)	20,145	76,185	133,450	190,055	246,355	303,000
November	(24,515)	38,005	100,145	163,315	223,070	288,225	350,920
December	(13,580)	54,380	122,010	190,625	255,865	326,470	394,650
January.......	(3,580)	69,405	142,010	215,650	285,865	361,495	434,650
February	5,670	83,305	160,510	238,800	313,615	393,895	471,650
March	9,920	89,655	168,960	249,400	326,265	408,745	488,550

*( ) Cash investment.

This chart reflects cash investment at various levels of response and shows at what point total cash investment is recouped. Investment is computed on the basis of an initial mailing of 100,000 pieces in October, followed by a continuation mailing of 1,000,000 in January. All costs of mailings, product costs, fulfillment and overhead are included. The attrition scale is reflected in the figures.

Analysis of the accumulated cash flow chart leads to some interesting observations:

1. The initial investment to cover the cost of the test mailing and first month of service came to $16,705.
2. Even though some revenue was coming in by the fourth month (January), the big investment in the continuation mailing brought the total investment up to $134,515.
3. The break-even point was reached in the twelfth month (September), when there was a small accumulated cash profit of $1,745.
4. From that point on, cash profits accumulated rapidly. At the end of 18 months, there was an accumulated cash profit of $89,655 against a peak investment of $134,575.

Break-even at the end of 12 months is generally considered quite satisfactory. The example cited shows why.
So it all boils down to this:

a. Time will tell the average amount of repeat business each new customer will generate. (If you can't afford to wait—estimate conservatively!)

295

b. A cash flow chart will graphically show the amount of peak investment and the time required to recoup investment. (Don't overlook any of the hidden costs in your operation!)

c. Rate of sales growth will be determined primarily by: (1) size of market; (2) amount of venture capital management is willing to expend; and (3), often, the limit of venture capital available to management.

The Hard-Core Support Group

There is a turning point in every mail order operation. The turning point is when "fickle" customers have been shaken out and a hard-core group supports the business. Another way of putting it is that, for every worthwhile proposition, there is a loyal group who will continue to purchase at an extremely high rate. This applies not only to subscription programs but to merchandise programs as well, even though in merchandise programs, for the most part, there is no prearranged pattern of repeat business. The chart which follows is hypothetical, but it is based on actual statistics of a firm selling a specific line of Christmas gift items.

The figures show repeat business percentages by years from a group of customers over an 11-year period. It is astounding that, while the repeat business percentage is only 34.2% the second year, this group is repeating at the fantastic rate of 83.8% 11 years later. It shows dramatically what can happen when a customer is satisfied and when continuing with the supplier becomes a habit.

Repeat Business Percentages

Year	% of Repeat
2d	34.2%
3d	60.0%
4th	71.2%
5th	75.9%
6th	76.0%
7th	79.3%
8th	79.9%
9th	80.9%
10th	79.8%
11th	77.8%
12th	83.8%

Once a marketer knows the percentage of repeat business which he can expect from his hard-core group, he can then have a real "fix" on what he can afford to invest in a new customer. If his figures were similar to those in the chart just cited, for instance, he would know that for every 1,000 new customers obtained he could expect 34.2% repeat business from this group in the second year. But more important, looking down the road, he would know how much repeat business he could expect in succeeding years. Knowing his profit per order, he can then easily determine the value of a customer over an extended period. It is because of the high profit potential of hard-core support groups that many major marketers are willing to invest in new customers with a view to getting their money back in many cases three to five years in the future.

When a giant book club like Doubleday's Literary Guild make a front end offer of four books for $1, they are probably investing about $6 in that new member. One can be sure that Doubleday, based on statistics, knows at what point they will get the $6 investment back and turn the investment into a profit.

How Catalog Firms Rate Customers

The ultimate method of evaluating customers on a profitable or nonprofitable basis was developed by the giant mail order firms many years ago. The Great Depression forced them to take a cold, hard look at their customer lists. And the recency-frequency-monetary method developed from this necessity.

The technique is comparable to the actuarial method of rating risks that insurance companies use. It estimates, from the past buying performance of categories of customers over a period of time (two years or four six-month seasons), how much these categories will buy again. If the selling cost ratio is too high to provide a profit, the category does not receive a mailing.

Referring to the original studies from which recency-frequency-monetary evolved, the late and great George Cullinan of Aldens stated:

"The elements or standards which controlled 90% of the reasons why customers repeat at a certain sales volume were found to be:

"1. *Recency* of the last order or orders before current mailing (weighted 35%).
"2. *Frequency* (whether a single or multiple) of ordering performance in the four seasons before current mailing (weighted 50%).
"3. *Monetary* value of the order or orders in a given season (weighted 15%).

"A customer category which ordered within the last six months before mailing (recency) and sent two or more orders during that period (frequency) for a combined total of over $20 (monetary) was just about the cream of the list. One which had ordered only once in the six months to a year before mailing for a total of less than $2 was probably the poorest segment of the list. The superiority of the first group mentioned over the second could be as high as ten to one."

Commenting on the results achieved through the application of R-F-M, Cullinan said, "The largest mail order company reduced the circulation of its semiannual 1,000-page catalog from 13 million to seven million to eight million. The second largest firm from 11 million to six million to 6.5 million. Others cut circulation even more, percentage-wise."

Alluding to the application of R-F-M for smaller mail order operations, he put forth these basic assumptions which may be used as guides for evaluating a customer list:

- All customers who order in the 12-month period before a catalog is mailed are twice as good as those whose last order came in from 12 to 24 months prior.
- All two-order customers are worth twice as much as one-order customers in the same period, whatever the period is.
- Customers who order 24−36 months prior to mailing are worth only 75% as much as those who order in the 12- to 24-month period before mailing.

"Correlating only these three factors in six simple groups (not the two or three dozen that can actually be arranged from the possible combinations) you have a range in value of about six to one between the top customers and the poorest . . . a good thing to know when budgeting mailings. It is the little fellow (in particular) with his smaller books, fewer orders per book, low average order and little or no installment credit who most needs answers to questions about circulation control."

Interpretation Is Vital to Success

At the outset of this chapter we pointed out the importance of interpreting figures in a meaningful way. Many a marketer has computer reports up to his ears. But, as often as not, reports are misinterpreted and apples are compared to oranges.

A dramatic example of the danger of misinterpretation is a case history of a well-known firm that sells goodwill items, advertising specialties, and collection messages to business firms by mail. They built a fine business. And rarely did their credit losses exceed 1.5% at year's end.

Searching for ways to expand their business, they came up with a bright idea. Why not sell consumer merchandise to their credit checked executives?

Response was terrific! Everything seemed to go well with their list. Paint guns, lawn mowers, cameras—just to mention a few items. The unit of sale ranged from $29.95 to $149.50. All orders were filled without question, because all orders came from business firms who had paid their bills.

Paper profit on this operation was truly excellent. It did indeed look as if this firm had hit the jackpot in a very big way. But several months later it turned out that bad debts weren't 1.5%—instead, they were in excess of 10%! What happened?

It seems that the marketing manager of this firm assumed that, because purchases of business necessities were paid for by the business firm, purchases of consumer goods items would be paid for by the business executive. False logic played tricks and nearly bankrupted the firm!

An example of how a marketer can arrive at false conclusions when he lacks all the necessary figures is cited by Tom Collins, executive vice president of RCS&A (New York). He states, "Back in 1965, I recall, we ran ads in two publications for Capitol Record Club and were completely misled by the results because all we had for a yardstick was an *average* allowable advertising cost per enrollment. The ad in *Playboy* came in well under the average allowable cost, and was considered a hit.

"The coupon cost in *Better Homes & Gardens* was about three times as much as we thought we could afford. What we had no way of knowing at that time was that the *Better Homes & Gardens* readers would end up buying three or four times as much from the club as the *Playboy* readers." Incomplete statistics are dangerous!

Perhaps the most dangerous exercise of all is interpreting figures on the basis of *averages*. Average percent of return really means very little. All it tells you is what your return is over a complete universe. It doesn't tell you where the profits or where the losses are coming from.

Many a firm selling via the mail order method nationally has learned, on analysis, that, while their distribution is national, their profit contribution is far from national. Sales derived from the home state are most often the most profitable. Analysis often discloses that the further you get from your home state, the less profitable your sales are.

A well-known firm selling via the catalog method followed the practice of advertising in publications on a national distribution basis. A sales analysis was made to determine sales per 100,000 households on a state-by-state basis. Figures developed by this analysis shook the very foundation of the establishment. Variances were expected, but not a range of from $307 in sales per 100,000 households in California to $5,560 per 100,000 households in the District of Columbia!

Statistics showed that, for a state to be profitable, it had to produce $2,000 or more in sales per 100,000 households. The first list on page 299 shows the states which qualified and combined to constitute the prime market.

Only 16 states and the District of Columbia met the criterion of $2,000 or more in sales per 100,000 households. More startling is the fact that 76% of total national sales came from these 17 areas.

The marketer could have stopped there. He did learn where 76% of his total national sales were coming from. But how about the cities within the states?

We all know that there are great differences in response between large cities and smaller cities. A three-digit ZIP Code analysis for five of the cities in Michigan illustrates the wide variances in response (second list on page 299).

298

State	Sales per 100 M Households
Connecticut	$5,141
Delaware	3,682
[District of Columbia]	5,560
Illinois	3,085
Indiana	2,404
Maine	3,139
Maryland	3,179
Massachusetts	2,653
Michigan	3,580
New Hampshire	3,495
New Jersey	3,206
New York	2,519
Ohio	4,864
Pennsylvania	3,302
Vermont	4,560
Virginia	3,342
Wisconsin	2,155

Michigan	ZIP Code	Customers per 100 M Population
Detroit	482	59
Flint	485	67
Lansing	489	121
Grand Rapids	495	83
Dearborn	481	936

Isn't it astounding that there were only 59 customers per 100 M population in the large city of Detroit vs. 936 per 100 M population in Dearborn, Michigan? It may be said, without much danger of contradiction, that—if a business is basically sound—the right application and interpretation of mathematics can make it dramatically profitable. Mathematics as applied to direct marketing is at the same time intriguing, fascinating, and frustrating. But the payoff can be great.

Self-Quiz

1. Name the five major factors involved in determining the break-even point for any product or service.

1. _____

2. _____

3. _____

4. _____

5. _____

2. When may the two-step method be more profitable than attempting to make a sale on the first effort?

_____

_____

3. The interval between time of receipt of order and delivery has
   ☐ No effect   ☐ Some effect   ☐ Considerable effect
   on customer satisfaction and acceptance.

4. Prompt order acknowledgment has
   ☐ No effect   ☐ Some effect   ☐ Considerable effect
   on customer satisfaction and acceptance.

5. Which of these three mail order markups is closest to the ideal mail order markup?
   ☐ 100%   ☐ 200%   ☐ 300%

6. Outside of a better markup, what other way is there to make your break-even point more easily attainable?

_____

_____

7. At what point do patterns of responses become quite projectable?
   ☐ Half-way point   ☐ Two-thirds point   ☐ 90% point

8. How can one best develop a projection scale for inquiries and/or orders?

_____

_____

9. What is meant by an attrition scale?

_____

_____

_____

_____

10. What is meant by cash flow?

_____

_____

11. What is meant by the hard-core support group?

_____

_____

_____

300

12. Define the recency-frequency-monetary formula.

Recency is _____

Frequency is _____

Monetary is _____

13. Using the assumptions of the R-F-M formula as a guide, you can expect that all customers who order two or more times within a measurable period are worth _____ as much as those who order only once within the same period.

14. What is the danger of interpreting figures by averages?

_____

_____

_____

Pilot Project

You have been given the assignment of selling a paint gun by mail to homeowners for $39.95.

Given the following set of facts, determine your break-even (number of orders required) per thousand pieces mailed.

1. Merchandise cost — $17
2. Order handling expense — 75¢
3. Shipping expense — $1.85
4. Cost of premium (free gift) — $1.25.
5. Administrative overhead — 10% of selling price
6. Returned goods — 21%
7. Refurbishing cost — 10% of merchandise cost
8. Estimated bad debts — 10%
9. Cost of mailing — $150 per 1,000, including a proportionate share of preparation costs

Chapter 14 Testing Techniques

There's an old saw in direct marketing. It goes like this: "If you don't know the answer — test." No one can argue with this sage advice. But, sad to say, too many direct marketers conduct invalid tests and too many direct marketers test trivia instead of the big things.

As direct marketers have become more sophisticated, they've moved away from trivia tests. Here are the types of trivia tests which were in vogue a decade or two ago. Which is more effective: three dots (. . .) to break up a sentence, or two dots (. .)? Is it more effective to underscore key words in a second color, or the same color? Does pink stock bring a greater response from females and blue from males, or vice versa? Does a tilted postage stamp increase response? Should an indented paragraph be on the top third of a letter, or the bottom third? Trivia all!

If you do test trivia of this nature, you will find differences between underscoring in the same color vs. a second color, differences between one color of paper stock vs. another, differences depending on where indented paragraphs appear. But chances are the differences will usually be minimal and probably statistically invalid.

What's more — trivia test results tend to flip-flop from one test to another.

Test the Big Things

Today's breed of direct marketing practitioners are leaving trivia to those who are still living in the '50s. They are testing the big things; they are looking for breakthroughs. There are six big areas from which breakthroughs emerge.

1. The products or services you offer.
2. The media you use (lists, print, and broadcast).
3. The propositions you make.
4. The copy platforms you use.
5. The formats you use.
6. The timing you choose.

Five of these areas for testing appear on most published lists these days. But testing new products and new product features is rarely recommended. And yet everything starts with the product or service you offer.

I've personally seen many direct marketers religiously test new ads, new mailing packages, new media, new copy approaches, new formats, and new timing schedules season after season, with never a thought to testing new product features. Finally, the most imaginative of creative approaches fail to overcome the waning appeal of the same old product. And still another product bites the dust.

This need not happen. For example, consider the most commonplace of mail order items — the address label. Scores of firms offer them — white stock, black ink. Competition is keen, prices all run about the same. But from this maze of competition a few emerge with new product features: gold stock, colored ink, seasonal borders, and so forth. Tests are made to determine appeal. The new product features appeal to a bigger audience.

Thinking up new product features and testing for appeal is one way to go. Pure research — seldom practiced — is another and usually more reliable route to follow. Here are just some of the questions which research can answer about any product or service.

What features in your product or service are favored over those of the competition?

What features offered by the competition are favored over yours?

What new features, not now available, would the consumer like to see in your product or service?

How much more does the consumer feel he would be willing to pay for additional features?

How do your prices compare with the competition's?

Product research, more often than not, isn't even considered until sales volume falls through the floor. Then someone says, in desperation, "Maybe we should hire some research outfit to find out what's wrong."

There's the case of the successful direct marketer who had enjoyed a consistent 15% sales growth for ten consecutive years. Then bang—sales dropped 30% in the eleventh year! What happened? Competition moved in. That's what happened. Competition with features the originator did not have.

So, with the disaster flags up, a research firm was hired. Research showed clearly the competition had three highly favored major features this marketer didn't have. These features were adapted and improved and two additional features, unearthed through research, were added. Presto! Sales leaped 40% the very next season. There is an important moral here: Don't wait for competition to force you to research your product or service. It could be too late.

Not only will product research lead the way to new testable features; it will give your creative people new life as well. For copywriters in particular, writing about new features is a dream come true. And research may even lead to new, untapped markets.

Questionnaire Mailings

Part and parcel of product improvement is learning about your customers, who they are, how they think, what their life styles may be. One of the most unusual questionnaires in the past decade was prepared and distributed by *Redbook*. This was a 100-part questionnaire run in the April 1972 issue. It took about one hour to complete.

There was no postage-free reply envelope provided. There was no incentive offered for replying. *Redbook* received over 120,000 completed questionnaires.

On the pages which follow we are reproducing the questionnaire in its entirety. One can only imagine the great value the editorial board derived from the profile established as a result of this questionnaire. It is safe to assume the profile was of equal value to the circulation promotion department of *Redbook*.

Too few marketers use questionnaires to learn more about their customers and prospects.

Please cut this page along the dotted line and use the form below to record your answers to the questionnaire.

Read each of the questions on the following pages carefully.

After reading each question, indicate your answer to it by circling the appropriate letter or letters opposite the question number on this page.

If there is any question that you prefer not to answer, skip it and go on to the next. All replies are anonymous and completely confidential. The value of the questionnaire will depend on the candor and thoughtfulness of your answers.

When you have completed the questionnaire and listed your answers below, put this page in a stamped envelope (a business-size, No. 10 is best) and mail it to:

> Dr. Carol Tavris
> Redbook Questionnaire
> P.O. Box 4088
> New York, New York 10017

The deadline for returns is April 30, 1972. But please do it as soon as you can.

1. A B C D E	27. A B C D E F	53. A B C D E F	79. A B C D
2. A B C D E	28. A B C D E F	54. A B C D E F	80. A___ B___ C___ D___ E___
3. A B C D E F	29. A B C D E F	55. A B C D E F	(fill in ages of children)
4. A B C D E	30. A B C D E F	56. A B C D E F	81. A B C D E F G
5. A B C D E	31. A B C D E F	57. A B C D E F	82. A B C D E
6. A B C D E	32. A B C D E F	58. A B C D E F	83. A B C D E
7. A B C D E	33. A B C	59. A B C D E F	84. A B C D E F
8. A B C D E	34. A B C D E	60. A B C D E F	85. A B C D E
9. A B C D E	35. A B C D E F	61. A B C D E	86. A B C D
10. A B C D E	36. A B C D	62. A B C D E F	87. A B C D E F G H I J
11. A B C D E	37. A B C D E F	63. A B C D E F	88. A B C D E F G H I J
12. A B C D E F	38. A B C D E	64. A B C D E F	89. A B C D E F G H I J
13. A B C D E F	39. A B C D E F	65. A B C D E F	90. A B C D E F G
14. A B C D E F	40. A B C D E F	66. A B C D E F	91. A B C D E F
15. A B C D E F	41. A B C D E	67. A B C D E F	92. A B C D E F G
16. A B C D E F	42. A B C D E F	68. A B C D E F	93. A B C D E
17. A B C D E F	43. A B C D E F	69. A B C D	94. A B C D
18. A B C D E F	44. A B C D	70. A B C D	95. A B C D E F
19. A B C D E F	45. A B C D E F G	71. A B C D	96. A B C D E F
20. A B C D E F	46. A B C D E F	72. A B C D	97. A B C D E
21. A B C D E F	47. A B C D E F	73. A B C D	98. A B C
22. A B C D E F	48. A B C D	74. A B C D	99. A B C D
23. A B C D E F	49. A B C D E F	75. A B C D	100. A B C D E F G H I J K
24. A B C D E F	50. A B C D E F	76. A B C	
25. A B C D E F	51. A B C D E F	77. A B C D E	
26. A B C D E F	52. A B C D E F	78. A B C D E	

1. Which sex has more advantages or privileges in this society? (On answer sheet, circle the letter before the statement that best expresses your viewpoint.)
   A. Men have many more than women.
   B. Men have more than women.
   C. There are advantages and disadvantages for each sex.
   D. Women have more than men.
   E. Women have many more than men.

2. What is the most effective way for women to overcome discrimination? (Circle A, B, C, D or E on answer sheet.)
   A. By working with men in organized groups.
   B. By working in exclusively female groups.
   C. By working individually to prove their abilities and educate men.
   D. It cannot be overcome under the present system; radical political change must come first.
   E. I do not think there is discrimination against women.

3. What is the *best* way for most women to develop their potential? (Circle A, B, C, D, E or F on answer sheet.)
   A. By being good wives and mothers only.
   B. By taking jobs that best utilize their feminine skills and qualities, such as nursing or social work.
   C. By taking jobs that most fulfill them as individuals.
   D. By joining women's groups that will develop their consciousness as women.
   E. By combining marriage, motherhood and work.
   F. By combining marriage or a love relationship and work.

Some people believe that personality differences between the sexes are biological in origin; others think that they are learned; others say that there are no differences at all. Which of the statements listed best expresses your viewpoint about the traits in entries 4 through 11?

4. Aggressiveness is:
   (Circle A, B, C, D or E on answer sheet.)
   A. More common in men, for biological reasons.
   B. More common in men, for cultural reasons.
   C. Equally common in both sexes.
   D. More common in women, for biological reasons.
   E. More common in women, for cultural reasons.

5. A capacity for deep feeling is:
   (Circle A, B, C, D or E on answer sheet.)
   A. More common in men, for biological reasons.
   B. More common in men, for cultural reasons.
   C. Equally common in both sexes.
   D. More common in women, for biological reasons.
   E. More common in women, for cultural reasons.

6. Independence is:
   (Circle A, B, C, D or E on answer sheet.)
   A. More common in men, for biological reasons.
   B. More common in men, for cultural reasons.
   C. Equally common in both sexes.
   D. More common in women, for biological reasons.
   E. More common in women, for cultural reasons.

7. Objectivity and rationality are:
   (Circle A, B, C, D or E on answer sheet.)
   A. More common in men, for biological reasons.
   B. More common in men, for cultural reasons.
   C. Equally common in both sexes.
   D. More common in women, for biological reasons.
   E. More common in women, for cultural reasons.

8. Nurturing capacity is:
   (Circle A, B, C, D or E on answer sheet.)
   A. More common in men, for biological reasons.
   B. More common in men, for cultural reasons.
   C. Equally common in both sexes.
   D. More common in women, for biological reasons.
   E. More common in women, for cultural reasons.

9. The ability to reason abstractly is:
   (Circle A, B, C, D or E on answer sheet.)
   A. More common in men, for biological reasons.
   B. More common in men, for cultural reasons.
   C. Equally common in both sexes.
   D. More common in women, for biological reasons.
   E. More common in women, for cultural reasons.

10. Preference for monogamy is:
    (Circle A, B, C, D or E on answer sheet.)
    A. More common in men, for biological reasons.
    B. More common in men, for cultural reasons.
    C. Equally common in both sexes.
    D. More common in women, for biological reasons.
    E. More common in women, for cultural reasons.

11. Empathy and intuition are:
    (Circle A, B, C, D or E on answer sheet.)
    A. More common in men, for biological reasons.
    B. More common in men, for cultural reasons.
    C. Equally common in both sexes.
    D. More common in women, for biological reasons.
    E. More common in women, for cultural reasons.

For entries 12 through 31, choose one of the statements that best expresses your feelings.

12. The communications media (for example, television and the press) degrade women by portraying them as sex objects or mindless dolls. (Circle A, B, C, D, E or F on answer sheet.)
    A. Strongly agree.   D. Slightly disagree.
    B. Generally agree.   E. Generally disagree.
    C. Slightly agree.   F. Strongly disagree.

13. Many women who do the same work as their male colleagues earn substantially less money. (Circle A, B, C, D, E or F on answer sheet.)
    A. Strongly agree.   D. Slightly disagree.
    B. Generally agree.   E. Generally disagree.
    C. Slightly agree.   F. Strongly disagree.

14. Most men do not take women seriously.
    (Circle A, B, C, D, E or F on answer sheet.)
    A. Strongly agree.   D. Slightly disagree.
    B. Generally agree.   E. Generally disagree.
    C. Slightly agree.   F. Strongly disagree.

15. If a woman wants to get ahead, there is little to stop her. (Circle A, B, C, D, E or F on answer sheet.)
    A. Strongly agree.   D. Slightly disagree.
    B. Generally agree.   E. Generally disagree.
    C. Slightly agree.   F. Strongly disagree.

16. I usually find the things men talk about more interesting than the things women talk about. (Circle A, B, C, D, E or F on answer sheet.)
    A. Strongly agree.   D. Slightly disagree.
    B. Generally agree.   E. Generally disagree.
    C. Slightly agree.   F. Strongly disagree.

17. I have often felt that men are more interested in my body than in me as a person. (Circle A, B, C, D, E or F on answer sheet.)

A. Strongly agree.   D. Slightly disagree.
B. Generally agree.   E. Generally disagree.
C. Slightly agree.   F. Strongly disagree.

18. A problem with our society is that women do the most important work—raising children—and get no recognition for it. (Circle A, B, C, D, E or F on answer sheet.)

A. Strongly agree.   D. Slightly disagree.
B. Generally agree.   E. Generally disagree.
C. Slightly agree.   F. Strongly disagree.

19. Women don't really deserve the same pay as men, since they are less reliable as workers. (Circle A, B, C, D, E or F on answer sheet.)

A. Strongly agree.   D. Slightly disagree.
B. Generally agree.   E. Generally disagree.
C. Slightly agree.   F. Strongly disagree.

20. I seem to be the kind of person who has more bad luck than good. (Circle A, B, C, D, E or F on answer sheet.)

A. Strongly agree.   D. Slightly disagree.
B. Generally agree.   E. Generally disagree.
C. Slightly agree.   F. Strongly disagree.

21. I am more at ease with a group of women than with a group of men. (Circle A, B, C, D, E or F on answer sheet.)

A. Strongly agree.   D. Slightly disagree.
B. Generally agree.   E. Generally disagree.
C. Slightly agree.   F. Strongly disagree.

22. Little children need full-time mothers. (Circle A, B, C, D, E or F on answer sheet.)

A. Strongly agree.   D. Slightly disagree.
B. Generally agree.   E. Generally disagree.
C. Slightly agree.   F. Strongly disagree.

23. I have always felt pretty sure my life would work out the way I wanted it to. (Circle A, B, C, D, E or F on answer sheet.)

A. Strongly agree.   D. Slightly disagree.
B. Generally agree.   E. Generally disagree.
C. Slightly agree.   F. Strongly disagree.

24. Women are exploited in this country as much as minority groups are. (Circle A, B, C, D, E or F on answer sheet.)

A. Strongly agree.   D. Slightly disagree.
B. Generally agree.   E. Generally disagree.
C. Slightly agree.   F. Strongly disagree.

25. Raising a child provides many rewards, but as a full-time job it cannot keep most women satisfied. (Circle A, B, C, D, E or F on answer sheet.)

A. Strongly agree.   D. Slightly disagree.
B. Generally agree.   E. Generally disagree.
C. Slightly agree.   F. Strongly disagree.

26. I find it easier to share my most important feelings with another woman than with a man. (Circle A, B, C, D, E or F on answer sheet.)

A. Strongly agree.   D. Slightly disagree.
B. Generally agree.   E. Generally disagree.
C. Slightly agree.   F. Strongly disagree.

27. The special privileges that men extend to women more than offset any discrimination they practice against them. (Circle A, B, C, D, E or F on answer sheet.)

A. Strongly agree.   D. Slightly disagree.
B. Generally agree.   E. Generally disagree.
C. Slightly agree.   F. Strongly disagree.

28. I usually feel pretty sure of myself even when people disagree with me. (Circle A, B, C, D, E or F on answer sheet.)

A. Strongly agree.   D. Slightly disagree.
B. Generally agree.   E. Generally disagree.
C. Slightly agree.   F. Strongly disagree.

29. I have rarely "played dumb" to please or impress a man. (Circle A, B, C, D, E or F on answer sheet.)

A. Strongly agree.   D. Slightly disagree.
B. Generally agree.   E. Generally disagree.
C. Slightly agree.   F. Strongly disagree.

30. The housewife/mother role does not really provide women with enough opportunity for self-fulfillment. (Circle A, B, C, D, E or F on answer sheet.)

A. Strongly agree.   D. Slightly disagree.
B. Generally agree.   E. Generally disagree.
C. Slightly agree.   F. Strongly disagree.

31. There's not much use for me to plan ahead because usually something happens to make me change my plans. (Circle A, B, C, D, E or F on answer sheet.)

A. Strongly agree.   D. Slightly disagree.
B. Generally agree.   E. Generally disagree.
C. Slightly agree.   F. Strongly disagree.

32. Imagine that you are at a small dinner party, enthusiastically discussing a book with a man you have just met. In the middle of your comments he says: "You have the most beautiful eyes I have ever seen." How do you feel? (Circle A, B, C, D, E or F on answer sheet.)

A. Flattered; he's made me feel feminine.
B. Pleased.
C. Neutral.
D. Irritated or annoyed.
E. Angry; he's insulted my intelligence.
F. Ambivalent; complimented but annoyed.

33. Mrs. R., the mother of two small children, works full time at a job she enjoys. Her children are in a day-care center run by trained teachers of whom she approves. How do you feel about Mrs. R.? (Circle A, B or C on answer sheet.)

A. I can't imagine a responsible mother neglecting her children like that.
B. I can't really criticize Mrs. R., but I think she is missing some of the most important experiences of being a mother.
C. I think it is great that she has such an arrangement.

34. Mr. and Mrs. T. share all household chores and the care of their three small children. Both work half time in order to maintain this family relationship. How do you feel about Mr. T.? (Circle A, B, C, D or E on answer sheet.)

   A. I could never respect such a man.
   B. I think doing housework and child care takes away from his masculinity.
   C. I admire him but would never want a marriage like that.
   D. I admire him and wish I were in a marriage like that.
   E. No feelings one way or the other.

35. (This question is for women with children only.) Suppose one day a perfect housekeeper and governess were to land on your doorstep, offering her services indefinitely without fee. How would you react? (Circle A, B C, D, E or F on answer sheet.)

   A. I would not avail myself of her offer.
   B. I would like to accept her offer, but would be reluctant to do so.
   I would accept her offer and *primarily* use the extra time to:
   C. Go to work full time.
   D. Go to work part time.
   E. Go back to school.
   F. Pursue my interests and hobbies.

36. How do you usually feel about menstruation *at the time* you have your period? (Circle A, B, C or D on answer sheet.)

   A. It is reassuring; it affirms my womanhood.
   B. I don't think about it; it's "just there."
   C. It makes me unhappy or irritated.
   D. It makes me resentful that men don't have a similar unpleasant experience.

37. In general, how did you feel about the way you looked when you were pregnant? (Circle A, B, C, D, E or F on answer sheet.)

   A. Very attractive and feminine.
   B. Funny and humorous.
   C. Clumsy and awkward.
   D. Very ugly and unfeminine.
   E. No feelings one way or the other.
   F. Not applicable.

38. In general, how did you feel mentally and emotionally when you were pregnant? (Circle A, B, C, D or E on answer sheet.)

   A. Marvelous, excited, happy.
   B. Normal or ordinary.
   C. Depressed, anxious or snappish.
   D. Alternated between emotional highs and lows.
   E. Not applicable.

39. Over-all, what was your reaction to the experience of childbirth? (Circle A, B, C, D, E or F on answer sheet.)

   A. The best experience I've ever had.
   B. Exciting and fascinating.
   C. Neither pleasant nor unpleasant; something to be got through.
   D. Unpleasant or depressing.
   E. The worst experience I've ever had.
   F. Not applicable.

40. If you breast-fed any or all of your children, how did you feel about it? (Circle A, B, C, D, E or F on answer sheet.)

   A. It affirmed my womanhood; men are cheated by not having a similar reassuring experience.
   B. It made me feel happy.
   C. I didn't think much about it.
   D. It made me feel unhappy or unfeminine.
   E. It made me resentful; men are lucky not to have to go through such an experience.
   F. Not applicable.

41. Taking everything together, how do you feel about your marriage or your present relationship? (Circle A, B, C, D or E on answer sheet.)

   A. Very satisfied.   D. Very dissatisfied.
   B. Relatively satisfied.   E. Not applicable.
   C. Relatively dissatisfied.

42. Over-all, is marriage what you had anticipated it would be? (Circle A, B, C, D, E or F on answer sheet.)

   A. It is definitely not what I had expected.
   B. In many ways it is not what I had expected.
   C. It is pretty much what I had expected.
   D. It is exactly what I had expected.
   E. I had no clear-cut expectations.
   F. Not applicable.

43. How important is sex to you in your relationship? (Circle A, B, C, D, E or F on answer sheet.)

   A. Very important.
   B. Important.
   C. Important because my husband or partner says it is.
   D. Not important.
   E. Very unimportant.
   F. Not applicable.

44. Many couples find that problems arise because of different sexual needs. Has this been an issue for you? (Circle A, B, C or D on answer sheet.)

   A. Yes; my husband or partner generally wants sex more often than I do.
   B. Yes; I generally want sex more often than my husband or partner does.
   C. No; we have sex about as often as each of us wants.
   D. Not applicable.

45. About how often do you reach orgasm during sexual intercourse? (Circle A, B, C, D, E, F or G on answer sheet.)

   A. Almost all the time.
   B. About three fourths of the time.
   C. About half of the time.
   D. About one fourth of the time.
   E. Infrequently or never, but this is not important to me.
   F. Infrequently or never, and this is a source of resentment or unhappiness for me.
   G. Not applicable.

46. Have you ever pretended to reach orgasm in order to please your husband or partner? (Circle A, B, C, D, E or F on answer sheet.)

   A. Frequently, and I am not bothered by this.
   B. Frequently, but I am resentful or unhappy about this.
   C. Occasionally.
   D. Rarely.
   E. Never.
   F. Not applicable.

47. How soon after your marriage was your first child born? (Circle A, B, C, D, E or F on answer sheet.)

A. Conceived before marriage.
B. Born within first year.
C. Born after one to three years.
D. Born after four to six years.
E. Born after six years.
F. Not applicable.

48. Were all your children planned? (Circle A, B, C or D on answer sheet.)

A. All were planned.
B. Some were planned, some not.
C. None were planned.
D. Not applicable.

Some women find routine household activities to be rewarding and fun; others just tolerate them; others find them unpleasant. For the activities listed in entries 49 through 57, choose the statement that best indicates your viewpoint.

49. Daily cooking for family. (Circle A, B, C, D, E or F on answer sheet.)

A. Very gratifying or a lot of fun.
B. Gratifying or fun.
C. I am indifferent or neutral.
D. Annoying or unpleasant.
E. Very annoying or very unpleasant.
F. Not applicable.

50. Sewing clothes for my family or myself. (Circle A, B, C, D, E or F on answer sheet.)

A. Very gratifying or a lot of fun.
B. Gratifying or fun.
C. I am indifferent or neutral.
D. Annoying or unpleasant.
E. Very annoying or very unpleasant.
F. Not applicable.

51. Keeping house (cleaning, cooking, dishwashing, laundry). (Circle A, B, C, D, E or F on answer sheet.)

A. Very gratifying or a lot of fun.
B. Gratifying or fun.
C. I am indifferent or neutral.
D. Annoying or unpleasant.
E. Very annoying or very unpleasant.
F. Not applicable.

52. Entertaining guests. (Circle A, B, C, D, E or F on answer sheet.)

A. Very gratifying or a lot of fun.
B. Gratifying or fun.
C. I am indifferent or neutral.
D. Annoying or unpleasant.
E. Very annoying or very unpleasant.
F. Not applicable.

53. Feeding infants. (Circle A, B, C, D, E or F on answer sheet.)

A. Very gratifying or a lot of fun.
B. Gratifying or fun.
C. I am indifferent or neutral.
D. Annoying or unpleasant.
E. Very annoying or very unpleasant.
F. Not applicable.

54. Supervising children's activities. (Circle A, B, C, D, E or F on answer sheet.)

A. Very gratifying or a lot of fun.
B. Gratifying or fun.
C. I am indifferent or neutral.
D. Annoying or unpleasant.
E. Very annoying or very unpleasant.
F. Not applicable.

55. Taking children shopping with me. (Circle A, B, C, D, E or F on answer sheet.)

A. Very gratifying or a lot of fun.
B. Gratifying or fun.
C. I am indifferent or neutral.
D. Annoying or unpleasant.
E. Very annoying or very unpleasant.
F. Not applicable.

56. Disciplining children. (Circle A, B, C, D, E or F on answer sheet.)

A. Very gratifying or a lot of fun.
B. Gratifying or fun.
C. I am indifferent or neutral.
D. Annoying or unpleasant.
E. Very annoying or very unpleasant.
F. Not applicable.

57. Decorating my home. (Circle A, B, C, D, E or F on answer sheet.)

A. Very gratifying or a lot of fun.
B. Gratifying or fun.
C. I am indifferent or neutral.
D. Annoying or unpleasant.
E. Very annoying or very unpleasant.
F. Not applicable.

58. Do you hire someone to help with housework? (Circle A, B, C, D, E or F on answer sheet.)

A. Full-time daily help.
B. Part-time daily help.
C. Help once or twice a week.
D. Help once or twice a month.
E. Help on special occasions.
F. Never have hired help.

59. Between you and your husband, who does the housework (cleaning, cooking, dishwashing, laundry) over and above that done by any hired help? (Circle A, B, C, D, E or F on answer sheet.)

A. I do all of it.
B. I do almost all of it.
C. I do over half of it.
D. We split the work 50-50.
E. My husband does over half of it.
F. Not applicable.

60. Between you and your husband, who handles routine child care? (Circle A, B, C, D, E or F on answer sheet.)

A. I do all of it.
B. I do almost all of it.
C. I do over half of it.
D. We split the work 50-50.
E. My husband does over half of it.
F. Not applicable.

61. How satisfied are you with this division of labor? (Circle A, B, C, D or E on answer sheet.)

A. Very satisfied.
B. Relatively satisfied.
C. Relatively dissatisfied.
D. Very dissatisfied.
E. Not applicable.

In general, at what age do you think it would be appropriate for a child to do the things listed in entries 62 through 68? Choose one of the age categories for each answer.

62. Decide what to eat. (Circle A, B, C, D, E or F on answer sheet.)

A. Ages 2-3.
B. Ages 4-5.
C. Ages 6-7.
D. Ages 8-9.
E. Ages 10-12.
F. Over 12.

63. Walk to school by himself. (Circle A, B, C, D, E or F on answer sheet.)

A. Ages 2-3.
B. Ages 4-5.
C. Ages 6-7.
D. Ages 8-9.
E. Ages 10-12.
F. Over 12.

64. Choose what to wear. (Circle A, B, C, D, E or F on answer sheet.)

A. Ages 2-3.
B. Ages 4-5.
C. Ages 6-7.
D. Ages 8-9.
E. Ages 10-12.
F. Over 12.

65. Stay overnight at a friend's house. (Circle A, B, C, D, E or F on answer sheet.)

A. Ages 2-3.
B. Ages 4-5.
C. Ages 6-7.
D. Ages 8-9.
E. Ages 10-12.
F. Over 12.

66. Have his or her own money. (Circle A, B, C, D, E or F on answer sheet.)

A. Ages 2-3.
B. Ages 4-5.
C. Ages 6-7.
D. Ages 8-9.
E. Ages 10-12.
F. Over 12.

67. Decide his or her own bedtime. (Circle A, B, C, D, E or F on answer sheet.)

A. Ages 2-3.   D. Ages 8-9.
B. Ages 4-5.   E. Ages 10-12.
C. Ages 6-7.   F. Over 12.

68. Travel a long distance alone. (Circle A, B, C, D, E or F on answer sheet.)

A. Ages 2-3.   D. Ages 8-9.
B. Ages 4-5.   E. Ages 10-12.
C. Ages 6-7.   F. Over 12.

Do you think boys and girls should be treated differently when they are growing up? For entries 69 through 75, choose the statement that best expresses your viewpoint. If you have children, please answer in terms of the way you actually rear them. If you do not have children or if your children are of one sex only, answer in terms of how you think you would act.

69. Encourage or approve of physical aggression. (Circle A, B, C or D on answer sheet.)

A. Appropriate for son only.   C. Appropriate for both.
B. Appropriate for daughter only.   D. Appropriate for neither.

70. Permit dependence on parent. (Circle A, B, C or D on answer sheet.)

A. Appropriate for son only.   C. Appropriate for both.
B. Appropriate for daughter only.   D. Appropriate for neither.

71. Encourage aspirations to be a doctor. (Circle A, B, C or D on answer sheet.)

A. Appropriate for son only.   C. Appropriate for both.
B. Appropriate for daughter only.   D. Appropriate for neither.

72. Teach to care for younger siblings. (Circle A, B, C or D on answer sheet.)

A. Appropriate for son only.   C. Appropriate for both.
B. Appropriate for daughter only.   D. Appropriate for neither.

73. Touch, kiss and cuddle child after age five. (Circle A, B, C or D on answer sheet.)

A. Appropriate for son only.   C. Appropriate for both.
B. Appropriate for daughter only.   D. Appropriate for neither.

74. Require such chores as washing dishes, dusting furniture, making beds. (Circle A, B, C or D on answer sheet.)

A. Appropriate for son only.   C. Appropriate for both.
B. Appropriate for daughter only.   D. Appropriate for neither.

75. Require such chores as mowing lawn, washing car, taking out garbage. (Circle A, B, C or D on answer sheet.)

A. Appropriate for son only.   C. Appropriate for both.
B. Appropriate for daughter only.   D. Appropriate for neither.

76. Which would you prefer to be, a husband or a wife? (Circle A, B or C on answer sheet.)

A. A husband.   C. Would not marry.
B. A wife.

77. What is your age? (Circle A, B, C, D or E on answer sheet.)

A. Under 20.   D. 30-35.
B. 20-24.   E. Over 35.
C. 25-29.

78. What is your marital status? (Circle A, B, C, D or E on answer sheet.)

A. Single.   D. Separated or divorced.
B. Married, first time.   E. Widowed.
C. Remarried.

79. How many children do you have? (Circle A, B, C or D on answer sheet.)

A. None.   C. Two or three.
B. One.   D. Four or more.

80. How old are your children? (Fill in the blanks on the answer sheet.)

A. Oldest child: _____   D. Fourth child: _____
B. Second child: _____   E. Others: _____ _____ _____
C. Third child: _____

81. Do you plan to have or adopt (more) children? (Circle A, B, C, D, E, F or G on answer sheet.)

A. Yes, one (more).
B. Yes, two or more.
C. I would like to but my husband would not.
D. My husband would like to but I would not.
E. No, neither my husband nor I want to.
F. Undecided.
G. Not married.

82. What is your religious affiliation? (Circle A, B, C, D or E on answer sheet.)

A. Protestant.   D. Agnostic.
B. Catholic.   E. Other.
C. Jewish.

83. How would you describe your political views? (Circle A, B, C, D or E on answer sheet.)

A. Very liberal.   D. Conservative.
B. Liberal.   E. Very conservative.
C. Moderate.

84. What is the highest level of education you have completed? (Circle A, B, C, D, E or F on answer sheet.)

A. Grade school.   D. College graduate.
B. High school.   E. Some graduate school.
C. Some college.   F. Advanced degree.

85. What is the approximate annual income of your family? (Circle A, B, C, D or E on answer sheet.)

A. Less than $5,000.   D. $15,001 to $25,000.
B. $5,000 to $10,000.   E. More than $25,000.
C. $10,001 to $15,000.

86. Are you presently working for pay outside the home? (Circle A, B, C or D on answer sheet.)

A. Have full-time job.   C. No; do volunteer work.
B. Have part-time job.   D. No.

Choose one of the following job categories to answer each question 87 through 90:

87. What is your husband's occupation? (Circle A, B, C, D, E, F, G, H, I or J on answer sheet.)

A. Professional with advanced degree (for example: doctor, lawyer).
B. Teacher, counselor, social worker, nurse.
C. Managerial, administrator, business.
D. White collar, sales, clerical, secretarial.
E. Artist, writer, etc.
F. Technician, skilled worker.
G. Semiskilled or unskilled worker.
H. Student.
I. Other.
J. Not applicable.

88. If you were employed before marriage, what was your occupation? (Circle A, B, C, D, E, F, G, H, I or J on answer sheet.)

A. Professional with advanced degree (for example: doctor, lawyer).
B. Teacher, counselor, social worker, nurse.
C. Managerial, administrator, business.
D. White collar, sales, clerical, secretarial.
E. Artist, writer, etc.
F. Technician, skilled worker.
G. Semiskilled or unskilled worker.
H. Student.
I. Other.
J. Not applicable.

89. If you are presently employed, what is your occupation? (Circle A, B, C, D, E, F, G, H, I or J on answer sheet.)

A. Professional with advanced degree (for example: doctor, lawyer).
B. Teacher, counselor, social worker, nurse.
C. Managerial, administrator, business.
D. White collar, sales, clerical, secretarial.
E. Artist, writer, etc.
F. Technician, skilled worker.
G. Semiskilled or unskilled worker.
H. Student.
I. Other.
J. Not applicable.

90. Did having children affect your working life in any of the following ways? (Circle A, B, C, D, E, F or G on answer sheet.)

A. I stopped working temporarily, with reluctance.
B. I stopped working temporarily, with pleasure.
C. I stopped working for good, with reluctance.
D. I stopped working for good, with pleasure.
E. I continued working.
F. I continued working, but on a part-time basis.
G. Not applicable.

91. Regardless of whether you are presently employed or not, what is your husband's attitude toward your working? (Circle A, B, C, D, E or F on answer sheet.)

A. Strongly approves of my working.
B. Generally approves of my working.
C. He is neutral or indifferent to my working.
D. He generally disapproves of my working.
E. He strongly disapproves of my working.
F. Not applicable.

92. Are you presently a member of any of these organizations for women? (On answer sheet, circle letters of all that apply.)

A. A women's political group (for example, Democratic, Republican or other party committee).
B. A local community group, charity, women's auxiliary or church organization.
C. The League of Women Voters.
D. A professional women's association (for example, women doctors).
E. A Women's Liberation discussion or action group.
F. The National Organization for Women.
G. I don't belong to any women's organization.

93. In general, how do you feel about your present employment situation? (Circle A, B, C, D or E on answer sheet.)

A. Very satisfied.
B. Satisfied.
C. Dissatisfied; I wish I didn't have to work.
D. Dissatisfied; I wish I had greater or different career involvement.
E. Not applicable.

94. If you are not presently employed, how do you generally feel about your situation? (Circle A, B, C or D on answer sheet.)

A. Very satisfied.
B. Satisfied.
C. Dissatisfied; I wish I had full- or part-time employment.
D. Not applicable.

95. Do you think you have been discriminated against *as a woman* in any of these ways? (On answer sheet, circle letters of all that apply.)

A. Admission to college or graduate school.
B. Hiring, promotions or job titling.
C. Salary.
D. In classes or counseling in high school.
E. The way men react to you when you are discussing things about which you have knowledge.
F. The way your parents reacted to your career ambitions.

96. What is your attitude toward the Women's Liberation Movement (WLM)? (Circle A, B, C, D, E or F on answer sheet.)

A. Strongly in favor.
B. Generally in favor.
C. Slightly in favor.
D. Slightly opposed.
E. Generally opposed.
F. Strongly opposed.

97. What kind of women do you think are *most* likely to join the WLM? (Circle A, B, C, D or E on answer sheet.)

A. Women with sexual problems.
B. Aggressive or angry women who dislike men.
C. Neurotic women who think they have been discriminated against.
D. Well-adjusted women with legitimate grievances.
E. Very healthy women fighting a sick system.

98. Do you think the WLM will affect *your* life? (Circle A, B or C on answer sheet.)

A. Yes, for the better.
B. Yes, for the worse.
C. Not especially.

99. If the WLM gets the things it wants, do you think your *daughter's* life will be affected? (Circle A, B, C or D on answer sheet.)

A. Yes; she will have more opportunities than I did.
B. Yes; she will have more difficulties than I did.
C. Not especially.
D. Not applicable.

100. Has the Women's Liberation Movement affected your feelings in any of the following ways? (On answer sheet, circle letters of all that apply.)

A. I like women more now.
B. I dislike women more now.
C. I get angry at men more often.
D. I am more sympathetic to men.
E. I resent male privileges more.
F. I feel better able to combine marriage and career.
G. I feel less able to combine marriage and career.
H. I am more aware of discrimination against women.
I. I feel closer to my husband.
J. I feel more distant from my husband.
K. My feelings haven't really changed.

REDBOOK

Pretesting for Most Appealing Products

Offering any new product for the first time is a gamble at best. But there are ways to hedge the bets. For example, for a book series published by Time-Life, they must learn which book in the series has the broadest appeal. Featuring the most appealing book in the series as the lead book greatly expands the universe of potential subscribers for the series. There are at least two ways for the publisher to determine the book in the series with the broadest appeal. (1) A questionnaire mailing listing all titles and requesting a ranking will give a clue; (2) actual test mailings featuring different lead books will likewise disclose relative appeal. The first method is far less costly.

An innovative approach, developed by *Reader's Digest,* for predetermining the relative appeal of merchandise offerings is worthy of study. Reproduced on the following pages is an eight-page questionnaire designed to determine product preferences among *Reader's Digest* prospects. The cost of this approach is peanuts against what it would cost to prepare a full-blown mailing package for each of six potential product offerings.

A-5

Reader's Digest
Pleasantville, N.Y. 10570

E 2438

```
              04566 21432    34678
              MR ROBERT STONE
              606 LAUREL AVE.
              WILMETTE. IL 60091
```

Dear Friend:

I am writing to ask for your help -- nothing more. For many years we have been able to offer a large number of very worthwhile, reasonably-priced products to our Digest friends and their families. We have been able to do this because our customers have been kind enough to tell us -- in advance -- what products were of most interest to them.

Now, we are asking you to help us. On the following pages we have briefly outlined six new products now in the planning stage here at Reader's Digest -- exciting new Home Entertainment products that we think you and your family will find useful and enjoyable. Would you help us by indicating those that appeal most to you.

It will only take a few minutes of your time to answer our survey and return it to us in the self-addressed, postage-paid envelope we have provided. But I want to thank you right now for spending these few minutes with us, helping us decide which of these products will provide our friends with exciting new adventures in listening pleasure and home convenience and enjoyment.

In order to make the results of this survey as complete as possible, as soon as possible, we would deeply appreciate your early reply to our questionnaire. We have used your name and address above merely for addressing purposes and your reply, of course, involves no commitment on your part at all.

Once again, our sincere thanks for your assistance in this important project. I can assure you it will help us continue to bring you what we consider to be the greatest bargains in home entertainment on the market today.

Yours very truly,

Carolyn Davis

How to Complete this Questionnaire

Inside, following each description of the six new Home Entertainment products the Reader's Digest is thinking of producing, please give us some idea of how likely you would be to send for each on 7 days' approval if it were offered to you through the mail. Please consider each product separately and mark *only one* square under each description to indicate:

I would probably order this product on approval for 7 days.	I might order this product on approval for 7 days.	I have some interest in this product, but am unlikely to order it on approval for 7 days.	I have almost no interest in this product.

Reader's Digest Digital Clock Radio

Lullaby yourself to sleep. Wake up to a polite buzzer or your favorite morning radio show . . . or both! Find out the time at a glance. Even bring yourself up to date on the weather, with the special federal government VHF Weather Alert.

This space-age designed console does it all—on AM and FM.

Look what you get in one precision-made, decorator styled package:

1. AM-FM Tuner—Ultra-sensitive AM-FM Tuner eliminates static, reproduces fine tonal shading with concert hall fidelity.

2. AM-FM Weather Alert Selector—Choose your radio band at the touch of a button.

3. Automatic Frequency Control—Found only in the finest FM units. So you'll find it here, built right in, to eliminate annoying drift from the station of your choice.

4. Automatic Gain Control—Extra power to pull in distant AM and FM stations loud and clear.

5. Flawless Reception—Sharp AM for sports, music, news; rich FM for non-stop music, concerts, talk shows.

6. Powerful Speaker—3½″ permanent magnet dynamic cone speaker.

7. Solid State—Provides instant on, instant off control, trouble-free operation.

8. Indirect Tuning—An ingenious feature. Makes fine tuning a breeze.

9. Fine Craftsmanship—Quality materials and highest inspection standards assure top performance, long life.

10. Sturdy Construction—Rugged chassis of high-impact design to resist shock, to last . . . and last . . . and last.

11. AC Outlet—Lets you plug in lamp, tape recorder, any electrical appliance of up to 300 watts.

12. VHF Antenna—Pulls in up-to-the-minute National Weather Service bulletins.

13. Cool Running Performance—A special thermistor keeps radio cool. Never a worry about "hot spot" marks on your fine furniture.

14. Speaker Jack—Everybody sleeping? Slip the bonus Pillow Speaker under your pillow, lull yourself to sleep without disturbing others. Comes with its own volume control, too. Not many do.

15. Bold-Face Numerals—Now you can easily read the exact time, to the second, day or night. Big, bold Digital Clock numbers are illuminated by radio's own neon light system.

16. Sleep Switch—Listen to up to 120 minutes of music while you drift off to sleep. Later, your radio goes to sleep, too . . . completely, automatically.

17. 24-Hour Timer—Triggers AM-FM radio or buzzer alarm or both whenever you want . . . set the alarm up to 24 hours in advance.

18. Snooze Bar—Go ahead, catch that "extra wink" of sleep. And do it without fear of over-sleeping. Simply push bar and alarm turns off . . . only to call you again in 10 minutes, as many times as you want.

19. Weather Alert—When you want the weather, there it is—at the push of a button. Ever hear of such convenience in a clock radio?

20. Earphone Jack—Plug in your BONUS Personal Earphone for quiet listening, without disturbing others.

21. Conference Call Monitor—Now telephone calls can be amplified for the whole family through the speaker of your clock radio, using your BONUS Conference Call Monitor. (Great for the businessman, too!)

22. Patch Cord Jack—Another BONUS feature, your Patch Cord allows you to tape the best of AM or FM on your tape recorder.

23. One Year Guarantee—One of the biggest features of all. Your AM-FM Digital Clock Radio comes with full One Year Guarantee on all parts and labor—not the 90-day warranty you've seen elsewhere.

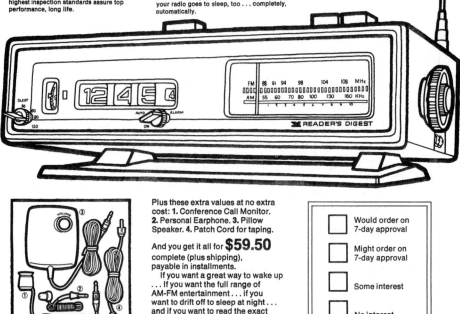

Plus these extra values at no extra cost: **1.** Conference Call Monitor. **2.** Personal Earphone. **3.** Pillow Speaker. **4.** Patch Cord for taping.

And you get it all for **$59.50** complete (plus shipping), payable in installments.

If you want a great way to wake up . . . If you want the full range of AM-FM entertainment . . . if you want to drift off to sleep at night . . . and if you want to read the exact time any time . . . then you want the new Reader's Digest exciting Digital Clock Radio.

☐	Would order on 7-day approval
☐	Might order on 7-day approval
☐	Some interest
☐	No interest

A

ALL READER'S DIGEST PRODUCTS CARRY OUR MONEY-BACK GUARANTEE OF SATISFACTION.

Reader's Digest
Classic-Folk Guitar and Complete
Beginner's Guitar Course

Great new fun for the whole family!

You might expect to pay $90 for the guitar alone — but you get all this for only $54.50 complete!

Rosewood concert-size classic-folk guitar. Six steel strings. 31½″ length. Metal tailpiece, metal gear tuning. Complete with shoulder strap, carrying bag, pick and pitch pipe for easy tuning. An outstanding value!

Look what else you get: the easiest and most enjoyable method we've ever seen to learn how to play . . . or how to play better. Color-coded chord cards slip right under the strings. Can be used over and over again. 24 different chords to learn right away. And a complete instruction book with 32 favorite songs for all ages that you will be playing beautifully in a matter of minutes!

Here is a truly unique, new Reader's Digest quality value that is fun, educational, easy and relaxing. Full one-year guarantee from Reader's Digest.

Complete outfit only **$54.50** (plus shipping), payable in installments.

- [ ] Would order on 7-day approval
- [ ] Might order on 7-day approval
- [ ] Some interest
- [ ] No interest

A ALL READER'S DIGEST PRODUCTS CARRY OUR MONEY-BACK GUARANTEE OF SATISFACTION.

Reader's Digest Fully Portable Electronic Pocket Calculator

Ever worry, as you approached the checkout counter with your filled-up cart of groceries, that you weren't going to have enough money to pay for it all? Or that you hadn't selected the most economical sizes of canned goods or cereals or hamburger?

Ever worry, as you wrote out checks for the month's bills, that you weren't going to have enough money in the bank to cover them all—or even that your bank balance might not be correct to begin with?

Ever worry, as you slaved over your income tax forms, that your arithmetic wasn't accurate and would be subject to review by the tax people? That your forms would be sent back because of a simple mistake?

Now, finally, you can spend well under $100 for a sophisticated, accurate, dependable, *electronic* calculator that does it all for you . . . that goes along with you, in your pocket . . . that adds, subtracts, multiplies, divides . . . that has an automatic square-root multiplier, on-off automatic clear power switch, negative indicator . . . that has an instant, silent 16-position

keyboard for right- or left-handed people . . . that has a six-digit entry with 12-digit readout . . . that needs no tape because it shows totals electronically, like a TV screen, on a large illuminated number display . . . that figures true credit balance in addition and subtraction . . . that has a floating decimal normally found only on much more expensive machines . . . that has a full one-year guarantee . . . and that measures a mere 3¼" x 6" and weighs a comfortable 20 ounces.

Plugs in at home or office. Uses rechargeable batteries at the store, in a car, on a plane, in a classroom. Clears the last entry without clearing the other calculations. Performs memory recall—needs no scratch notes or re-entry of intermediate answers.

And the actual size is as shown!

Its size is tiny—and so is its price. But it's a giant in the ways it saves you time, work and money.

Only **$69.50** (plus shipping), payable in installments. Batteries included.

Bright "TV screen" readout

Mini-portable

Rechargeable

Floating Decimal

Memory Recall

Clear entry

Silent-touch keyboard

Adds, subtracts, multiplies, divides

Negative indicator

Battery indicator

AC adaptor

Reverse key

(Shown Actual Size)

A mini-computer— right in your pocket!

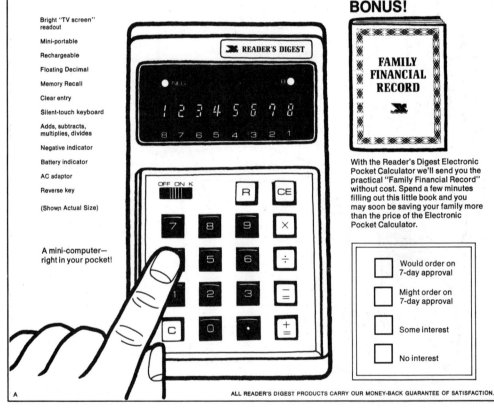

BONUS!

FAMILY FINANCIAL RECORD

With the Reader's Digest Electronic Pocket Calculator we'll send you the practical "Family Financial Record" without cost. Spend a few minutes filling out this little book and you may soon be saving your family more than the price of the Electronic Pocket Calculator.

☐ Would order on 7-day approval

☐ Might order on 7-day approval

☐ Some interest

☐ No interest

A

Reader's Digest Nature Kit

A brand-new, all-in-one way to see nature close up—and discover the endless array of our "secret" world!

A new hobby—and an exciting new way to have fun *learning!*

Look what you get: 16 power portable microscope, 8 power binocular, 324-page Reader's Digest book called *An Invitation to Wonder*, and a handsome shoulder bag to tote it all with you.

Here is an investment for every parent who is concerned about the world his or her children will be living in . . . for youngsters who need to know more about our natural world . . . for vacationers and campers who want to get closer to nature . . . for everyone who collects stamps, coins, shells, minerals and other small objects.

2-Stage 16 Power Microscope

Primary stage. Observe specimens up to 1¾" x 2". See them 16 times bigger than life. *See-through stage.* Observe specimens in their own environment. See them 8 times bigger than life.

Fine stage adjustment brings up every subject clear and sharp.

Built-in light source with on/off switch brings out every detail. Battery powered. (Batteries included.)

Two dissecting instruments for the amateur biologist or zoologist.

Three specimen collecting containers . . . specimen hold-down clip . . . microphotography camera adapter for all instamatic cameras . . . custom field carrying case.

Completely portable with rugged polyethylene construction built for outdoors.

Ideal not only for amateur naturalists—but for stamp collectors, coin collectors, rock "hounds," butterfly collectors, photographers, hobbyists of all ages.

8 x 30 Removable Binoculars

Precision molded, stronger-than-steel fiberglass. Shockproof, waterproof, it even floats. The all-purpose 8-power glasses lift out from the microscope compartment. Has its own neck strap.

Ideal for birdwatching, moon watching, wildlife observation. A really rugged instrument that can increase your enjoyment of all outdoor activities: hunting, fishing, camping, flying, skiing, boating, auto races, horse races, football and baseball, much more. A camera adapter is included for telephotography.

"An Invitation to Wonder" Field Book

A big, new Reader's Digest book that can help your family experience the reality of life around you—first hand. Spiral bound, 324 pages big, giant-sized 9" x 12". Filled to brimming with rare and wonderful full-color photographs. Designed in four parts to help you explore the mysteries and marvels of nature in an exciting, "fun" way: 1. The Miracle of Living Things. 2. Exploring in Your Own Backyard. 3. Protecting Our Precious Heritage. 4. Earth in All Her Glory.

The microscope/binocular with picture-filled Reader's Digest book, rugged shoulder case—the entire Nature Kit complete.

Only **$59.50** total
(plus shipping),
payable in installments.

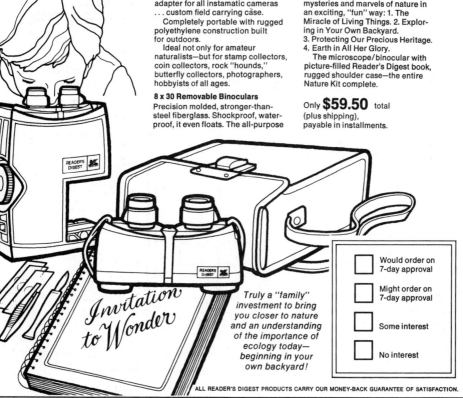

Truly a "family" investment to bring you closer to nature and an understanding of the importance of ecology today—beginning in your own backyard!

☐	Would order on 7-day approval
☐	Might order on 7-day approval
☐	Some interest
☐	No interest

A

ALL READER'S DIGEST PRODUCTS CARRY OUR MONEY-BACK GUARANTEE OF SATISFACTION.

Reader's Digest
Do-It-Yourself
Rug Making Kit

Want to make something new . . . easy . . . beautiful?
Want to discover the fun of a brand-new hobby? Now
you can create your own stunning versions of the new
popular art form called the Bernat "Latch-Hook
Technique."

Everything is provided for you in one complete kit.
No experience required—no looms or other fancy
equipment needed.

Choose from nine authentic, original designs and
make a 22" x 36" rug or tapestry. Kit contains 40 skeins
of pre-cut wool yarn with 360 strands per packet. Also
included: color-stenciled, color-coded rug canvas . . .
latch-hook . . . rug binding . . . and complete, illustrated,
full-color instructions that tell you and show you how to
go on and make all sorts of beautiful things: pillows,
chair cushions, fireside seats, ottoman covers, wall
hangings and many more decorator accent items for
your home.

Enjoy the lasting satisfaction of personal accomplishment . . . create fine gifts which are truly "handmade"
. . . and begin a whole new hobby that's easy, relaxing,
fun! Your Rug Making Kit can be just the beginning of a
brand-new, easy-to-do-it-yourself activity.

Only **$29.95** complete
(plus shipping),
payable in installments.

☐	Would order on 7-day approval
☐	Might order on 7-day approval
☐	Some interest
☐	No interest

ALL READER'S DIGEST PRODUCTS CARRY OUR MONEY-BACK GUARANTEE OF SATISFACTION.

316

Reader's Digest
6-Band Globemaster Portable Radio

Enjoy the fun of radio again. Now dial six full bands in one remarkable instrument: AM, FM, Shortwave, Police, Air, Marine—all full bands (not partial, not combined) so you and your family can go adventuring, via radio, around the world! Guaranteed to pull in stations up to 10,000 miles away!

A turn of the Dial-O-Map can take you to a different time, a different place. Dial the Police band and pick up calls to patrol cars . . . dial the Air band and eavesdrop on plane-to-plane communications . . . dial the Marine band and monitor ship-to-shore broadcasts . . . dial FM and listen to static-free, high fidelity FM . . . and dial AM for music, news, sports.

Globemaster is the ultimate in radio sets, now for a new low price from Reader's Digest! **Look what you get:**

- Time zone Dial-O-Map
- Instant band selector
- Color-coded tuning
- Twin telescoping antennas
- Fine tuning, squelch, volume controls
- Pluggable, portable—take it along with you or plug it in at home
- Automatic Frequency Control for FM
- Precision jack system
- Built-in bar antenna for AM, Marine
- Easy-access battery compartment
- Solid state circuitry
- 8 OHM 4" x 6" speaker
- Decorator styled
- Padded cabinet
- Shock-resistant construction
- Spring-loaded dial cover
- Full one-year guarantee from Reader's Digest

All for only **$84.50** complete
(plus shipping)
and you can pay in installments

Now radio is fun again—with the Reader's Digest 6-band Globemaster Portable Radio!

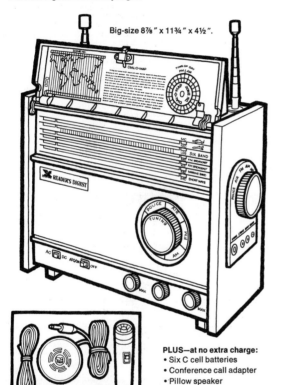

Big-size 8⅞" x 11¾" x 4½".

PLUS—at no extra charge:
- Six C cell batteries
- Conference call adapter
- Pillow speaker
- Hand microphone for public address
- Cassette patch cord for taping
- External antenna wire
- Personal ear plug
- Two booklets (Shortwave, and VHF Band Guide, Marine Band Guide)

☐	Would order on 7-day approval
☐	Might order on 7-day approval
☐	Some interest
☐	No interest

A

If you have any further comments on the products described in this folder, or
suggestions for other products you would like, we would welcome your views here.

_____

_____

_____

_____

_____

_____

_____

_____

_____

_____

_____

_____

_____

_____

_____

_____

_____

_____

_____

Focus Interviews

Still another avenue of research open to direct marketers is what is commonly known as the focus interview. Feelings about the value of such interviews are divided. Those who put little value on focus interviews point out that what people tell you they will do and what they actually do are usually two different things. They further point out that people tend to answer questions in the way they think will make them appear intelligent. These criticisms are valid, in my opinion.

However, I have seen great things come from focus interviews. Trained psychologists should conduct such interviews. Seasoned interpretation is a key factor in making focus interviews valuable.

On one occasion I was privy to the transcripts of a focus interview conducted by a trained psychologist for a major direct marketer. A panel of typical customers were brought together to discuss attitudes about buying merchandise by mail and attitudes about the offerings of this direct marketer in particular. In confirmation of the fact that people tend to tell little white lies when interviewed—everyone in the group had purchased merchandise from this firm, but only one admitted that he had! On this basis, one could conclude the focus interview was a complete failure. But here are some of the things which came out of it.

1. The majority of those interviewed stated that the direct marketer consistently offered off-brand merchandise. The fact was that this marketer consistently offered merchandise produced by such well-known manufacturers as G.E., Polaroid, and Westinghouse.
2. Interviews disclosed very clearly that the group felt merchandise was overpriced. In fact, all merchandise offerings were indeed very fairly priced. Each offering was a good value.

Armed with this information, the marketer made major changes in promotion pieces, putting much greater emphasis on major brand names; proof of value was stepped up; and testimonials proving customer satisfaction were used to back the major points.

So, focus interviews should not be ruled out. As I say, seasoned interpretation is the key to their value.

Telescopic Testing

In general advertising, Starch reports are used regularly to determine readership of advertising. Starch reports have also been helpful in measuring the readership of direct response print advertising. But because, by the very nature of direct response advertising, effectiveness can be measured by actual responses, the effectiveness of ads is measured much more easily.

For many decades A-B splits have been considered *the* way to test ads in publications. Availability of A-B splits was a breakthrough of sorts, in that publications found a way to run two entirely different ads on an every-other-copy basis in a single edition. When the coupons were counted, the advertiser could be reasonably certain ad A did definitely have more pulling power than ad B—or vice versa.

But the advertiser never did know what would happen if he had been able to run ad C against A and B, and additionally, ads D, E, F, and G—all simultaneously, all in the same edition, all under *measurable* conditions. There was no way to know.

But now it is possible through a technique appropriately known as telescopic testing. Telescopic testing is simply the process of telescoping an entire season of test ads into one master test program. (Telescopic testing was alluded to in Chapter 11.)

319

Regional editions of publications, and other developments, make telescopic testing possible. Indeed, with regional editions you can telescope a year's testing sequences into a single insertion, testing a multiplicity of ads simultaneously.

TV Guide offers the optimum opportunity for telescopic testing. It publishes 84 different regional editions. So testing ten or 15 different ads or ad variations simultaneously is simple. *Time,* with eight regional editions, makes it possible to test nine different ads or ad variations simultaneously.

Telescopic testing sounds complicated, but it really isn't. This is not to say it isn't essential that tests be structured properly to make results measurable, meaningful, and projectable. It is!

Tom Collins, a pioneer in telescopic testing, has established this rule of thumb for estimating the minimum circulation you should buy for your ad tests to make results meaningful.

First, start by assuming you need an average of 200 responses per appeal to be statistically valid. Then, multiply 200 times your allowable advertising cost per response. Finally, multiply again by the number of key numbers in the test. This will give you the total minimum expenditure required to get meaningful results.

To clarify the technique further, let's say you want to test four new ads against a control ad, which we will call ad A.

Your tests for the four new ads against the control ad will be structured as follows: A vs. B; A vs. C; A vs. D; A vs. E.

Thus we have a total of five ads requiring eight different keys. (Ad A, the control ad, is being tested against a different ad in four separate instances and therefore requires four different keys.)

To read the results in this kind of test, we simply convert ad A to 100% in all regions being tested, and the other ads to plus or minus 100%, depending on results achieved. In this way, ad C can be compared with ad E, for instance, even though they were not directly tested against one another.

Now, let's say we want to test these four new ads in *TV Guide* against the control ad. Further, let's assume, using the Collins formula, we need a circulation of two million plus to get 200 or more replies for each side of each two-way split.

Here's the type of schedule which would be placed in *TV Guide* to accomplish the objective.

Split 1 — Ad A vs. Ad B		*Split 2 — Ad A vs. Ad C*	
Edition	Circ.	Edition	Circ.
San Francisco Metro	604,932	Philadelphia	515,213
Pittsburgh	330,249	Cleveland	297,169
Detroit	221,279	Kansas City	188,533
N. Texas	178,137	W. New England	184,665
E. N.Y. State	162,833	No. Carolina	174,514
Iowa	157,303	Colorado	164,991
Phoenix	152,394	N. Illinois	123,599
W. Illinois	53,248	Gulf Coast	95,952
N. Indiana	84,238	Minn. – St. Paul	102,379
Nashville	76,253	Central California	87,878
	2,020,866	S.E. Texas	85,555
			2,020,448

Split 3—Ad A vs. Ad D		Split 4—Ad A vs. Ad E	
Edition	Circ.	Edition	Circ.
So. Ohio	464,461	E. New England	595,604
Michigan State	269,412	Chicago Metro	293,454
W. N.Y. State	196,688	Wisconsin	227,519
Central Indiana	181,632	Central Florida	183,464
San Diego	157,790	Seattle–Tacoma	150,582
N. New England	157,906	Oklahoma State	168,330
Portland	126,235	St. Louis	107,610
E. Virginia	122,727	Utah–Idaho	79,987
Kansas State	88,026	Oregon State	56,630
Tucson	56,360	E. Illinois	75,520
N. Dakota	33,745	Missouri	84,910
E. Washington State	100,865		2,023,610
Evansville–Paducah	65,407		
	2,021,254		

Note: A careful study of the markets selected for each split (region) will show that all markets are balanced geographically.

A recap of this structured test reads as follows: Five simultaneous ad tests, distributed among 45 markets, with a total circulation of 8,086,178, at a total cost of $19,950, or a CPM of $2.47. Historically, winning ads from this type of structured test can be determined within two to three weeks of issue date!

Telescopic testing is not limited to regional editions of publications. Newspaper inserts serve as an ideal vehicle for telescopic testing. The test pieces are intermixed at the printing plant before shipping to the newspaper. However, all test pieces must be exactly the same size. Otherwise, newspapers cannot handle them on their automatic inserting equipment.

Full page card inserts in magazines are still another way to test a multiplicity of ads simultaneously. Scores of magazines now accept such inserts.

It is important to remember that, in telescopic testing, we are looking for breakthroughs—not small differences. As Collins puts it, "We are not merely testing ads, we are testing *hypotheses*.

"Then when a hypothesis appears to have been proven by the results, it is often possible to construct other, even more successful ads, on the same hypothesis."

Test hypotheses seem to fall into four main categories:

1. What is the best *price* and/or offer?
2. Who is the best prospect?
3. What is the most appealing product *advantage?*
4. What is the most important ultimate *benefit?* (By "ultimate benefit" we mean the satisfaction of such basic human needs as pride, admiration, safety, wealth, peace of mind, and so on.)

U.S. School of Music is a prime example of an advertiser who uses hypotheses in determining the type of ads to be developed for telescopic testing. Let's take our second test hypothesis as an example: Who is the best prospect? U.S. School of Music established this hypothesis: "A middle-aged woman interested in piano is a better prospect than a teen-age male interested in guitar."

To test the soundness of this hypothesis, two ads were prepared with identical copy. The headline for both was, "The Secret of Teaching Yourself Music." The only difference was that one ad carried a photo of a female middle-aged piano player (tying into the hypothesis); the other ad carried a photo of a male teen-age guitar player (testing the validity of the hypothesis). The ad with the photo of the male teen-age guitar player did 55% better than the one with the photo of the female middle-aged piano player!

Shown below are the control ad and two of eight new ads tested against the U.S. School of Music control. Here are the scores of the eight new ads against the control ad: (1) 41% poorer, (2) 11% better, (3) 30% poorer, (4) 67% poorer, (5) 56% poorer, (6) 36% poorer, (7) 72% poorer, (8) 55% better. So the final score reads: Six losers and two winners.

And therein lies the great value of telescopic testing. Under the old A-B split method, if only No. 1 had been tested against the control, the control ad would have prevailed, chewing up many additional thousands of dollars of the advertising budget. And Ad No. 2, which was but 11% better, would have required much retesting. It could have been a year down the road before the advertiser got down to Ad No. 8, which was the real breakthrough.

Three ads from nine-way split used by U.S. School of Music: Ad A was control ad. Ad B did 56% poorer than the control. Ad C, with the only change being a photograph, pulled 55% better than the control.

Three ads from nine-way split used by U.S. School of Music: Ad A was control ad. Ad B did 56% poorer than the control. Ad C, with the only change being a photograph, pulled 55% better than the control.

There is but one question which may run through the minds of astute advertisers about the validity of telescopic testing. It is this: "Can the results of telescopic testing derived from broad audience consumer magazines like *TV Guide* be reliably applied to special interest publications like *McCall's, Ladies' Home Journal,* and *Psychology Today?*" The best person to answer this question is Collins, who says, "We've now measured over 200 different ads through the medium of telescopic testing. Each time we have reconfirmed in special interest publications—control ad vs. breakthrough ad—the breakthrough ad has emerged the big winner."

Innovative Direct Mail Tests

Just as wisdom dictates that we look for breakthroughs in print advertising tests, so it dictates we look for breakthroughs in direct mail tests. In Chapter 2, we got an insight about the vast differences experienced in mailing list tests. In Chapter 8, we learned of

322

the vast differences in response depending on propositions. In Chapter 9, we learned of the great differences in response depending on mailing packages. In Chapter 2, we likewise learned the importance of timing. It is in these key areas, plus product testing, that real breakthroughs are possible. The secret of finding breakthroughs is in being innovative in your tests — testing for the big things.

Consider this case history, which is a classic example of how breakthroughs come about in direct mail selling. A publisher who sells business services by mail and through space advertising decided to test an unusual hypothesis. His hypothesis was, "Subscribers to a magazine are more likely to respond to a direct mail solicitation if a preprint of a forthcoming advertisement is enclosed with the mailing piece."

To test the hypothesis, the publisher made arrangements with the trade publication to rent the entire subscription list for a two-way test. One-half of the subscription list would receive the basic mailing package with a preprint of a forthcoming full page ad.

The other half of the subscription list would receive the basic mailing package without the preprint of the forthcoming ad.

The mailing was made 30 days prior to the appearance of the full page ad in the publication. Difference in results was dramatic. The mailing package featuring the preprint outpulled the standard mailing package without the preprint by 107%.

The 107% increase takes into account the increased pull of the preprint mailing package only. It is more than likely the preprint mailing increased readership of the full page ad when it appeared in the publication the following month. If that is true, increased response from the ad was an extra bonus.

But let's not assume any extra benefits from the space advertising. Let's apply the cold arithmetic which successful direct marketers use. Let's see how many orders we need in excess of break-even on our preprint mailings to pay for the mailings, plus the space advertising.

For this purpose we have taken a group of trade publications at random from Standard Rate & Data, showing circulation for each and cost of a black and white page at the time this manuscript was prepared.

We've assumed a mailing cost of $150 per thousand for our preprint mailing, a profit contribution of $7.50 per order (profit contribution = selling price less product cost and overhead), therefore a break-even of 2% for the mailing.

Chart 1, Break-Even Point, clearly indicates the very small increase over break-even needed for the preprint mailing to absorb all advertising cost, without counting orders which would come from the space ad — all of which would bring a clear profit of $7.50 each.

Chart 1. Break-Even Point

Publication	Circulation	Cost 1 page b&w	*Add. orders needed to pay cost of ad	% increase needed for pre-print mailing
Modern Manufacturing Pub.	94,872	$1,990	259	0.27%
Administrative Management	49,326	1,420	189	0.38
Air Conditioning and Re- frigeration Business	43,233	1,250	166	0.38
Package Engineering	51,221	1,780	237	0.46
National Petroleum News . . .	21,631	1,280	171	0.79
Industrial Photography	38,849	1,395	186	0.48
Product Engineering . .	107,551	1,730	224	0.21

*Profit contribution = $7.50 per order

So the break-even point certainly seems attainable. For example, the preprint mailing to the *Modern Manufacturing* subscription list would have to pull only 2.27% instead of 2% to pay all mailing costs, plus space advertising; *Product Engineering*, 2.21%; etc.

But direct marketers want to do better than break even. They want to make money. Let's apply our example. Let's say we do 107% better than break-even. Here are how some of the profit figures would look, after paying all direct mail costs and all space costs. (At 107% of break-even we'd pull 41.4 orders per thousand, giving us a profit of $160.50 per thousand after paying mailing costs.)

Chart 2. Profit Figures

Publication	Quantity mailed	Total mailing profit	Space cost	Net profit
Modern Manufacturing .	94,872	$15,225	$1,990	$13,235
Package Engineering .	51,221	8,220	1,780	6,440
Product Engineering ..	107,551	17,261	1,730	15,531

As you can see from these profit figures, even if the preprint mailing did only 25% to 50% better than break-even, it would still be a good deal for the direct marketer.

Testing for breakthroughs. There's where the real profit possibilities are.

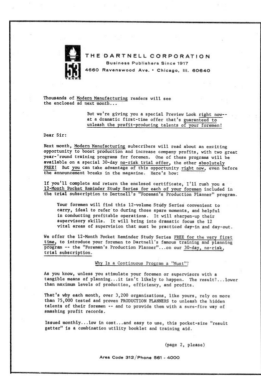

Testing Components vs. Testing Mailing Packages

In the endless search for breakthroughs, the question continually arises: In direct mail, should we test components or mailing packages? There are two schools of thought on this, but the prevailing one is that the big breakthroughs come about by testing completely different mailing packages vs. testing individual components within a mailing package. Something can be learned from each procedure, of course. But, in my opinion, the more logical procedure is to first find the big differences in mailing packages and then follow with tests of individual components. Some of the components in the losing packages can make the winning packages even better.

Under package testing, you start with a complete concept and build all the components to fit the image of the concept. Consider the differences between these two package concepts:

Package #1:
9 × 12 envelope
8-page letter stapled together
8½ × 11 order form, with perforated stub

Package #2:
#10 window envelope
8½ × 11 computer letter — printed both sides
4-page illustrated circular
order form, 8½ × 3⅔

The differences between these two package concepts are considerable. Chances are great that there will be a considerable difference in response. Once the winning package evolves, component tests make considerable sense. Let us say the 9 × 12 package is the winner. A logical subsequent test would be to fold the same inserts into a 6 × 9 envelope. A reply envelope may be considered as an additional test. Computerizing the first page of the eight-page letter could be still another test.

Determining Sample Sizes

The most nagging question of all relating to testing techniques is, "How big should my sample be in order to get valid results?" Probability tables (Chapter 2) are the ultimate answer for the purist. However, a careful study of the tables will indicate that certain percentages of expected response, at certain error limits, require fantastic test quantities. To be statistically accurate for certain expected responses at certain error limits could require budgets well beyond the realm of practicality. For instance, it is conceivable that statistical accuracy could require 100,000 mailing pieces on each side of a test. If you were testing six different packages, each against the control package, a total of 1.2 million mailing pieces would be required. At an average cost of $150 per thousand mailing pieces, total test budget would be $180,000. Obviously — impractical.

Orlan Gaeddert, specialist in circulation research at Time-Life for 16 years, gives some alternatives to this problem in an interview he had with Rose Harper, president of Lewis Kleid Co.

To the question "When are large samples necessary; when are small ones adequate?" Gaeddert answers:

"The proper sample size is determined by two factors.
— the normal variation that is anticipated for any random sample
— the degree of risk that the user is willing to accept

"You can always make your sampling tolerance as small as you like by increasing the sample size. Do keep in mind, however, that to cut the tolerance in half, you must increase the sample fourfold. This axiom holds for two random samples drawn in exactly the same way.

"The risk factor involves subjective judgment. When you know your product and market, you can accept the larger risks of relatively small samples. When trying a new product, or a novel promotional concept, it is desirable to minimize risks by running larger tests — perhaps retesting — before making a decision.

"The acceptable risk is also conditioned by what you are testing. Low markups require larger samples since there is little room for error. Price tests demand high accuracy and large samples. A large sample is needed initially if you want to track payments or later purchases.

"When profit potential is small — often true of 'one shots' — it is not worth using large samples or extensive retesting. Occasionally a new product test or an experiment with a new procedure has very high costs. You may, for example, wish to minimize exposure in the market place. In such instances, one must take calculated risks and use minimum size samples.

"When testing two packages with roughly similar costs, you can stand rather large sampling tolerances. If the costs are quite different, the solution is complicated."

To the question, "How big is the variation for typical samples?" Gaeddert answers:

"Chances are that the tolerances for your tests are wider than you think. Assuming that your testing procedures are well controlled and that you are using perfect Nth name samples, a typical test of 10,000 should pull within 10% of the true value about two-thirds of the time. The other one-third of your tests will be off by 10 to 20%. In only 38% of your tests can you hope to be within 5% (+ or −) of the true value. If you don't have the ideal Nth name sample or have more than the normal number of blemishes in the procedure, your tolerances will be wider than this — perhaps much wider.

"The example assumes 1% response from a 10,000 mailing for a total of 100 orders. The easiest way to approximate the expected variation for this situation is: 1 standard deviation $= \sqrt{\text{orders}}$. Next, from a normal probability table you find that 68% of the errors should fall within one standard deviation (high or low) from the true value. Other formulas apply to other sampling plans and problems. If you dislike formulas, try breaking your usual sample into four or five sub-samples. You will get a vivid demonstration of sample variation.

"Where does this leave the old saw about needing 100 orders from a test? Well, if you can live with results that might easily be off by 10–15%, then use a guideline. The point is, *you* must decide how much risk you can accept for various test situations. Then choose the sample sizes that suit you instead of those that fit somebody else.

"If you still insist on using someone else's rules, the following seem to strike the right balance between cost and risk for a variety of direct mail situations:

Packages, promotion concepts:	10,000 to 25,000 per panel
Price tests:	50,000 to 100,000 per panel
	5,000 is a practical unit for a straight list test. 'Regression' tests may require 50,000 or more."

To the question, "How can direct marketers get more out of list tests?" Gaeddert answers:

"I find that experience is the great teacher in list testing. Sampling theory can't apply very well when dealing with non-random samples, interlist duplication and the host of other messy problems one encounters. So by all means tap the hard won knowledge that your list broker has.

326

"List testing is like a flour sifter with a coarse screen. That is why sequential sampling is a sound and universal practice. If a small sample looks promising, try a bigger bite. Then another chunk if that holds up. Incidentally, sampling variation runs both ways. So if a list has a good track record but looks a little weak in the current test, it too may be worth a retest.

"When testing outside mail order lists, a standard sample unit of 5,000 is practical. In some cases you may go lower, thus buying a limited amount of information about a greater range of lists for the same total test expenditure. I would not, however, test a list with less than 2,500.

"A sample of more than 10,000 is seldom justifiable. Believe it or not, the proportion of the list used in testing has hardly any effect on sample variation (unless you test more than one-quarter of the total).

"On the other hand, when testing the very largest lists — particularly compiled lists — you are probably searching for a few segments that work. This may involve a 'regression' test or other advanced statistical techniques. A test of 50,000 would be a good starter — 25,000 an absolute minimum. Sometimes 100,000 or more names are necessary.

"Regression testing is a fairly recent idea and a good one. Unfortunately, the term includes a confusing variety of techniques and test designs. All of these methods, however, have the same goal. First, to identify the few critical selection factors and, second, to predict the relative response from the better segments of the list. The complexities are such that you must have competent help in planning and analyzing a study of this sort. Incidentally, my own view is that improved selectivity tools beyond regression will be developed and exploited in the next few years."

To the question, "What is the best strategy for testing new products?" Gaeddert responds:

"I doubt that there is one best strategy, but you might put this maxim on your checklist: Bring everything you've learned about marketing (and testing) with you. Then prepare to learn the rules of the new game as the test returns come back.

"The following ideas apply best to those new products which appear to have large potential. Scale everything down for a limited interest product, substituting marketing experience for testing as necessary.

"The price and the nature of the promotion, and the usable list volume all have huge leverage on projected profitability, hence on the go/no-go decision. You are searching for the optimum mix, and yet not all of the combinations can be tested. There are too many things to guess at as it is; so you can't afford to scrimp on testing.

"*Pricing:* You should try at least two significantly different price levels. The new product, or the market segments it appeals to, may have substantially different price sensitivity than your current lines. If so, this is worth knowing.

"*Offer and package:* Marketing pros disagree over the role of promotion testing in deciding the viability of a new product. I have seen a number of cases where the whole decision to launch depended on finding the right kind of selling proposition and the correct positioning. In my judgment, it pays to test alternative promotions if you have two or three quite different concepts or offers to try. Refinements in copy, brochure, or envelope probably should be left for a later stage of testing.

"*Market depth (list) testing:* Our preconceptions about the ultimate sales penetration and about the target segments are rarely accurate. List testing, or 'spectrum' testing as you have called it, Rose, yields clues about how deeply to mail. These clues go beyond the immediate response percentages. You will also see which segments are responding in a well-designed 'spectrum' test. Note that in this application, a list test is a two dimensional sample. You are *sampling the universe of lists* as well as the people on the

327

particular lists chosen. In practice there is no rigorous way to project to those other untested lists. Nevertheless, the projection must be made—so intuition, insight and luck are essential ingredients.

"*Simulation,* a tool borrowed from operations research, can be invaluable in deciding what to test, how big to test, and what to watch for after a launch."

Gaeddert's testing concepts are based on considerable wisdom and experience gained over a 16-year period. Suffice it to say that testing is a never ending process, one which requires wisdom, ingenuity, experience.

Testing with the obvious advantage of *measurable results* is one of the factors which makes direct marketing a truly exciting endeavor. Good luck in all your efforts!

Self-Quiz

1. What are the six big things to test?

   1. _____

   2. _____

   3. _____

   4. _____

   5. _____

   6. _____

2. What is an effective way to predetermine appeal for a proposition aside from making advertising tests?

   _____

   _____

3. What is the chief criticism leveled against focus interviews?

   _____

   _____

4. Define telescopic testing.

   _____

   _____

   _____

5. Test hypotheses seem to fall into four main categories:

   1. _____

   2. _____

   3. _____

   4. _____

328

6. Describe the theory behind an advertising preprint mailing.

_____

_____

_____

7. Which is preferable, testing components or testing mailing packages?

_____ Testing components   _____ Testing mailing packages

8. The proper sample size for a list test is determined by two factors.

1. _____

_____

2. _____

_____

9. You can accept the larger risks of relatively smaller samples when:

_____ You know your product and market.

_____ You are trying a new product, or a novel promotional concept.

10. Low markup items require larger samples because _____ _____

_____

11. If you want to track payments or later purchases from a list source, a ☐ small ☐ large sample is required initially.

12. Rules of thumb to follow in list testing:

1. When testing packages and promotion concepts, test _____M to _____M per panel.

2. For price tests use _____M to _____M per panel.

3. Use _____M for a straight list test.

4. Regression tests may require _____M, or more.

13. When price testing you should:

_____ Try at least two significantly different prices.

_____ Test two or more prices in small increments.

329

Pilot Project

You are the new advertising manager for a publisher of a stock market service known as *Stock Trends*. The service is issued twice monthly and sells for $60 a year, or two months for $15. All subscriptions are sold by mail. Average pull is 1%, with 80% of subs being for a two-month trial.

Over the past 15 years, the publisher has done very little mailing package testing. As a matter of fact, one control package has been used season after season, the only changes being in updating copy. The mailing package consists of the following components:

> #10 white mailing envelope with corner card.
> 2-page letter, printed both sides, black and red ink.
> 1-page circular, printed on one side, brown ink, buff stock. (Circular lists the benefits of the service and includes testimonials from satisfied subscribers.)
> Order form, size $8\frac{1}{2} \times 3\frac{2}{3}$, printed on green stock, green ink. (Proposition is: two months for $15, or 12 months for $60.)
> Standard postage-free reply envelope, white stock, black ink.

You have been assigned the task of coming up with some real breakthroughs by devising new formats, vastly different from the control mailing package. You have clearance to test your new packages against the control mailing package.

Describe each of four new mailing packages in detail and determine the quantity of each to be tested against the control.

INDEX

A

A-B split-run testing, 250–59, 319
Abercrombie & Fitch Co., 7
Ad-a-card/Ad-an-envelope, 90
Additive approach (to a control package), 203
Adler, Aaron, 19
Adler, Mort, 134–35
Advertising Manager's Handbook, mailing package, 188–89, *illus.* 191
AIDA, 192
Ambassador Leather Goods, 224, 226
American Heritage, sample ad, 249
American Network, 89
American Television & Communications, 116
Angerman, Virgil D., 128, 187

B

Baier, Martin, 53
Better Homes & Gardens, subscriber profile, 42
Bell & Howell, mailing package, 16, 19, *illus.* 19
Big List, The, 134
Bind-in cards. *See* Insert cards
Blumenfeld, Sol, 201
Booklet format, 180
Book-of-the-Month Club, 249
Bounce back propositions, 162
Branham-Moloney, Inc., 87
Break-even point, 282–85
Bucket brigade, 193
Bringe, Paul, 199
Broadcasting. *See* Radio commercials; Television commercials
Broadside format, 180
Brochures. *See* Circulars
Brokers, mailing list, 44, 128, 266–67
Buffalo *Courier Express,* 91
Buffalo *Evening News,* 91
Business Buyer's Guide, 134

C

Cable Family Shopping Center, 112, *illus.* 117
Cablemart, 112
Cable Television, 109–17
catalog sales, 114
costs, 111
direct mailing supports, 110–11, 113, 115
interactive, 116
Calling lists, telephone, 140, 150
Campaign Communication Institute of America, Inc., 137
Card inserts. *See* Insert cards
Carlson, Len, 214
Catalogs, 211–28
arrangement of merchandise, 215–16
color, 218–19
copy, 219–20, 222
covers, 216
customer lists, 212, 215
graphics, 216–18, 228
guarantees, 220
incentives, 222–24
layout, 217–18, 228
order forms, 224, 226–227
sales analysis, 227–28
showrooms, 213
space allotments, 216, 228
specialty catalogs, 213
testimonials, 220
themes, 213
CATV. *See* Cable television
Charter proposition, 161
Circulars, 179–80, 183–85, 204
Cluster-of-diamonds copy, 244–45
C.O.D. orders, 156
Collins, Tom, 203, 233n, 298, 320
Color vs. black/white ads, 76–77, 96, 218
Columbia House, 103
Comics sections, 89–90
Commercial credit cards, 2, 31, 157, 224
Commercials. *See* Radio commercials; Television commercials
Compiled lists, 58, 134
Computer letters, 201, *illus.*, 202
Conditional sale incentives, 160
Confidence level, in probability, 51, 52
Consumers Communication Corporation, 132
Contests, 160
Conversion promotion, 285–88
Co-ops, 125–35
costs, 132
newspaper, 132–34
package inserts, 128
post card, 127–28, *illus.* 126, 127, 128
special interest, 125, 128
Copywriting techniques, 176–205
catalog copy, 219–20, 222
circular copy, 183–85, 204
classic mailing package, 179, 183–89
color, 204
enclosures, 187, *illus.* 186
envelopes, 183
formats, 179–81, 204, *illus.* 181
letter copy, 189–201, 204, samples, 198
formula letters, 192–93
lead copy, 190–92, 201, 203
length, 196–97
P.S., 197
order forms, 186–87
print copy, 233–51
graphics, 249–50
headlines, 234–37, 242
lead copy, 242–43
price justification, 248–49
reply format, 250
semantics, 238–39
testimonials, 247–48
testing response, 250–59
unique feature, 245–47
product appeal, 177–79, 201
reader involvement, 182–83, *illus.* 181, 184
typography, 187, 189, *illus.* 188
Costs, advertising
color, 77, 87, 89, 96
estimates, 282–91
break-even point, 282, 284–85, 289–90
conversion rates, 285–88
filling orders, 282, 284
markup, 289–90
response patterns, 290–92
space
cable television, 111
co-ops, 132
magazines, 68, 74, 75
newspapers, 83–84, 87, 89, 90
radio, 122
television, 102, 104–6, 108
telephone solicitation, 139
Cousins, Norman, 146
C.P.A., 159
C.P.I., 159
Credit cards, 2, 31, 157, 224
Credit ratings, 14–15
Culturological market segmentation, 56–57

D

Direct mail catalogs. *See* Catalogs
Direct mail lists. *See* Mailing lists
Direct marketing executive, 34–37
Direct Mail/Marketing Association, 37
Direct response copy. *See* Copywriting techniques, *subhead* print copy
Direct response lists. *See* House lists
Discount catalog houses, 213
Discounts, as incentives, 161
Donelley mail co-op, 125, 132, 134
Duplication of names, on lists. *See* Name duplication
Dutch door inserts, 87, *illus.* 88

E

Economic market segmentation, 56
El Segundo, California interactive cable TV pilot project, 116, 120
Encyclopedia sales propositions, 159, 164, 245

Envelope manufacturers, 266
Error limit, in probability, 51–
    53. 54–55
European direct marketing, 32–
    33
Evans, Jacob A., 103
Exchanging lists, 44
Extractive approach (to a control
    package), 203

F
Fairfax Agencies, 87
Family Weekly, 87
Fan dance copy, 245
Film Corporation of America,
    134
Fingerhut Manufacturing Co.,
    163
Flagwaver, 132–34, *illus.* 133
Folder format, 179–80
Foreign direct marketing, 32–
    33
Formats, for mailing packages,
    179–81, 204
    circulars, 179–80, 183–85
    classic package, 179–180,
        183, 185–186, 189, *illus.*
        190
    illustrated letters, 180
    invitations, 180, *illus.* 181
    reader involvement, 182–83,
        187, *illus.* 181, 182, 184
    self-mailers, 180
    simulated telegrams, 181
Foster & Gallagher, 213
Franklin Mint, 156
Free gift incentives, 161, 162–
    64, 187, 224, *illus.* 186
Free trial incentives, 160
Frequency of placing magazine
    ads, 74–75
Fulfillment handling, 287–89
Fund-raising copy, 200

G
Gans, Leo, 14
Geographic market segmenta-
    tion, *chart,* 50
    factor analysis, 61
    ZIP Code areas, 57–58, 59–63
Geographic testing
    mailing lists, 50
    prime newspaper markets, 91
    regional magazine editions,
        66–69
Get-a-friend proposition, 160,
    165
Gift incentives. *See* Free gift
    incentives
Gift plans, multiple, 162
Guarantees, 157–58, 220, 250
    third-party, 158
Guaranteed buy-back proposi-
    tion, 161
Guzofsky, Elliott, 109

H
Hanover House, 213
Heritage Book Club telephone
    solicitation campaign, 142–

44
Hewlett-Packard mailing pack-
    age, 16, *illus.* 18
Holland, Leonard G., 134
House lists (direct response
    lists), 42, 58, 134

I
Illustrated letters, 180
Incentives. *See* Propositions
Industrial Marketing, 128
    action cards, *illus.* 127
Innovative approach (to a con-
    trol package), 203
Insert cards
    co-ops, 134
    magazines, 73, 78, 250
    newspapers, 83, 250
Installment credit, 8
Intangible selling, 20–21, 199
Invitation format, 180, *illus.* 181
Isaac, Ted, 132, 134

J
Jefferson, Chad, 189
Job cost estimate form, 271
Job cost revision form, 272
Job envelope, 269, 279
Job ticket-space ad form, 274

K
"Keeper" gift plans, 163
Kestnbaum, Bob, 45, 285, 291
Kiplinger boom-or-bust letter,
    193, *illus.* 21
Kobs, Jim, 176n, 179, 183

L
Layout estimate form, 269
Lead copy, 191–92, 201, 203;
    See also Copywriting tech-
    niques
Letter copy, 189–201, 204
    computer letters, 201, *illus.*
        202
    formula letters, 192–93
    lead copy, 190–92, 201
    length, 196–97
    multiversioned copy, 200
    samples, 198
Lettershops, 268
Limit of error, in probability, 51,
    52, 54, 55
List brokers, 44, 128, 266–67
List managers, 44–46
Lists. *See* Calling lists, tele-
    phone; Mailing lists
Literary Guild, 246
Load-up propositions, 161, 164
Long-term offers, 158–59
Los Angeles Times-May Co. du-
    plication system, 48–49

M
Machine gun copy, 245
Madison House, 158
Magazine ads
    color vs. black/white, 76–77
    copy. *See* Copywriting tech-
        niques, *subhead* print
        copy

costs
    color, 77
    CPR, 74, 75
    regional, 68
    frequency of ad, 74–75
    insert cards, 73, 78
    pilot publications, 69, 71–72
    positioning ad, 68, 77–78
    regional editions, 66–69
    renewals, 158–59
    response patterns, 73–74
    size of ad, 75–76
    shopping advertising pages,
        67
    subject groupings, 69–71
    testing, 68–69, 250–59
    timing of ad, 74
Mail response lists, 58
Mailing lists, 13–14, 42–65
    age of, 44, 49
    Big List, The, 134
    brokers, 44, 128
    cable TV as support, 110–11,
        113, 115
    compiled lists, 58, 134
    costs, 102
    customer rating, 296
    exchanges of, 44
    geographic testing, 50
    house lists, 42, 58
    mail response lists, 58
    name duplication
        costs, 47
        elimination of, 47–48
        Los Angeles Times-May Co.
            duplication elimination
            system, 48–49
        use of, for market segmenta-
            tion, 58
    performance charts, 50
    profiles of, 42–44
    projections, probability, 51–
        55
    rentals of, 44–45
    size of mailing, 51–55
    testing response, 49–55, 326–
        27
    use of, for market segmenta-
        tion, 58. *See also* Market
        segmentation
Mailing packages, 176–205
    checklist, 205
    color, 204
    enclosures, 187, *illus.* 186
    envelopes, 183, 204
    formats 2, 5–6, 179–81, 204
        circulars, 179–80
        classic packages, 179, 183–
            89
        illustrated letters, 180
        invitations, 180, *illus.* 181
        reader involvement, 182–
            83
        self-mailers, 180
        simulated telegram, 181
    improving a package, 201–3
    letter copy. *See* Letter copy

product appeal, 177–79
testing, 325
typography, 187–89, *illus.*
188
Mailing schedule, 277
Market Development Corporation, 43
Market segmentation, 53–63
evaluation of, 59–63
geographic, 57–58, 59–63
mailing lists use, 58
psychographic, 56–57
regression analysis, 62–63
Marshall, Walter, 287, 288
May Co.-Los Angeles Times duplication system, 48–49
Merge and purge, 47–48, *chart,*
48
Merlite Co., 247
Metro Sunday comics, 89
Metromail co-op, 125
Metropolitan groupings, 60–61
Miles Kimball, 213
Multiple gift plans, 162
Multiproduct propositions, 161
Mystery gift propositions, 163

N
Name duplication, on lists
costs, 47
elimination of, 47–48
Los Angeles Times-May Co.
duplication system, 48–
49
use of, for market segmentation, 58
National Business Lists, 14
National Cash Register, 11–13
National Network, 89
National Research Bureau, 158
Negative option propositions,
161
New York Times Sunday magazine, 91
New Yorker, 66
Newspaper advertising, 82–
96
ad-a-card, ad-an-envelope, 90
card inserts, 83
color vs. black/white, 96
comics, 89–90
copy. *See* Copywriting techniques, *subhead* print
copy
costs, 83–84, 87, 89, 96
dutch door inserts, 88
geographic testing, 91
positioning ad, 95
preprints, 82–86
response patterns, 94–95
ROP format, 90–91
size of ad, 95
syndicated supplements, 87–
88, 134
testing, 91–92, 250–59
timing, 92–94
Newspaper Preprint Corporation, 82, 83

North American Publishing Co.,
127, 132
O
Old American Insurance Co., 59,
60
Order forms, 186–87, 224–27
Order handling, 287–88
"Overkill," 155, 159
Overwraps, 222
P
Paperback book card inserts,
134
Parade, 87
Payment terms, as incentive,
156–57
Periodical ads. *See* Magazine
advertising
Piggyback incentives, 162
Pilot publications, 69, 71–72
Polaroid award-winning package, 183, *illus.* 182
Position of ads, 68, 77–78, 95
Positive option propositions, 161
Preprints, 82–86
Prime newspaper test markets,
91
Print media. *See* Magazines;
Newspapers
Printers, 267–68
Printing quotation form. 273
Probability equation, 51–53
Probability tables, 51–52, *illus.*
52, 53, 54–55
Product appeal, in copy, 177–78
Production techniques, 263–79
checklist, 276
forms, 269–78
Profiles of mailing lists, 42–44
Propositions, success of, 160–65
believability, 159
case histories, 154
discounts, 155
free gifts, 155
guarantees, 157–58
overkill, 155
payment terms, 156–57
short-term/long-term, 158–59
Psychographic market segmentation, 56–57
Publishers Clearing House, 182
Puck Group comics, 89
Purchase order form, 270
R
Radio Advertising Bureau, 120
Radio commercials, 120–24
Rapp, Stan, 66n, 286
Rebus illustration, 249
Regional editions, 66–69
Regression testing, 327
Remnant space, 87
Rentals of lists, 44–45
Repeat business factor, 292–96
Response factor, in probability,
51, 52
Response patterns. *See also*
Testing response
magazine ads, 73–74

mailing lists, 51–55
newspaper ads, 94–95
projecting, 290–92
Response tally form, 278
*Retail Advertising and Sales
Promotion Manual,* 158
Retailing vs. direct marketing,
6–9
Reverse time scheduling, 263–
64
Roman, Murray, 137
Ronco Products Co., 103
Ross, Maxwell C., 193, 219
S
Scheduling, production, 263–64
Schwab, Victor, 237
Seasonal advertising, 49–50,
74, 92–94
Self-mailers, 180
Semantics, 238–39
Short-term offers, 158–59
SIC classifications, 13–14
Simulated telegrams, 181
Size of ads, 75–76, 95
Sloan, Al, 16
Snyder, Ray, 49, 50
Southern Living, 47
Space, buying of
magazines, 68, 75–78
newspapers, 95
Specialty mail order houses, 213
Spencer Gifts, 213, 219
Split-run testing, 250–59, 319
String-of-pearls copy, 245
Subscription renewals, 159
Sunday-Metro, 87
Sunset House, 213, 214, 219,
222, *illus.* 217
Suppliers, 265
*Sweet's Architectural Catalog
File,* telephone campaign,
141–42, 149
Syndicated newspaper supplements, 87–88
Syndicators, 9, 16–20
T
Tape-recorded telephone ads,
145–46, 149, *samples,* 146–
49
Telegrams, simulated, 181
Telephone solicitation, 137–
51
case histories, 141–44
costs, 138
lists, 140, 150
operator techniques, 143,
144–45, 150–51
professional marketing agencies, 140–41, 150
taped messages, 145–49
testing, 140
uses of, 138–39, 145
Telescopic testing, 250–59,
319–22
Television Bureau of Advertising, Inc. (TvB), survey,
100–102

Television commercials
  advertising budgets, 100, 102
  cable. *See* Cable television
  costs, 102, 104–6, 108
  lead-producing ads, 104
  length of, 101, 106
  program ratings, 104–5, 108
  support ads, 103–4, 106, 108
  time slots, 101, 102, 104, 105–8
Terms of payment, as incentive, 156–57
Testimonials, 220, 247–48
Testing response
  direct mail test, 322–24

interviews, 319
magazines, 3–4, 68–72, 250–59
mailing lists, 49–55
newspapers, 91–92, 250–59
questionnaires, 302–10
size of test, 325
techniques, 302–29
telephone, 140
telescopic testing, 250–59, 319–22
Theta-Com, 116
Third-party guarantee, 158
Timing ads, 49–50, 74, 92–94
TV Guide, 2

Two-step promotions, 285–86
Typography, 187–88, 203, *illus.* 188
W
WinCraft, 220, *illus.* 221
Writing copy, *See* Copywriting techniques
Y
Yes-no proposition, 160, 162
Young, James Webb, 246
Young Family Index, 43
Z
ZIP Code Segmented Marketing Evaluation, 59–63